T0180940

Lecture Notes in Computer Science

Lecture Notes in Artificial Intelligence   14741

Founding Editor

Jörg Siekmann

Series Editors

Randy Goebel, *University of Alberta, Edmonton, Canada*
Wolfgang Wahlster, *DFKI, Berlin, Germany*
Zhi-Hua Zhou, *Nanjing University, Nanjing, China*

The series Lecture Notes in Artificial Intelligence (LNAI) was established in 1988 as a topical subseries of LNCS devoted to artificial intelligence.

The series publishes state-of-the-art research results at a high level. As with the LNCS mother series, the mission of the series is to serve the international R & D community by providing an invaluable service, mainly focused on the publication of conference and workshop proceedings and postproceedings.

Toyotaro Suzumura · Mayumi Bono
Editors

New Frontiers
in Artificial Intelligence

JSAI International Symposium on Artificial Intelligence
JSAI-isAI 2024, Hamamatsu, Japan, May 28–29, 2024
Proceedings

 Springer

Editors
Toyotaro Suzumura
The University of Tokyo
Tokyo, Japan

Mayumi Bono
National Institute of Informatics
Tokyo, Japan

ISSN 0302-9743   ISSN 1611-3349 (electronic)
Lecture Notes in Artificial Intelligence
ISBN 978-981-97-3075-9   ISBN 978-981-97-3076-6 (eBook)
https://doi.org/10.1007/978-981-97-3076-6

LNCS Sublibrary: SL7 – Artificial Intelligence

This Springer imprint is published by the registered company Springer Nature Singapore Pte Ltd.
The registered company address is: 152 Beach Road, #21-01/04 Gateway East, Singapore 189721, Singapore

If disposing of this product, please recycle the paper.

Preface

The Sixteenth JSAI International Symposia on Artificial Intelligence (JSAI-isAI) was held on May 28–29, 2024, at Act City Hamamatsu, Shizuoka, Japan. JSAI-isAI has hosted several international workshops every year since 2009, and they are supported by JSAI. It provides a unique and intimate forum where AI researchers gather and share their knowledge in a focused discipline. Since 2022, JSAI-isAI has been held with the JSAI Annual Conference to achieve synergies between the two events. Although JSAI is a Japanese society and is mainly run in Japanese, the JSAI Annual Conference has an international session, providing a forum for presentations and exchanging opinions in English. From 2023, the JSAI Annual Conference participants could participate and present their papers at JSAI-isAI free of charge, and more participants than ever before were seen taking part in JSAI-isAI and engaging in active discussions, and presenters at JSAI-isAI had the same framework for submission recommendations to New Generation Computing (published by Springer), the international journal of JSAI, as presenters at the JSAI Annual Conference.

The Eighteenth International Workshop on Juris-informatics (JURISIN 2024) addressed legal issues from the perspective of information science. It covered various topics, including models of legal reasoning, argumentation agents, legal ontologies, legal knowledge bases, computerized legal education, AI legal problems, legal document analysis, and natural language processing for law. The Eighth International Workshop on Scientific Document Analysis (SCIDOCA 2024) focused on various aspects and perspectives of scientific document analysis for their efficient use and exploration. The International Workshop on Artificial Intelligence of and for Business (AI-Biz 2024) focused on the vast business and AI technology fields. It covered various topics, including investment strategy, stock market, mergers and acquisitions, online advertisement, knowledge extraction, power market, collaborative multi-agent, visualization, COVID-19 infections, classification, fake news, wide and deep learning, but it is not limited to them. The BIAS Workshop on Fairness and Diversity Bias in AI-driven Recruitment (BIAS 2024) focused on the functionalities of these technologies to encompass their profound implications on the social and ethical dimensions of hiring practices, to explore how these technologies shape notions of fairness and diversity bias globally, and to seek collaborative efforts to move towards a more equitable and just landscape.

This volume is the proceedings of JSAI-isAI 2024. From the 30 papers submitted to JURISIN 2024, the 15 papers submitted to SCIDOCA 2024, the 8 papers submitted to AI-Biz 2024, and the 10 papers submitted to BIAS 2024, 21 papers were selected based on a single-blind review by at least two reviewers and the quality of the extended versions of the papers was carefully checked by the program committee members. The acceptance rate was about 33% (21 papers out of 63 papers), ensuring the quality of the proceedings. We hope this book will introduce readers to the state-of-the-art research outcomes of JSAI-isAI 2024 and motivate them to organize and participate in JSAI events in the future.

May 2024

Toyotaro Suzumura
Mayumi Bono
Hiroki Kanezashi
Ken Satoh
Katsumi Nitta
Nguyen Le Minh
Setsuya Kurahashi
Carlotta Rigotti
Eduard Fosch-Villaronga

Organization

Program Committee Chairs

Toyotaro Suzumura	University of Tokyo, Japan
Mayumi Bono	National Institute of Informatics, Japan
Hiroki Kanezashi	The University of Tokyo, Japan
Ken Satoh	National Institute of Informatics, Japan
Nguyen Le Minh	Japan Advanced Institute of Science and Technology, Japan
Setsuya Kurahashi	University of Tsukuba, Japan

AI-Biz 2024

Workshop Leader

Takao Terano	Chiba University, Japan

Workshop Co-leader

Setsuya Kurahashi	University of Tsukuba, Japan
Hiroshi Takahashi	Keio University, Japan

Steering Committee

Chang-Won Ahn	Vaiv Company Inc., South Korea
Ernesto Carella	University of Oxford, UK
Reiko Hishiyama	Waseda University, Japan
Manabu Ichikawa	Shibaura Institute of Technology, Japan
Yoko Ishino	Yamaguchi University, Japan
Hajime Kita	Kyoto University, Japan
Hajime Mizuyama	Aoyama Gakuin University
Chathura Rajapaksha	University of Kelaniya, Sri Lanka
Masakazu Takahashi	Yamaguchi University, Japan
Alfred Taudes	Vienna University, Austria
Shingo Takahashi	Waseda University, Japan
Takashi Yamada	Yamaguchi University, Japan

| Matthias Raddant | Kiel University, Germany |
| Chao Yang | Hunan University, China |

BIAS 2024

Workshop Chairs

| Carlotta Rigotti | Leiden University, The Netherlands |
| Eduard Fosch-Villaronga | Leiden University, The Netherlands |

Program Committee

Mark W. Kharas	Norwegian University of Science and Technology, Norway
Roger Andre Søraa	Norwegian University of Science and Technology, Norway
Alexandre Puttick	Bern University of Applied Science, Switzerland
Mascha Kurpicz-Briki	Bern University of Applied Science, Switzerland
Guðbjörg Linda Rafnsdóttir	University of Iceland, Iceland
Ragna Kemp Haraldsdóttir	University of Iceland, Iceland

JURISIN 2024

Workshop Chairs

| Ken Satoh | Center for Juris-Informatics, Japan |
| Katsumi Nitta | Center for Juris-Informatics, Japan |

Steering Committee

Yoshinobu Kano	Shizuoka University, Japan
Takehiko Kasahara	Toin University of Yokohama, Japan
Nguyen Le Minh	Japan Advanced Institute of Science and Technology, Japan
Makoto Nakamura	Niigata Institute of Technology, Japan
Yoshiaki Nishigai	Chiba University, Japan
Katsumi Nitta	Center for Juris-informatics, Japan
Yasuhiro Ogawa	Nagoya City University, Japan
Seiichiro Sakurai	Meiji Gakuin University, Japan

Ken Satoh	Center for Juris-informatics, Japan
Satoshi Tojo	Japan Advanced Institute of Science and Technology, Japan
Katsuhiko Toyama	Nagoya University, Japan
Masaharu Yoshioka	Hokkaido University, Japan

Advisory Committee

Trevor Bench-Capon	University of Liverpool, UK
Henry Prakken	Utrecht University, The Netherlands
John Zeleznikow	Victoria University, Australia
Katsumi Nitta	Center for Juris-informatics, Japan
Robert Kowalski	Imperial College London, UK
Kevin Ashley	University of Pittsburgh, USA

Program Committee

Ryuta Arisaka	Kyoto University, Japan
Giuseppe Contissa	University of Bologna, Italy
Marina De Vos	University of Bath, UK
Wachara Fungwacharakorn	National Institute of Informatics, Japan
Saptarshi Ghosh	Indian Institute of Technology Kharagpur, India
Randy Goebel	University of Alberta, Canada
Guido Governatori	Charles Sturt University, Australia
Tokuyasu Kakuta	Chuo University, Japan
Yoshinobu Kano	Shizuoka University, Japan
Mi-Young Kim	University of Alberta, Canada
Nguyen Le Minh	Japan Advanced Institute of Science and Technology, Japan
Davide Liga	University of Luxembourg, Luxembourg
Réka Markovich	University of Luxembourg, Luxembourg
Makoto Nakamura	Niigata Institute of Technology, Japan
María Navas-Loro	Universidad Politécnica de Madrid, Spain
Ha-Thanh Nguyen	Center for Juris-Informatics, Japan
Katsumi Nitta	Center for Juris-informatics, Japan
Yasuhiro Ogawa	Nagoya City University, Japan
Adrian Paschke	Freie Universität Berlin, Germany
Juliano Rabelo	University of Alberta, Canada
Livio Robaldo	University of Swansea, UK
Víctor Rodríguez Doncel	Universidad Politécnica de Madrid, Spain
Seiichiro Sakurai	Meiji Gakuin University, Japan
Ken Satoh	Center for Juris-informatics, Japan

Jaromir Savelka	Carnegie Mellon University, USA
Akira Shimazu	Japan Advanced Institute of Science and Technology, Japan
Satoshi Tojo	Asia University, Japan
Katsuhiko Toyama	Nagoya University, Japan
Vu Tran	Institute of Statistical Mathematics, Japan
Bart Verheij	University of Groningen, The Netherlands
Sabine Wehnert	Leibniz Institute for Educational Media — Georg Eckert Institute, Germany
Yueh-Hsuan Weng	Tohoku University, Japan
Hannes Westermann	University of Montreal, Canada
Hiroaki Yamada	Tokyo Institute of Technology, Japan
Masaharu Yoshioka	Hokkaido University, Japan
May Myo Zin	Center for Juris-Informatics, Japan
Thomas Ågotnes	University of Bergen, Norway

SCIDOCA 2024

Workshop Chairs

Nguyen Le Minh	Japan Advanced Institute of Science and Technology, Japan
Yuji Matsumoto	RIKEN Center for Advanced Intelligence Project, Japan
Vu Tran	Institute of Statistical Mathematics, Japan

Program Committee

Nguyen Le Minh	Japan Advanced Institute of Science and Technology, Japan
Noriki Nishida	RIKEN Center for Advanced Intelligence Project, Japan
Vu Tran	Institute of Statistical Mathematics, Japan
Yusuke Miyao	University of Tokyo, Japan
Yuji Matsumoto	RIKEN Center for Advanced Intelligence Project, Japan
Yoshinobu Kano	Shizuoka University, Japan
Akiko Aizawa	National Institute of Informatics, Japan
Ken Satoh	Center for Juris-informatics, Japan
Junichiro Mori	University of Tokyo, Japan
Kentaro Inui	Tohoku University, Japan

Nguyen Ha Thanh   Center for Juris-informatics, Japan
Nguyen Minh Phuong   Japan Advanced Institute of Science and
                                       Technology, Japan
Tung Le   University of Science, VNU-HCM, Vietnam

Sponsored by

The Japan Society for Artificial Intelligence (JSAI)

The Japanese Society for Artificial Intelligence

Contents

SCIDOCA 2024

AI-Biz 2024

Artificial Intelligence of and for Business (AI-Biz 2024)

Takao Terano[1], Setsuya Kurahashi[2] and Hiroshi Takahashi[3]

[1] Chiba University of Commerce
[2] University of Tsukuba
[3] Keio University

1 The Workshop

The objective of the Artificial Intelligence of and for Business (AI-Biz 2024) is to foster the concepts and techniques of "Business Intelligence (BI)." in Artificial Intelligence. BI should include such cutting-edge techniques as data science, agent-based modeling, complex adaptive systems, and IoT. The application areas include business management, finance engineering, service sciences, manufacturing engineering, and so on.

AI-Biz 2024 invites one excellent lecturer. It also consists of five cutting-edge research papers and two invited papers. The workshop theme focuses on various recent issues in business activities and the application technologies of Artificial Intelligence to them.

The AI-Biz 2024 is the seventh workshop hosted by the SIG-BI (Business Informatics) of JSAI. The workshop includes the vast fields of business and AI technology and Investment Strategy, Stock Market, Mergers and Acquisitions, Online Advertisement, Knowledge Extraction, Power Market, Collaborative Multi-agent, Visualization, COVID-19 Infections, Classification, Fake News, Wide and Deep Learning, and so on.

2 Acknowledgment

As the organizing committee chair, I would like to thank the steering committee members. The members are leading researchers in various fields:
Chang-Won Ahn, VAIV Company, Korea
Ernesto Carella, University of Oxford, UK
Reiko Hishiyama, Waseda University, Japan
Manabu Ichikawa, Shibaura Institute of Technology, Japan
Yoko Ishino, Yamaguchi University, Japan
Hajime Kita, Kyoto University, Japan
Hajime Mizuyama, Aoyama Gakuin University, Japan
Matthias Raddant, Kiel University, Gemany
Chathura Rajapaksha, University of Kelaniya, Sri Lanka
Masakazu Takahashi, Yamaguchi University, Japan
Shingo Takahashi, Waseda University, Japan

Alfred Taudes, Vienna University, Austria
Takashi Yamada, Yamaguchi University, Japan
Chao Yang, Hunan University, China

The organizers would like to thank JSAI for its financial support. Finally, we wish to express our gratitude to all those who submitted papers, steering committee members, invited speakers, reviewers, discussants, and the attentive audience. We are extremely grateful to all the reviewers. We would like to thank everybody involved in the sympodia organization who helped us in making this event successful.

Time Series Network Analysis for Profit Dynamics in Pre-owned Luxury Goods Market Based on Network Motifs

Tengfei Shao[1]([✉])[ID], Yuya Ieiri[2][ID], and Shingo Takahashi[1][ID]

[1] Graduate School of Creative Science and Engineering, Waseda University,
Shinjuku, Tokyo 169-8555, Japan
`tengfei.shao@toki.waseda.jp`
[2] Graduate School of Information, Production, and Systems, Waseda University,
Kitakyushu, Fukuoka 808-0135, Japan

Abstract. This study introduces a pioneering Time Series-based Transaction Pattern Analysis model for scrutinizing profit dynamics within the pre-owned luxury goods domain via network motifs. By employing a model that integrates network motif analysis with time series, this study aims to elucidate the transactional patterns that govern market efficiency and profitability. Utilizing data from a Japanese enterprise specializing in pre-owned luxury goods, this investigation highlights the critical role of specific transaction patterns, identified as network motifs, in enhancing our understanding of market dynamics. The findings demonstrate the model's capability in revealing insights into the temporal and structural aspects of transactions, thus offering a comprehensive tool for optimizing sales strategies and market operations. Beyond contributing to the theoretical understanding of network motifs in economic contexts, this study provides actionable insights for market practitioners.

Keywords: Pre-owned luxury goods · Time series analysis · Network motifs

1 Introduction

Owing to its inherent complexity and the high value of its offerings, the luxury goods market has historically been a focal point of economic and sociological studies [1]. However, the burgeoning sector of pre-owned luxury goods, despite its substantial influence on consumer behavior, price dynamics has frequently been overlooked [2,3]. The industry's unique challenges call for sophisticated analytical approaches to decode the intricate dynamics between buyers and sellers, thereby generating actionable insights.

A promising avenue for elucidating these complex interactions is through the lens of network analysis, specifically focusing on network motifs [4]. Recognized as statistically significant subgraphs or patterns recurring within larger networks, network motifs adeptly encapsulate complex interactions. Their successful deployment in understanding networks across biological, social, and technological domains [5,6] underscores their potential in dissecting the convoluted

© The Author(s), under exclusive license to Springer Nature Singapore Pte Ltd. 2024
T. Suzumura and M. Bono (Eds.): JSAI-isAI 2024, LNAI 14741, pp. 5–20, 2024.
https://doi.org/10.1007/978-981-97-3076-6_1

networks of interactions within the pre-owned luxury goods market, thereby offering a structured analytical model [7].

Moreover, time series analysis, as shown by Feng et al. [8] in their study of luxury car ownership trends, and agent-based models, as used by Doshi et al. [9] for influencer marketing simulations, are crucial for understanding consumer behavior over time. These methods reveal demand patterns and assist in decision-making for businesses and policymakers, enhancing market trend predictions and insights into consumer preferences.

In response to the challenges presented by the temporal complexities inherent in these market dynamics, this study introduces a Time Series-based Transaction Pattern Analysis (TSTPA) model. This innovative model utilizes network motifs to systematically construct topological models of transactions within the pre-owned luxury goods market, subsequently analyzing these models temporally with attributes such as profit and ROI. Herein, ROI, a pivotal financial metric, is employed to quantify the efficiency of investments by comparing the net profit from selling pre-owned luxury goods against the original purchase price. Hence, the study's primary objectives are delineated as follows:

1. To develop a novel TSTPA model, incorporating a new algorithm (Algorithm 2) and integrating network motifs with time series analysis to examine the impact of transaction patterns on benefits.
2. To empirically validate the TSTPA model using data obtained in collaboration with a pre-owned luxury goods market firm aiming to enhance market efficiency based on these insights.

2   Related Work

2.1   Pre-owned Luxury Goods Market

The pre-owned market for luxury goods has emerged as an area with significant potential for societal and economic enhancement. This evolving domain has recently garnered considerable academic interest, with numerous studies delving into consumer behavior, particularly focusing on the motivations behind preferences for pre-owned and vintage luxury items [10]. Additionally, other research avenues have expanded this discourse, exploring the wider socioeconomic impacts of the pre-owned luxury goods market, thereby affirming its crucial role within the contemporary consumer ecosystem [11].

While these investigations have substantially deepened our understanding of market dynamics and consumer attitudes, they predominantly focus on profitability [12,13]. This approach fails to capture the full economic picture. For instance, a luxury item costing $ 20,000 that generates only $100 in profit could technically be considered "profitable", yet its ROI remains markedly low.

Notably, there exists a pronounced gap in the literature regarding strategies that could aid suppliers in optimizing the profitability of this market. This study aims to bridge this gap by employing a novel approach that integrates time-series analysis with network motif-based ROI analysis. This model is designed to unveil the complex purchasing behaviors and trends within the pre-owned luxury goods market. Strategic sales strategies are then formulated based on insights gathered from the model analysis and recommended to suppliers.

In summary, by systematically identifying and categorizing pre-owned luxury goods clusters based on time series, this model enables a detailed ROI analysis. Consequently, the application of this innovative approach has the potential not only to significantly enhance profitability but also to contribute to the broader economic efficiency of the pre-owned luxury goods market.

2.2   Network Analysis

Social network analysis, applied across diverse networks from online platforms to recommendation systems, benefits from the identification of influential nodes, as shown by Jiang et al. [14], which is crucial for understanding the expansion of complex systems like the pre-owned luxury goods market.

Network motifs, identified as repetitive patterns within larger networks by Schwarze and Porter [15], play a key role in our TSTPA model by highlighting trade patterns that influence ROI in this market. Despite their potential, the specific application of network motifs to the pre-owned luxury goods market remains underexplored, with existing studies [13,16] focusing on clustering for improved satisfaction and efficiency without a deep dive into ROI impacts.

In contrast to the traditional utilization of time series analysis within network studies, exemplified by the assessment of complex networks' topological graph measurements for time series classification and clustering [17] and the employment of network science principles and algorithms to facilitate a more comprehensive analysis of time series data across various real-world systems [18], this investigation pioneers the application of network motifs to examine the temporal and structural trade dynamics in the luxury goods market. Our innovative methodology integrates network motifs with time series analysis to unveil a distinct perspective on the trade dynamics and ROI influences within the pre-owned luxury goods market for the first time.

Our study diverges significantly from traditional clustering research by Husein et al. [20] and Li et al. [21] through its innovative use of network motifs to analyze directed, time-series data. While the mentioned studies apply K-means for segmenting customer data and managing energy storage, respectively, our method advances by incorporating temporal patterns and network analysis. This approach not only identifies clusters but also uncovers the intricate dynamics of the pre-owned luxury goods market, offering a more comprehensive understanding of its economic efficiency. Moreover, while Newman et al. [19] introduced modularity for graph clustering, these techniques primarily cater to undirected graphs. Our study advances the field by proposing a novel algorithm that leverages network motifs for analyzing complex, directed, and time-series data, aiming to enhance the pre-owned luxury goods market's economic.

3   Method

The Time Series-based Transaction Pattern Analysis model is conceived as a dedicated analytical tool, leveraging time series methodologies to examine transactional dynamics within the pre-owned market for luxury goods. Central to this model, as illustrated in Fig. 1, is its architectural core, which integrates two innovative algorithms. The first algorithm is designed to construct a sophisticated network from time series data, facilitating the identification of network motifs within this construct. The second algorithm is tasked with evaluating ROI by leveraging the topological configurations while also undertaking an exhaustive examination of transactional seasonality patterns.

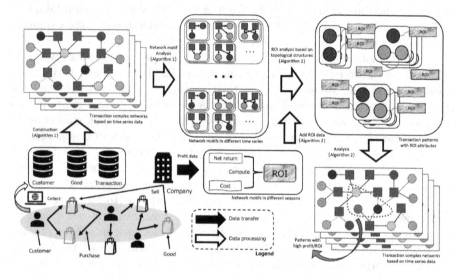

Fig. 1. Time Series-based Transaction Pattern Analysis Model

This model's workflow progresses from the crucial data collection phase towards the ultimate goal of formulating empirically supported sales strategies for the market, predicated on the identified clusters. A thorough discussion of the model, beginning with data collection and proceeding through to strategy formulation, will be elaborated on in the following sections of this document.

3.1   Data Collection

The data collection model for this research is structured around four essential elements: goods, customer, transaction, and profit data. Here, "goods data" pertains to the names and unique identifiers of pre-owned luxury goods. "Customer data" is defined as the names and unique identifiers of individuals. "Transaction data" encapsulates the relationships between the good unique identifiers and the

---

Algorithm 1. Network Construction and Network Motif Computation

---

1: **Input:** C, G, T ▷ Sets of Customers, Goods, Transactions
2: **Output:** $NetworkMotifs \leftarrow \emptyset$
3: **procedure** MAIN(C, G, T)
4:     **for all** (y, s) in unique years and seasons in T **do**
5:         $T_{ys} \leftarrow \{(c, g, t) \in T | t$ in year y and season $s\}$ ▷ Network construction
6:         $G_{ys} \leftarrow (C \cup G, \{(c, g)|(c, g, t) \in T_{ys}\});$ **for** $m \in \{3, 4, 5\}$
7:             $Subgraphs \leftarrow$ *enumerate all m-sized subgraphs of* $G_{ys};$ **for all** $sg \in$
    $Subgraphs$ ▷ Network motif computation
8:                 $Z \leftarrow (O_{sg} - E_{sg})/\sigma_{sg};$ **if** $Z >$ threshold **then** $NetworkMotifs$.add(sg)
9:     **end for**
10:     **return** $NetworkMotifs$
11: **end procedure**

---

customer unique identifiers. "Profit data" includes the original pricing and net profit associated with each item within the transactions. In order to facilitate the construction of the network, the above data is saved in the form of sets; that is, similar data is saved in the same set. The process of data acquisition initiates with the establishment of collaborative arrangements with companies in the pre-owned luxury goods sector, followed by consultations with industry experts to fully capture the attributes of the goods. After identification, the data undergoes cleaning and preprocessing to ensure its integrity.

3.2   Network Construction and Network Motif Computation

Following the data collection, Algorithm 1 employs a method designed for the efficient detection of network motifs to compute network themes, as described in Newman's subsequent work [22]. The focus of the current study is on network motifs of sizes 3, 4, and 5, grounded in two fundamental principles.

The proposed Algorithm 1 offers a methodology for identifying statistically significant motifs within complex networks derived from transactional data involving customers, goods, and transactions. The initial step involves preprocessing the transactional data (T), which is segregated by unique combinations of years and seasons, facilitating a temporal analysis of network dynamics. For each segregated dataset (T_{ys}), a network (G_{ys}) is constructed where nodes represent customers and goods and edges signify transactions. This step ensures that the motif detection analysis is contextualized within specific time frames, allowing for the identification of temporal patterns in customers and goods interactions.

Subsequently, the algorithm focuses on the enumeration and analysis of all subgraphs of sizes 3, 4, and 5, aiming to uncover recurring structural patterns that exceed expected frequency thresholds based on Z-score analysis [22]. The Z-score calculation $(Z = (O_{sg} - E_{sg})/\sigma_{sg})$ compares the observed frequency of a subgraph (O_{sg}) against its expected frequency in a random network (E_{sg}), normalized by the standard deviation (σ_{sg}). Subgraphs with Z-scores exceeding a predefined threshold are deemed statistically significant and are added to the

---

Algorithm 2. Analysis of ROI and Profit in Network Motifs

1: **Input:** NetworkMotifs, ProfitData   ▷ Network motifs and profit data with costs
2: **Output:** BestMotifByROI, BestMotifByProfit
3: **procedure** MAIN(NetworkMotifs, ProfitData)
4:     $\mathcal{S} \leftarrow \emptyset$; $\mathcal{R} \leftarrow \emptyset$
5:     **for all** motif m in NetworkMotifs **do**   ▷ Profit analysis for all network motifs
6:         $S_m \leftarrow$ extract subgraph for m; $C_{\text{total}} \leftarrow 0$; $R_{\text{total}} \leftarrow 0$
7:         **for all** node n in S_m **do**
8:             **if** node n is product **then**
9:                 C_{total} += ProfitData$[n].cost$; R_{total} += ProfitData$[n].revenue$
10:            **end if**
11:        **end for**
12:        $\mathcal{S}.add(S_m)$; $Profit \leftarrow R_{\text{total}} - C_{\text{total}}$; $ROI \leftarrow Profit/C_{\text{total}}$
13:        $\mathcal{R}.add(\{m, ROI, Profit\})$
14:    **end for**
15:    $BestMotifByROI \leftarrow \arg\max_{m \in \mathcal{R}}(\mathcal{R}[m].ROI)$ ▷ Profit/ROI analysis for all network motifs
16:    $BestMotifByProfit \leftarrow \arg\max_{m \in \mathcal{R}}(\mathcal{R}[m].Profit)$
17:    **return** $BestMotifByROI, BestMotifByProfit$
18: **end procedure**

---

set of network motifs ($NetworkMotifs$). This process not only highlights motifs that are unlikely to have occurred by chance but also underscores their potential significance within the network's structure and dynamics.

3.3 Analysis of ROI and Profit in Network Motifs

This algorithm offers a novel approach to analyzing network motifs within transactional data networks by integrating economic metrics such as ROI and profit. By examining the cost data associated with transactions and goods within these networks, the algorithm identifies motifs—recurring, significant patterns—that are not only structurally important but also economically efficient. The process involves extracting motifs from the network, assigning costs to each node within these motifs based on the provided cost data, and calculating the total cost, total revenue, profit, and ROI for each motif. This allows for a comparative analysis of motifs to determine which ones offer the highest economic value, thereby providing valuable insights into optimizing network structures for financial efficiency.

The Algorithm 2 presents an advanced methodology for assessing the economic performance embedded within network motifs. Utilizing NetworkMotifs and ProfitData as its primary inputs, the algorithm meticulously evaluates the financial dimensions of these structural patterns. Network motifs, which represent significant recurring patterns within a network, are analyzed in conjunction with financial data that assigns cost and revenue to each constituent node. This approach facilitates a detailed examination of the economic activities characterizing each motif, enabling the algorithm to compute total costs and revenues, from which it derives profit and ROI for each identified motif.

In operational terms, the algorithm iterates over each network motif, aggregating financial data for the nodes involved to calculate the *C_total* and *R_total*. These figures inform the computation of *Profit* and *ROI*, calculated as *R_total - C_total* and *Profit/C_total*, respectively. This process underpins the algorithm's capability to identify motifs that are not only structurally significant but also economically advantageous, offering a unique lens through which the financial efficiency (ROI) and economic value (profit) of network patterns can be evaluated. The conclusion of this analysis is the identification of motifs that yield the highest ROI and profit, providing invaluable insights for decision-makers into the most financially beneficial network configurations. This novel application of network motif analysis in the realm of economic and business analytics heralds a significant advancement in strategic planning and resource optimization efforts within various organizational contexts.

After processing Algorithm 1 and Algorithm 2, we can compare all network motifs in different periods, that is, different years and seasons, and compare their ROI, profit, and number of occurrences to conduct a further in-depth study of the pre-owned luxury goods trading model.

4   Experiment

To assess the TSTPA model, our study embarked on a collaborative venture with a Japanese firm specializing in the pre-owned market for luxury goods. Our data collection spanned transactions from 2018 to 2020, amassing a dataset of 256,210 entries, primarily bifurcated into acquisitions and sales of pre-owned luxury items. This investigation focused exclusively on transactions involving individual consumers, explicitly excluding B2B sales. The company's operations encompass both online storefronts and brick-and-mortar outlets, with physical store transactions numbering 29,021 and online transactions slightly higher at 29,298.

Recognizing the potential influence of the shopping environment on consumer behavior, our analysis was conducted separately for physical store data. For the purposes of this study, we primarily utilized transaction data from physical stores. An initial scrutiny of the transaction data was undertaken to identify potential brand keywords. These data were subsequently cross-referenced with local expertise to gauge their transaction frequency. This process facilitated the establishment of connections between these keywords and specific pre-owned luxury items, laying the groundwork for cluster discovery.

Following the data cleansing protocol, we eliminated invalid and erroneous values. Employing Algorithm 1, we constructed eight distinct networks based on the collected data from physical stores, corresponding to the seasons of Spring, Summer, Autumn, and Winter for the years 2019 and 2020. Moreover, Algorithm 1 was utilized to analyze the thematic networks within these eight networks, identifying all network motifs ranging from size 3 to 5. Subsequent analyses were conducted using Algorithm 2, specifically extracting all sub-networks that conformed to the network thematic structures of sizes 3 to 4 identified by Algorithm 1.

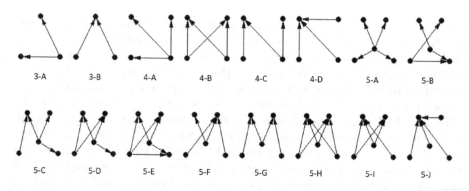

Fig. 2. Discovered network motifs

In our comprehensive analysis of the luxury goods market, we have delineated a variety of network motifs that elucidate the intricate patterns of transactions. As depicted in Fig. 2, these motifs are expressed as directed graphs, each node and link capturing distinct roles and interactions within the market framework. Nodes that receive links represent items—luxury goods whose flow we are tracking. In contrast, nodes that initiate links stand for customers, the dynamic market participants driving the commerce. Links themselves symbolize the act of purchasing, a fundamental activity that fuels the entire network. Such simpler motifs may encapsulate straightforward exchanges between a customer and a single item, reflective of individual transactions.

The network motifs presented in Fig. 2 illustrate a diversity of transactional forms within the luxury goods market, each serving as a microcosm of the market's dynamic interplay. The simpler motifs, such as 3-A and 3-B, represent direct transactions where a single customer acquires a luxury item. These basic interactions are foundational to the market and indicative of straightforward consumer purchases. In contrast, more elaborate motifs like 4-C and 5-D, where multiple customers are connected to a single product node, suggest bulk purchasing or items that attract multiple bids, a phenomenon common in high-end auctions or exclusive releases.

Intermediate complexities are observed in motifs such as 4-A and 4-B, where customers purchase from multiple product nodes, and 5-A and 5-B, depicting situations where customers are linked to several items, and those items, in turn, link back to other customers. These patterns may reflect scenarios where customers engage in a series of transactions, potentially trading within a closed network or participating in a consignment arrangement. Such motifs are emblematic of a more interconnected market where goods circulate among participants, signaling vibrant trade and a diversity of consumer preferences and purchasing strategies.

The most intricate motifs, for instance, 5-G and 5-J, with their interwoven customer and product nodes, point towards a sophisticated network of exchanges, possibly embodying trade-in scenarios, bundled purchases, or complex buyer-seller relationships with intermediaries. The presence of these complex motifs within the network hints at a mature market with participants who are not merely engaged in one-off transactions but are part of a larger, more intricate system of commerce. Understanding the nuances and implications of these patterns is key to grasping the full scope of transactions within the luxury goods market, as each motif reflects specific buyer behaviors, market trends, and the fluidity of luxury goods as they navigate through various echelons of economic exchange.

5   Results

Our comprehensive analysis of network motifs across various seasonal periods from 2019 to 2020 offers profound insights into transaction dynamics. As shown in Fig. 3, two figures on the left encapsulate the fluctuations in network motif frequencies across various motif sizes (3, 4, and 5) over sequential seasons, starting from Spring 2019 to Winter 2020. This graphical representation employs a logarithmic scale on the y-axis to effectively display the wide range of motif frequencies, which span several orders of magnitude. Each line, distinguished by unique colors and markers, correlates to a distinct network motif within the specified size category, thus allowing for a comparative analysis of motif dynamics over the observed periods. The right table categorizes the discovered network motifs by their frequency and Z-scores across different seasons from 2019 to 2020, providing insight into how often certain transaction patterns occur and their statistical significance. The result is segmented into eight columns representing the seasonal periods. The Z-score indicates how statistically significant the motif's frequency is compared to what would be expected by chance.

Focusing on Size 3 motifs, such as 3-A and 3-B, we observe that motif 3-A has frequencies like 0.0017 in Spring 2019 and exhibits consistently high Z-scores of 0.995 across all seasons. This pattern, despite its low frequency, demonstrates a statistically significant presence, suggesting an essential but niche transaction pattern within the market. Conversely, motif 3-B showcases a remarkably high frequency, nearing ubiquity with values such as 0.9983 in Spring 2019, coupled with similar high Z-scores. The contrast between the rare occurrence of 3-A and the pervasive presence of 3-B across all seasons illuminates the diverse interaction landscape within the market, from niche, strategic transactions to widespread, fundamental trading activities.

Delving into the complex structures represented by the Size 4 motif, we notice that motif 4-D presents an almost constant high frequency, with values like 0.9976 in Spring 2019 and significant Z-scores peaking at 16.2, indicative of its overrepresentation and importance in the market's transaction network. Such patterns suggest a robust, possibly central transaction structure that persists across seasons, reflecting stable and significant market operations, potentially pointing to established supply chains or critical distribution mechanisms that are essential for the market's functionality. The high Z-scores across most motifs confirm that the observed frequencies are not due to random variation but are reflective of underlying transaction patterns within the market.

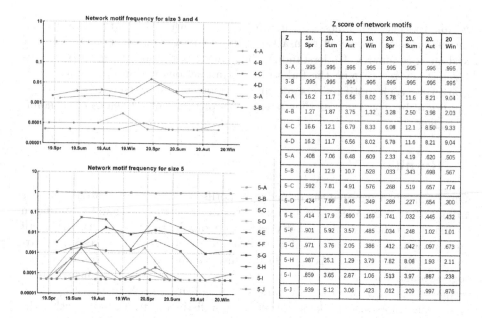

Z	19. Spr	19. Sum	19. Aut	19. Win	20. Spr	20. Sum	20. Aut	20 Win
3-A	.995	.995	.995	.995	.995	.995	.995	.995
3-B	.995	.995	.995	.995	.995	.995	.995	.995
4-A	16.2	11.7	6.56	8.02	5.78	11.6	8.21	9.04
4-B	1.27	1.87	3.75	1.32	3.28	2.50	3.98	2.03
4-C	16.6	12.1	6.79	8.33	6.08	12.1	8.50	9.33
4-D	16.2	11.7	6.56	8.02	5.78	11.6	8.21	9.04
5-A	.408	7.06	6.48	.609	2.33	4.19	.620	.505
5-B	.614	12.9	10.7	.528	.033	.343	.698	.567
5-C	.592	7.81	4.91	.576	.268	.519	.657	.774
5-D	.424	7.99	8.45	.349	.289	.227	.654	.300
5-E	.414	17.9	.690	.169	.741	.032	.445	.432
5-F	.901	5.92	3.57	.485	.034	.248	1.02	1.01
5-G	.971	3.76	2.05	.386	412	.042	.097	.673
5-H	.987	25.1	1.29	3.79	7.82	8.08	1.93	2.11
5-I	.859	3.65	2.87	1.06	.513	3.97	.887	.238
5-J	.939	5.12	3.06	.423	.012	.209	.997	.876

Fig. 3. Frequency and Z score of Network motifs

The analysis of Size 5 motifs, particularly motifs like 5-B and 5-D, showcases their seasonal variability and the intricate dynamics of the market. For instance, motif 5-B transitions from a frequency of N (indicating a negligible occurrence) in Spring 2019 to more noticeable frequencies and significant Z-scores, such as 12.9 in Summer 2019, highlighting the impact of seasonal changes on complex transaction networks. This fluctuation in the representation and significance of such motifs underscores the market's adaptability and responsiveness to external factors, including consumer trends, economic conditions, and seasonal influences. It reflects the necessity for market participants to remain agile, adjusting strategies to navigate the evolving landscape of the goods sector effectively. Algorithm 2 was then applied to amalgamate the cost of goods into the product nodes of each sub-network, subsequently calculating the total benefit, average ROI, and frequency within each network.

For sale and ROI, we concentrated exclusively on size 4 network motifs for assessing profit and ROI, excluding sizes 3 and 5. This decision was grounded in the recognition that size 4 motifs provide a more comprehensive understanding of complex transaction patterns, offering a balance between granular detail and overarching market dynamics.

For the specific focus on size 4 network motifs in the assessment of sales and ROI, two key studies provide substantial support for this methodological choice. First, the study by Ning et al. [24], "Detection of Four-Node Motif in Complex Networks," introduces a methodology specifically for extracting and analyzing four-node motifs in complex networks. This research highlights the significance

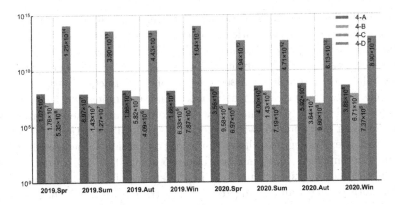

Fig. 4. Size 4 Network motifs for sale data

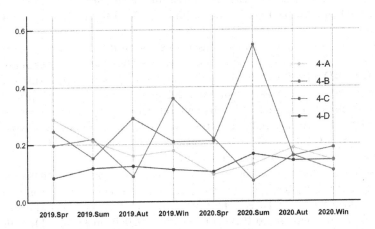

Fig. 5. Size 4 Network motifs for ROI data

of size 4 motifs in understanding complex network structures, which is crucial for analyzing intricate transaction networks with implications for profit and ROI. The approach by Ning et al. proposes an efficient algorithm that employs a two-way spectral clustering method to reduce computational complexity, thereby enabling more precise identification and analysis of these motifs in large datasets, such as those encountered in transaction networks.

Moreover, Jiang et al. [25] in their work "Analyzing Online Transaction Networks with Network Motifs," further underscore the utility of network motifs for investigating online transaction networks. While their study primarily emphasizes smaller motifs, the analytical framework they develop is equally applicable to size 4 motifs, providing insights into the local topology of transaction networks. By extending their motif-based analysis to size 4 motifs, one can derive a nuanced understanding of transaction dynamics, which is essential for optimizing sales strategies and improving ROI. This work demonstrates how motif-based analyses, including those focusing on size 4 motifs, can enhance our understanding of online transaction networks' structural characteristics, thereby offering valuable insights into profit maximization and ROI enhancement strategies.

These studies collectively affirm that concentrating on size 4 network motifs offers a balanced approach to dissecting complex transaction patterns, situating this choice as strategically beneficial for comprehending and leveraging the intricacies of sales and ROI dynamics within complex networked environments.

As shown in Fig. 4 and 5, we also focused specifically on the total sale and ROI for web themes. Figure 4 shows the total transaction value of each network motif in different years and quarters. Figure 5 shows the ROI of each trading model in different years and quarters. In the spring of 2019, the total sale for 4-D was notably high, amounting to over 125 trillion JPY, which underscores the motif's dominant role in market transactions during this period. This trend continued across all seasons, with 4-D maintaining the highest total sale among the identified motifs, peaking in the autumn of 2020 with sales exceeding 6.12 trillion JPY.

ROI is a key performance metric assessing the profitability of motifs relative to their sales. Despite 4-D's significant sales, its ROI varied across seasons. In spring 2019, 4-D's ROI was 0.084, indicating lower investment returns compared to its total sales. By contrast, in summer 2020, 4-C achieved an exceptional ROI of 0.547, demonstrating a highly efficient return despite lower sales frequency compared to 4-D. Additionally, a T-test ($p < 0.05$) was applied to assess differences between 4-C and 4-D across periods, revealing significant variances except for summer 2019, autumn 2020, and winter 2020.

These figures illuminate the market's transaction structure efficiency, with 4-C's higher ROI suggesting that less common transaction patterns may offer greater profitability than those represented by 4-D. Seasonal variations in 4-D's ROI, such as an increase to 0.158 in autumn 2020 from spring 2019, indicate market dynamic shifts, possibly due to changes in consumer demand, pricing strategies, or inventory levels.

Moreover, while 4-D dominated the total sale across all seasons, indicating a high volume of transactions, it did not consistently yield the highest ROI. This highlights that a high frequency and volume of transactions do not necessarily equate to the most profitable outcomes. The varied ROI performance across seasons for different motifs suggests that market participants might benefit from strategies that balance transaction frequency with profitability.

In summary, the results of our analysis using the TSTPA model have successfully demonstrated the model's capability in identifying and quantifying network motifs within the market. Through meticulous examination of the total sales and ROI of these motifs across different seasons, the TSTPA model has uncovered patterns that reveal potential seasonality in market transactions.

6   Discussion

The results of our study utilizing the TSTPA model provide a nuanced understanding of the transactional dynamics within the pre-owned luxury goods market. This discussion seeks to interpret the implications of our findings and explore how they may be applied to the operation and strategy development.

The prevalence of certain network motifs, particularly size 4 motifs like 4-D, throughout all seasons suggests a consistent consumer behavior pattern and transactional structure. The high Z-scores indicate that these motifs are not random occurrences but are integral to the market's fabric [23]. The persistence of these motifs could be attributed to consumer loyalty to certain luxury brands, habitual purchasing behaviors, or the success of marketing strategies that funnel transactions into predictable patterns [26].

The ROI variability observed across seasons for different motifs reflects the market's sensitivity to external factors, such as economic trends, marketing campaigns, and seasonal consumer preferences [27]. For instance, the higher ROI associated with less frequent motifs like 4-C during the summer of 2020 could be indicative of targeted marketing strategies that capitalize on summer trends or events. It suggests that while high-frequency motifs contribute significantly to total sales, focusing on specific, less common transaction patterns could yield greater profitability.

Moreover, the meticulous examination of network motifs across the contrasting landscapes of 2019 and 2020, as illustrated in Figs. 3 and 4, offers an insightful lens through which the ramifications of the COVID-19 pandemic on the pre-owned luxury goods market are discerned. Specifically, the dynamic shifts in network motifs' frequencies and ROIs between these years underscore the profound impact of global disruptions caused by the pandemic. In 2019, characterized by economic stability and conventional consumer behavior, the frequency and ROI of motifs, such as 4-D, depicted in Fig. 4, suggest a market driven by traditional transaction patterns with steady profitability. However, transitioning into 2020, the advent of COVID-19 catalyzed a significant transformation in consumer behavior and market dynamics. This is particularly evident in the alteration of motif 4-C's ROI, as depicted in Fig. 5, which remarkably increased in the summer of 2020, highlighting an agile market response to the pandemic's constraints, with an evident pivot towards online transactions and digital engagement strategies. The comparative analysis of these figures not only illustrates the market's resilience but also its capability to adapt to the accelerated digital transformation necessitated by the pandemic.

Furthermore, the analysis extends beyond mere transactional frequencies, delving into the economic essence of these shifts, as depicted in the ROI variations across 2019 and 2020 within Fig. 5. The adaptation to pandemic-induced market conditions is mirrored in the strategic reorientation towards motifs that facilitated higher ROIs, despite lower transaction frequencies. This strategic pivot, necessitated by the pandemic's restrictions, underscores the importance of digital agility and the ability to harness analytical insights from network motifs to navigate through tumultuous periods. The increased ROI of less frequent motifs, such as 4-C during the pandemic, suggests a nuanced market response, leveraging digital platforms to sustain consumer engagement and profitability. These figures serve as a blueprint for future resilience, emphasizing the critical role of data-driven strategies in anticipating and addressing shifts in consumer behavior and market conditions.

The findings from our TSTPA model analysis offer actionable insights for businesses operating within the pre-owned luxury goods market. Diversification of Sales Strategies: While it may be tempting to focus on the most frequent transaction patterns that guarantee volume, our study highlights the importance of diversifying strategies to also tap into less frequent, higher ROI motifs. Seasonal Marketing Approaches: The revealed seasonality in motif prevalence and ROI suggests that businesses could benefit from adapting their marketing strategies according to seasonal trends, potentially aligning inventory and promotions with the expected fluctuations in consumer purchasing behavior. Consumer Behavior Analysis: The consistent appearance of certain motifs can help businesses identify and understand the purchasing habits of their customers, allowing for more personalized and effective customer engagement strategies. Inventory Management: The variation in ROI across seasons and motifs can guide inventory decisions, ensuring that stock levels align with expected sales trajectories to maximize profitability.

While our analysis has offered valuable insights into the market through the examination of network motifs and seasonal variability, it is important to acknowledge its limitations for a comprehensive understanding. Lack of Real-Time Data Analysis: The study does not incorporate real-time data analysis, which limits its ability to capture current trends and the immediate effects of digital marketing strategies on consumer behavior and ROI in the pre-owned luxury goods market. Limited Scope on Specific Items and Brands: A notable limitation of our research is that it analyzes trends at a macro level, focusing on transaction patterns without delving into specific details regarding which brands or items within these transaction models yield higher ROIs or sales volumes. This oversight means that while we can identify general patterns and profitable transaction types, we lack the granularity to provide targeted recommendations for investors or businesses looking to capitalize on specific brands or items within the luxury goods sector.

To address the limitations, future research directions should encompass the integration of real-time data analysis to enhance the accuracy of market trend predictions. Furthermore, expanding the research scope to include detailed analyses of specific items and brands will provide deeper insights into transaction patterns.

7   Conclusion

This study introduces an innovative Time Series-based Transaction Pattern Analysis model that leverages network motifs and time series analysis to investigate the pre-owned luxury goods market. The findings underscore the model's effectiveness in identifying transaction patterns that significantly impact market dynamics and profitability. By examining various network motifs' frequency, structure, and associated ROI, the research highlights the intricate interplay between transaction patterns and market efficiency. The analysis reveals that certain motifs, particularly those with higher ROIs, offer potential insights into optimizing transaction structures for enhanced economic performance.

Furthermore, the study's application to a real-world dataset from a Japanese firm specializing in pre-owned luxury goods validates the TSTPA model's practical utility. It identifies seasonal trends in transaction patterns and their potential implications for sales strategies, inventory management, and marketing approaches. The research underscores the importance of diversifying sales strategies and aligning marketing efforts with identified transaction patterns to capitalize on seasonal variations and consumer behavior insights.

Future research should aim to refine the TSTPA model by incorporating real-time data analysis to capture evolving market trends and consumer preferences more accurately, especially focusing on brands. By delving deeper into the analysis of different brands and items, future studies will be poised to offer insights that are not only more precise but also actionable, catering to the dynamic needs of the luxury goods market.

Acknowledgements. This work was supported by JST SPRING, Grant Number JPMJSP2128. We also extend our deepest gratitude to Prof. Reiko Hishiyama for her assistance.

References

1. Gurzki, H., Woisetschlager, D.M.: Mapping the luxury research landscape: a bibliometric citation analysis. J. Bus. Res. **77**, 147–166 (2017)
2. Aliyev, F., Urkmez, T., Wagner, R.: A comprehensive look at luxury brand marketing research from 2000 to 2016: a bibliometric study and content analysis. Manag. Rev. Q. **69**, 233–264 (2019)
3. Bindi, B., Bandinelli, R., Fani, V., Pero, M.E.P.: Supply chain strategy in the luxury fashion industry: impacts on performance indicators. Int. J. Prod. Perform. Manag. **72**(5), 1338–1367 (2023)
4. Webster, C.M., Morrison, P.D.: Network analysis in marketing. Australas. Mark. J. (AMJ) **12**(2), 8–18 (2004)
5. Kim, H.K., Kim, J.K., Chen, Q.Y.: A product network analysis for extending the market basket analysis. Expert Syst. Appl. **39**(8), 7403–7410 (2012)
6. Schiessl, D., Dias, H.B.A., Korelo, J.C.: Artificial intelligence in marketing: a network analysis and future agenda. J. Mark. Anal. **10**(3), 207–218 (2022)
7. Kuzmin, A., Bykov, V., Kazaryan, M., Danko, T., Sekerin, V.: Market of luxury goods and sales forecasting using the network analysis. Int. J. Appl. Bus. Econ. Res. **15**(21), 439–450 (2017)
8. Feng, Y., Luo, J.: When do luxury cars hit the road? Findings by a big data approach. In: 2016 IEEE International Conference on Big Data (Big Data). IEEE (2016)
9. Doshi, R., Ramesh, A., Rao, S.: Modeling influencer marketing campaigns in social networks. IEEE Trans. Comput. Soc. Syst. **10**(1), 322–334 (2022)
10. Thomsen, T.U., Holmqvist, J., von Wallpach, S., et al.: Conceptualizing unconventional luxury. J. Bus. Res. **116**, 441–445 (2020)

11. Turunen, L.L.M., Leipamaa-Leskinen, H.: Pre-loved luxury: identifying the meanings of second-hand luxury possessions. J. Prod. Brand Manag. **24**(1), 57–65 (2015)
12. Beard, N.D.: The branding of ethical fashion and the consumer: a luxury niche or mass-market reality? Fash. Theory **12**(4), 447–467 (2008)
13. Shao, T., Teraoka, F., Ishizaki, K., Hishiyama, R.: Discovering multiple clusters of second-hand luxury goods for profit improvement using network motif. In: Rocha, A., Adeli, H., Dzemyda, G., Moreira, F. (eds.) WorldCIST 2022. LNCS, vol. 470, pp. 438–448. Springer, Cham (2022). https://doi.org/10.1007/978-3-031-04829-6_39
14. Knoke, D., Yang, S.: Social Network Analysis. SAGE Publications (2019)
15. Schwarze, A.C., Porter, M.A.: Motifs for processes on networks. SIAM J. Appl. Dyn. Syst. **20**(4), 2516–2557 (2021)
16. Shao, T., Ieiri, Y., Hishiyama, R.: Discovering multiple clusters of sightseeing spots to improve tourist satisfaction using network motifs. IEICE Trans. Inf. Syst. **104**(10), 1640–1650 (2021)
17. Silva, V.F., Freitas, V., et al.: Novel features for time series analysis: a complex networks approach. In: Data Mining and Knowledge Discovery, vol. 36, no. 3, pp. 1062–1101 (2022)
18. Silva, V.F., Silva, M.E., Ribeiro, P., Silva, F.: Time series analysis via network science: concepts and algorithms. In: Wiley Interdisciplinary Reviews: Data Mining and Knowledge Discovery, vol. 11, no. 3, p. e1404 (2021)
19. Newman, M.E., Girvan, M.: Finding and evaluating community structure in networks. Phys. Rev. E **69**(2), 026113.1–026113.15 (2004)
20. Husein, A.M., Setiawan, D., Kolose Sumangunsong, A.R., Simatupang, A., Yasmin, S.A.: Combination Grouping Techniques and Association Rules For Marketing Analysis based Customer Segmentation. SinkrOn (2022)
21. Li, Z., et al.: Energy Storage Charging Pile Management Based on Internet of Things Technology for Electric Vehicles. Processes (2023)
22. Newman, M.E.: Fast algorithm for detecting community structure in networks. Phys. Rev. E 69(6), 066133.1–066133.5 (2004)
23. Kapferer, J.-N., Bastien, V.: The Luxury Strategy: Break the Rules of Marketing to Build Luxury Brands. Kogan Page (2009)
24. Ning, Z., Liu, L., Yu, S., Xia, F.: Detection of four-node motif in complex networks. In: Cherifi, C., Cherifi, H., Karsai, M., Musolesi, M. (eds.) COMPLEX NETWORKS 2017. sCI, vol. 689, pp. 115–126. Springer, Cham (2018). https://doi.org/10.1007/978-3-319-72150-7_37
25. Jiang, J., et al.: Analyzing online transaction networks with network motifs. In: Proceedings of the 28th ACM SIGKDD Conference on Knowledge Discovery and Data Mining, pp. 3098–3106. ACM (2022)
26. Chevalier, M., Mazzalovo, G.: Luxury Brand Management: A World of Privilege. Wiley, Hoboken (2012)
27. Wagner, T., Hennigs, N., Siebels, A.: The impact of economic crises on consumer behavior in the luxury segment. J. Bus. Res. **112**, 433–440 (2020)

A Study on the Propagation Process of New Knowledge in Organizations

Yoshiki Matsubara[✉] and Setsuya Kurahashi[iD]

University of Tsukuba, 3-29-1 Otsuka, Bunkyo-ku, Tokyo 112-0012, Japan
yooooki@gmail.com

Abstract. Currently, the emergence of technologies that significantly alter the framework of existing business operations, such as generative AI and Web3, along with the growing importance of globally demanded knowledge and skills such as Digital Transformation (DX) and Green Transformation (GX), is evident. In Japan, there is a growing need for reskilling. However, many companies and employees are unable to adapt to technological and social changes, remaining at low productivity levels. This study aims to construct a simulation model that explores how companies adapt to the demand for new knowledge in society, depending on their organizational structure. The results revealed that differences in organizational structure can affect the speed of knowledge propagation and business performance utilizing new knowledge. Specifically, in organizations with employees having high learning capabilities, the acquisition of existing knowledge within the company is quick, but there is a failure to adapt to new knowledge demanded by society. Additionally, it was found that organizations with a flat, non-hierarchical structure improve performance more quickly compared to those with defined hierarchies. Thus, this simulation was able to replicate the process of knowledge propagation influenced by organizational structure and corporate activities. Future efforts will focus on adding parameters to better represent the reality of organizations, conducting additional research to enhance the model's validity, and aiming to apply it in the formulation of strategies in actual organizations.

Keywords: Agent Based Model · Multi Agent Simulation · Organization Learning

1 Introduction

1.1 Background

Currently, the emergence of technologies such as generative AI, Web3, and others that are significantly changing the existing framework of business operations is creating a need for organizations to acquire new knowledge. Japanese government has clearly stated that it will invest 1 trillion yen over 5 years in reskilling, which is of great importance to the country as a whole [11]. On the other hand, the

T. Suzumura and M. Bono (Eds.): JSAI-isAI 2024, LNAI 14741, pp. 21–34, 2024.
https://doi.org/10.1007/978-981-97-3076-6_2

current measures are not necessarily successful in acquiring new knowledge. In fact, the survey shows that only 40% of companies have implemented measures aimed at knowledge acquisition, such as providing reskilling opportunities, and among these, only 60% of employees feel that the measures are effective [12].

1.2   Related Work

Research on Organizational Knowledge Creation and Organizational Learning. Previous studies in organizational knowledge management include Nonaka and Umemoto's (1996) SECI model, which outlines a cyclical four-phase process of knowledge creation and sharing within organizations [1]. Argyris (1977) introduced double-loop learning, emphasizing the reassessment of underlying assumptions in organizational decision-making [7]. Hedlund (1994) advocated for a shift from hierarchical to network-based (N-form) organizations for better knowledge integration [9]. Kaschig (2013) identified key measures for knowledge retention, emphasizing personalized strategies over standardized approaches [8].

Research on Knowledge Propagation and Management in Organizations Using Agent Models. Previous studies in organizational knowledge management and decision-making processes incorporate various simulation and modeling techniques. Bonabeau (2002) highlighted the significance of Agent-Based Models in designing effective organizations, focusing on measuring organizational performance changes in response to parameter variations, and noting the qualitative insights gained during simulation design [10]. Kikuchi and Kunigami et al. (2019) provided a formal description of the MDDM (Managerial Decision-Making Model) using agent model logs, simulating top-down and bottom-up decision-making processes in organizations and validating the model's consistency with actual business cases [4]. Fujita and Nakase (2007) emphasized the importance of knowledge management for organizational knowledge transfer, demonstrating through multi-agent simulation that the introduction of a knowledge database and a knowledge manager can lead to improved worker performance [6]. Hashimoto and Fujiwara et al. (2013) implemented Nonaka's SECI model in a multi-agent simulation to examine knowledge propagation in organizations. The study investigates how the match rate between knowledge needed for tasks and employee knowledge changes under various parameters [5].

1.3   Research Questions

As described above, various studies have been conducted on organizational learning and knowledge management, and attempts have been made to elucidate the theory with an agent model. On the other hand, what has been mainly discussed in the research to date is how an organization learns in response to a single piece of knowledge. Inherently, however, it is conceivable that the knowledge required by companies and the knowledge required by society may differ.

Specifically, while it is necessary to acquire knowledge related to DX for mid-term growth, the acquisition of analog business knowledge precedes the acquisition of knowledge for the current corporate performance. Therefore, we assume that the knowledge required by companies and the knowledge required by society may differ. We then aim to construct a simulation model that expresses how the two types of knowledge propagation take place in an organizational structure, focusing mainly on socially required knowledge. In addition, the simulation model in this study will utilize an agent-based model. The reason for this is the importance of interaction. Knowledge propagation in an organization is assumed to be greatly influenced by the interactions among employees and the activities of the organization.

2 Methodology

This study aims to represent a more realistic organizational structure by adding parameters such as learning ability and hierarchy to the simulation model of Hashimoto and Fujiwara et al. (2013). Therefore, we first explain the model of Hashimoto and Fujihara et al. (2013), which is the basis of this experiment.

2.1 Overview

The SECI model is modeled using agent simulation. As mentioned earlier, the SECI model has a spiral structure of four processes as the process by which employee knowledge is shared with the organization, and knowledge is constantly updated as each process is repeated. The knowledge propagation in this process is represented using the tag model. First, in the socialization phase, the tag value changes to that of one employee with a certain probability due to interaction between employees. In this phase, the tag sequence of the interacting partner is treated as tacit knowledge because it is not disclosed to the entire organization. The next phase is the externalization phase, in which tacit knowledge is converted to formal knowledge, and employees with knowledge tags that are similar to the task tags are extracted. Next, in the combination phase, a new manual is created from the knowledge tags of the extracted employees. Finally, the internalization phase, in which the created manuals are dropped into the knowledge tags of the individuals, transforms formal knowledge into tacit knowledge. Again, the knowledge tag is transformed into the value of the manual's tag by a certain probability.

2.2 Implementation of New Parameters and Activities

New elements are added based on the model of Hashimoto and Fujiwara (2013) to allow for a more realistic representation of organizational structure and comparison by organizational structure.

- Learning ability: the higher the learning ability, the easier it is to update tags during socialization and internalization

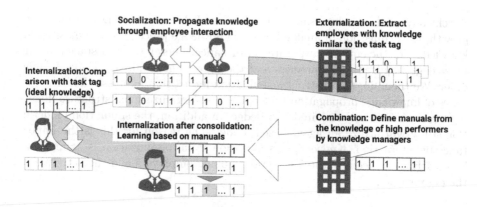

Fig. 1. This figure shows the SECI model with agent based simulation [5].

- Hierarchy: knowledge is more likely to be propagated from employees in higher hierarchies to those in lower hierarchies and vice versa during socialization.
- Culture tag: Compare not only the similarity of task tags, but also the culture of the company and its employees, and measure the combined results in terms of performance.
- Termination/Hiring: Add termination and hiring activities as company activities (Fig. 1).

In this simulation, knowledge tags and culture tags are introduced. Knowledge tags and culture tags are vectors consisting of N elements, where each element s_k and c_k consists of M patterns, where N and M represent the diversity of knowledge, respectively; the larger the value, the more complex the knowledge. We also introduce a new knowledge tag as an important element of this study. The new knowledge tag is the knowledge required by society, such as Digital Transformation (DX) and Green Transformation (GX), which have been seen in recent years, and is the target knowledge that organizations should aim to acquire.

Company Agents. Company has knowledge tags and culture tags as attributes. Company actions include updating firm knowledge, firing employees, and hiring. Updating firm knowledge involves ranking the employees in a firm based on their performance, extracting the top few percent, and defining new firm knowledge tags from the knowledge tags held by these high performers. In other words, in this study, the corporate knowledge tag is not defined in a fixed manner, but is treated as something that is dynamically updated by high performing employees in a company.

Employee Agents. Employees have knowledge tags, culture tags, learning capabilities, and organizational hierarchy as attributes. Employee agents share knowledge, self-learn, and execute tasks.

3 Implementation of the SECI Model in This Study

We expanded the SECI model which modeled in previous study. In this study, performance is calculated in the phase of "Execution of Operations" in order to demonstrate the effectiveness of the process. In addition, the termination and hiring process will be introduced according to the performance by the execution of operations. The model for calculating the probability of knowledge acquisition in the SECI model is based on Hashimoto and Fujiwara et al. (2013), and new elements such as learning ability and hierarchy are added in this study.

Socialization. In the socialization phase, knowledge is shared, i.e., one employee's knowledge tag is updated to another employee's knowledge tag, through interaction among employees. The probability that an element s of the knowledge tag of one employee i is updated to an element s' of the knowledge tag of another employee i' is defined as follows

$$\begin{cases} p_{ii'} = \alpha(1 - d_{ii'})(r_i + \frac{1}{N})^{o_i l_{ii'}} & for \quad P_i \geq P_{i'} \\ p_{ii'} = \alpha(r_i + \frac{1}{N})^{o_i l_{ii'}} & for \quad P_i < P_{i'} \end{cases} \tag{1}$$

$$d_{ii'} = P_i - P_{i'} \quad 0 \leq d_{ii'} \leq 1 \tag{2}$$

$$o_i = \frac{1}{a_i} \tag{3}$$

$$l_{ii'} = \frac{l_i}{l_{i'}} \tag{4}$$

Here r_i is the similarity between employee i's knowledge and the new knowledge calculated using the Hamming distance h_i, and is a value that indicates how well the employee is able to fulfill the knowledge required by society when viewed from the knowledge base. Also, P_i represents the performance of employee i, a_i the learning ability, and l_i the layer. Note that the Hamming distance has a smaller value the higher the similarity, but in r, the closer the distance is, the higher the value should be expressed, so it is calculated as follows.

$$r_i = 1 - h_i \tag{5}$$

In addition, d_i means the difference in performance between the employee at the source of knowledge sharing and the employee at the destination of knowledge sharing. In other words, if the performance of the sharing source is low, the motivation to inherit knowledge from it is considered to be small, and thus the inheritance probability is adjusted to be lower. The o_i is calculated from the learning ability of the shared employee, and the higher the learning ability, the more likely the employee is to acquire knowledge. Furthermore, $l_{ii'}$ is calculated from the hierarchy of each interacting employee, and is set so that the update probability increases when the hierarchy of the sharing source is higher than that of the sharing destination, and decreases when the opposite is true. This assumes teaching, in which knowledge is transferred from supervisor to subordinate. Finally, α serves as a parameter that represents the efficiency of knowledge acquisition for the organization as a whole. Note that the combination of employees with which the interaction occurs is randomly set by the regular network of order 4.

Externalization. The Representation phase identifies the knowledge of employees who are excellent performers. Each employee is ranked according to his or her performance, and the top few percent are identified as high performers.

Combination. In the Combination phase, the knowledge tags of the extracted high performers are combined and set as the knowledge required for the new enterprise. The merging method is determined by majority voting for each element of the knowledge tag. In other words, if three knowledge tags [1,0,1], [0,0,0], and [0,1,1] are extracted, [0,0,1] is newly set as the knowledge required by the company.

Internalization. In the internalization phase, employees learn the knowledge required by the newly established firm and their knowledge tags are updated. The probability that an element s of a knowledge tag held by an employee i is updated to an element $s^{Company}$ of the company's knowledge tag is defined as follows

$$p_i = \alpha(r_i + \frac{1}{N})^{o_i} \qquad (6)$$

Execution of Operations. Each employee's knowledge tag is updated through the four processes represented in the SECI model. Employees calculate performance by performing tasks based on the knowledge they have acquired. Performance is calculated by knowledge tag and culture tag as follows

$$P_i = \beta r_i + (1 - \beta)r_i^{culture}, \quad 0 \leq \beta \leq 1 \qquad (7)$$

In addition, β represents the preferences that firms have. In other words, the closer β is to 1, the more a firm values business knowledge, and the closer β is to 0, the more it values culture fit.

Where r_i is calculated from the similarity between the employee's knowledge tag and the new knowledge tag. In other words, performance is calculated such that the closer the employee's knowledge tag is to the socially required knowledge tag, the higher the value. In addition, $r_i^{culture}$ is calculated using the Hamming distance $h_i^{culture}$, which is the similarity between the employee's culture tag and the company's culture tag, as follows

$$r_i^{culture} = 1 - h_i^{culture} \qquad (8)$$

Performance is thus determined by the degree to which the employee's knowledge matches the new knowledge and the cultural fit with the company.

Dismissal and Hiring. Termination is based on the performance of the employees in the company, and the bottom few percent are selected and removed from the company's employee list. In the firing and hiring process, employees with low performance are fired and an equal number of agents are hired as employees. Note that at the time of initial hiring, the agents' behavior is set so that employees with knowledge required by society are hired, and thereafter, the agents' behavior is set so that they inherit the attributes including the tags of the high-performing employees so that the performance of the firm as a whole is enhanced.

Measurement Items. In the simulation process, the average $\bar{p}$ of employee performance, the average $\bar{r}$ of agreement with the corporate knowledge tag, and the average $\bar{r}^{culture}$ of agreement with the corporate culture tag are measured for each ticks, and the changes over time are visualized, changes in corporate performance and the knowledge propagation process of the organization. The evaluation formulas for each measurement item for n number of employees are as follows

$$\bar{p} = \frac{1}{n} \sum_{i=1}^{n} P_i \tag{9}$$

$$\bar{r} = \frac{1}{n} \sum_{i=1}^{n} r_i \tag{10}$$

$$\bar{r}^{cultrue} = \frac{1}{n} \sum_{i=1}^{n} r_i^{cultrue} \tag{11}$$

4 Results

4.1 Validation of the Model

In order to use this simulation model, we will validate the model's usability. The validation method follows previous studies and compares the change in the speed of knowledge propagation when the complexity of knowledge is varied and when the organizational learning efficiency is varied.

Impact of Knowledge Complexity. One of the parameters, Knowledge tag length, represents the number of elements in a knowledge tag. In the tag model, the greater the number of elements, the more complex the attribute, and the longer it is expected to take to transform the culture. Therefore, in this validation, the usefulness of the model is verified by changing the Knowledge tag length and comparing the transition to the acquisition of corporate knowledge across the organization. As a result, it was found that the larger the value of Knowledge tag length, the longer it takes to acquire corporate knowledge, as shown in Fig. 2.

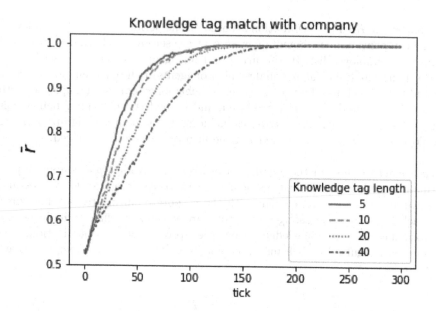

Fig. 2. Impact of Knowledge Complexity

Impact of Overall Learning Efficiency. Then, one of the parameters, α, represents the overall learning efficiency. The image of the parameter is that it indicates whether the environment in which employees are placed, such as having learning tools in place, makes it easier for them to acquire knowledge. It is commonly applied to all employees who are members of the organization, and the higher the value, the easier it is to acquire knowledge during internalization and socialization. Therefore, in this validation, the usefulness of the model is tested by varying α and comparing the transition to the acquisition of corporate knowledge across the organization. As a result, it was found that the larger the value of α is, the shorter the time to achieve the acquisition of corporate knowledge becomes, as shown in Fig. 3.

Basic Parameter Settings. The basic parameters to be used in this experiment are set as in Table 1.

Effects by Learning Ability and Organizational Structure

Comparison by Learning Capacity. Employee type, which represents the ability to learn, is represented by [1,4], with higher values indicating easier knowledge acquisition. The percentage of employee types in the organization and changing process of percentage are compared. The four patterns in Table 2 are set for the ratio of employee types in the organization. Then, we will observe the changes over time by running the test 30 times and taking the average of the measurement items.

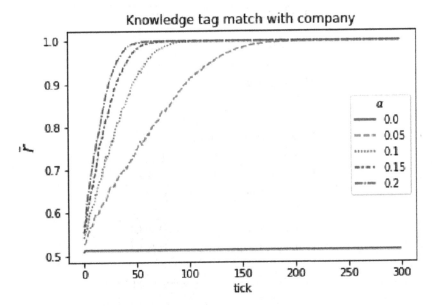

Fig. 3. Impact of overall learning efficiency

From Fig. 4, it can be seen that the case with the most people with high learning ability achieves the fastest match with the corporate knowledge, while the case with all people with low learning ability takes the longest time to achieve it. On the other hand, from Fig. 4, performance is highest in the case where everyone has low learning ability, and in the case where most people have high learning ability, initial performance is high, but the increase stops at a certain value and eventually the performance becomes the lowest. This means that organization with high learning ability achieves the knowledge propagation required by the company at an early stage, but fail to capture the social requirements. This situation suggests that even in organizations with high learning ability, effective knowledge acquisition may not be achieved if the knowledge to be acquired is only from within the organization.

Comparison by Hierarchy. The organizational hierarchy is denoted by [1, 4]. During socialization, knowledge is more likely to be propagated from employees in higher hierarchies to those in lower hierarchies. In addition, the larger the difference in hierarchy, the greater the propagation effect. In order to compare the change in the transition of the knowledge acquisition process according to the proportion of employees in each hierarchy in an organization, the four patterns are prepared as Table 3. Then, we will observe the changes in the time series by running the test 100 times and taking the average of the measurement items.

From Fig. 5, the matching to the company knowledge tag does not change depending on the hierarchical structure of the organization. On the other hand, in the performance of Fig. 5, the case where all members are in the same hierarchy

Table 1. Basic parameter settings

parameter	value
Number of employees	40
Skill tag length: N	40
Culture tag length: N	40
Number of tag factors: M	2
Learning efficiency ratio: α	0.05
Company preference: β	1
High performer ratio	0.025
Low performer ratio	0.025
Ticks	300
Employee's layer: l	[1,2,3,4]
Employee's type: o	[1,2,3,4]

Table 2. Percentage of employee types

Organization type	employee type			
	1	2	3	4
All with low learning ability Type	1.0	0.0	0.0	0.0
Most of them have low learning ability	0.5	0.3	0.15	0.05
Most people have high learning ability	0.05	0.15	0.3	0.5
Each type is equally present	0.25	0.25	0.25	0.25

is the easiest to rise, and the performance is lower in the case of three or more layers. This can be attributed to the difficulty of socialization. In other words, knowledge is easily transferred from employees at higher levels of the hierarchy to those at lower levels, so that when employees at higher levels of the hierarchy possess knowledge that is socially required, it is easier to transfer it to employees at lower levels. However, the cases in which knowledge transfer should occur are those in which the employee higher in the hierarchy is performing well, otherwise, negative knowledge transfer may occur, and the propagation of new knowledge will stagnate. As a result, it is assumed that the highest performance is achieved in organizations where the volatility of knowledge transfer by hierarchy is small, and where all employees are in the same hierarchy.

5   Discussion

The study presented three main findings through an agent simulation model. Firstly, the multi-agent simulation model based on the SECI model of the previous study was extended to more closely resemble a realistic organization. As a result, we confirmed that the behavior of the model changes correctly when the

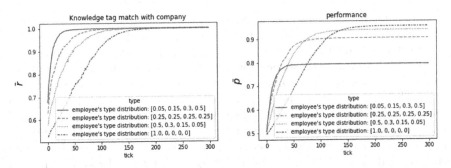

Fig. 4. Organization with employee type 4, i.e., those with more people with high learning ability, is faster in fitting the company knowledge tag. On the other hand, organization where all employees are 1 is the slowest in acquiring the company knowledge. Note that the value for the first tick is different because the measurement items are measured after the first tick of the SECI model process. Regarding performance, organization with all employees type 1 has the best performance and organization with the most type 4 has the worst performance.

Table 3. Hierarchy type percentage

Organization type	employee layer			
	1	2	3	4
No hierarchy	1.0	0.0	0.0	0.0
2 hierarchies	0.5	0.5	0.0	0.0
3 hierarchies	0.33	0.34	0.33	0.0
4 hierarchies	0.25	0.25	0.25	0.25

parameters are varied. Secondly, organizations with a higher proportion of quick learners can adapt faster, though they may initially focus too much on existing knowledge, delaying the integration of new, essential knowledge. To prevent this situation, introducing new knowledge from external sources, such as through hiring or external training, might be proposed as a solution to enhance performance effectively. Hiring simulation will be modeled in future research. Thirdly, the model illustrated the impact of organizational hierarchy on performance, indicating that flatter structures facilitate better knowledge transfer and performance improvements. This is consistent with the perception stated in Shiraishi (2010) that flattening, which reduces the number of hierarchies, has contributed to the recovery of firms' performance [2]. However, completely eliminating hierarchy is not deemed practical, highlighting a need for a balanced approach that includes the benefits of middle management [3]. Future research will expand the model's parameters and explore various organizational structures to understand knowledge propagation better. This includes examining how different network types affect knowledge spread and changing the value of β to express the more complex cases because 1 is quite extreme and simplified case. Although the simulation aligns with theoretical expectations, validating the model against real-world data is essential to improve its relevance and applicability. Future plans include conducting surveys to compare the simulation's outcomes with actual organizational performance, aiming to refine the model for practical use. The study acknowledges the limitations of focusing solely on the SECI model for knowledge propagation and suggests extending the simulation to encompass knowledge creation. It also reflects on the nuanced process of knowledge sharing within organizations, considering the potential gaps in capturing the subtleties of tacit knowledge exchange. In conducting this study, we interviewed Mr. Fujiwara, the author of Hashimoto and Fujiwara et al. (2013). He stated that the model proposed in the paper was regarded as having useful results in the field at the time of writing. They proposed two specific measures based on the model: (1) personnel transfers should be a mixture of employees who are transferred in long and short cycles, and (2) employees with good communication skills should experience a variety of workplaces. Regarding point 1, he said that employees who are transferred on a long cycle are expected to improve the quality of their knowledge, but the quality fluctuates widely, so by combining them with employees who are transferred on a short cycle, the organization can improve quality while minimizing fluctuation. Regarding point 2, the paper stated that by promoting communication across group boundaries, knowledge acquisition will increase as a whole. The role of the simulation model is to provide hints of what kind of impact can occur in reality by changing parameters such as the transfer cycle of employees (which is defined as the period of employment in the paper) and the scope of interaction among employees, and by using factors that can be moved as measures as parameters, the model can be used in the field. The model can be utilized in the field by setting parameters that can be moved as measures. Unfortunately, no actual measures have been implemented based on the results, but this is due to the fact that the parameters of the model could not be identified as realistic, and the results were difficult to interpret because they were analyzed using hypothetical values rather than technical problems. In other words, I understood that the values of parameters such as how long is a transfer cycle and how is the distance between an employee and an out-group defined in reality may not be clear in reality. However, in my opinion, it is possible to divide the employee transfer cycle into short, medium, and long-term periods without identifying the values so strictly, and to actively encourage employees who are evaluated as having good communication skills to participate in projects that cross over group boundaries. In such cases, it is necessary to separately measure the effectiveness of the measures to see if the quality of knowledge has improved. As there are cases where the results of simulation models are used in actual workplaces, we would like to create opportunities to use the models developed in this study in business settings.

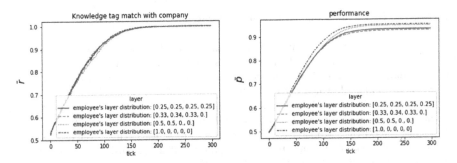

Fig. 5. No differences by organizational structure of layers are observed with respect to match to company knowledge tags. Performance is highest in organizations with no layers and performance is lowest when the layer is more than 3.

6   Conclusion

In this study, we aimed to construct a simulation model of how existing and new knowledge, if any, are propagated by the firm structure. As a result, by extending the model based on the SECI model of the previous study, we were able to construct a new model consistent with the previous study. In the next step, we will incorporate actions such as hiring personnel with new knowledge and acquiring knowledge by attending external study groups into the model in order to test the hypothesis and obtain implications for specific measures to address issues such as what measures should be taken to efficiently propagate new knowledge in each organizational structure.

References

1. Nonaka, I., Takeuchi, H.: The Knowledge-Creating Company. Toyo Keizai Inc. (1996). (in Japanese)
2. Shiraishi, H.: The impact of expanding the number of managers through flattening on employee development - exploring the long-term risks inherent in the expansion of the number of managers. Res. Bull. Works Rev. **5**(9), 1–12 (2010). (in Japanese)
3. Ito, H., Moriya, F.: An economic theory of middle management: monitoring function, information transfer function and middle dilemma. Jpn. Inst. Labour **51**(11), 47–59 (2009). (in Japanese)
4. Kikuchi, T., Kunigami, M., Takahashi, H., Toriyama, M., Terano, T.: Description of decision making process in actual business cases and virtual cases from organizational agent model using managerial decision-making description model. J. Inf. Process. **60**(10), 1704–1718 (2019). (in Japanese)
5. Hashimoto, G., Fujiwara, T., Suzuzki, M., Okuda, H., Ise, J., Shioya, M.: Multi-agent based simulation of knowledge propagation in organizations. IEEJ Trans. Electron. Inf. Syst. **133**(9), 1770–1778 (2013). (in Japanese)
6. Fujita, Y., Nakase, A., Nakayama, Y., Toriumi, F., Ishii, K.: Knowledge management modeling in organization. IPSJ SIG Tech. Rep. **90**(1), 52–61 (2007). (in Japanese)

7. Argyris, C.: Double loop learning in organizations. Harv. Bus. Rev. **55**(5), 115–125 (1977)
8. Kaschig, A., et al.: Organizational learning from the perspective of knowledge maturing activities. IEEE Trans. Learn. Technol. **6**(2), 158–176 (2013)
9. Hedlund, G.: A model of knowledge management and the N-form corporation. Strateg. Manag. J. **15**(S2), 73–90 (1994)
10. Bonabeau, E.: Agent-based modeling: methods and techniques for simulating human systems. Proc. Natl. Acad. Sci. **99**(suppl 3), 7280–7287 (2002)
11. Nikkei Asia. Prime Minister Kishida's policy statement: "1 trillion yen over 5 years" to support reskilling[Translated from Japanese] (2022). https://www.nikkei.com/article/DGXZQOUA30ACD0Q2A930C2000000/. Accessed 3 Oct 2022
12. Persol Innovation. Reskilling Support Service "Learning Coach", Fixed-point survey on reskilling, vol. 2 (2023 edition) [Translated from Japanese] (2023). https://persol-innovation.co.jp/news/2023/0616-4/. Accessed 20 June 2023

Research on Improving Decision-Making Efficiency with ChatGPT

Hiroyasu Seita and Setsuya Kurahashi[✉]

Graduate School of Tsukuba University, Tsukuba, Japan
{s1830138,kurahashi.setsuya.gf}@u.tsukuba.ac.jp

Abstract. ChatGPT, a generative AI released in 2022, quickly gained global attention and reached 100 million users within two months of its release. Since then, its applications have expanded beyond a simple search engine to include customer support, content generation, translation, and educational support. In this study, we examined the possibility of using ChatGPT in decision-making scenarios to reduce the time required for decision-making. The results of a game-based experiment showed that a single person interacting with ChatGPT could produce decision-making results equivalent to an extensive discussion by multiple people. This suggests that there are advantages in terms of reduced decision-making time and workload.

Keywords: Generative AI · ChatGPT · Gaming · Decision-making · Lead Time Reduction

1 Introduction

This chatbot is a generative AI developed by Sam Altman and colleagues at OpenAI and released in November 2022. It is characterized by its ability to converse with users in natural language using a large-scale language model. Its applications are diverse, including customer support, content generation, translation, and educational support. Recently, applications in the medical, financial, and legal fields are also being considered. In conventional decision-making, when there are conflicts of interest or contradictions, discussions involving multiple parties are required, which often take an enormous amount of time and effort. In addition, it often requires a variety of knowledge and information, including legal, scientific, technical, and accounting knowledge, and the optimal solution must be selected from among a variety of possibilities. In these situations, ChatGPT has the potential to significantly reduce decision-making lead time and effort.

2 Prior Research

Several studies have been conducted on the effectiveness of AI support in decision making; Mohammad Hossein Jarrahi (2018) focused on the complementarity between humans and AI, examining their respective strengths in organizational decision-making

© The Author(s), under exclusive license to Springer Nature Singapore Pte Ltd. 2024
T. Suzumura and M. Bono (Eds.): JSAI-isAI 2024, LNAI 14741, pp. 35–46, 2024.
https://doi.org/10.1007/978-981-97-3076-6_3

processes characterized by uncertainty, complexity, and randomness. They found that the strength of AI lies in its superior computational processing power and analytical approach to augment human cognitive abilities when dealing with complexity, whereas the strength of humans lies in their ability to provide a holistic and intuitive approach to uncertainty and randomness. Anne D. Trunk, Hendrik Birkel, E. Hartmann (2020) pointed out that AI might not only help reduce inherent problems in the decision-making process but may amplify them. In contrast, Christoph Keding, Philip Meissner (2021) introduced a binet-based decision experiment targeting 150 senior executives, examining individual perceptions of AI-driven decision-making. Contrary to prior research on algorithm aversion, they found that adopting an AI-based advisory system positively impacted decision-making quality. The application of AI in the decision-making process remains a divisive topic. The complex decision-making process with conventional AI requires an enormous amount of manpower to process a large amount of information obtained as a result of AI searches and multi-person discussions for a variety of situations. In addition, while conventional AI only searches for relevant information and communicates it to decision makers, ChatGPT is unique in that it understands and responds to the intent of the questioner who needs to make a decision in a dialogic format. ChatGPT is unique in that it understands and responds to the intent of the questioner in a dialogic format. Moreover, it provides rich and well-organized information in an objective and easy-to-understand manner. Answers are sufficient but not wasteful because they are based on the way things should be, and because it is an interpersonal conversation, there is a sense of reality as if one is discussing with an in-person person. These characteristics make it easier for the questioner to accept the answers as opinions and to reach a consensus without unnecessary rejection. These features suggest that using ChatGPT in the decision-making process may reduce the time and manpower required for decision-making.

3 Research Objective

Using ChatGPT in the decision-making process may reduce the necessary manpower. Hence, the research hypothesis is: "By utilizing ChatGPT, a decision-maker, even if alone, can make decisions equivalent to those made after discussions among multiple individuals."

4 Research Method

We will test this hypothesis using a game. In this study, we compare the decision-making processes of participants and ChatGPT by changing the content of the episodes and the order of decision-making for a decision-making task of high difficulty. For this purpose, it is necessary for the research method to be flexible in setting highly difficult decision-making tasks and to allow participants to make decisions as if they were real events that happened to them, even if the tasks set are fictitious. In games as a research method, it is relatively easy to include complex situations in episodes and to incorporate devices to create a sense of realism. Therefore, while games are creative works, they are characterized by the fact that players' own experiences and feelings are reflected in the episodes and are undeniably treated as real-life problems of the participants. For these reasons, this study attempted to test the hypothesis using games as a means of observing the decision-making process. In the experiment, participants were divided into several groups and played a game.

The game participants were working graduate students: 14 (9 males and 5 females) for test 1, 12 (10 males and 2 females) for test 2.

Test 1: After dividing the participants into several groups, Episode 1, which includes conflicting solutions, is presented to each participant individually. Participants first make an individual decision and answer Yes/No to the outcome. Next, each group discusses and decides Yes/No as a group. The group is then presented with their opinions on Episode 1 as presented by ChatGPT. The group then discusses again and decides Yes/No. The initial group discussion time is 15 min, and the group discussion time after the presentation of ChatGPT's opinion is also 15 min. A similar procedure was followed in another episode 2. The contents of the episodes are shown in Table 1.

Test 2: Similarly, another episode 3 is presented to the participants. Participants first make their individual judgments. Then, in the reverse order of Test 1, ChatGPT opinions are presented first, and each individual makes a decision without group discussion and expresses his/her opinion with Yes/No. Then, a group discussion is held, and the group makes a decision as a group and states its opinion with Yes/No. After reading ChatGPT's opinion, 15 min are allotted for individual decision-making, and the time allotted for the subsequent group discussion is 15 min as well. The contents of the episodes 3 are shown in Table 2.

Table 1. Episodes of Test 1

Episode 1	Episode 2
The Omicron strain is now available and is spreading to young people. You have been tasked with promoting vaccination in your community. The risk of infection is increasing, although the rate of serious illness among young people is low. On the other hand, there are whispers that vaccination may cause transient painful swelling, fatigue, and fever, as well as infertility and taste blindness, and there are concerns about liability issues in the event of health problems caused by vaccination. Ms. X, who is in her 20s, says she does not dare to be vaccinated because of the risk of side effects. Would you recommend that Ms. X be vaccinated? A. Recommend B. Do not recommend	You are a restaurant manager. The number of bankruptcies in the restaurant industry has skyrocketed during the pandemic, and you are facing great difficulties. Restaurants are still considered to be places with a high risk of infection, and this time, too, restaurants were required to take some kind of countermeasures. Under these circumstances, a proposal was presented to check vaccination and test negative records for employees and customers working in restaurants. Would you refuse entry to a restaurant to an employee or customer who does not have a vaccination/negative test record? A. Allow B. Refuse

Table 2. Episodes of Test 2

Episode 3
Mr. B of mask manufacturer Company A is responsible for shipping. Due to the recent outbreak of coronas, medical institutions nationwide are strapped for masks. Company A supplies 10,000 masks per day to medical institutions nationwide, but has an excess backorder that exceeds its production capacity. One day, during the outgoing inspection process, a mask was found to be slightly damaged visually, and when more inspections were conducted, the defect rate was estimated to be 0.5%. Under normal circumstances, the masks should have failed the inspection, but if they are not shipped, many healthcare workers will be at risk of infection. Mr. B, do you ship these masks? Yes, I will ship. No. Do not ship

5 Research Results

5.1 Comparison of Changes in Yes/No Ratios by Decision-Making Process

In Test 1, there was a change in the group decision-making results compared to the individual decision-making results (Yes/No ratio). However, there was no change in the group discussion results after the subsequent presentation of ChatGPT opinions, which were the same as the decision-making results during the group discussion (see Fig. 1). On the other hand, in Test 2, similarly, there was a change in the individual and individual decision-making results after ChatGPT's opinion presentation, but no change when compared to the results of the subsequent group discussion (see Fig. 2).

In other words, individual decision-making results after viewing ChatGPT opinions were equivalent to the discussion results without viewing ChatGPT opinions.

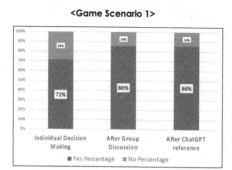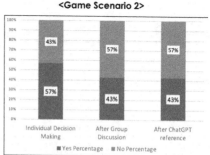

Fig. 1. Change in Yes/No ratio in the decision-making process for Test 1

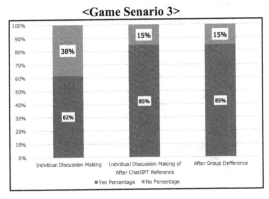

Fig. 2. Change in Yes/No ratio in the decision-making process in Test 2

5.2 Linguistic Analysis of Decision-Making Processes Using ChatGPT

By comparing the results of applying co-occurrence analysis to the series of decision-making processes using ChatGPT conducted in Test 2, we will examine how ChatGPT affects the decision-making process. First, we conducted a co-occurrence analysis of ChatGPT's views, followed by a co-occurrence analysis of participants' reasons for decision-making in each process (decision-making based solely on ChatGPT's views and subsequent group discussions) conducted using ChatGPT's views for Episode 3. Finally, we analyzed the co-occurrence of reasons for decision-making in the group discussions. The results of these co-occurrence analyses are shown in Fig. 3a–c. The results were compared with the opinions of ChatGPT in Episode 3.

From the co-occurrence analysis results in Fig. 3a, b:

1. Shipment of masks, considering quality risk and prioritizing the safety of health care workers.
2. Communication with the counterparties before shipment.
3. Implementation of quality measures

These are common, indicating that the reasons for the decisions made by the individuals were derived from the views of ChatGPT.

Figure 3c also shows that, from the group discussions

1. Shipments are made after clearly communicating the possibility that defective products may be included due to an emergency situation.
2. Defective products are shipped as irregular processing.
3. Ship first, consider immediate countermeasures, and consider how to deal with defective products in the future.

These are common and indicate that the reasons for the individual's decision were derived from the ChatGPT's views. The reasons for decisions made by group discussions also derive from the ChatGPT's views. Taken together, the reasons for decisions, both by individuals and by group discussions, are derived from ChatGPT's views.

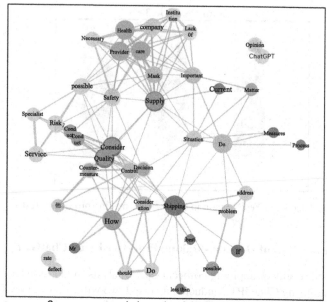

a.   Co-occurrence analysis results of the views expressed by ChatGPT

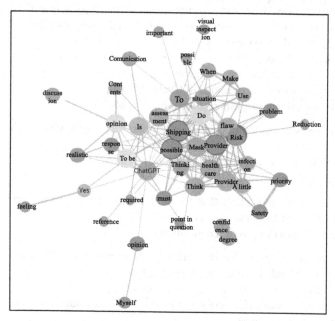

b.   Co-occurrence analysis results of reasons for decision making by individual participants using ChatGPT views

Fig. 3. Co-occurrence analysis of ChatGPG opinions and participants' reasons for their decisions in each decision process.

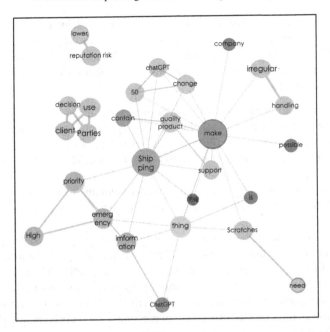

c.Co-occurrence analysis results for reasons for decision-making in subsequent group discussions

Fig. 3. (*continued*)

5.3 Investigation of the Effectiveness of Repeated Discussions as a Measure to Reduce Distrust of ChatGPT

In the results of the above test, some members expressed negative opinions about the GPT. This is considered to be a low level of conviction with the GPT and may hinder its effectiveness in the process of implementing measures after they are formulated. Repeated discussions with the GPT as a practice to increase the level of conviction could be considered, and the effectiveness of this practice will be tested.

The following research hypotheses were developed

Hypothesis; Repeated discussions with GPTs will decrease negative views of GPTs. The validation procedure was as follows.

Test3 was conducted using the following experimental procedure. The first subject is given episode 4. (See Table 3) After a 20-min discussion among participants, we repeated the discussion on GPT and measures within the same time period, and extracted negative opinions from the discussion. The test participants were 34 working graduate students. 34 working graduate students, 27 males and 7 females. Figure 4 shows the results of the co-occurrence analysis of the countermeasures proposed in the participants' discussions and those proposed by chatGPT in its discussions with the participants. The repeated discussions with chatGPT after the discussions by the participants revealed that, in addition to the countermeasures proposed in the discussions by the participants, chatGPT proposed to discuss them in advance with the relevant departments. The following is the evaluation of chatGPT given by the participants during the discussions with chatGPT.

<Member's remarks>

- The method of examining countermeasures using ChatGPT is very interesting.
- I felt that it would provide a foothold for considering effective countermeasures while avoiding human disadvantages (discovery and group blind spots).
- The fact that we are dealing with AI allows us to ask neutrally what we should have done as a company.
- The team was also able to suggest and discuss medium- to long-term issues that are difficult to notice from the on-site perspective, such as education and fostering a workplace culture.
- The answers from the chatGPT were similar to ours, and it provided an opportunity to think about the role that humans should play as AI develops in the future.
- With regard to creating a climate conducive to communication, as suggested in the participants' discussion, the chatGPT further proposes the following five measures.

    (1) Improvement of communication channels; (2) Promotion of teamwork (e.g., regular team meetings); (3) Improvement of communication skills (training/training); (4) Promotion of awareness-raising (educational activities to raise awareness of quality control); and (5) Supervisor leadership (promotion of communication and awareness raising) were mentioned.

    In response to the chatGPT measures, participants stated that the implementation of the above measures to create a corporate culture is expected to make the organization more effective in preventing fraud.

- The team's conclusion, based on the opinions of the chatGPT, is that long-term education and system building are necessary to prevent such fraud.In addition, although their opinions differed from those of the GPT, many of them were positive about the GPT's measures, such as incorporating the GPT's findings and developing better countermeasures.

Table 3. Episodes of Test 3

A company Y, an automobile manufacturer, has a large backlog of orders due to the recent eco-car boom and wants to increase productivity as much as possible. He realized that since he already knows whether the product has "passed" or "failed" before inputting the results, he should change the order of the work and input the inspection results after sending the inspected products to the subsequent process if they have passed. At the time, Mr. C's process is about to be overflowing with cars waiting for inspection. Will Mr. C follow through with this new idea? Mr. X, the factory manager, has told the workers to go beyond the norm and implement any idea that can increase production by even one more unit! If we don't implement these improvements, we will have to spend one million yen a year. If we don't implement this improvement, we will lose one million yen a year, and our boss will be in a bad position.

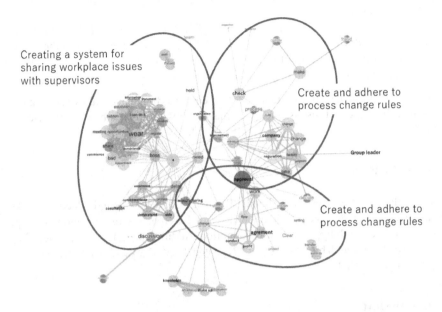

a. Co-occurrence analysis of measures presented by participants in discussions

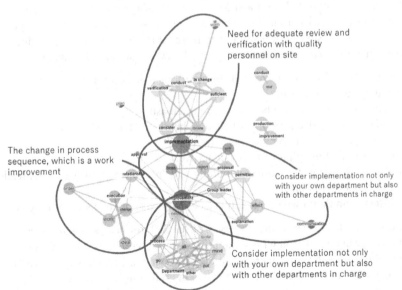

b. Co-occurrence analysis results for reasons for decision-making in subsequent group discussions

Fig. 4. Co-occurrence analysis of ChatGPG opinions and participants' reasons for their decisions in each decision process.

They also differed from the GPT in their opinions, but were positive about the GPT's measures.

- We did not find any negative opinions about GPT, and our distrust of GPT diminished as we discussed with them. Even when they differed from the opinions of the CHAT-GPT, they did not reject all of them, but rather constructively incorporated some of them, leading to better planning of countermeasures.

In conclusion, no negative evaluation of chatGPT was found in the above evaluations, suggesting that repeated discussions with chatGPT may mitigate the negative view of chatGPT.

6 Conclusions

Based on the results of Test1 and Test2, "By using ChatGPT, a single decision maker can make a decision that is equivalent to a decision based on discussion among multiple people." This research hypothesis was supported. Additionally, the results of test 3 are also support the research hypothesis that "Repeated discussions with GPTs will decrease negative views of GPTs."

7 Discussion

The experimental results of Tests 1 and 2 indicate that using ChatGPT for decision making can be as effective as a group discussion with multiple people, even with one person. This suggests the possibility of a significant increase in decision-making productivity. After the game, the following comments were observed from the participants:

- It was found that decisions were made by clarifying risks and taking countermeasures so that they can be shipped.
- It is easy to make a decision because there is a reason.
- The outcome of the decision did not change, but the certainty increased.
- ChatGPT's professional opinion was helpful.
- ChatGPT's impartial opinions were persuasive.
- In the team discussion, the team that initially said "no" changed to "yes" after reading back ChatGPT's opinion.
- If it differs from their own opinion, it is a clue to revise or change their judgment.

Experimental results show that the use of ChatGPT for decision making can be as effective as a group discussion with several people, even with one person. This suggests the possibility of a significant increase in decision-making productivity. Observations of participants' opinions after the game yielded the following comments:

- It was found that decisions were made by clarifying risks and taking countermeasures so that they can be shipped.
- It is easy to make a decision because there is a reason.
- The outcome of the decision did not change, but the certainty increased.
- ChatGPT's professional opinion was helpful.
- ChatGPT's impartial opinions were persuasive.

- In the team discussion, the team that initially said "no" changed to "yes" after reading back ChatGPT's opinion.
- If it differs from their own opinion, it is a clue to revise or change their judgment.

There were some positive comments about the use of ChatGPT, such as.On the other hand, some were skeptical or concerned about the use of ChatGPT, as follows.

- ChatGPT can use data to make accurate judgments, but only humans can make true "judgments."
- It only provides general information and does not influence decision-making.
- There is concern that ChatGPT reinforces one's own confirmation bias.

However, as shown in the results of Test 3, no such negative opinions were found in the other cases where discussions were repeated with ChatGPT. This result may be due to the fact that ChatGPT, unlike conventional AI, not only displays search results, but also provides expert-like advanced knowledge that captures the context of the episode, making it useful for decision making and persuasive in its unbiased opinions.

While the practical significance of this study is that it demonstrated that decision-making costs can be significantly reduced, its academic significance is that the ChatGPT was recognized as a multifaceted, objective, and balanced view that eliminated opportunistic biases and had a significant impact on decision-making. The second academic significance is that ChatGPT was shown to be persuasive and effective through repeated discussions just as among humans.

8 Limitations and Future Directions of this Study

Limitations of this study include concerns that the quality and content of more complex episodes might yield different results and the small number of subjects. Future research should examine how the content of the ChatGPT questions, the words, the words themselves, and their context, or linguistic structure, affect the ChatGPT responses and people's views of those responses, and how they affect people's decision-making outcomes and sense of conviction These are important research topics, both practically and academically, and are the subject of future research.

References

Jarrahi, M.H.: Artificial intelligence and the future of work: human-AI symbiosis in organizational decision making. Bus. Horiz. **61**(4), 577–586 (2018)

Trunk, A.D., Birkel, H., Hartmann, E.: On the current state of combining human and artificial intelligence for strategic organizational decision making. Bus. Res. **13**, 875–919 (2020)

Keding, C., Meissner, P.: Managerial over-reliance on AI-augmented decision-making processes: how the use of AI-based advisory systems shapes choice behavior in R&D investment decisions. Technol. Forecast. Soc. Change **171**, 120970 (2021)

Vaswani, A., Shazeer, N., et al.: Attention is all you need. In: Proceedings of the 30th Conference on Neural Information Processing Systems (NIPS) (2017)

Müller, H., Mancuso, F.: Identification and analysis of co-occurrence networks with NetCutter. PLOS J. (2008). https://journals.plos.org. Accessed 28 Jan 2024

Stam, D., de Vet, A., Barkema, H., Dreu, C.D.: Suspending group debate and developing concepts. J. Prod. Innov. Manag. **30**, 48–61 (2013)

Álvarez-Gálvez, J.: Network models of minority opinion spreading. Soc. Sci. Comput. Rev. (2016). https://journals.sagepub.com. Accessed 28 Jan 2024

Cheng, V., Wong, S.-C., Chuang, V.W., et al.: The role of community-wide wearing of face mask for control of coronavirus disease 2019 (COVID-19) epidemic due to SARS-CoV-2. J. Infect. **81**(1), 107–114 (2020)

Kim, G., Park, S.: Understanding restaurant users' attitudes towards self-service ordering via kiosks during the COVID-19 pandemic: an application of the theory of anxiety. Tourism Hospitality Res. **24**(1) (2020)

Jeong, J.-Y., Lee, H.: Determinants of restaurant consumers' intention to practice COVID-19 preventive behavior: an application of the theory of planned behavior. Nutr. Res. Pract. (2021). https://doi.org/10.4162/nrp.2021.15.S1.S79. Accessed 28 Jan 2024

Mascarenhas Danabal, K.G., Magesh, S., Saravanan, S.: Attitude towards COVID-19 vaccines and vaccine hesitancy in urban and rural communities in Tamil Nadu, India – a community-based survey. BMC Health Serv. Res. **21**, Article no. 994 (2021)

Oderanti, F., De Wilde, P.: Dynamics of business games with management of fuzzy rules for decision making. Int. J. Prod. Econ. **128**(1), 96–109 (2010)

Yiannakoulias, N., Gordon, J.N., Darlington, J.: The decision game: a serious game approach to understanding environmental risk management decisions. J. Risk Res. **23**(1) (2020)

First International Workshop on Fairness and Diversity Bias in AI-Driven Recruitment (BIAS 2024)

The BIAS project, a four-year research initiative co-funded by the European Commission and the Swiss State Secretariat for Education, Research, and Innovation, aims to identify and mitigate diversity biases in AI applications within the labor market. This project is expected to yield two main outcomes. First, the development of the Debiaser, an innovative and reliable technology utilizing natural language processing (NLP) and case-based reasoning (CBR) for recruitment and selection purposes. Second, the BIAS project seeks to deepen our understanding of diversity biases and fairness in AI applications within the labor market, advancing the interdisciplinary field of worker studies and facilitating capacity building within the HR community. To achieve these objectives, extensive consultation and co-creation efforts have been undertaken with diverse stakeholders, including HR practitioners, AI developers, policymakers, trade unions, civil society organizations, and scholars.

This first international workshop on fairness and diversity bias in AI-driven recruitment (BIAS 2024) aligned with this participatory approach, extending the discussion beyond Europe and convening brilliant scholars with diverse backgrounds and expertise. Held as part of the International Symposia on AI hosted by the Japanese Society of Artificial Intelligence (JSAI-isAI), BIAS 2024 spanned two days and featured interactive panel presentations and discussions exploring fairness and AI in the labor market from various legal, technological, and practical perspectives.

To ensure a robust program, we issued a call for papers and engaged consortium partners of the BIAS project to review and select the most suitable submissions for presentation. Authors received personalized feedback, and a selection of papers was chosen for inclusion in the post-proceedings volume.

We extend our gratitude to the Advisory and Program Committees of JURISIN 2020, all authors who contributed to BIAS 2024, and the Organizing Committee of JSAI-isAI.

Sincerely,

Carlotta Rigotti
Eduard Fosch-Villaronga

Governing AI in Hiring: An Effort to Eliminate Biased Decision

Muhammad Jibril[✉][iD] and Theresia A. Florentina[iD]

Universitas Gadjah Mada, Yogyakarta 55281, Indonesia
{muhammad.jibril,theresiaaverinaflorentina}@mail.ugm.ac.id

Abstract. The existence of bias and discrimination in the employment sector, especially hiring, is nothing new. The presence and the use of artificial intelligence (AI), however, may either address or worsen this issue. Unfortunately, the scarcity of AI regulation left this issue unaddressed. Therefore, this study aims to analyze the current laws and policies on the use of AI in hiring and make guidelines for policymakers in governing the use of AI in hiring. This study found that the only existing law specifically on the use of AI in hiring is the New York City Local Law 144 of 2021 regarding Automated Employment Decision Tools. There are, however, a plethora of bills and policies on AI as well as AI in employment. Subsequently, this study suggests that policymakers governing AI in employment consider the definition of AI tools, the scope of AI usage, the permissible human involvement in the employment process, the scope of employment, and the compliance measures.

Keywords: Artificial Intelligence · Regulation · Employment Bias Mitigation

1 Introduction

The process of hiring employees incurs both direct and indirect costs [1]. Hiring the wrong employee and then replacing them would incur subsequent costs. Thus, it is logical that organizations want to minimize these kinds of expenditures. One way of reducing these expenditures is by implementing AI in the recruitment process. It is reported that 23% of Australian Public Sector agencies used AI in hiring in 2022 [2]. In addition, a survey found that 92% of 259 HR leaders are planning to implement AI in their HR departments, one of them being in recruitment and hiring [3]. This is because AI is more efficient than humans [4,5]. The recruitment process, however, is not only a delicate issue for the organizations but also applicants. The European Union AI Act thus categorizes recruitment as high-risk AI systems because it impacts a person's livelihood as well as their future career outlooks [6]. Unfortunately, a study found that applicants who belong to a minority ethnic group face discrimination in acquiring employment [7]. This kind of discrimination may also occur in AI-based recruitment.

AI, just like any other tool, may be used either for good or bad doings. For example, a kitchen knife can be used to prepare dinner, but it can also be used

T. Suzumura and M. Bono (Eds.): JSAI-isAI 2024, LNAI 14741, pp. 49–63, 2024.
https://doi.org/10.1007/978-981-97-3076-6_4

for homicide. A computer may be used by a clerk to do their company's administrative tasks, but it can also be used to hack into other people's computers. Likewise, the use of AI in hiring has its pros and cons. For example, 12 out of 279 promotion decisions were overturned by the Australia Promotion Review Committees in the annual report of 2021–22 [8]. These overturns were caused by an outsourced recruitment specialist who utilized AI in the process wherein it was found that the selection process using the AI was not entirely based on merits [8]. Another notable case is the case of Amazon AI recruiting tools that are negatively biased towards women [9]. In other words, it is found that AI may produce biased decisions either in hiring or other employment actions such as promotion.

Nonetheless, although there is a vast amount of research on AI in the employment sector, it seems that research on how to regulate this phenomenon is still lacking. Many domains of law intersect with AI and employment such as data protection, transparency, fairness, anti-discrimination, etc. This paper, however, will focus on the domain of mitigating bias in the utilization of AI in hiring. This study will start by laying down the pros and cons of AI in hiring. Subsequently, this study will analyze the current laws and policies that address AI in the employment sector. Lastly, this study will aid policymakers in governing AI in the employment sector.

2   AI in Hiring: Benefits and Detriments

The utilization of AI in hiring presents numerous values for an organization. Studies found that machine learning, an application of AI, would cut a big chunk of repetitive administrative tasks in a hiring process [4,5]. In other words, automating these tasks would cut the time-consuming processes inherent in the hiring process [10]. This is supported by a study that shows that AI has at least 25% faster speed to process information and make decisions [11]. Moreover, holding tests and conducting interviews would incur costs for the organization [12]. Albeit AI hiring tools are arguably costly, AI hiring tools serve as an excellent investment for long-term use for organizations due to their efficiency and effectiveness [13]. This in turn, would lead to a reduction of expenditure in the hiring process and thus would benefit the organization.

Machine learning would not only benefit an organization in terms of its balance sheet but also impact the quality of hiring, i.e., acquiring suitable fit candidates [14]. In addition, a recent study shows that AI-based hiring also influences applicants' organizational commitment and their justice perceptions towards the hiring process [15]. In other words, applicants identify AI-based hiring to provide better fairness than conventional hiring [16]. Moreover, in terms of providing fairness, a study found that AI would provide more transparency compared to humans because it follows a specific set of rules that can be traced [17]. However, transparency would depend on the organization's policy, i.e., whether they are willing to open the information on how the aforesaid rules or algorithm performs [18]. It is conceded that ensuring transparency in AI-based hiring may prove to be difficult because the stakeholders must understand well how AI works, which can be challenging [15,19]. Thus, transparency may become a virtue or vice, depending on the policy adopted by the organization.

There is, however, one benefit of using AI in hiring that must be explicitly addressed, which is eliminating human biases. Conventional hiring processes are undoubtedly prone to human biases, which, in turn, lead to unfairness [20]. Many biases may occur in a hiring process, such as gender bias, ethnic bias, anchoring and adjustment bias, ingroup bias, cliche bias, label bias, or like-me bias [21]. These biases may be eliminated given that AI recruiting tools are more objective and not biased compared to humans [22]. Besides removing these biases, AI may also be utilized to evaluate prior biased decisions in the hiring process [10]. Thus, the implementation of AI in recruitment would produce an inclusive, diverse, and dynamic workplace [23].

Notwithstanding the fact that AI may reduce human biases in the hiring process, it is conceded that this feat is a double-edged sword that could bring harm to applicants. Detriment towards applicants comes from the fact that human intervention in AI-based hiring is inevitable. Fundamentally, AI's behaviour would depend on the algorithm it is designed with [21]. In addition, AI needs to analyze data patterns wherein the dataset itself must be provided by the user [24]. Consequently, AI is dependent on human assistance to make correct inferences in order to provide fair decisions [15]. Nonetheless, this also shows that biased AI and biased humans differ in the fact that if AI shows bias, unlike humans, it can be addressed and corrected [20]. It is thus accepted that hiring AI would not wholly remove human biases [12].

On the grounds that AI is reliant on human involvement, it is thus not farfetched to assume that the human operator itself may deliberately model the said AI to be biased [19,24]. This kind of scenario is possible to happen. Biased AI, however, is not only caused by deliberately designing its algorithms to be biased. The developer's bias may be mirrored by the AI [2]. Prior employee demographics data may also cause the AI to be biased [25]. For instance, previous employee demographic data from Amazon reveals a gender gap in employment, which led to the AI algorithm being mimicked by penalizing applicants who are recognized as female [9]. This shows that a single dataset may cause an unethical and unjustifiable recruitment decision. Therefore, the process of developing an AI-hiring tool should be executed with meticulous attention to detail [23]. Ultimately, considering the benefits of employing AI in hiring would outweigh its potential harm, it is argued that to prevent these unwanted incidents, AI-based hiring should be regulated rather than simply banned. The first step in governing AI-based hiring is to benchmark the current existing regulations to learn their merits and shortcomings as well as understand the salient features established in each of the regulations.

3   The Status Quo of AI-Based Hiring Regulation

3.1   Laws

New York City. New York City Local Law 144 of 2021 regarding Automated Employment Decision Tools (AEDT), the Bias Audit Law, up to this study, was a one-of-a-kind regulation regarding AI-based hiring. The Bias Audit Law, which amends Chapter 5 of Title 20 of the Administrative Code of the city of New York, was enforced by the New York City Department of Consumer and Worker Protection (DCWP). One of the things that should be mentioned about this law is its definition of AEDT.

Article §20-870 of the Bias Audit Law defines AEDT as *"any computational process, derived from machine learning, statistical modeling, data analytics, or artificial intelligence that issues simplified output, including a score, classification, or recommendation, that is used to substantially assist or replace discretionary decision making for making employment decisions that impact natural persons [...]"*. It is observed that the law sets AEDT to encompass a broader scope than AI. This shows us that biases may transpire not only in AI but also in other computational processes. In addition, this law uses the term employment decisions, which subsequently explains that it comprises both hiring and promotion. This gives us a hint that the utilization of automation in practice is not only for the hiring process but also for the promotion process. Consequently, the promotion process must also be considered when making the regulatory framework for using automation in hiring. Employment decisions also do not necessarily mean the final decision in employment because the law defines it as a *"means to screen"*, i.e., including the screening process. Thus, AEDT may be utilized in more than one employment scenario and more than one stage of a process.

The main objective of the Bias Audit Law is to prevent biased decisions through automation. The law requires the employer and employment agency (AEDT user) to conduct an impartial bias audit on the AEDT through an independent auditor, publicly publish the said bias audit result, and give notifications to applicants of the usage of the said AEDT. It should be noted that this law puts obligations only towards AEDT users, i.e., the developer and publisher of AEDT does not have a responsibility to do a bias audit. In support of the Bias Audit Law, it is submitted that assigning obligations to the right individual is an important aspect that should be kept in mind by policymakers. Responsibility should be carried by the AEDT user and not the vendor because the vendor arguably would design the algorithm by order of the AEDT user. Moreover, this is supported by the fact that the data used in the audit must be provided by the AEDT user and not the vendor. In conclusion, the Bias Audit Law shows that the compliance measures of audit, as the name implies, are the salient feature of the said law. This law also gives a hint on determining the definition of AI. Other than New York City, it was observed that the European Union (EU) is one of the parties actively formulating a legal framework for AI, notwithstanding the fact that there are still limited enacted EU laws that explicitly regulate AI in hiring.

European Union. The General Data Protection Regulation (GDPR) is the law that regulates data protection in many realms, one of it being data protection in Automated Decision-Making (ADM), accommodated through Article 22 concerning Automated individual decision-making, including profiling. In the GDPR, AI hiring tools are classified as ADM because their decisions are based on automated algorithms. Subsequently, Article 22 (1) of GDPR stated *"The data subject shall have the right not to be subject to a decision based solely on automated processing [...]"*. The notable nomenclature used by GDPR in this article is 'solely', which requires further analysis.

The consequence of using the nomenclature *'solely'* is that the ADM regulated by GDPR is one without human involvement, i.e., full usage of ADM [26, 27]. This is substantially different from other legal constructions used in other policies wherein the regulated automated processing usually involves human involvement, i.e., partial usage of ADM. A study argued that the legal constructions adopted by Article 22 of GDPR are insufficient to address harm arising from algorithmic management or in the context of risk arising from ADM [27]. It is said to be insufficient because most of the ADM used today, including in employment, is still algorithmically assisted by human operators [27]. It is submitted that this argument stands because such legal constructions would be too narrow and thus cannot reach partial usage of ADM. Moreover, the use of AI in hiring is still developing. The adaptations of GDPR amongst EU member states, however, come in different approaches, from the simple to the most complex: negative, neutral, procedural, and proactive [28]. France is one of the states that is proactive in drafting adaptations and making additional provisions for its laws.

A study found that French law is one of the most innovative and complex in regulating and implementing Article 22 of GDPR [28]. French law not only regulates ADM in the context of its data protection but also governs the usage of semi-ADM and full ADM in different manners, such as (1) judicial, (2) administrative, and (3) all other kinds [28, 29]. For example, in the judicial field, the usage of ADM to assess personality is prohibited. For the administrative field, the use of ADM is not permitted, except that ADM is allowed if all the requirements and safeguards are fulfilled. For private fields, there are much fewer restrictions. The French, other than separating the regulations into each field, also added rights endowed to the applicant in their law, such as the right to receive notification of the contestation outcome [28]. This provides transparency to the recruitment process, giving the applicant the right to recheck and challenge the decision. In summary, the EU GDPR establishes the importance of determining the scope of AI usage on AI in hiring. Nonetheless, although the EU GDPR and the NYC Bias Audit Law have been regulating AI in hiring, it seems that those are the only existing regulations regulating AI in hiring. Thus, it is beneficial to look at the existing bills and other policies that try to govern AI in hiring.

3.2   Bills and Guidance

The legal framework of AI in hiring is still very limited. However, many policy-makers are trying to regulate this issue, such as California's Bill AB331, which requires the deployer (the user of the automated decision-making tool) to perform an impact assessment of the automated decision tool. This is similar to the Bias Audit Law obligations to audit AEDT. Another note is Canada's Artificial Intelligence and Data Act, which addresses the biased output of AI systems. Recently, the EU Parliament and the EU Council, after lengthy negotiations, reached a provisional agreement on the AI Act, which is claimed to be the most comprehensive AI regulation in the world [30,31]. However, the act has not yet been officially adopted and published. The AI Act is a harmonized rule on AI systems that adopts a risk-oriented approach [32]. AI in the act is classified into four types based on the degree of the user dependence on the decision by AI and possible risk to health and violation of fundamental rights that are (1) minimal risk, (2) limited risk, (3) high risk, and (4) unacceptable risk. The level of risk determines conditions and standards that must be fulfilled, whereas the higher the risk, the more requirements must be fulfilled. Employment in the AI Act falls into the high-risk classification. The AI act determines employment to encompass all employment relations such as recruitment, promotion and termination, task allocation, monitoring and evaluation, and all relations-based work contracts [6]. Likewise, the United States is also on the track to provide a harmonized AI Act through the Algorithmic Accountability Act (AAA) 2023, which was first introduced in 2019. Unfortunately, this bill failed to pass Congress three consecutive years after the year it was introduced. Nonetheless, this act is designed to serve as a framework addressing the use, risk, and flawed design of ADS in the United States, requiring companies to conduct 'Algorithmic Impact Assessment' and 'Annual Summary Reports' to the Federal Trade Commission (FTC). In brief, these bills show us that the obligation to do an assessment or audit of the AI and define the scope of employment is fundamental. Other than bills, one of the policy types that should be mentioned is guidance.

One of the prime examples of guidance is Australia's guidance material for using AI-assisted recruitment tools published by the Australia Merit Protection Commissioners (MPC). Australia has been working on making regulations regarding AI [33]. Nonetheless, it is observed that Australia does not have any laws on the use of AI [34]. It is conceded that Australia has several policies on AI, such as the Artificial Intelligence Ethics Framework or Automated Decision-Making Better Practice Guide. However, none of these regulates AI-based hiring. Thus, the guidance published by the MPC is currently the only policy that may be referred to in Australia on the topic of AI-based hiring.

The MPC guidance mainly provides direction for government agencies in procuring AI hiring tools and using them, which may be summarized as comparing providers, considering providers' transparency, evaluating the tool's effectiveness, checking whether the tools have biases, confirming that the tools can be modified, reviewing the tools privacy policies, hiring in-house expertise, educating staff on bias hazard, and minding data protection issue. The guidance defines

AI-assisted and automated tools as *"any recruitment tools that aim to minimise or remove direct human input. Types of AI-assisted and automated tools include resume scanners, video interviews, or psychometric tests which are reviewed by AI or an automated process"* [2]. The approach used by the MPC in defining the use of AI in hiring seems more general than the approach used in The Audit Bias Law of NYC. The main tenet is any tools that minimise human input, whereas, in the Bias Law, it must substantially assist decision-making. Nonetheless, it is observed that the scope of the definition is pretty much like the Audit Bias Law, which encompasses all kinds of automated processes. In addition, like Bias Law, the guidance indicates that the agencies are accountable for the decisions made by the AI, i.e., the user and not the vendor. In conclusion, the MPC guidance presents us with the significance of defining the scope of human involvement in AI systems. Accordingly, all of these regulations and policies' salient features thus give us a hint at the essential aspects of governing AI in hiring.

4   Governing AI-Based Hiring

The scarcity of AI regulation has led major countries to compete in regulating AI [35]. It is observed that existing laws that may address harm sourced from AI in hiring (e.g., the GDPR), albeit not perfect, may provide some protection. However, the lack of regulation of AI in hiring, seeing the high risk it possesses, may lead to detriments towards applicants, such as biased decisions. Therefore, in the pursuit of governing the use of AI to provide fairness for applicants, this paper aims to guide policymakers in determining aspects that need to be considered in regulating AI-based hiring.

This paper submitted that the aspects that are fundamental to be governed are the definition of AI, the scope of AI usage, the amount of human involvement permitted, the scope of employment, and the compliance measures that are going to be imposed. These aspects were chosen because they were observed to be the salient features of the current regulations and policies on AI in hiring, as discussed in the preceding section. Moreover, policymakers seem to have differing opinions on these aspects thus it is crucial to stipulate them in the regulation to avoid confusion and ambiguity. The explanation for each of the aspects is described in the following subsection.

4.1   Defining AI

The foremost subject that needs to be considered by policymakers is defining what to refer to as the "AI" itself. New York City uses the term automated employment decision tools, which encompasses any computational process (including AI). Similarly, the US Algorithmic Accountability Act of 2022 defines AI as an automated decision system that includes computational systems, software, or processes that produce outputs for decision-making. However, the US Algorithmic Accountability Act of 2022 excludes passive computing infrastructure, an intermediary technology that does not influence the output of a decision, such as web hosting. The GDPR, albeit it does not elaborate further on the term, also uses the terms automated means, automated processing, and automated individual decision-making.

The Australia MPC, however, seems to distinguish between *AI-assisted tools* and *automated tools* because its nomenclature is '*AI-assisted and automated tools*'. Likewise, the California Assembly Bill 331 also differentiates the terms '*artificial intelligence*' and '*automated decision tool*' (ADT). AI in the California Assembly Bill 331 is defined as a machine-based system that is capable of making predictions, recommendations, or decisions that influence a real or virtual environment when given a set of human-defined objectives. Next, ADT denotes an exclusively developed system that makes or is a controlling factor of a consequential decision (has a significant effect on the individual) that utilizes AI. It is submitted that AI and automated tools (automation) are indeed distinct subjects.

Automation is a system that can do repetitive tasks automatically based on explicit pre-programmed rules and will only work within those commands and rules [36]. Conversely, AI is utilized for non-repetitive tasks and is able to make decisions by learning from information that it has [37]. Thus, Automation does not necessarily mean AI because automation is not always equipped with AI. For example, some still utilize traditional software or mechanization, such as integrated traffic light systems that do not require the implementation of AI [36, 38]. Automation, however, may be combined with AI to produce an intelligent process automation (IPA) [37]. Consequently, AI and automated tools cannot be used interchangeably.

Policymakers thus must set the scope of the "AI" definition in conjunction with their needs, i.e., whether they want to govern only AI or also automated tools. Nonetheless, it is suggested that policymakers adopt an expansive definition, such as NYC's definition of AEDT, which encompasses any computational process to reduce the chance of biased decisions in the employment field, which in turn would promote diversity and inclusivity. Defining AI, however, would inevitably also define what kind of AI usage is governed.

4.2 The Scope of Usage

First, it should be established for the purpose of this study that full usage of AI is one without human involvement, wherein partial usage may range from minimal to lots of human involvement in the process. Policymakers, of course, may choose to regulate all kinds of usage or just some of it without regulating the other. For instance, the Bias Audit Law defines automated tools as tools that '*substantially assist or replace discretionary decision making*'. This phrase is further explained under Article § 5-300 of The Rules of the City of New York, which means that it either (i) totally removes human decision-making, (ii) the AI output is weighted more than any criterion, or (iii) if the AI output is used to overrule conclusions derived from other factors. Thus, NYC only governs full and heavy usage of AI, whereas minimal use of AI in hiring is not subject to the Bias Audit Law.

Australia MPC seems to have the same approach as NYC wherein the notable difference is that in the guidelines published by the MPC, the nomenclature it uses is *'minimise human input'* rather than *'substantially assist'*. There is, however, no further explanation of the scope of such minimizing human input in the MPC's guideline. Nonetheless, *'minimise'* may be simply understood as having AI reduce human involvement to the least possible amount, thus making AI output the major factor in decisions. This would have the same effect as NYC's *'substantially assist'* term. The GDPR, however, differs from NYC and Australia MPC, wherein the GDPR only governs the full usage of AI.

In conclusion, the use of AI in hiring that is governed by existing laws is the one where the employer is heavily or fully dependent on the AI. It is observed that the approach taken in these existing laws is influenced by the competition in AI leadership. Regulating only a small part of AI usage, i.e., the heavily or fully dependent ones, would open the room for technological innovation. However, a too tight of a scope such as the ones in the GDPR would be too lenient and in turn, would fail to address the potential harm in AI [27]. Therefore, policymakers must strike the right balance between protecting against AI potential harm and pushing technological innovation in governing the usage of AI. Nonetheless, striking such a balance is not an easy task, seeing that governing the scope of AI usage would entail the discussion of human involvement in the hiring process because the relationship between human involvement and AI in the hiring process is inextricably intertwined.

4.3 Human Involvement

Human involvement is an integral part of AI and the leading cause of AI-biased decisions. It is settled that AI-biased decisions come from human biases, whether conscious or unconscious. Thus, it is argued that limiting human involvement in AI would reduce the occurrence of biased decisions, i.e., pushing AI dependency. This is because AI is inherently objective and has no unconscious bias compared to humans [22]. AI cannot assess complex human emotions and feelings [39], at least for now. Thus, using AI purely based on facts and not on emotions or sympathies would build objective standards and transparency [40]. Conversely, increasing human involvement in AI would in turn escalate the occurrence of biased decisions. However, it is observed that there is a concern about whether AI itself can be free of human biases [21]. Policymakers thus may adopt one of the approaches available to determine the permissible amount of human involvement in the AI-based hiring process.

First, policymakers may reduce the permissible amount of human involvement in the hiring process and thus increase AI dependency, i.e., AI output is the major factor in decision-making. Nonetheless, it should be noted that reducing is not equivalent to eliminating. AI still requires human involvement to produce correct inferences and a form of control [15]. Qamar et al. suggested that one of the ways to control the possibility of biases in AI-based hiring is to monitor the dataset provided to the AI [19]. This approach, consequently, demands a more comprehensive and stringent audit obligation on the AI and its system.

Contrarywise, the second approach requires a lot of human involvement and minimises AI dependency, which in turn would require a heavier obligation towards the user to ensure that the hiring decision they produce is not biased. This approach may be taken because a study argues that the empathy and emotions of the applicants must be assessed in the recruitment process so that the decision made is not merely an output of the AI algorithm but the recruiter as well [13]. As a result, the main object of the audit shall be the organization, and thus, the AI audit obligation may be laxer than the first approach. That is because empathy in the recruitment process may distort judgement, encourage bias and make it less effective to make a wise decision [41,42]. Policymakers may also offer these approaches as options for organizations to choose from. Next, another subject that should be a point of concern for policymakers is defining what constitutes employment.

4.4 Defining Employment

It is imperative to define the scope of employment governed by AI-based hiring regulations, considering that several regulations and policies have different approaches. For instance, in the New York Bias Audit Law and Australia MPC Guidance for Using AI-assisted recruitment tools, employment solely means the AI use in the scope of recruitment [2]. Subsequently, some bills, like California Assembly Bill 331, have a broader scope, whereas employment is defined to be one of the definitions of "*consequential automated decision*". Section 1 Chapter 25 (d) (1) of California Assembly Bill 331 gives an extensive definition of employment, which includes payment, promotion, hiring, termination, and automated task allocation. However, some laws or policies regulate in much general concept without further defining the scope of employment, like GDPR, which only states *decisions based solely on automated processing*. This definition implies that the GDPR generally applies to automated decision-making tools, which may be inferred to extend to all parts of employment as long as it impacts individuals. In conclusion, not all kinds of employment are regulated by the existing laws, and some only regulate specific activities in employment.

The current practice of governance of the scope of employment in AI-based hiring differs worldwide. For example, AI-based hiring is widely used in the United States. Therefore, there are a lot of available detailed frameworks regulating AI usage in the context of the recruitment process. However, the existing AI laws are far behind in addressing and keeping up with the emerging innovation. Currently, many companies have adopted AI not only for recruitment purposes but also to assess and evaluate employees and even provide feedback for employees to upgrade their performance, such as what happened in Omega Corp, Amazon, Enaibele, MetLife, and Unilever [43]. Similarly, the Australian government has utilized AI to promote the employee's job role [44]. These examples are just several technological innovations that are left unaddressed in the current framework. In other words, many other fields of employment also adopt AI in the process and will eventually continue to grow over time.

In conclusion, AI in employment not only denotes the process of recruitment but also may include uses of AI within work relations between a private or public company with employees such as recruitment, evaluation, promotions, and termination. Therefore, it is essential to determine to which extent the AI hiring regulation applies. It is thus suggested that policymakers should address not only short-term and rigid laws on the "common" AI used recently in the country but also address the potential development and innovation of AI in employment. This, in turn, will equip the regulation with a clear scope of employment to help form a comprehensive AI law. Accordingly, this will ease the mapping process of the regulation and mitigate the risk that might occur in specific events in employment. In addition, a clear scope of employment stage will aid in determining the proper responsibility and sanction if necessary. Nonetheless, all of this effort to define the scope of AI usage, as well as the definition itself, would become a futile effort if the regulation were not equipped with compliance measures. Thus, the following section suggests that policymakers should regulate compliance measures in the form of audits and in-house expert obligations, as well as penalties and enforcement.

4.5   Compliance Measures

Audit and In-House Expert. Ensuring the utilization of AI adheres to the regulations should come from both internal and external parts of the organizations. One of the common methods to do this is via audit. An audit can be done on AI tools to assess the impact of the AI on certain groups. Many AI laws and policies require AI auditing as a mandatory checklist before users are permitted to use AI in their employment processes. This measure aims to keep track of the usage of AI to be fair and accountable, i.e., eliminating biases. One prominent example of AI Auditing is the one regulated under the Bias Audit Law. The law obliges company users of AEDT to conduct Auditing with independent auditors and follow the stipulated requirements. According to Article § 5-300 of The Rules of the City of New York, an independent auditor is a person or group capable of exercising objective and impartial judgement to AEDT performance. The Bias Audit Law sets out further the requirements to be considered as an independent auditor, such as they must not be involved in using or developing the said AEDT. Similar to the Bias Audit Law, the United States, through AAA 2023, mandated algorithmic impact assessments (AIAs), which is the '*evaluation of an automated decision system or augmented critical decision process and its impact on consumers*' addressing the biases, effectiveness, and other factors prior and after the processing which obligation puts toward the deployer. AAA requires the deployer to actively consult independent auditing, internal parties (employees), and external parties (impacted group, advocates, and tech experts) in performing AIAs.

Other than imposing the obligation to do an audit with independent auditors, policymakers may also impose the obligation to create an in-house AI professional division or committee. Policymakers may also require an in-house AI professional to be embedded in the organization's existing internal audit division. A study submitted that the development, implementation, and maintenance of AI-hiring tools should be integrated with the organization's HR [23]. The main task of these HR professional committees would be to oversee and evaluate the algorithm applied in the AI [45]. This will have a significant impact on minimising tool failures and thus ensuring tool accountability [46]. Another task of this committee should be to educate staff on the risk of bias, which would help reduce findings from the auditors. Nonetheless, such obligations to do audits and hire in-house experts without penalty would become an unfinished law, *lex imperfecta*, which is typically not enforceable. Therefore, policy-makers must stipulate penalties and how to enforce them in their policies.

Penalty and Enforcement. Penalties are important because employment decisions are both high-impact and high-risk decisions and, thus, should not be taken lightly by organizations that utilize AI. Enforcement through non-compliance measures is therefore essential, and it is observed that policymakers can adopt different approaches to imposing penalties. First, the Bias Audit Law imposes civil penalties for violation of the requirements in Subchapter 25 of the law, wherein each of the violations of the requirements will be treated as a separate violation that brings a separate penalty. Moreover, subsequent penalties would lead to a more significant penalty. Similarly, California's Bill AB331 also imposes an administrative fine per violation and can be given rise daily for non-compliance. The Enforcement of the Bias Law provision must be brought before the court by the New York City's corporation counsel or its designee to be enforced.

Next, penalties are differentiated into two types in the AIDA depending on the severity of the violation, namely administrative monetary penalties (AMPs), the lightest sanction that the government can directly impose on the violator, and regulatory non-compliance, penalties for more severe infringement, which the fault must be proven through court. California's Bill AB331 also requires public attorneys to bring a civil action against ADT deployers who are violating the law. Meanwhile, the EU AI Act provides decentralized enforcement of the law, wherein the act mandates Member States to provide necessary measures like penalties, including administrative fines, for infringements of the act. Furthermore, The Act requires Member States to take necessary measures to properly implement all of the conditions in the act. In conclusion, policymakers must set out to stipulate penalties for breach of audit or in-house expert obligations. It is suggested that civil penalties are the way to go seeing that in the context of AI-based hiring it falls into the private sector rather than public one.

5   Conclusion

The utilization of AI in the hiring process has been increasing worldwide. Albeit using such an AI system may bring both benefits and detriments to society it seems that this issue is still underregulated. The New York City Bias Audit Law is currently the only regulation that specifically addresses the issue of AI in hiring. Policymakers worldwide, however, have been trying to govern the issue of AI in hiring, which can be seen from the plethora of bills and policies. These bills and policies show that there is an urgent need for regulations to prevent the occurrence of AI-biased decisions. Lastly, this paper believes that determining AI definition, its usage, the amount of human involvement permitted, the scope of employment that is about to be governed, and the compliance measures are imperative when policymakers want to govern AI in hiring. Nonetheless, there is room for further research on this issue, as AI potential may become both a virtue and a vice. Moreover, employment decisions are a high impact as well as a high-risk decision that need to be saved from biased factors.

Acknowledgments. This study does not receive any funding.

Disclosure of Interests. The authors have no competing interests to declare that are relevant to the content of this article.

References

1. Muehlemann, S., Strupler Leiser, M.: Hiring costs and labor market tightness. Labour Econ. **52**, 122–131 (2018). https://doi.org/10.1016/j.labeco.2018.04.010
2. The Merit Protection Commissioner: Guidance Material for Using AI-Assisted Recruitment Tools (2022). https://www.mpc.gov.au/resources/guidance/myth-busting-ai-assisted-and-automated-recruitment-tools
3. Eightfold AI: The Future of Work: Intelligent by Design |Eightfold AI's 2022 Talent Survey. Eightfold AI (2022)
4. Rab-Kettler, K., Lehnervp, B.: Recruitment in the times of machine learning. Manag. Syst. Prod. Eng. **27**, 105–109 (2019). https://doi.org/10.1515/mspe-2019-0018
5. Hmoud, B., Varallyai, L.: Will artificial intelligence take over human resources recruitment and selection? Netw. Intell. Stud. **7**, 21–30 (2019)
6. European Commission: Proposal for a Regulation of The European Parliament and of The Council Laying Down Harmonized Rules on Artificial Intelligence (Artificial Intelligence Act) and Amending Certain Union Legislative (2021)
7. Adamovic, M.: When ethnic discrimination in recruitment is likely to occur and how to reduce it: applying a contingency perspective to review resume studies. Hum. Resour. Manag. Rev. **32**, 100832 (2022). https://doi.org/10.1016/j.hrmr.2021.100832
8. Merit Protection Commissioner: Merit Protection Commissioner Annual Report 2021–22. Merit Protection Commissioner (2022)
9. Dastin, J.: Amazon scraps secret AI recruiting tool that showed bias against women. In: Ethics of Data and Analytics. Auerbach Publications (2022)
10. Singh, E.P., Doval, J.: Artificial intelligence and HR: remarkable opportunities, hesitant partners. Presented at the 4th National HR Conference on Human Resource Management Practices and Trends (2019)
11. Kuncel, N.R., Klieger, D.M., Ones, D.S.: In Hiring, Algorithms Beat Instinct (2014). https://hbr.org/2014/05/in-hiring-algorithms-beat-instinct

12. Al-Alawi, A.I., Naureen, M., AlAlawi, E.I., Naser Al-Hadad, A.A.: The role of artificial intelligence in recruitment process decision-making. In: 2021 International Conference on Decision Aid Sciences and Application (DASA), pp. 197–203 (2021). https://doi.org/10.1109/DASA53625.2021.9682320

13. Brishti, J.K., Javed, A.: The Viability of AI-Based Recruitment Process: A Systematic Literature Review (2020). http://urn.kb.se/resolve?urn=urn:nbn:se:umu:diva-172311

14. Shet, S., Nair, B.: Quality of hire: expanding the multi-level fit employee selection using machine learning. IJOA **31**, 2103–2117 (2023). https://doi.org/10.1108/IJOA-06-2021-2843

15. Yu, J., Ma, Z., Zhu, L.: The configurational effects of artificial intelligence-based hiring decisions on applicants' justice perception and organisational commitment. ITP (2023). https://doi.org/10.1108/ITP-04-2022-0271

16. Ochmann, J., Laumer, S.: Fairness as a determinant of AI adoption in recruiting: an interview-based study. In: DIGIT 2019 Proceedings (2019)

17. Hoddinghaus, M., Sondern, D., Hertel, G.: The automation of leadership functions: would people trust decision algorithms? Comput. Hum. Behav. **116** (2021). https://doi.org/10.1016/j.chb.2020.106635

18. Dijkkamp, J.: The Recruiter of the Future, a Qualitative Study in AI Supported Recruitment Process (2019). http://essay.utwente.nl/80003/

19. Qamar, Y., Agrawal, R.K., Samad, T.A., Chiappetta Jabbour, C.J.: When technology meets people: the interplay of artificial intelligence and human resource management. JEIM **34**, 1339–1370 (2021). https://doi.org/10.1108/JEIM-11-2020-0436

20. Polli, F.: Using AI to Eliminate Bias from Hiring (2019). https://hbr.org/2019/10/using-ai-to-eliminate-bias-from-hiring

21. Soleimani, M., Intezari, A., Pauleen, D.J.: Mitigating cognitive biases in developing AI-assisted recruitment systems: a knowledge-sharing approach. Int. J. Knowl. Manag. **18**, 1–18 (2021). https://doi.org/10.4018/IJKM.290022

22. Van Esch, P., Black, J.S., Ferolie, J.: Marketing AI recruitment: the next phase in job application and selection. Comput. Hum. Behav. **90**, 215–222 (2019). https://doi.org/10.1016/j.chb.2018.09.009

23. Han, D.: The Rose: Artificial Intelligence in the Current Hiring Process. Brigham Young University Scholars Archive, vol. 3 (2020)

24. Mirowska, A., Mesnet, L.: Preferring the devil you know: potential applicant reactions to artificial intelligence evaluation of interviews. Hum. Res. Manag. J. **3**, 364–383 (2022). https://doi.org/10.1111/1748-8583.12393

25. Gay, D.S., Kagan, A.M.: Big data and employment law: what employers and their legal counsel need to know. ABA J. Labor Employ. Law **33**, 191–210 (2018)

26. Lukacs, A., Varadi, S.: GDPR-compliant AI-based automated decision-making in the world of work. Comput. Law Secur. Rev. **50**, 105848 (2023). https://doi.org/10.1016/j.clsr.2023.105848

27. Abraha, H.: Regulating algorithmic employment decisions through data protection law. Eur. Labour Law J. **14**, 172–191 (2023). https://doi.org/10.1177/20319525231167317

28. Malgieri, G.: Automated decision-making in the EU member states: the right to explanation and other "suitable safeguards" in the national legislations. Comput. Law Secur. Rev. **35**, 105327 (2019). https://doi.org/10.1016/j.clsr.2019.05.002

29. Loi n°2018-493 du 20 juin 2018, modifying the previous 'Loi n° 78-17 du 6 janvier 1978 relative a l'informatique, aux fichiers et aux libertes' (2018)

30. European Parliament News: EU AI Act: First Regulation on Artificial Intelligence. https://www.europarl.europa.eu/news/en/headlines/society/20230601STO93804/eu-ai-act-first-regulation-on-artificial-intelligence. Accessed 24 Jan 2024

31. Press Release | Artificial Intelligence Act: Deal on Comprehensive Rules for Trustworthy AI. https://www.europarl.europa.eu/news/en/press-room/20231206IPR15699/artificial-intelligence-act-deal-on-comprehensive-rules-for-trustworthy-ai. Accessed 24 Jan 2024

32. Delvaux, M.: Report with recommendations to the Commission on Civil Law Rules on Robotics | A8-0005/2017 | European Parliament - (2015/2103(INL)) (2017)

33. Department of Industry, Science and Resources: Positioning Australia as a Leader in Digital Economy Regulation - Automated Decision Making and AI Regulation - Issues Paper (2022)

34. Department of Industry, Science and Resources: Safe and Responsible AI in Australia Consultation (2024)

35. Panait, C., Ljubenkov, D., Alic, D.: Striking the balance between innovation and regulation in AI - is Europe leading the way or lagging behind? Europuls Policy J. EU Affairs **1**, 27–45 (2021)

36. Robb, D.: AI vs. Automation. https://www.eweek.com/big-data-and-analytics/ai-vs-automation/. Accessed 31 Jan 2024

37. Donepudi, P.K.: Application of artificial intelligence in automation industry. Asian J. Appl. Sci. Eng. **7**, 7–20 (2018). https://doi.org/10.18034/ajase.v7i1.42

38. Haanen, R.: Automation vs AI & ML. https://redmarker.ai/posts/automation-vs-ai-ml. Accessed 31 Jan 2024

39. Hunkenschroer, A.L., Kriebitz, A.: Is AI recruiting (un)ethical? A human rights perspective on the use of AI for hiring. AI Ethics **3**, 199–213 (2023). https://doi.org/10.1007/s43681-022-00166-4

40. Wisskirchen, G., Biacabe, B.T., Bormann, U., et al.: Artificial Intelligence and Robotics and Their Impact on The Workplace. IBA Global Employment Institute (2017)

41. Hougaard, R., Carter, J., Afton, M.: Connect with Empathy, But Lead with Compassion (2021). https://hbr.org/2021/12/connect-with-empathy-but-lead-with-compassion

42. Bloom, P.: Against Empathy: The Case for Rational Compassion. Ecco (2016)

43. Tong, S., Jia, N., Luo, X., Fang, Z.: The Janus face of artificial intelligence feedback: deployment versus disclosure effects on employee performance. Strateg. Manag. J. **42**, 1600–1631 (2021). https://doi.org/10.1002/smj.3322

44. Skatssoon, J.: Automated Selection Bungling APS Recruitment. https://www.governmentnews.com.au/automated-selection-bungling-aps-recruitment/. Accessed 05 Jan 2024

45. Malik, A., Budhwar, P., Patel, C., Srikanth, N.R.: May the bots be with you! delivering HR cost-effectiveness and individualised employee experiences in an MNE. Int. J. Hum. Resour. Manag. **33**, 1148–1178 (2022). https://doi.org/10.1080/09585192.2020.1859582

46. Fernandez, J.: The ball of wax we call HR analytics. SHR **18**, 21–25 (2019). https://doi.org/10.1108/SHR-09-2018-0077

Navigating the Artificial Intelligence Dilemma: Exploring Paths for Norway's Future

Maka Alsandia$^{(\boxtimes)}$

Iver Trøans Vei 8, 7018 Trondheim, Norway
alsandiamaka@gmail.com

Abstract. This position paper delves into the complex intersection of Artificial Intelligence (AI) deployment, human rights implications, and discriminatory practices in recruitment within Norway. In response to the global discourse on AI regulatory frameworks, the adoption of Fundamental rights impact assessments, inspired by the recent EU AI Act is advocated. Moreover, a critical knowledge gap and a reliance on abstract ethical principles is identified, and Norway is urged to align its national strategy with emerging international standards. Drawing attention to systemic discrimination in the labor market, particularly against non-ethnic Norwegians, the need for rigorous risk assessments before deploying AI systems in recruitment is emphasized. The government's acknowledgement of a lack of competence in the public sector and recent steps toward AI regulation are recognized, but these also prompt a call for comprehensive measures aligning with human rights principles.

Keywords: discrimination · recruitment · human rights

1 Introduction

Where do we stand today regarding Artificial Intelligence (AI) and its implications for human rights? It is commonly referred to as, and arguably watered down by the term, "algorithmic bias". In contrast to other technological advancements such as biotechnology or pharmaceuticals, AI has managed to evade scrutiny. Governments worldwide, including in Norway, seem to have granted an unimpeded path to technology developed by multibillion-dollar IT companies potentially harboring vested interests. As international discourse steers away from an ethics-based approach towards a legal and human rights-based perspective, Norway seems to be lagging in this pivotal shift.

To define AI for this discourse, the definition provided in the newly approved EU AI Act is used:'An AI system is a machine-based system designed to operate with varying levels of autonomy and that may exhibit adaptiveness after deployment and that, for explicit or implicit objectives, infers, from the input it receives, how to generate outputs such as predictions, content, recommendations, or decisions that can influence physical or virtual environments' [1].

T. Suzumura and M. Bono (Eds.): JSAI-isAI 2024, LNAI 14741, pp. 64–74, 2024.
https://doi.org/10.1007/978-981-97-3076-6_5

On one hand, AI has been hailed by proponents as groundbreaking technology that can outperform humans in many respects. On the other hand, concerns have been raised as early as 2018 about the human rights violations of AI systems [2]. These authors [2] identified six fields of human activities where AI has been deployed, resulting in considerable human rights impacts: 1) Criminal Justice (risk assessments); 2) Finance (credit scores); 3) Healthcare (diagnostics); 4) Content Moderation (standards enforcement); 5) Human Resources (recruitment and hiring), and; 6) Education (essay scoring). A more recent comprehensive analyses of AI and its impact on human rights, includes specific cases, both those previously raised and those not previously raised, such as AI's impact on LGBTQIA+ individuals [3].

These concerns have led to the United Nations High Commissioner for Human Rights to urge governments to incorporate a human rights approach into AI regulatory frameworks [4]. At the regional level, a significant development has occurred: the Artificial Intelligence Act (AI Act) was approved by the EU parliament on 13th of March 2024. The EU AI Act identifies high-risk areas for AI deployment, including in recruitment, such as CV-sorting software for recruitment procedures. The act imposes stringent obligations before deploying AI systems in identified high-risk public domains. It mandates the implementation of adequate risk assessment and mitigation systems to ensure the high quality of datasets feeding the system, thereby minimizing risks and discriminatory outcomes [1].

Despite the aforementioned calls to address AI-generated human rights violations through human rights law, there still exists a global and national knowledge gap on the subject. The primary approach emphasized in IT literature has been ethics- abstract ethical principles [5] that cannot serve as a regulatory framework for AI. Moreover, some argue that the ethics approach is ineffective [6]. Research mapping and analyzing the current AI ethics literature presents an interesting conclusion: solutions proposed by the public and private sectors to address ethical challenges differ considerably [7]. It also highlights the underrepresentation of certain regions in the AI ethics debate, indicating a power imbalance in the international discourse. Notably, Norway is not participating in the global discourse [7], nor is the Norwegian government providing concrete guidelines and risk-mitigating measures for the public sector in the adoption of AI systems [8].

Jobin et al. [7] concluded that: a) there is a need to interpret ethical principles into practice and seek harmonization between AI ethics codes (soft law) and legislation (hard law) as vital steps for the global community, and b) there is a necessity for '...clarifying how AI ethics guidelines relate to existing national and international regulation' [7].

2   Background on the Norwegian Context

Norway has declared high ambitions in digitalization and positions itself as a frontrunner in this, including AI [10]. The National Strategy for AI does make a reference to human rights, but the plan envisages digitalization-friendly legislation and operates under the assumption that the'public sector is highly competent, and there is high-quality registry data spanning over decades' [9]. However, it has also been claimed that the strategy lacks substantial practical guidelines for AI implementation and favors business matters over human rights [10]. While the national strategy for AI emphasizes public trust, the public does not seem to be the primary audience [10], begging the question: what and whose purpose does it serve? The National Strategy for AI is also largely congruent with an AI-ethics approach promulgated by the private sector, despite the pitfalls of this approach [5,6]. Some contend that fostering public trust in AI is likely to diminish scrutiny and may even undermine certain societal obligations of AI producers [7]. Moreover, Norwegian society is particularly vulnerable to fostering public trust in AI given their generally high faith in the government.

Current government policy has a clear goal for the increased use of artificial intelligence in the public sector, describing AI use to deliver more precise and user- adapted services, increasing the societal benefit of its operations, streamlining operations and work processes, and reducing risk [9]. While acknowledging the potential negative consequences associated with the use of AI, the primary concern is expressed regarding the uncertainty about its use, which may cause the public sector to be unnecessarily hesitant, missing out on important opportunities to improve services or streamline processes [8]. Thus, this policy emphasizes that the deployment of AI is essentially left to the public sector itself based on principles without clear regulation. Moreover, the Norwegian Parliament is notably absent from the AI debate. Between 2016 and 2021, there were only 23 references to AI none of these pertaining to the rules of use of AI in the public sector [8].

While there is a widespread assumption that human rights literacy prevails in Norway, the reality is quite different. For example, Lile [11] showed a deficiency in human rights education. It could therefore be argued that this lack of human rights education and understanding is likely to extend to a lack of understanding regarding the human rights implications of AI systems, including its discriminatory implications on recruitment. In the human rights periodic review, Norway is encouraged to ensure that ethnic minorities, among other things, have access to employment [12]. The government, under the heading'Enhancing Innovation Capacity using AI,' provides on its website the results of a survey indicating a lack of competence in the public sector to understand the ramifications of AI [9]. Remarkably, this acknowledgment stands in stark contrast with the premise of the National Strategy for AI where the public sector is described as highly competent. However, the government's efforts to commission a survey and acknowledge the outcomes can be seen as a positive step in the right direction. Other positive developments include a substantial amount of money allocated to AI research [13] and a newly established Ministry of Digitalization entrusted with the mandate to oversee AI.

The National Equality and Anti-discrimination Ombudsman has recently launched guidelines on the use of AI [14]. This also marks a promising development, hopefully shifting the AI public debate from the ethics to the legal realm and prompting the government to adopt these guidelines in the national AI strategy. However, these guidelines fail to refer to potential discriminatory outcomes of AI systems in recruitment, nor do they draw attention to existing systemic discrimination of non- ethnic Norwegians in recruitment. This is despite the fact that this is the only agency overseeing the implementation of the national act on equality and non-discrimination.

A report commissioned by the Anti-discrimination and Inclusion Ombudsman [15] shows that the Anti-discrimination Tribunal received 575 complaints in 2022, indicating an increase from the previous year. The breakdown by the public domain was: Employment: 178 cases, public administration: 47, Education: 21, access to housing: 15, Police, legal system: 6. The majority of cases (178) concern discrimination in the labor market, including based on nationality [15]. These are only reported cases, indicating that the number of unreported cases can be higher. Additionally, the Ombudsman stresses that the legal practice of the burden of proof in cases concerning discrimination has been interpreted in violation of EU law [15].

It is striking that to the contrary of the evidence of systemic and widespread discrimination in the labor market, there has never been a case brought before the Norwegian court on discrimination in employment based on ethnicity. This is presumably due to the burden of proof that lies on the complainant (Pers. Comm. - Confirmed in a phone conversation with a legal adviser at the anti-discrimination ombudsman's office in October 2023).

Back in 2016, a study concluded that ethnic Norwegians were favored over second- generation immigrants at the initial screening of the applications, thus many of the applicants called for the interview were ethnic Norwegians [16]. In legal terms, this can amount to discrimination based on ethnicity. Hence potentially violating International Convention on the Elimination of All Forms of Racial Discrimination which Norway is party to and national law on anti- discrimination [17]. Even though this research gave some insight into the recruitment process, it only looked at the initial phase of hiring: selection of the candidates for the interview. Other quantitative analyses indicate that there is extensive discrimination against minority candidates despite regulations, visions, and slogans about increased diversity [18]. This research collected and analyzed the data covering all phases of the recruitment process, from invitation to interview to the final selection of candidates. These analyses indicated that candidates with an ethnic minority background are systematically treated differently. A central explanation for the findings was that employers in the state have a high degree of freedom and emphasize subjective and less transparent criteria such as "personal suitability", despite the public sector being subject to stricter regulations than private companies [19]. Public administration is obliged by guidelines issued by the government to call for interview at least one person with an immigration background [18] in addition to the law on anti-discrimination, which forbids discriminations among other things based on gender ethnicity, nationality, and sexual orientation [15].

These studies demonstrated that it is not necessarily sufficient to overcome the initial obstacle and be called for an interview, even for applicants with high formal qualifications. A visible ethnic minority background reduces the likelihood of being selected as the first candidate as much as the lack of relevant education. The article concludes that these findings should be a source of concern for political authorities [19]. Other vulnerable groups in recruitment include women because of their underrepresentation in the labor market on executive positions and potentially also LGBTQIA+ individuals.

Research conducted to examine the causes of underrepresentation of women in the management position found that there is still fewer female than male managers in Norway's state bureaucracy [20]. Even though organizational barriers were not identified as a cause of the problem, Storvik and Schøne [20] concluded that one possible reason for women's underrepresentation could be that female managers apply for management positions less often than their male colleagues. Reasons offered for women not applying included potential anticipated discrimination rather than lack of ambition or self-confidence, which hinders women's movement into higher management positions in the state bureaucracy [20].

3   Examining AI Deployment in the Public Sector: Recruitment and the Pertinent Legal Framework

Information on AI deployment in Norway is very scarce, especially concerning its use for recruitment purposes. Moreover, there is a certain secrecy surrounding the actual use of AI. Some public sectors do not disclose the use of AI systems, but there are indications that AI predictive models are being used [8], raising questions about adherence to transparency and good governance, which are cornerstones of democracy and the rule of law that Norway prides itself on.

Survey-based research conducted in 2019 among the biggest municipalities mapping actual and future deployment of AI in the public sector found some level of deployment of AI in HR management [21]. Although response rates were relatively low (83 respondents) around 15% of respondents indicated that AI systems have been adopted in HR management. When questioned about future deployment, the HR management sector displayed a mid-range value for intention to adopt AI systems in the future (scored of 3 on a Likert scale of 0 to 7) [21]. The deployment of AI in the public sector was as of 2021 in its initial stage [22].

The Norwegian Parliament has added legal provisions to two national legal acts in 2021 and 2022 without much political discourse providing for more lenient rules for use of data. Tax law §5–11 [23] provides tax authorities with a power to process personal data for compiling, profiling, and automated decision-making [8]. Similarly a legal provision of the social welfare act §4 was added [24] in 2021, giving NAV (Norwegian Labour and Welfare Administration) authorization for fully automated processing of personal data. The provision does not regulate profiling. However, it follows from NAV's procedural circulars that profiling may be included in automated case processing, even though this is not mentioned in the law or preparatory works [8].

Article 92 of the Norwegian Constitution (the part of the constitution that has incorporated human rights) states: "The authorities of the State shall respect and ensure human rights as they are expressed in this Constitution and in the treaties concerning human rights that are binding for Norway." Article 98 of the constitution states: "All people are equal under the law. No human being must be subject to unfair or disproportionate differential treatment." [25].

The Equality and Anti-discrimination Act §5 stipulates that "The United Nations International Convention on the Elimination of All Forms of Racial Discrimination (...) shall apply as Norwegian law". Following, §6 states: "Discrimination on the basis of gender, pregnancy, leave in connection with childbirth or adoption, care responsibilities, ethnicity, religion, belief, disability, sexual orientation, gender identity, gender expression, age, or combinations of these factors is prohibited. 'Ethnicity' includes national origin, descent, skin color, and language" [17]. §24 of the same legal act lays down the following obligations: "Public authorities shall in all their activities make active, targeted, and systematic efforts to promote equality and prevent discrimination as specified in section 6. This duty shall include an obligation for public authorities to preclude harassment, sexual harassment, and gender-based violence, and to counter stereotyping. Public authorities issue a statement on what they are doing to integrate considerations relating to gender and non-discrimination into their work. Public authorities shall describe what they are doing to convert equality and non-discrimination principles, procedures, and standards into action. Public authorities shall provide an assessment as to what has been achieved as a result of these efforts and outline expectations with regard to future efforts in this area. The statement shall be provided in the annual report, another report issued annually, or another document available to the general public" [17].

Despite the legal framework for anti-discrimination outlined above, implementation of it is rather patchy. The report published in December 2022 by Rambøll Management Consulting and Vestlandsforsking illustrates AI deployment in the public sector, including in recruitment, and to what extent there is compliance with the above- described laws [26]. Researchers conducted a survey aimed at assessing the use of AI in the public sector, particularly where personal data or individual data are involved in AI projects. They also mapped to what extent public sectors were aware of the implications of AI systems on discrimination as proscribed by national law. According to the report, a total of 200 organizations completed the survey out of the 491 organizations invited to participate. Sixty organizations participating in the survey indicated that they had projects (or activities) utilizing AI. An equal number reported having concrete plans for AI projects. Furthermore, 39 of these respondents stated that they handled personal data or individual data in the respective AI project. These organizations have AI projects in different public services and in public administration, including using AI for improving decision-making processes, and some used AI for recruitment purposes [26]. This work did not investigate this further, nor did they inquire about discrimination as pertaining to recruitment, but investigated generally to what extent discriminatory outcomes of AI systems were considered. According to the report, only 3% of those surveyed believed that AI increases the risk of discrimination. Thus, the overwhelming majority of the respondents did not consider discrimination as a risk factor in AI systems. Moreover, public sector employers expressed their views concerning the legislation that is not adapted to AI, including the overarching principle in General Data Protection Regulation, such as storing minimal data for a minimal period of time [26]. Interestingly, the report showed that public sector employees consider existing legislation as a hindrance for deploying AI rather than using it as a guiding principle. At the same time, while they seem to be aware of some sort of legislation that presents an obstacle to deploying AI because of its promise and utility, they are not aware of the law on discrimination and AI's potential impact on discrimination. The report concluded that the risk of discrimination also increases when knowledge about discrimination in the sense of the Equality and Anti-Discrimination Act is not included in the project from the beginning. The survey and interviews show that there is little attention and a lack of knowledge about discrimination in the legal sense. Furthermore, the second factor that can contribute to increasing the risk of discrimination is rhetoric around AI as an 'objective' tool and about datasets that can be corrected to become entirely 'correct and complete,' or as in the AI regulation, to "...find a balance (or compromise) between the best possible and feasible" [26].

Thus, there is a political expectation and pressure on the public sector to digitalize their services, and AI systems are part of that digitalization. At the same time, reports such as [26] offer valuable insight into the question this article is concerned with - discrimination in recruitment. Even though it lacks a specific focus on discrimination in hiring, it gives a glimpse into some of the AI projects being used in recruitment. Given the lack of public discourse or absence thereof on discriminatory outcomes of AI systems in recruitment, it can be inferred that AI deployment in recruitment might suffer the most from poor data sources and oversight, leading to discriminatory outcomes. The urgency of this matter cannot be overstated. Addressing this issue at the initial stage of launching AI is imperative to prevent amplified discrimination in the labor market under the guise of the perceived "objectivity" of AI approaches. As the European Commission White Paper on Artificial Intelligence states: "bias and discrimination are inherent risks of any societal or economic activity. Human decision- making is not immune to mistakes and biases. However, the same bias when present in AI could have a much larger effect, affecting and discriminating many people without the social control mechanisms that govern human behavior" [27].

4   Position Statement

Considering the implications of AI on human rights and discriminatory practices in recruitment, the lack of expertise in the public sector in determining the impact of AI systems and the absence of public discourse, Norway could address these issues in line with the emerging international discourse and a new EU AI act [28]. For instance, by introducing Fundamental rights impact assessments. Other related actions may entail: 1) Establishment of a panel of AI experts tasked with overseeing the deployment of AI systems and providing recommendations; 2) Developing mandatory guidelines for the public sector, informed by the panel's expertise and including fundamental rights impact assessment, and; 3) Institute a course on the human rights implications of AI, as is in accordance with the legal provision allowing for the assignment of specific national responsibilities in research or teaching, as stipulated in § 1–3 of the university and high school act [29]. This course could be mandated for major universities with IT programs, particularly those graduating a significant number of IT engineers, to bridge the gap between IT knowledge and its societal implications.

In relation to fundamental rights impact assessment, they should be carried out by independent legal experts together with hiring managers and HR staff, with a clear mandate for the legal experts to make evaluations and recommendations. Moreover, the government needs to actively engage in capacity-building for diverse stakeholders, primarily in the public sector, AI developers, and the public at large, ensuring that AI systems do not lead to discriminatory outcomes. It is crucial to adopt a new national strategy aligned with the EU Artificial Intelligence Act and incorporate guidelines proposed by the equality and non-discrimination ombudsman. Additionally, it is important to develop contextual understanding based on the social, cultural, and political context in Norway, enhancing the grasp of nuanced impacts on human rights. This is particularly important regarding recruitment and inclusion of immigrants and ethnic minorities. Considering the historical background of the treatment of Sami people and Kven minorities, one can assume that historical data is flawed. Proposing Fundamental rights impact assessments for AI systems in the public sector faces challenges due to some potential resistance. Public sectors currently value the freedom to conduct recruitment autonomously, often prioritizing subjective criteria. Thus, convincing such institutions to adopt risk assessments may be challenging due to a lack of awareness regarding discriminatory outcomes in their practices or denial thereof. However, overcoming these hurdles is crucial for the trustworthy deployment of AI systems and safeguarding the right to employment. AI developers might also resist initially, perceiving these assessments as bureaucratic obstacles. Yet, overcoming these challenges is essential for the deployment of AI and human rights protection, particularly in recruitment.

5   Conclusion

Exploration into Norway's AI landscape illuminates both promises and challenges. Despite aspiring to be a digitalization and AI frontrunner, these findings raise concerns about absence of public and political discourse on existing systemic discrimination on labour market and its implication for AI systems. Moreover, presumed competence within the public administration and the quality of available data raise concerns. From a legal standpoint, there appear to be frequent breaches of International Conventions on Elimination of All forms of Racial Discrimination and national anti-discrimination law, particularly noticeable in recruitment practices that systematically discriminate against non-ethnic Norwegians.

The call to address AI's impact on human rights and discriminatory recruitment practices aligns with the emerging international discourse and recently approved EU AI Act. Essential strategies include proposing comprehensive measures like mandated Fundamental rights impact assessments, establishment of a panel of AI experts tasked with overseeing the deployment of AI systems and providing recommendations. In addition, developing mandatory guidelines for the public sector, informed by the panel's expertise and Institute a course on the human rights implications of AI for major universities.

While substantial funds allocated to AI research and the establishment of a Ministry of Digitalization are commendable initiatives, the true litmus test lies in translating these initiatives into effective actions. Acknowledging the systemic discrimination in recruitment is crucial for developing contextual understanding.

To meet its strategic objectives and become a global leader in digitalization, Norway must integrate a Human Rights approach into its AI policy. This involves not only adhering to international obligations but also addressing systemic discrimination and fostering public trust.

As Norway stands at the nexus of technological innovation, the chosen path will define its digital future. The incorporation of a Human Rights approach is not merely a legal or ethical imperative but a strategic necessity to ensure an inclusive, unbiased, and trustworthy AI ecosystem for future generations.

Acknowledgments. The author thanks Dr. Glenn Dunshea for assistance and proofreading. Additionally, the author expresses gratitude to the anonymous reviewers for their comments, which have enhanced the paper.

Disclosure of Interests. The author has no competing interests to declare that are relevant to the content of this article.

References

1. AI Act | Shaping Europe's digital future. https://digital-strategy.ec.europa.eu/en/policies/regulatory-framework-ai. Accessed 24 Mar 2024
2. Bavitz, C., Kim, L.: Artificial Intelligence & Human Rights: Opportunities & Risks. Rochester, NY (2018). https://doi.org/10.2139/ssrn.3259344
3. Smuclerova, M., Kral, L., Drchal, J.: 2. AI Life Cycle and Human Rights Risks and Remedies. In: Artificial Intelligence and Human Rights. Oxford University Press, Oxford (2023)
4. Türk addresses World Standards Cooperation meeting on human rights and digital technology. OHCHR. https://www.ohchr.org/en/statements/2023/02/turk-addresses-world-standards-cooperation-meeting-human-rights-and-digital. Accessed 25 Dec 2023
5. Yam, J., Skorburg, J.A.: From human resources to human rights: impact assessments for hiring algorithms. Ethics Inf. Technol. **23**(4), 611–623 (2021). https://doi.org/10.1007/s10676-021-09599-7
6. Munn, L.: The uselessness of AI ethics. AI Ethics **3**(3), 869–877 (2023). https://doi.org/10.1007/s43681-022-00209-w
7. Jobin, A., Ienca, M., Vayena, E.: The global landscape of AI ethics guidelines. Nat. Mach. Intell. **1**(9), 389–399 (2019). https://doi.org/10.1038/s42256-019-0088-2

8. Broomfield, H., Lindtveld, M.N.: Snubler Norge inn i en algoritmisk velferds-dystopi? Tidsskrift velferdsforskning **3**, 1–15 (2022). https://doi.org/10.18261/tfv. 25.3.2

9. Norwegian Ministry of Local Government and Modernisation. The National Strategy for Artificial Intelligence. regjeringen.no (2020). https://www.regjeringen.no/en/dokumenter/nasjonal-strategi-for-kunstig-intelligens/id2685594/. Accessed 24 Mar 2024

10. Holderbein, K., Krüger, S., Wilson, C.: Trust for sale: a critical reading of the Norwegian National Strategy for AI. Nor. Medietidsskrift **28**(2), 01–06 (2021). https://doi.org/10.18261/ISSN.0805-9535-2021-02-07

11. Lile, H.S.: The realisation of human rights education in Norway. Nord. J. Hum. Rights **37**(2), 143–161 (2019). https://doi.org/10.1080/18918131.2019.1674007

12. Bachelet, M.: Letter from united nations human rights office of the high commissioner to the minister of foreign affairs (2019). https://www.ohchr.org/sites/default/files/lib-docs/HRBodies/UPR/Documents/Session33/NO/HC_letter_33rdSession_Norway.pdf

13. Gundersen, M.: Regjeringen med milliardsatsning på KI. NRK. https://www.nrk.no/norge/regjeringen-med-milliardsatsning-pa-kunstig-intelligens-1.16546093. Accessed 25 Nov 2023

14. Vik, K.T.A.: Innebygd diskrimineringsvern: En veileder for å avdekke og forebygge diskriminering i utvikling og bruk av kunstig intelligens. The Equality and Discrimination Ombudsman LDO 2023 (2023)

15. Commissioned Report. Diskrimineringsretten 2022: rettsutvikling på likestillings-og diskrimineringsfeltet, med gjennomgang av relevante lovendringer, forvaltnings-og rettspraksis." Likestillings- og diskrimineringsombudet LDO 2023 (2022). https://www.ldo.no/globalassets/_ldo_2019/_bilder-til-nye-nettsider/rapporter/ldo_diskrimineringsrettsrapporten_2022_elektronisk_utgave.pdf

16. i Oslo, U., Garbo, G.L.: Ansetter Knut framfor Muhammed. https://www.forskning.no/partner-arbeid-transport/ansetter-knut-framfor-muhammed/431416. Accessed 24 Feb 2024

17. Lov om likestilling og forbud mot diskriminering (likestillings- og diskrimineringsloven) - Lovdata. https://lovdata.no/dokument/NL/lov/2017-06-16-51. Accessed 24 Feb 2024

18. Statens personalhåndbok 2020 (2020)

19. Bjørnset, M., Sterri, E.B., Rogstad, J.: Gjennom nåløyene. Søkelys På Arb. **38**(3–4), 226–241 (2021). https://doi.org/10.18261/issn.1504-7989-2021-03-04-05

20. Storvik, A.E., Schøne, P.: In search of the glass ceiling: gender and recruitment to management in Norway's state bureaucracy1. Br. J. Sociol. **59**(4), 729–755 (2008). https://doi.org/10.1111/j.1468-4446.2008.00217.x

21. Mikalef, P., Fjørtoft, S.O., Torvatn, H.Y.: Artificial intelligence in the public sector: a study of challenges and opportunities for Norwegian municipalities. In: Pappas, I.O., Mikalef, P., Dwivedi, Y.K., Jaccheri, L., Krogstie, J., Mäntymäki, M. (eds.) I3E 2019. LNCS, vol. 11701, pp. 267–277. Springer, Cham (2019). https://doi.org/10.1007/978-3-030-29374-1_22

22. Broomfield, H., Reutter, L.: Towards a data-driven public administration: an empirical analysis of nascent phase implementation. Scand. J. Public Adm. **25**(2), 73–97 (2021). https://doi.org/10.58235/sjpa.v25i2.7117

23. Lov om skatteforvaltning (skatteforvaltningsloven) - Kapittel 8 Opplysningsplikt for skattepliktige, trekkpliktige mv. - Lovdata. https://lovdata.no/dokument/NL/lov/2016-05-27-14/KAPITTEL_8#%C2%A78-16. Accessed 16 Mar 2024

24. Lov om folketrygd (folketrygdloven) - Lovdata. https://lovdata.no/dokument/NL/lov/1997-02-28-19. Accessed 16 Mar 2024

25. The Constitution of the Kingdom of Norway - Lovdata. https://lovdata.no/dokument/NLE/lov/1814-05-17. Accessed 23 Mar 2024

26. Corneliussen, H.G., Iqbal, A., Seddighi, G., Andersen, R.: Bruk av kunstig intelligens i offentlig sektor og risiko for diskriminering Kunnskapsgrunnlag for arbeidet med å forebygge diskriminerende effekter ved bruk av kunstig intelligens i offentlig virksomhet (2022). https://www.vestforsk.no/sites/default/files/2023-03/VFrapport7_2022_KI_i_offentlig_sektor.pdf

27. White Paper on Artificial Intelligence: a European approach to excellence and trust - European Commission. https://commission.europa.eu/publications/white-paper-artificial-intelligence-european-approach-excellence-and-trust_en. Accessed 24 Mar 2024

28. Lov om universiteter og høyskoler (universitets- og høyskoleloven) - Kapittel 1. Lovens formål og virkeområde - Lovdata. https://lovdata.no/dokument/NL/lov/2005-04-01-15/KAPITTEL_1-1#KAPITTEL_1-1. Accessed 21 Mar 2024

29. Artificial Intelligence Act: deal on comprehensive rules for trustworthy AI | News | European Parliament. https://www.europarl.europa.eu/news/en/press-room/20231206IPR15699/artificial-intelligence-act-deal-on-comprehensive-rules-for-trustworthy-ai. Accessed 25 Feb 2024

JURISIN 2024

Preface

The Eighteenth International Workshop on Juris-Informatics (JURISIN 2024) was held with a support of the Japanese Society for Artificial Intelligence (JSAI) in association with JSAI International Symposia on AI (JSAI-IsAI 2024) in Hamamatsu, Japan on 28–29 May.

JURISIN is an international workshop on legal informatics and has been held annually in Japan since 2007. Relevant topics range from models of legal reasoning, argumentation agents, legal ontologies, legal knowledge bases, computerized legal education, AI legal problems, legaldocument analysis, natural language processing for law, etc.

There were 30 submissions. Each submission was reviewed by 3 program committee members. The committee decided to accept 12 papers, but one paper was withdrawn. Thus, this volume contains 11 papers. In addition to the 11 oral presentations, there were two invited talks by Mihoko Sumida from Hitotsubashi University, Japan and Francesca Toni from Imperial College, UK.

We would like to thank the JURISIN 2024 steering committee, the program committee, all those who submitted papers, and the organizing committee of JSAI-IsAI 2024 for the publication of the JURISIN 2024 proceedings.

March 2024

Ken Satoh
Nguyen Le Minh

Addressing Annotated Data Scarcity in Legal Information Extraction

May Myo Zin$^{(\boxtimes)}$ [ID], Ha Thanh Nguyen[ID], Ken Satoh[ID],
and Fumihito Nishino[ID]

National Institute of Informatics, Tokyo, Japan
{maymyozin,nguyenhathanh,ksatoh,nishino}@nii.ac.jp

Abstract. Named Entity Recognition (NER) models face unique challenges in the field of legal text analysis, primarily due to the scarcity of annotated legal data. The creation of a diverse and representative legal text corpus is hindered by the labor-intensive, time-consuming, and expensive nature of manual annotation, leading to suboptimal model performance when trained on insufficient or biased data. This study explores the effectiveness of Generative Pre-trained Transformers (GPT) in overcoming these challenges. Leveraging the generative capabilities of GPT models, we use them as tools for creating human-like annotated data. Through experiments, our research reveals that the pre-trained BERT model, when fine-tuned on GPT-3 generated data, surpasses its counterpart fine-tuned on human-created data in the legal NER task. The demonstrated success of this methodology underscores the potential of large language models (LLMs) in advancing the development of more reliable and contextually aware Legal NER systems for intricate legal texts. This work contributes to the broader goal of enhancing the accuracy and efficiency of information extraction in the legal domain, showcasing the transformative impact of advanced language models on addressing data scarcity issues.

Keywords: Information Extraction · Legal NER · Annotated Data Augmentation

1 Introduction

Legal information extraction plays a vital role in modern legal practice, though it poses unique challenges and complexities. Legal texts are widely recognized for their complex and ambiguous language, often posing challenges for those not well-versed in legal terminology. Moreover, a substantial portion of legal data is unstructured, lacking a predefined format. Extracting information from such unstructured text demands AI-powered Natural Language Processing (NLP) algorithms. In this context, Named Entity Recognition (NER) plays a crucial role in precisely identifying and extracting specific entities. Legal NER extends beyond names of individuals, places, or organizations to include names of laws,

T. Suzumura and M. Bono (Eds.): JSAI-isAI 2024, LNAI 14741, pp. 77–92, 2024.
https://doi.org/10.1007/978-981-97-3076-6_6

procedures, catchphrases, and conceptual entities [1–4]. Through the application of NER, the automated extraction and classification of the legal entities are streamlined, enhancing the efficiency of analyzing and comprehending legal texts.

The automation of NER in legal texts represents a frontier in the intersection of Artificial Intelligence (AI) and legal practice, marked by both its critical importance and its formidable challenges. Unlike general texts, legal documents are characterized by a dense use of specialized terminology, inherent ambiguity, and complex sentence structures, making the accurate extraction of named entities a task traditionally reliant on manual effort. Historically, the automation of legal NER has been stymied by several factors. The nuanced nature of legal language, with its precise yet context-dependent meanings, presents a significant obstacle for conventional NLP algorithms. Additionally, the scarcity of structured, annotated datasets has traditionally made it difficult to train models with the requisite accuracy and specificity for legal applications. To ensure effective performance, comprehensive training on a diverse and representative dataset is crucial.

In the field of law, where resources are frequently scarce, it is imperative to generate extra data to bolster the training process and enhance the performance of NER. The creation of datasets involves generating new examples relevant to the specific domain or application, ensuring that the model encounters a broad spectrum of instances and fosters adaptability to various scenarios. Equally critical is the annotation phase, where datasets are labeled with entity information. This annotation serves as a guide during training, providing the model with supervised learning signals to establish connections between specific text patterns and corresponding entity labels.

The conventional methods employed for labeled data creation bring about significant challenges, particularly in their resource-intensive nature. These established practices, often reliant on human efforts for data collection and the manual assignment of labels or annotations, exact a toll on vital resources such as labor, time, and, potentially, financial investments. Given that state-of-the-art large language models (LLMs), such as OpenAI's GPT series, have demonstrated remarkable zero-shot and few-shot performance across diverse tasks, it becomes imperative to investigate how LLMs can effectively mitigate costs associated with labeled data creation task.

This paper investigates how leveraging the capabilities of GPT-3 and GPT-4 can contribute to automating the process of generating annotated data. By leveraging the advanced NLP capabilities of these models, we aim to streamline and optimize the labor-intensive tasks involved in the preparation of training datasets for legal information extraction. The ultimate goal is to enhance the efficiency and cost-effectiveness of deploying advanced LLMs for such tasks, thereby opening new avenues for improved performance and broader applicability in the legal domain. As a case study, we focus on a specific task involving the identification and extraction of entities or facts within contractual case descriptions.

This work makes notable contributions to artificial intelligence (AI) and Law research by introducing an approach that integrates the GPT model with a pre-trained language model for legal entity extraction task. Notably, the methodology employs GPT models for creating annotated data, streamlining the process and reducing manual efforts. The subsequent fine-tuning of the pre-trained BERT [16] model on GPT generated dataset enhances its proficiency in entity extraction from contractual case descriptions. In unraveling the capabilities of GPT models in this legal NER task, our investigation revolves around the following pivotal research questions:

RQ1: Can GPT models contribute to generating human-like annotated data for developing a robust Legal NER model?

RQ2: How does the quality of the training data generated by a GPT model compare to the training data created manually?

RQ3: Can a Legal NER model, trained or fine-tuned on data generated by a GPT model, outperform the direct utilization of the GPT model for legal entity extraction?

2 Related Work

In the legal domain, there are various proposals to formalize legal information in the form logical predicates. One such system is PROLEG [5], which capable of representing and reasoning about contract status and derive information such as its validity or the right or reason of a rescission. However, a key challenge is the automatic transformation of input text into logical facts. Primarily, translating texts describing contract events into logical facts requires manual coding, making the process inefficient in terms of cost and time. This manual approach also poses issues with updates, as any subsequent changes demand manual creation. To address this, bridging the gap between NLP and this logical system is crucial for the automatic retrieval of all relevant entities or facts from text to populate the PROLEG fact knowledge base.

Entity or fact extraction from contractual legal cases was performed by Navas-Loro et al. in 2019 [6]. These legal cases consist of different events related to the status of the sale and purchase contract. The authors used NLP tools and rules to extract event-centric entities or facts and then transformed those facts into frames, returning the logic clauses (i.e., PROLEG fact formulas) of the input case description. While their proposed approach has successfully processed all the example cases generated by legal researchers, it does have several limitations. Notably, it cannot recognize appositions or naming statements. New rules are required to detect various forms of alternative paraphrasing. Furthermore, additional frames capable of representing diverse legal situations, along with corresponding rule sets for populating them, need to be developed. However, it is important to acknowledge that natural language is inherently complex, and making it impractical to create rules that cover all possible scenarios. Later, in 2023, a deep learning-based model with a transfer learning approach, Legal-CaseNER [7], was developed. This involved fine-tuning a pre-trained language model, BERT [16], on the annotated contractual case descriptions, successfully extracting contractual facts or entities. While this approach proves effective in achieving high accuracy in entity extraction, it necessitates a larger dataset with manual annotations.

Addressing the need for annotated data can be achieved through the application of data augmentation techniques [8–10]. This approach involves creating new data by modifying existing data points [11]. The augmented data can be derived from existing labeled data [12,13] and used directly in supervised learning [14]. Alternatively, the augmented data can be effectively utilized in semi-supervised learning for unlabeled data, incorporating consistency regularization techniques [15]. The recent advancements in AI, driven by the emergence of Large Language Models (LLMs), have significantly enhanced the automation of complex language tasks, such as text generation, translation, and question answering, achieving unprecedented levels of sophistication and accuracy. Researchers in the field of NLP have begun exploring the potential of using LLMs to assist in the task of annotating corpora or generating annotated corpora, achieving promising results across several applications [17–19]. However, it remains uncertain whether comparable levels of performance can be achieved when annotating legal case descriptions, particularly those involving sale and purchase scenarios. Legal texts present unique challenges due to their intricate nature, given that individuals or entities can play diverse roles such as sellers, buyers, minors, rescinders, threateners, and victims. The intricacies of legal language and the multifaceted roles involved in legal cases may pose challenges that differ from other applications where LLMs have shown success. Further investigation is required to assess the effectiveness of LLMs in annotating legal case descriptions and to determine their adaptability to the nuances inherent in this specific domain.

3   Named Entity Recognition

The primary purpose of NER is to identify and categorize important information, known as entities, within text data. An entity can be a single word or a sequence of words that refer to the same category. In a specific example related to a contractual legal case, as depicted in Fig. 1, the entity detection system might detect the word "John" and categorize it as the "SELLER".

In the contract negotiation , John SELLER disclosed that he had sold his ... ...

Fig. 1. Entity detection in contractual legal case - John identified as the seller.

The process of NER typically involves several steps, and the exact number can vary based on the specific approach and methodology used. However, a generalized outline often includes the following key steps.

Data Collection: It involves the process of collecting or creating a representative set of texts or documents that align with the objectives of the NER task. These texts should cover a diverse range of scenarios and language use.

Data Annotation: Human annotators, guided by predefined annotation guidelines, play a crucial role in this process. Consistency among annotators is essential to ensure uniform and reliable annotations. They contribute to the creation of labeled datasets, which serve as the foundation for training NER models. Annotation tools facilitate this task by providing a platform for annotators to label entities in text data efficiently. There are various annotation tools available for NER. Some widely used NER annotation tools include Label Studio, LabelBox, LightTag, Doccano, and Prodigy.

While various events may be associated with the status of a sale and purchase contract, our attention is specifically directed towards events involving:

- The agreement of the contract between parties.
- Rescission of the agreement, either due to one of the parties being a minor or as a result of duress (threatening) imposed on one of the parties.

The desired entity categories associated with these events are outlined in Table 1.

Model Selection and Training: In the context of recognizing important words or phrases (i.e., entities) within legal texts, both rule-based and machine learning (ML) approaches play crucial roles. In a rule-based approach, domain experts meticulously craft predefined patterns, rules, and heuristics to identify entities within legal texts. These rules are designed based on a deep understanding of legal language and context, ensuring that specific terms or expressions indicative of important information are accurately captured. This method relies on explicit logic defined within the rules, enhancing transparency and interpretability as the decision-making process is clearly outlined. However, the effectiveness of rule-based systems may be limited to scenarios explicitly covered by the rules, and they may struggle with generalizing to new or complex data patterns that fall outside the predefined rules. On the other hand, ML models such as Bidirectional LSTMs [20,21] or Transformer [22] architectures like BERT and GPT leverage advanced algorithms to automatically learn and identify important words or phrases within legal texts. These models can discern intricate patterns, relationships, and semantic nuances within the data, enabling them to generalize effectively to new, unseen examples. With proper training data, ML models can adapt to diverse legal domains and tasks, making them versatile for a wide range of applications. This adaptability and generalization capability make ML models particularly valuable for handling complex legal texts where explicit rules may not cover all scenarios comprehensively.

Evaluation: The evaluation of the NER system involves assessing its performance on either a designated validation set or a separate test set. Precision (P),

Table 1. Entity categories in Sale and Purchase case descriptions.

Entity Category	Definition
SELLER	The party or entity that offers goods, services, or property for sale. In a transaction, the seller is the one transferring ownership or providing the specified goods or services
BUYER	The party or entity that acquires or intends to acquire goods, services, or property through a transaction. The buyer is the one making the purchase and gaining ownership or use of the specified items
POTENTIAL_BUYER	An individual or entity that is considering or exploring the possibility of making a purchase
CONTRACT_NAME	The name or title assigned to a legally binding agreement between two or more parties
PURCHASE_PRODUCT	The specific item, product, or service that is being bought or acquired by the buyer in a transaction
PURCHASE_PRICE	The agreed-upon monetary value or consideration that the buyer agrees to pay to the seller in exchange for the purchase of a product, service, or property
PURCHASE_DATE	The date on which a purchase agreement is executed or the date when ownership of the purchased item is transferred from the seller to the buyer
MINOR	The party who has not reached the age of legal adulthood, typically under the age of 18, when the agreement was made
THREATENER	The individual or entity that employs coercion, intimidation, or threats to compel another party to undertake a specific action, such as initiating a contract cancellation
VICTIM	The party or entity that is subjected to duress, threats, or coercion
DURESS_DATE	The date when the coercive or threatening circumstances arose, prompting one party to feel compelled to cancel the existing agreement against their will
RESCINDER	The party or entity that initiates the cancellation or rescission of a contract or agreement
RESCIND_DATE	The date on which a contract or agreement is officially canceled, revoked, or rescinded

recall (R), and *F1* score are commonly used and widely accepted metrics in NER evaluations. These metrics provide a balanced assessment of the NER system's performance by considering both false positives and false negatives.

4 Experiments

4.1 Data Preparation

To annotate data for NER task, it is essential to specify the class to which each token in the sentence belongs. Existing datasets available on the Internet come in various formats, such as CoNLL, which can be challenging for human beings to digest. The following annotation format is considered to be quite user-friendly for both creating and reading annotations.

In the contract negotiation, [John Smith](SELLER) disclosed that he had sold his [vacant land](PURCHASE_ PRODUCT) to [David Martin](BUYER) through a [Land Purchase Agreement](CONTRACT_ NAME). The agreed-upon price was [$200,000](PURCHASE_ PRICE), with the transaction set to be completed on [April 2, 2023](PURCHASE_ DATE). Notably, [David Martin](MINOR), the buyer, was a minor at the time the agreement was made. Subsequently, on [April 15, 2023](RESCIND_ DATE), [David Martin](RESCINDER)initiated the rescission of the contract.

In this annotation format, square brackets "[ ]" are used to delineate the boundary of the entity, while parentheses "( )" are employed to indicate the entity label or category within it. To automatically transform this annotation format into a format directly compatible with HUGGING FACE'S TRAINER CLASS[1], we employ a preprocessing approach similar to that of the NER DATA MAKER[2]. For initial seed data, we manually create 150 samples in this annotation format.

Data Augmentation: As the initial set of 150 samples proves inadequate for the development of a robust NER model, we adopted two approaches for augmenting additional training data: manual and GPT-generated. Through manual efforts, we created 6,300 new annotated samples from the initial set by introducing entity variations, synonym replacement, and paraphrasing.

In parallel, we generated 6,300 annotated data samples using GPT-3 and an additional 6,300 samples with GPT-4. To instruct the GPT model to generate annotated data in the user-friendly format mentioned at the beginning of the section, the prompt was structured as follows:

Generate 10 different case descriptions (i.e., summaries) of a purchase agreement in a human-written style, each summarizing details such as the seller, buyer, contract_ name, purchase_ product, purchase_ date, purchase_ price,

---

[1] https://huggingface.co/learn/nlp-course/chapter7/2?fw=pt.
[2] https://gist.github.com/jangedoo/7ac6fdc7deadc87fd1a1124c9d4ccce9.

minor (i.e., the party who has not reached the age of legal adulthood, typically under the age of 18, when the agreement was made), threatener (i.e., the individual or entity that employs coercion, intimidation, or threats to compel another party to undertake a specific action, such as initiating a contract cancellation.), victim (i.e., the party or entity that is subjected to duress, threats, or coercion), duress_ date (i.e., the date when the coercive or threatening circumstances arose, prompting one party to feel compelled to cancel the existing agreement against their will), rescind_ date (i.e., the date on which a contract or agreement is officially canceled, revoked, or rescinded), rescinder (i.e., the party or entity that initiates the cancellation or rescission of a contract or agreement), etc. Also, consider entering into an agreement first and then canceling it due to various reasons, including minor cases, threats, or forceful cancellations. Make sure to incorporate real names, dates, accurate financial information, and other relevant details. Please write in a paragraph and use "[]" and "()" to annotate entities.

Learn annotations from the following example case:
[*** an example of an annotated case from seed data ***]

Please avoid replicating the structure and writing style of the provided examples. Instead, create diverse formats and writing styles, such as human-written purchase case summaries, while ensuring accurate annotations. Incorporate names of individuals, companies, or organizations from various countries across Asia and Europe. Display dates in varied formats and styles, encompassing different conventions. Introduce distinct currency symbols and currency types within each summary, ensuring variety across the information provided. Occasionally express purchase prices in words rather than numbers. Utilize various rationales for contract agreement, cancellation, or termination. Moreover, incorporate a range of verbs or synonyms in the generated summaries to enhance diversity.

This well-crafted prompt is designed to guide the GPT model in generating diverse case descriptions with accurate annotations. By "*diverse*", we mean not only variations in entities among cases but also diversity in the structure and word usage within each case.

Evaluation Test Sets: We have prepared four test sets for evaluation purposes. The initial test set, labeled "**seenTest**", consists of 50 samples that comprehensively cover and align with the scope of the initial seed data. To enhance the diversity of our evaluation, we created three extra unseen test sets, each consisting of 20 samples. These sets were collaboratively crafted with input from different individuals. Evaluating the NER model on our "unseen" or "out-of-distribution" test sets involves assessing its performance on data that differs significantly from the training data. This helps determine the model's ability to handle unexpected scenarios and provides insights into its generalization capabilities beyond the specific patterns encountered during training. We refrained from providing any samples as examples during the unseen test sets creation process. The approach differed for each contributor:

unseenTest1: The first person received information about the scope and specific events related to the cases under consideration. This allowed them the liberty to create cases freely. Although the resulting unseen test set remains within our considered events, the structure of each case significantly diverges from our training data.

unseenTest2: The second person, without any information about the scope, was tasked with creating various events related to purchase case scenarios. This unseen test set falls within the domain of sale and purchase case scenarios, encompassing several events. Some aligning with our considered events, while others deviate.

unseenTest3: For the third person, we provided the freedom to create any contractual cases. Consequently, the third unseen test set consists of several contractual cases, with only a small portion related to sale and purchase scenarios.

These test sets provide a comprehensive evaluation of the model's performance across various scenarios, including cases with structures different from the training data, diverse purchase scenarios, and a mix of contractual cases. The objective is to evaluate model's generalization capabilities and its performance in real-world scenarios not explicitly covered in its original training data.

4.2   NER as Token Classification Task

Token classification is a type of sequence labeling task where each token in a sequence is assigned a specific label. In the context of NER, the goal is to recognize and classify entities within a given text. The input to the model is a sequence of tokens (words or subword units), and the output is a label assigned to each token, indicating whether it belongs to an entity and, if so, what type of entity it is.

Instead of training the model from scratch, we employ transfer learning. We fine-tune a pre-trained $BERT_{BASE}$ model for our specific NER task using corresponding annotated data. This ML model has various hyperparameters such as learning rate, batch size, warm-up steps, and the number of training epoch. These hyperparameters are not learned from the data but are set before training. Fine-tuning these hyperparameters is crucial for achieving optimal model performance. For each experiment, we conduct multiple training sessions with different hyperparameter configurations. The set that performs best on the validation set is then selected. Emphasizing the importance of balanced model generalization to address overfitting and underfitting, we incorporate cross-validation. This technique involves splitting the dataset into multiple folds, training and validating the model on different combinations. The inclusion of cross-validation enhances the reliability of our evaluation, particularly in datasets with limitations. Additionally, we implement Early Stopping to prevent overfitting problem.

4.3   NER as Zero-Shot Entity Extraction Task

This study aims to utilize the GPT model to generate annotated data for building a robust NER model. However, the key questions arise: *"Why use the GPT model to create NER data when it can be directly applied to entity extraction tasks? Is it possible that a model trained or fine-tuned on GPT-generated labeled data performs better than using the GPT model directly for legal entity extraction?"*. To answer these questions, we conduct a zero-shot GPT NER task by directly applying the GPT model. The following prompt is designed to instruct the GPT model on how to extract the desired entities from a user input test case:

Extract the following information from the given case summary:
Seller:
Buyer:

.

.

.

Rescind Date (i.e., the date on which a contract or agreement is officially canceled, revoked, or rescinded):
Please provide the information exactly as it appears in the provided summary without additional paraphrasing. If a specific entity type is not present in the case summary, indicate it with "N/A". Ensure accuracy and attention to detail in capturing relevant information.

Case Summary:
*[*** user input test case ***]*

To ensure that the GPT model fully comprehends the entities we aim to extract, we furnish the definition or explanation of each entity category in the prompt. Explanations are excluded for easily understandable categories like seller, buyer, purchase product, purchase price, and purchase date. The explanations of each category can be found in Table 1. Additionally, we instruct the model not to paraphrase or rewrite but to extract the exact text spans for each entity category, if present, from the user input case.

4.4   Results and Discussion

In our experiments, we employed *text-davinci-003* for GPT-3 and *gpt-4-0613* for GPT-4. By leveraging their capabilities, we explore their effectiveness not only in creating diverse and coherent NER annotated data but also in extracting entities from user input data. We then compare their usefulness in each task. The key findings are presented in Table 2, revealing significant insights. The BERT-based NER model, initially fine-tuned on a seed dataset, demonstrates satisfactory performance with a score of 0.92 across all evaluation metrics on the **seenTest** set. However, this model struggles to generalize to unseen test data, indicating a need for additional data for fine-tuning to enhance its robustness. The initial seed dataset is insufficient in capturing the complexities present in

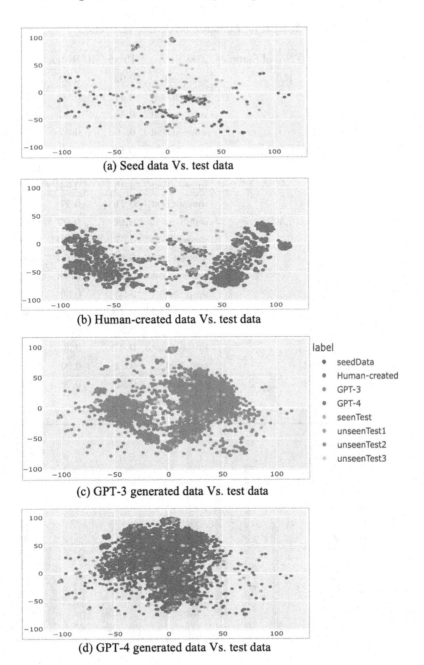

(a) Seed data Vs. test data

(b) Human-created data Vs. test data

label
- seedData
- Human-created
- GPT-3
- GPT-4
- seenTest
- unseenTest1
- unseenTest2
- unseenTest3

(c) GPT-3 generated data Vs. test data

(d) GPT-4 generated data Vs. test data

Fig. 2. Augmented training data and test data (seenTest, unseenTest1, unseenTest2, unseenTest3) visualized using *t-SNE* dimensionality reduction after encoding with the Sentence Transformer model "*all-MiniLM-L6-v2*". The scatter plot shows the distribution of sentence embeddings in a 2D space, where each point represents a sentence and is color-coded based on its data source.

Table 2. NER performance on diverse test sets.

Approach	No. of Samples	Test Set	Precision	Recall	F1
Seed Data	150	seenTest	0.92	0.92	0.92
		unseenTest1	0.51	0.50	0.50
		unseenTest2	0.45	0.50	0.47
		unseenTest3	0.16	0.24	0.19
Manual	6,300	seenTest	**0.96**	0.96	0.96
		unseenTest1	0.58	0.56	0.57
		unseenTest2	0.45	0.54	0.49
		unseenTest3	0.21	0.27	0.23
GPT-3	6,300	seenTest	**0.96**	**0.97**	**0.97**
		unseenTest1	0.67	**0.70**	**0.68**
		unseenTest2	**0.61**	**0.64**	**0.62**
		unseenTest3	0.28	**0.48**	**0.35**
GPT-4	6,300	seenTest	0.93	0.80	0.86
		unseenTest1	**0.78**	0.58	0.66
		unseenTest2	0.57	0.36	0.45
		unseenTest3	**0.41**	0.30	0.34
Zero-Shot-gpt3-NER	-	seenTest	0.82	0.90	0.86
Zero-Shot-gpt4-NER	-	seenTest	0.92	0.90	0.91

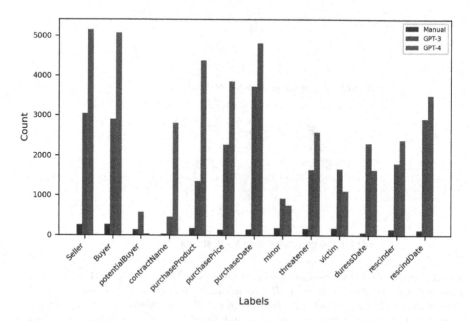

Fig. 3. Comparison of entity counts among three types of augmented datasets.

the unseen test sets, as illustrated in Fig. 2(a). The model needs more diverse and representative training data to improve its performance on new and unseen examples.

Upon augmenting the dataset with an additional 6,300 manually created samples, there is a notable improvement in performance across all test sets. Surprisingly, the model fine-tuned on data generated by GPT-3 surpasses the performance of the model fine-tuned on human-created data. This suggests that generating annotated data using GPT-3 is an efficient alternative to manual creation, offering a substantial advantage in terms of time and resource savings. Furthermore, the annotations in the GPT-3 generated data exhibit a high level of accuracy. Figure 2(b) illustrates that human-created data lacks the diversity required for effective generalization, leading to poor performance on unseen test scenarios. In contrast, GPT-3 generated data (Fig. 2(c)) demonstrates greater diversity, covering a wider range of scenarios and contributing to the improved generalization capability of the NER model. These findings emphasize the efficiency and effectiveness of GPT-3 in rapidly producing diverse and accurate annotated data, highlighting its potential as a valuable tool in training NER models. This observation directly addresses the research questions, specifically **RQ1** and **RQ2** as outlined in Sect. 1.

In the process of optimizing prompts for the GPT model, we experimented with various prompt versions, ultimately selecting the most effective one for GPT-3. This selected prompt was also applied to GPT-4. Although GPT-4 can generate annotated data with varied structures, as shown in Fig. 2(d), and diverse entity values for each category, as depicted in Fig. 3, manual analysis revealed instances where GPT-4 occasionally exhibited some missing annotations (especially for PURCHASE_DATE, DURESS_DATE, and RESCIND_DATE), leading to performance degradation when compared with GPT-3 generated data. However, it still shows improvement on two unseen test sets: **unseenTest1** and **unseenTest3** when compared with human-created data.

In addressing research question **RQ3**, we conducted a performance comparison between a BERT-based NER model fine-tuned on GPT-3 generated data and two alternative models, namely Zero-Shot-gpt-3-NER and Zero-Shot-gpt4-NER. The conclusion drawn from the comparison, as shown in Table 2, is that using the GPT model for creating annotated data is a more effective approach for the entity extraction task when compared to the other two models. This suggests that the GPT-3 generated data, when used to fine-tune a BERT-based NER model, outperforms the other models in terms of entity extraction accuracy or performance on the task being evaluated.

5   Conclusion

In this study, we explore the efficacy of GPT models as both data creators and annotators for improving the legal entity extraction task. We address three

key research questions, and our experimental results indicate that GPT models
have the potential to generate annotated legal data for the tasks related to legal
information extraction. Remarkably, the performance of a BERT-based model
fine-tuned on the dataset created by GPT-3 surpasses that of a model fine-tuned
on human-annotated data. These findings highlight the promising prospect of
leveraging LLMs for automatic data creation and annotation, showcasing their
ability to enhance the performance of NER by providing a reliable additional
training data. The results also demonstrate that utilizing GPT models in collaboration with other pre-trained language models, such as BERT, can lead
to improved performance in the specific tasks. We anticipate that the insights
gained from this research will contribute to the development of methods aimed at
further enhancing the quality of data generated by LLMs. By enabling individuals to autonomously create data for their model training, we aspire to facilitate
the democratization of legal AI, making advanced tools and technologies more
accessible to a broader audience.

6   Limitations and Future Work

Our study has certain limitations that should be acknowledged. Firstly, our
approach focuses solely on prompt engineering for optimizing GPT-3 performance. To fully guide the GPT-4 model, it would be advantageous to extend
our prompt engineering techniques. Additionally, the initial dataset used in our
experiments only covers the specific events within contractual legal cases related
to sale and purchase agreements. In future iterations, we aim to expand our
dataset to encompass all relevant events. Another constraint of our study is
the financial limitations that restricted our ability to conduct large-scale experiments with the proposed data creation methods. Consequently, our findings may
not be entirely representative of larger datasets or diverse populations. Moreover, although we have observed some annotation errors in the data generated
by GPT, particularly with GPT-4, we have refrained from making modifications
and opted to use it as is. Therefore, in the future, we will explore methodologies
for automatic error detection and correction. This proactive approach aims to
enhance the overall quality of the generated data, ensuring that it aligns more
closely with the desired accuracy standards.

Acknowledgments. This work was supported by JSPS KAKENHI Grant Numbers,
JP22H00543 and JST, AIP Trilateral AI Research, Grant Number JPMJCR20G4.

References

1. Cardellino, C., Teruel, M., Alonso Alemany, L., Villata, S.: A low-cost, high cov-
   erage legal named entity recognizer, classifier and linker. In: 16th Edition of the
   International Conference on Artificial Intelligence and Law, ICAIL 2017, London,
   UK, pp. 9–18 (2017)

2. Mandal, A., Ghosh, K., Ghosh, S., Mandal, S.: A sequence labeling model for catchphrase identification from legal case documents. Artif. Intell. Law **30**, 325–358 (2021). https://doi.org/10.1007/s10506-021-09296-2

3. Çetindağ, C., Yazıcıoğlu, B., Koç, A.: Named-entity recognition in Turkish legal texts. Nat. Lang. Eng. **29**(3), 615–642 (2023)

4. Darji, H., Mitrović, J., Granitzer, M.: German BERT model for legal named entity recognition. In: 15th International Conference on Agents and Artificial Intelligence, ICAART 2023, Lisbon, Portugal, vol. 3, pp. 723–728 (2023)

5. Satoh, K., et al.: PROLEG: an implementation of the presupposed ultimate fact theory of Japanese civil code by PROLOG technology. In: Onada, T., Bekki, D., McCready, E. (eds.) JSAI-isAI 2010. LNCS (LNAI), vol. 6797, pp. 153–164. Springer, Heidelberg (2011). https://doi.org/10.1007/978-3-642-25655-4_14

6. Navas-Loro, M., Satoh, K., Rodríguez-Doncel, V.: ContractFrames: bridging the gap between natural language and logics in contract law. In: Kojima, K., Sakamoto, M., Mineshima, K., Satoh, K. (eds.) JSAI-isAI 2018. LNCS (LNAI), vol. 11717, pp. 101–114. Springer, Cham (2019). https://doi.org/10.1007/978-3-030-31605-1_9

7. Zin, M.M., Nguyen, H.T., Satoh, K., Sugawara, S., Nishino, F.: Improving translation of case descriptions into logical fact formulas using LegalCaseNER. In: 19th International Conference on Artificial Intelligence and Law, ICAIL 2023, Braga, Portugal, pp. 462–466 (2023)

8. Feng, S.Y., et al.: A survey of data augmentation approaches for NLP. arXiv preprint arXiv:2105.03075 (2021)

9. Meng, Y., Huang, J., Zhang, Y., Han, J.: Generating training data with language models: towards zero-shot language understanding. In: Advances in Neural Information Processing Systems 35, pp. 462–477 (2022)

10. Chen, J., Tam, D., Raffel, C., Bansal, M., Yang, D.: An empirical survey of data augmentation for limited data learning in NLP. Trans. Assoc. Comput. Linguist. **11**, 191–211 (2023)

11. Yang, Y., et al.: Generative data augmentation for commonsense reasoning. arXiv preprint arXiv:2004.11546 (2020)

12. Ding, B., et al.: DAGA: data augmentation with a generation approach for low-resource tagging tasks. arXiv preprint arXiv:2011.01549 (2020)

13. Liu, L., Ding, B., Bing, L., Joty, S., Si, L., Miao, C.: MulDA: a multilingual data augmentation framework for low-resource cross-lingual NER. In: 59th Annual Meeting of the Association for Computational Linguistics and the 11th International Joint Conference on Natural Language Processing, vol. 1, pp. 5834–5846 (2021)

14. Wei, J., Zou, K.: EDA: easy data augmentation techniques for boosting performance on text classification tasks. arXiv preprint arXiv:1901.11196 (2019)

15. Xie, Q., Dai, Z., Hovy, E., Luong, T., Le, Q.: Unsupervised data augmentation for consistency training. In: Advances in Neural Information Processing Systems 33, pp. 6256–6268 (2020)

16. Devlin, J., Chang, M.W., Lee, K., Toutanova, K.: BERT: pre-training of deep bidirectional transformers for language understanding. In: NAACL-HLT, vol. 1, p. 2 (2019)

17. Ding, B., Qin, C., Liu, L., Bing, L., Joty, S., Li, B.: Is GPT-3 a good data annotator? arXiv preprint arXiv:2212.10450 (2022)

18. Frei, J., Kramer, F.: Annotated dataset creation through large language models for non-English medical NLP. J. Biomed. Inform. **145**, 104478 (2023)

19. Gilardi, F., Alizadeh, M., Kubli, M.: ChatGPT outperforms crowd-workers for text-annotation tasks. arXiv preprint arXiv:2303.15056 (2023)

20. Graves, A.: Generating sequences with recurrent neural networks. arXiv preprint arXiv:1308.0850 (2013)
21. Zaremba, W., Sutskever, I., Vinyals, O.: Recurrent neural network regularization. arXiv preprint arXiv:1409.2329 (2014)
22. Vaswani, A.: Attention is all you need. In: Advances in Neural Information Processing Systems, vol. 30 (2017)

Enhancing Legal Argument Retrieval with Optimized Language Model Techniques

Aleksander Smywiński-Pohl[1] and Tomer Libal[2]

[1] Computer Science Institute, AGH University of Krakow, Kraków, Poland
apohllo@agh.edu.pl

[2] Department of Computer Science, Luxembourg University, Luxembourg City, Luxembourg
tomer.libal@uni.lu

Abstract. Understanding the meaning of legal concepts appearing in regulations is essential to both legal experts and lay people. The main way to explain these terms involves sifting through extensive case law and identifying court opinions regarding the interpretations of the concepts in certain scenarios. Automating this task can be achieved by using argument retrieval techniques. In this paper, we build on the extensive results in [1] and present six approaches for potentially improving the results. These approaches are then tested and compared on the same data set. By careful experiment design and extensive testing we were able to improve the NDCG@10 score by 12% points on the evaluation subset and by 13% points on the test subset, setting a new state-of-the-art result for the dataset of statutory interpretation.

Keywords: Legal argument retrieval · Language model optimization · Explaining legal concepts · Legal information systems

1 Introduction

An important challenge for legal professionals is legal research [2] due to the ever changing statute and case law. This challenge stems from the fact that laws are written in an abstract and vague way [3], which is then explained, defined and interpreted in case law [4].

A key step in legal research is the ability to decide about the value of an abstract and vague legal concept, given a certain context. For example, the concept "Useful improvement" from American Patent Law[1], is taking a negative interpretation in WEST VIEW RESEARCH v. BAYERISCHE MOTOREN WERKE, where the court decided that "There is nothing in the specification to support this representation that the inventions provide new and improved systems, protocols or methods of securing wireless transactions from interception by unauthorized users"[2].

---

[1] Patents 35 U.S. Code §101.

[2] https://cite.case.law/f-supp-3d/226/1071/.

T. Suzumura and M. Bono (Eds.): JSAI-isAI 2024, LNAI 14741, pp. 93–108, 2024.
https://doi.org/10.1007/978-981-97-3076-6_7

Given a new patent idea, an important part of the research required in order to determine whether it makes a useful improvement or not, is to determine which of the existing case law describes a similar patent and then, what was the court decision regarding the usefulness of the improvement. In our previous work [5], we have considered what level of factual information is required in order to identify the most relevant positive and negative examples of court rulings regarding a certain concept.

Another approach, taken by Šavelka in his doctoral thesis [1], is to identify those sentences in case law, which contain the highest level of information for understanding the legal concept. In [6], Šavelka and Ashley confirm that pre-trained large language models can be fine-tuned to efficiently identify those sentences.

In this paper, we suggest six possible improvements over the ones mentioned in [6]. Our results show that at least one suggestion can significantly improve the finding of such sentences. The goals of the paper are several. We first would like to add to the state-of-the-art in discovering explanatory sentences in case law. Second, one of the key difficulties in [1] was reviewing the annotations done by students. In this paper, we show that the quality of the result is not worse, if only two options are used for classifying sentences, which also reduces the annotation effort. Lastly, we test one of the assumptions in [7] that a greater number of tokens allowed by language models can increase the quality of the result. We also test the impact of larger variants of the language models as well as a voting scheme which naturally stems from the fact that in each experiment four separate models are trained.

In the next section, we introduce the approach taken by Šavelka and Ashley and especially, their best performing model, which we will use as our baseline for the experiment. Section 3 will introduce the six possible improvements, that are evaluated in Sect. 4. In the last section, we conclude the findings and discuss how they might be used, in combination with our previous work, to help in understanding legal terms.

2 Relevant Work

This research concerns the task of discovering sentences for argumentation about the meaning of statutory terms. This task, introduced by Šavelka and Ashley, is defined in [7] as a specific type of legal argument retrieval, by itself defined by Ashley and Walker [8] as the merging of legal information retrieval and legal argument mining.

The task of legal information retrieval [9] is concerned with finding documents containing specific information, such as court cases relating to specific legal concepts. The task of argument mining [10], on the other hand, focuses on understanding the structure of arguments within legal documents. Legal argument retrieval is therefore the task of retrieving the arguments within a large body of legal documents [8].

In terms of explaining statutory terms, the JusticeBot project [11] uses case law argument extraction to create legal expert systems. Another approach to reason with case law, based on abstract dialectical frameworks, is described in [12], where also a review of earlier similar methods is given.

When considering language models for case law argument retrieval, one should mention Legal-BERT [13], a legal language model, which we discuss later in Sect. 3. In [14], an even larger legal language model is assembled and used to detect bias and other harmful elements in legal texts.

In this paper, we focus on extending the work in [7] and especially on the fine-tuned language models mentioned in [6], and defined in [1]. For a further overview of the research on legal argument retrieval, information retrieval and argument mining, we refer the reader to [7]. In their work, Šavelka and Ashley define the process of discovering sentences in case law regarding the meaning of statutory terms as a sentence ranking task for given queries.

While in [7], they have experimented with various ranking algorithms and approaches, in [1], they have shown that fine-tuning a language model outperforms carefully designed experiments, already for the current amount of data that they have assembled.

In order to train and test their model, Šavelka and Ashley have assembled a dataset of almost 27 thousand sentences from court case decisions. These sentences were retrieved from the Caselaw access project[3] and where selected according to the sentences containing specific occurrences of a list of chosen legal concepts. For the full list of legal concepts, we refer the reader to Šavelka's Doctorate thesis [1]. In addition to sentences, Šavelka and Ashley store also the full case, opinions within the case and the paragraph containing the concept. Due to restrictions on the maximal size of the input query which can be given to the language model they have fine-tuned, in this work they have opted for using sentences only. For their experiment, they have chosen to fine-tune the language model RoBERTa base, which is a pre-trained transformer-based language model developed by Facebook AI.

The task considered by Šavelka and Ashley is to return, given legal concept, a list of sentences which best explain the legal meaning of the concept. Such sentences can be definitional sentences [7] that state explicitly in a different way what the statutory phrase means or state what it does not mean, by providing an example, instance, or counterexample of the phrase, and sentences that show how a court determines whether something is such an example, instance, or counterexample. In order to be able to train and assess the models, the dataset was annotated by law students where each sentence was annotated by two students. The annotators assigned each sentence a category denoting whether it has a *high, certain, potential* or *no value* to understanding the legal concepts.

Since they have already identified the list of possible sentences for each legal concept, which are the sentences containing an exact quote of a concept, the task is reduced to sorting these sentences and have those with the highest value first. The use of pre-trained language models means that the researchers have not given a precise method for computing the categories above, but instead fine-tuned the model on examples which they believe demonstrate how such a

---

[3] https://case.law.

method should behave. The difference between the approaches discussed in [6] is therefore the choice of examples used in fine-tuning.

Another parameter of their experiment (called k) is the number of sentences to return for a certain term. They opted for two different numbers, which are $k = 10$ and $k = 100$. With $k = 10$, for each concept, the 10 best sentences are returned, while for $k = 100$, the best 100 are returned. The rationale behind returning 100 sentences is that in legal research, it is common for legal professionals to go over a substantial number of case decisions in order to best understand a legal concept. However measuring the score with $k = 10$ shows how valuable sentences are at the very top of the result, so improving that score makes the legal research much more efficient. This is the reason we have decided to use this value as the primary optimization target.

In order to train and evaluate the quality of their fine-tuned models, the researchers used Normalized Discounted Cumulative Gain score, very popular in information retrieval [15]. For the task of argument mining they first defined $S_j = (s_1, \ldots, s_n)$, where s_i for $0 < i \leq n$ is a sentence for concept j in the i-th place in the list of retrieved sentences. They then used, for the purpose of assigning a value for each S_j, and for a given k, a normalized discounted cumulative gain as follows:

$$NDCG(S_j, k) = \frac{1}{Z_{jk}} \Sigma_{i=1}^{k} \frac{rel(s_i)}{log_2(i + 1)} \tag{1}$$

where $rel(s_i)$ is the value of each sentence for the understanding of a concept (3 for *high* value to 0 for *no value*) and Z_{jk} normalizes the result by dividing it with the value of the ideal sorting of the sentences. The reader is invited to consult with [15] for a detailed explanation of this measure.

For the purpose of fine-tuning their best model, they have used examples pairing the sentences with the provision of the legal concepts, where the provisions were defined as the smallest text in the regulation expressing a statutory provision regarding the legal concept. Lastly, they have divided their data into 6 folds, 4 of which were used for training in a 4-fold cross-validation setup (in each training one of the folds is used as the evaluation fold and 3 remaining folds are used to train the model) and 2 for final testing. In order to ensure proper distribution of the data among the folds, they have classified each legal concept into one of four categories and ensured the same number of elements of each category are in each fold.

Their result of running the model on the validation and test folds for $k = 10$ and $k = 100$ is summarized in Table 1. In the next section, we define six modifications to the experiment above.

3   Methodology

In this section, we discuss several issues related to the definition of the task as well as the features of the model that was used in [6].

Table 1. Result summary for the BERT sp2snt model [1].

	NDCG@10	NDCG@100
Validation	.71 ± .19	.80 ± .14
Test	.68 ± .21	.77 ± .17

[R1] **Does state-of-the-art models such as DeBERTa or domain-specific models such as Legal-BERT give better results than RoBERTa?** We have decided to test DeBERTa v.3 [16,17] and Legal-BERT [13] as alternatives, specifically to find out if it is better to use a general-purpose model that gives state-of-the-art results on typical NLP tasks or a domain-specific model such as Legal BERT.

[R2] **Does inclusion of the concept in the text passed to the model improve the results of the model?** It is apparent that even if only the concept and the sentence are considered, the model gives meaningful results. So a natural question that stems from these observations is whether the inclusion of the concept, together with the sentence and the provision would improve (or maybe degrade) the results obtained by the model.

[R3] **Is it possible to obtain similar results by using a binary, rather than 4-values classification?** We investigate this problem by clustering the *high* and *certain* value into general type of *relevant* sentences and *potential* and *no value* into general type of *irrelevant* sentences. In both cases the model is finally used just to sort the sentences (rather than classify them according to the scheme), so this reduction in expensiveness does not influence the perceived function of the system for the prospective user. To give a fair comparison with the previous research, we use the original scale of values when computing the scores. The binary scale is used only for training.

[R4] **Does the limit on the input size in the RoBERTa model (512 subtokens) impact the results of the model?** The memory requirements related to the computation of the attention in a typical transformer implementation is quadratic with respect to the length of the input sequence. As a result the authors of BERT decided they will train the model only on texts up to 512 subtokens. On the other hand there has been much research related to models that accept longer sequences, such as *flash attention* [18] or *approximated computation* of the attention as presented in [19]. DeBERTa [16] uses the traditional attention mechanism (i.e. quadratic memory consumption), but it also introduced an innovation with respect to the representation of the position of tokens in the text. In that model, the attention is computed separately for the tokens content and tokens position, and the positions are relative, rather than absolute. By introducing this invention the model allows to process sequences of arbitrary length and it achieves state-of-the-art in a number of NLP task, when models of similar sizes are considered.

[R5] **What is the impact of the size of the model on its performance?** Since the authors have decided to follow a cross-validation scheme for evaluating the performance of the model, considering only "base" models, typically having approx. 100 million parameters, was a good decision, since larger models require much more computation. Given that the accessibility of computing power is growing, we have decided to check what would be the benefit of using larger models. It is apparent that these models give very good results for tasks such as passage retrieval [20], so taking them into account should answer the question if the additional computational effort is worth its cost. Since even models of modest sizes, like RoBERTa-large or DeBERTa-large require a lot of computation, the number of experiments for these models is still limited in our setting.

[R6] Does a voting among the trained models improve the results on the held-out corpus? All experiments use 4 folds for training, which produces 4 models. Therefore we can utilize them all in a voting scenario. We have used a procedure of computing the distribution of classes according to each model and then making the final decision by taking the average of the probabilities.

We have added one additional tweak that was used in all experiments. In [2] the F1 score of a model on the cross-validation split was computed and then the best model according to that measure was tested on the held-out splits. However the target metrics used to judge the performance of the model were NDCG@10 and NDCG@100. In our experiments we computed these metrics during training and have used NDCG@10 to select the "best" model. We have decided to use $k = 10$, since we believe that in practical settings, the user is interested in getting the most relevant results at the very top of the result list, which is reflected by a lower k.

Regarding hyper-parameter optimization, we have followed a rational approach (with respect to the computing resources we have), which was achieved by a manual experimentation with the hyper-parameters. We have mainly modified the batch size and the learning rate, to find a configuration that would yield the best results for a given model and a problem configuration. Since for each such configuration we have to train 4 models, we could not perform a grid-search among all possible hyper-parameter configurations. In most cases, a learning rate 2e-5 with a linear decrease schedule produced the best results. The batch size was usually set to utilize all of the available VRAM.

4   Experiments

In this section, we describe the results of experiments which were conducted in order to test the six questions presented in the previous section.

The experiments compute how well different algorithms have managed to order sentences from case law with regards to their relevancy for explaining legal concepts.

In the last part of this section, we discuss a more qualitative, albeit more subjective, analysis of the baseline model and our best model. We check which sentences have been identified as the most relevant (top 10) by each algorithm and which group of results would better serve in order to explain the meaning of the "useful improvement" concept from American patent law.

4.1   General vs Domain-Specific Models

We have started with the training of the RoBERTa-base model as our baseline, to make sure that the results we obtain and the general configuration of the environment we are using matches that in the original research. The results of these experiment are given in Table 2. For each model we report the mean result on the *evaluation* datasets (i.e. the result on the one split that was held-out when the model was trained on the remaining splits). We also report the result on the *test* dataset, that is the held-out split (number 5 and 6) the model was neither trained or evaluated on. The test dataset is the same for all 4 trained models in the given experiment setup and we report the mean scores of these models. This reporting scheme applies to all the other experiments, if not explicitly stated otherwise.

Table 2. The results of the training of different models: RoBERTa-base, DeBERTa-base and Legal-BERT-base in the cross-validation setting. The *Eval* results are the mean results for the 1 held-out split, while *Test* are the mean results on the two splits that were not used for training or evaluation.

	Eval NDCG		Test NDCG	
Model	**@10**	**@100**	**@10**	**@100**
Original	0.710	0.800	**0.680**	**0.770**
RoBERTa-base	**0.778**	**0.840**	0.675	0.759
DeBERTa-base	0.710	0.818	0.662	0.756
Legal-BERT-base	0.729	0.818	0.634	0.742

The *original* are the results reported by Šavelka and Ashely in [6]. We have obtained quiet different results for the evaluation subsets in our experiment, with NDCG@10 improved by +6.8 pp. and NDCG@100 improved by +4.0 pp., which we judge a successful reproduction of their results. The differences might stem from the different hyper-parameters used to train the model and the different random generator seed, which influences the order of the data the models are trained on, as well as the fact that we selected the best model using NDCG@10, rather than the F1 score. The results on the Test dataset are however slightly worse in both settings: −0.5 pp. for NDCG@10 and −1.1 pp. for NDCG@100.

We have also trained models base on DeBERTa-base and Legal-BERT-base, to find out if it is beneficial to use a domain-specific model like Legal-BERT for the statutory interpretation task and what is the impact of a state-of-the-art model like DeBERTa-v3-base. The results obtained by DeBERTa-base and Legal-BERT-base on the evaluation datasets are very similar, they obtain 0.710 and 0.729 NDCG@10 and 0.818 and 0.818 NDCG@100 respectively. However when comparing to the results produced by RoBERTa-base, we have found out that they are worse in all settings. Although DeBERTa-base gives slightly better results on the evaluation subset than the original RoBERTa-base model (for the NDCG@100 score), it is worse than the RoBERTa-base model we have trained ourselves. Similar results are obtained for Legal-BERT-base. Regarding the scores obtained on the test subset, these models are worse than the original and the reproduced model.

So the answer to R1 seems negative already after the first experiment. Even though these results are not that encouraging, we have decided to use both DeBERTa and Legal-BERT in the remaining experiments, since the difference on the evaluation set is not huge and they were as good or better than the original model on that subset. What is more, DeBERTa is the only model that allows us to easily check if giving a longer limit for the input would yield better results.

4.2   Concept Inclusion

The authors of [6] decided to use three types of inputs for the models:

1. *sentence* from judgment,
2. *concept* + *sentence* from judgment,
3. *provision* + *sentence* from judgment,

to fine-tune a model that would be able to decide if the sentence is relevant or not. The last configuration was the most successful and we refer only to the results obtained by this configuration in our experiments. However it is apparent that it would be very easy to test the following input:

4. *concept* + *provision* + *sentence* from judgment.

We have tested this setup in the second experiment. The actual order of the elements was changed to: concept + sentence + provision, since in the case the text would be longer than the limit allowed by the model, we prefer the provision, rather than the sentence to be truncated. The possible benefit of this setup is the fact that the model receives a clear indication of the concept we are interested in. The downside of this setup is the fact that the input is longer, so more information might be truncated, if the input is longer than the limit accepted by the model. We elaborate on that problem in Sect. 4.4.

The results of that experiment are given in Table 3 in rows marked as 1–3. For the RoBERTa-base model the results regarding all metrics are worse than in the setup without the concept, which is an interesting outcome of our experiments. The largest drop is with respect to the NDCG@10 score, which is definitely not a good outcome. On the other hand, the results for the other models are generally slightly better when the concept is included. DeBERTa-base gained 2.4 pp. NDCG@10 on the evaluation set, at the same time it lost 0.8 pp. NDCG@100 score on the test set. For Legal BERT the results are almost identical for each setup.

Thus, the answer to R2 is not clear at this stage, since the effect of the presence of the concept is inconsistent. As a result, we have decided to include the concept in the remaining experiments only for the DeBERTa,

Table 3. The comparison of the results for various training setups. The results reported in parentheses are the differences with respect to the best previous configuration of a given model and they are reported in percentage points. Compared configurations: **Concept** – with inclusion (*yes*) of the concept in the input text, **Values** – 4-value or binary classification, **Length** – with context length extended to 768 subtokens.

	Model	Features	Eval NDCG		Test NDCG	
			@10	@100	@10	@100
	Original		0.710	0.800	0.680	0.770
		Concept				
1)	RoBERTa-base	yes	0.693 (−8.5)	0.814 (−2.6)	0.653 (−2.1)	0.741 (−1.8)
2)	DeBERTa-base	yes	0.734 (2.4)	0.821 (0.2)	0.671 (0.9)	0.748 (−0.8)
3)	Legal-BERT-base	yes	0.730 (0.1)	0.820 (0.2)	0.634 (0.0)	0.745 (0.3)
		Values				
4)	RoBERTa-base	2	**0.778** (0.0)	**0.853** (1.2)	0.673 (−0.1)	0.768 (0.9)
5)	DeBERTa-base	2	0.746 (1.2)	0.839 (1.8)	**0.710** (3.9)	**0.772** (2.4)
6)	Legal-BERT-base	2	0.710 (−2.0)	0.823 (0.5)	0.624 (−1.0)	0.743 (0.1)
		Length				
7)	DeBERTa-base	768	0.745 (1.2)	0.831 (1.0)	0.681 (1.0)	0.761 (1.3)

which benefited the most from its presence. All in all, comparing the results to the scores in the original publication, we have improved the results on the evaluation set for the DeBERTa model, but the results on the test set remained worse for all trained models.

4.3 Binary Classification

In the next group of experiments we wanted to find out if it is beneficial to keep a fine-grained distinction of relevancy as in the original work or whether it is possible to reduce the problem to just a binary classification. Šavelka in his PhD thesis [1] indicated the problems related to the annotation of the dataset. The task was pretty challenging for the annotation team and the annotations were inconsistent among the annotators. We believe that the annotation process could be improved if the number of relevancy classes was reduced. Yet such a change could lead to a worse performance of the models. Still, at the end, the model is used to sort[4] the sentences with respect to their relevance – the end user does not see the scores of the classification model – so it might be the case that the final sorting is almost the same or even better when the number of classes is reduced.

The results of this experiment are given in Table 3 in rows marked as 4–6. It is surprising to see that even though the number of values was reduced to only

---

[4] In general the model is able to perform the classification, since we can select a certain probability threshold (or just take the most problable class) and judge that a given sentence falls into given category. However the outcome is used by multiplying the probability by the value of the class, so at the end it is used to sort the sentences.

2, for the DeBERTa-base model all NDCG scores were better for that setting. The evaluation NDCG@10 improved by 1.2 pp., NDCG@100 by 1.8 pp. What is more, the test NDCG@10 improved by 3.9 pp. and NDCG@100 by 2.2 pp. It is a sign that at least for this model the reduced value set is easier to grasp. It should be noted that for this model the results of NDCG@10 on the test subset are better by 3 pp. than the results reported in the original research.

For the other models the improvement was not that apparent. For RoBERTa-base, there was a slight improvement in NDCG@100 for evaluation (+1.2 pp.) and test (+0.9) subsets. In the case of Legal BERT, the results at NDCG@10 were worse with the reduced number of values, both for the evaluation (−2.0 pp.) and test (−1.0 pp.) subsets.

Still, it is not obvious if such a reduction should be performed during the annotation, since that would lead to a different value scheme. Yet, it would be advisable to check if the binary classification yields higher annotation agreement and also to see what is the biggest source of confusion for the annotators. If it is in fact the distinction between "no value" and "potential value" or between "high value" and "certain value" then maybe at least one of these groups should be collapsed.

This problem requires further investigation, but the results obtained in our experiment suggest that in **at least for some of the models, the answer to R3 is positive, i.e. a simpler classification scheme might give similar or even better results as observed by the end user of the system.**

4.4   Length Limit

Regarding the length limit, we have first checked if there are any text examples with a number of tokens surpassing the 512 subtoken limit imposed by the RoBERTa tokenizer. Generally, the majority of examples fall into the 512 length limit, but there are some sentences that go far beyond that limit. For the train subset there are examples as long as 1200 subtokens and for the test subset there are examples as long as 2500 subtokens.

We have experimented only with DeBERTa regarding the length limit, since only that model (among the tested ones) allows to set a higher limit on the input text. The results of our experiment are presented in Table 3 in the row marked as 7 and are compared to the training when this model was trained in the original 4-value scheme. **We can observe that for this setting the model is able to gain approx. 1 pp. for each measure, which gives a positive answer to R4.** Still the results are slightly worse as compared to the setting when the binary classification scheme is applied for this model. Similarly to the previous experiments, we observe that the results on the evaluations subsets are better than in the original experiment, but for the test set we can hardly get better results. The impact of the input length was further investigated in the following experiment.

4.5   Model Size

In the last setup of experiments related to the parameters of the model we have selected the model size. The reason to change that parameter in the last experiments was the fact that these models require much more computation than the base models. Moreover Legal-BERT is available only in the *base* size, so it is excluded from these experiments.

Table 4. The comparison of results with respect to the model size and the voting scheme. The variants of the DeBERTa model include: *not-binary*: 4-value classification *no-length* context length: 512. In the case of the voting results we refer to the best result of a given model obtained previously on the test set.

Model			Eval NDCG		Test NDCG	
			@10	@100	@10	@100
Original			0.710	0.800	0.680	0.770
		Size				
1)	RoBERTa	large	0.780 (0.2)	0.847 (0.7)	0.692 (1.7)	0.766 (0.7)
2)	DeBERTa	large	0.823 (7.7)	**0.878** (3.9)	0.757 (4.7)	**0.786** (1.4)
3)	DeBERTa-not-binary	large	**0.830** (8.5)	0.876 (3.7)	**0.790** (8.0)	**0.786** (1.5)
4)	DeBERTa-no-length	large	0.824 (7.8)	0.872 (3.4)	0.765 (5.5)	0.785 (1.4)
		Voting				
5)	RoBERTa-base	yes			0.730 (5.5)	0.780 (2.1)
6)	RoBERTa-large	yes			0.704 (1.2)	0.782 (1.6)
7)	DeBERTa-base	yes			0.715 (0.5)	0.783 (1.2)
8)	DeBERTa-large	yes			**0.817** (2.7)	**0.801** (1.5)
9)	Legal-BERT-base	yes			0.674 (4.0)	0.768 (2.4)

The results of the experiment are presented in Table 4 in rows marked as 1–4. Taking into account the results of the experiments on the smaller models, for RoBERTa-large we have taken the setup without concept and with 4-value classification. For DeBERTa-large as the reference setup we included the concept, took binary classification and extended the context length (768 subtokens). Since the results for DeBERTa large were very good, we also included ablation experiments: *not-binary* was a variant with the original, 4-value classification, while *no-length* was a variant with the original 512 subtokens length limit.

Generally, in all cases the large versions of the models performed better, giving a positive answer to R5, but the improvement was much dependant on the variant of the model. For RoBERTa-large there was only a slight improvement ranging 0.2–0.7 on the validation sets, and 0.7–1.7 on the test sets. However for the larger version of DeBERTa we have observed much better results than for the base version. For the best setup, with the original 4-value classification we have observed 8.5 and 8.0 pp. NDCG@10 score improvement for the evaluation and test sets respectively as well as 3.7 and 1.5 pp NDCG@100 score improvement for the evaluation and test sets respectively. That result was especially encouraging since for most of the former experiments we have observed an improvement on the evaluation set which did not yield any improvement on the test set. The NDCG@10 scores for this setup were 12 pp. and 11 pp. better on the evaluation and test sets respectively than in the original research, which we judge a very good improvement.

4.6 Voting

As a final improvement for obtaining better relevance scores we have tested the voting scheme among the trained models. Although such a scheme requires each sentence to be passed through 4 models, we decided to check if it gives any improvement. This was also tempting, since for each experimental setup we have trained 4 models, so there was not much additional computational power involved in that experiment.

The results of this final experiment are given in Table 4 in rows marked as 5–9. **It is apparent that for all configurations, the additional voting step improves the results, giving a clearly positive answer to R6.** For RoBERTa and Legal-BERT, the improvement is the largest (5.5 pp. and 4.0 pp. NDCG@10 score respectively). For these models the improvement of the NDCG@10 is better than the improvement on NDCG@100. On the other hand, the last base model – DeBERTa – has the smallest improvement with respect to the NDCG@10 score (0.5 pp.). For the large models the improvement is more modest: 2.7 and 1.2 pp. NDCG@10 for DeBERTa and RoBERTa respectively, while for NDCG@100 it is 1.2 and 2.1 pp. respectively.

This final addition gave the best-model so far, DeBERTa-large and additional boost which yielded the **new state-of-the-art results on the statutory interpretation dataset: 0.817 NDCG@10 score and 0.801 NDCG@100 score for the test subset**. This is more than 13 pp. and 3.1 pp. better respectively than the scores reported in the original research. Once again, we have to stress that the large improvement on NDCG@10 score is very important, since a potential user of a legal information system is mostly interested in the results at the very top, which is reflected by the NDCG@10 score.

There is also one phenomenon which needs explanation, i.e. better NDCG@10 than NDCG@100 score for the best model setup. This is an uncommon, but not erroneous result. From theoretical standpoint this is perfectly fine: a dataset with 20 relevant results and 80 irrelevant results might be sorted in a way that 10 relevant results would be put at the beginning and 10 relevant results at the end of 100-result window, which gives better NDCG@10 than NDCG@100 score. However, from a practical point of view, it is rather hard to train a model with such a behavior. We believe that this is due to the fact that when selecting the best model during the training process, we used NDCG@10 on the evaluation set to judge which model is the best. In most of the cases this has not lead to better NDCG@10 score, but for this particular experiment it yielded such an outcome.

4.7   Qualitative Assessment of the "Useful Improvement" Concept

To better understand the impact of the improvements given by our method, we have manually assessed the results of the baseline model (RoBERTa-base) without voting, with the results of our best method (DeBERTa-large with voting) for the "useful improvement" concept. We will call this method "the best model" even though it is a combined result of 4 models. We have concentrated on the top-10 results, since for this setting the improvement was the largest.

Table 5 gives the comparison of scores assigned to the results by the baseline and by our best model as well as top-10 sentences selected by the best model (the last column). The numerical scores are to be interpreted as in the original research, i.e. 3 is "high value', 2 is "certain value", 1 is "potential value" and 0 is "no value". The interesting observation is that there is a completely different distribution of the scores obtained by the baseline model and the best model. The baseline model returns mostly sentences scored as 2, there is only one sentence with 0, 1 and 3 score in the top-10 results. So the baseline model returns sentences that have certain value, but there are better examples in the dataset.

On the other hand, the bast model gives results with a combination of 3 s and 0 s – there are 4 "high value", 5 "no value" and only 1 sentence with "potential value". So there is much more contrast in the results given by that model. By analyzing the sentences returned by that model, it is apparent that there are many very useful results and the model puts one useful result ("high value" result) at the very top. Inspection of the sentences that have 0 assigned shows the source of the confusion for the model – it is the fact that the concept can be used in different contexts, not only in the context of patent law. So these examples clearly explain what is a useful improvement, but not in that context. This is the reason they scored 0.

This is just the analysis for one concept from the test set, but it shows what could be another improvement for the method for concepts that appear in many different contexts. If for a given concept we could identify all relevant pieces of legislation, i.e. all the different meaning of the concept that appear in legal cases, we could construct an improved version of the algorithm. For instance, we could run exactly the same model with the sentence coming from the case and the different provisions defining the possible context of the concept as the last argument for the model. If the model would score a given sentence with a provision we are not interested in higher than with the provision we are interested in, such an example could be filtered out or given a penalty. This possible improvement for the method is left for future research.

Table 5. The comparison of the reference scores assigned to the sentences returned by the baseline model and the best combination of models for the concept "useful improvement". The last column is the sentence selected by the best combination of models.

Baseline	Best	Best sentence
2	3	In Du Bois v. Kirk, 158 U. S. 58, 15 Sup. Ct. 729, 39 L. Ed. 895, it was decided that the application of an old device to meet a novel exigency and to subserve a new purpose was a useful improvement; and patentable
2	0	A building increases the value of the lot where built, and therefore, is a useful improvement, inasmuch as it improves the property in a useful way
2	3	In Du Bois v. Kirk, 158 U. S. 58, 15 Sup. Ct. 729, 39 L. Ed. 895, it was held that "the application of an old device to meet a novel exigency and to subserve a new purpose" was a useful improvement and patentable, and that the fact that defendant was able to produce the same result by another and different method did not affect plaintiff's right to an injunction"
2	0	Therefore, a building is a useful improvement
1	2	It represents a useful improvement, rendering more practical the employment of the automatic discharging device in place of the old hand ladle method
2	0	The repairs to the sugar mill were a useful improvement, and certainly enhanced its value if they prevented it from becoming altogether useless
2	3	Tbe use of by-p-ass conduits and steam jets to improve circulation was unknown in the prior art, and their addition to progressive kilns constituted a new and useful improvement, greatly improving tbe process of drying lumber in such kilns and increasing tbe value of tbe finished product"
0	0	We must concede that a building is a useful improvement for the purposes of §416
2	0	Apparently, it is understood in that opinion that a building is not a useful improvement because it is not erected for improving the light, comfort and sanitary condition of the property
3	3	A slight improvement of an old machine is a useful improvement But, if the alleged invention should be absolutely hurtful or injurious, it is no improvement- it is not "a useful invention," and, it is your province to determine, from the evidence of witnesses experienced in the subject-matter, the validity of this objection

5   Conclusion

In this paper, we have experimented with 6 variants to the state-of-the-art in argument retrieval. Among the six variants, two have shown improvement over the original experiment. By combining DeBERTa-base with the use of only two values to classify the value of sentences, we have obtained an improvement of 3% for NDCG@10 and 0.2% for NDCG@100. A more significant improvement was obtained with the use of larger models and by adding the voting mechanism. For NDCG@100, we have obtained a 3% improvement while for NDCG@10, we have obtained, on the test set, a significant 13%.

The approach taken in this paper is to compare different methods based on the same data set. We are currently in the process of constructing our own data set over European case law. Among the immediate next directions we take are: experimenting with the accuracy of models trained on the case law of one continent in retrieving arguments in case law of another continent; training models to identify arguments in sentences with no mention of the legal concept we try to explain; and improving the retrieval of arguments by considering not only the concepts they are to explain, but further context which might help finding the most relevant arguments in case law.

The above 3 elements, as well as the current one, are part of our attempt to build Legal Question-Answering Systems [21]. They are part of a project to improve access to justice and is planned as part of a chatbot which combines formal legal reasoning over legislation with argument retrieval over case law.

Further work will also include the release of software capable of giving accurate and explainable legal advice on topics such as data and consumer protection.

Acknowledgement. This research was supported by the Polish National Centre for Research and Development - Pollux Program under Grant WM/POLLUX11/5/2023 titled "Examples based AI Legal Guidance" as well as POIR.01.02.00-00-0154/16 titled "Big Data Game Content Engine: mBaaS game engine enabling access to Big Data as game content for developers" and by the Luxembourg National Research Fund under grant C22/IS/17228828/ExAILe. We gratefully acknowledge Polish high-performance computing infrastructure PLGrid (ACK Cyfronet AGH) for providing computer facilities and support within computational grant no. PLG/2023/016304.

References

1. Savelka, J.: Discovering sentences for argumentation about the meaning of statutory terms. Ph.D. thesis. University of Pittsburgh (2020)
2. Sanderson, J., Stamboulakis, D., Kelly, K.: A Practical Guide to Legal Research. Lawbook Co. (2021)
3. Endicott, T.: Vagueness and law. In: Vagueness: A Guide, pp. 171–191. Springer, Cham (2011)
4. MacCormick, D.N., Summers, R.S.: Interpreting Statutes: A Comparative Study. Routledge (2016)
5. Libal, T., Smywiński-Pohl, A.: Giving examples instead of answering questions: introducing legal concept-example systems. In: JURIX (2023)

6. Savelka, J., Ashley, K.D.: Discovering explanatory sentences in legal case decisions using pre-trained language models. In: Findings of the Association for Computational Linguistics: EMNLP 2021, pp. 4273–4283 (2021)
7. Šavelka, J., Ashley, K.D.: Legal information retrieval for understanding statutory terms. Artif. Intell. Law 1–45 (2022)
8. Ashley, K.D., Walker, V.R.: From information retrieval (IR) to argument retrieval (AR) for legal cases: report on a baseline study. In: JURIX 2013, pp. 29–38 (2013)
9. Sansone, C., Sperlí, G.: Legal information retrieval systems: state-of-the-art and open issues. Inf. Syst. **106**, 101967 (2022)
10. Habernal, I., et al.: Mining legal arguments in court decisions. Artif. Intell. Law 1–38 (2023)
11. Westermann, H., Benyekhlef, K.: JusticeBot: a methodology for building augmented intelligence tools for laypeople to increase access to justice. In: Proceedings of the Nineteenth International Conference on Artificial Intelligence and Law, pp. 351–360 (2023)
12. Al-Abdulkarim, L., Atkinson, K., Bench-Capon, T.: A methodology for designing systems to reason with legal cases using abstract dialectical frameworks. Artif. Intell. Law **24**, 1–49 (2016)
13. Chalkidis, I., Fergadiotis, M., Malakasiotis, P., Aletras, N., Androutsopoulos, I.: LEGAL-BERT: the Muppets straight out of law school. In: Findings of the Association for Computational Linguistics: EMNLP 2020, pp. 2898–2904. Association for Computational Linguistics (2020)
14. Henderson, P., et al.: Pile of law: learning responsible data filtering from the law and a 256gb open-source legal dataset. In: Advances in Neural Information Processing Systems, vol. 35, pp. 29217–29234 (2022)
15. Järvelin, K., Kekäläinen, J.: Cumulated gain-based evaluation of IR techniques. ACM Trans. Inf. Syst. (TOIS) **20**(4), 422–446 (2002)
16. He, P., Liu, X., Gao, J., Chen, W.: DeBERTa: Decoding-enhanced BERT with Disentangled Attention (2021)
17. He, P., Gao, J., Chen, W.: DeBERTaV3: Improving DeBERTa using ELECTRA-Style Pre-Training with Gradient-Disentangled Embedding Sharing (2021)
18. Dao, T., Fu, D.Y., Ermon, S., Rudra, A., Ré, C.: FlashAttention: Fast and Memory-Efficient Exact Attention with IO-Awareness (2022)
19. Child, R., Gray, S., Radford, A., Sutskever, I.: Generating Long Sequences with Sparse Transformers (2019)
20. Kobyliński, Ł., et al.: PolEval 2022/23 challenge tasks and results. In: 2023 18th Conference on Computer Science and Intelligence Systems (FedCSIS), pp. 1243–1250. IEEE (2023)
21. Libal, T., Smywiński-Pohl, A.: Giving examples instead of answering questions: introducing legal concept-example systems. In: Proceedings of the Nineteenth International Conference on Artificial Intelligence and Law, pp. 287–292 (2023)

Overview of Benchmark Datasets and Methods for the Legal Information Extraction/Entailment Competition (COLIEE) 2024

Randy Goebel[1], Yoshinobu Kano[2], Mi-Young Kim[3(✉)], Juliano Rabelo[1], Ken Satoh[4], and Masaharu Yoshioka[5]

[1] Department of Computing Science and Alberta Machine Intelligence Institute, University of Alberta, Edmonton, AB, Canada
{rgoebel,rabelo}@ualberta.ca
[2] Faculty of Informatics, Shizuoka University, Hamamatsu, Shizuoka, Japan
kano@inf.shizuoka.ac.jp
[3] Department of Science, Augustana Faculty, University of Alberta, Camrose, AB, Canada
miyoung2@ualberta.ca
[4] National Institute of Informatics, Chiyoda-ku, Tokyo, Japan
ksatoh@nii.ac.jp
[5] Faculty of Information Science and Technology, Hokkaido University, Sapporo-shi, Hokkaido, Japan
yoshioka@ist.hokudai.ac.jp

Abstract. We summarize the 11th Competition on Legal Information Extraction and Entailment (COLIEE 2024). In this eleventh edition, the competition included four tasks on case law and statute law. The case law component includes an information retrieval task (Task 1), and the confirmation of an entailment relation between an existing case and a selected unseen case (Task 2). The statute law component includes an information retrieval task (Task 3), and an entailment/question-answering task based on retrieved civil code statutes (Task 4). Participation was open to any group based on any approach. Ten different teams participated in the case law competition tasks, most of them in more than one task. We received results from 10 teams for Task 1 (26 runs) and 6 teams for Task 2 (18 runs). On the statute law task, there were 12 different teams participating, most in more than one task. 8 teams submitted a total of 20 runs for Task 3, and 8 teams submitted a total of 23 runs for Task 4. We describe the variety of approaches, our official evaluation, and analysis of our data and submission results.

Keywords: COLIEE2024 · legal information retrieval · legal information entailment

1 Introduction

The objective of the Competition on Legal Information Extraction/Entailment (COLIEE) is to encourage the development of state of the art for information

T. Suzumura and M. Bono (Eds.): JSAI-isAI 2024, LNAI 14741, pp. 109–124, 2024.
https://doi.org/10.1007/978-981-97-3076-6_8

retrieval and entailment methods using legal texts. It is usually co-located with JURISIN, the Juris-Informatics workshop series, which was created to promote community discussion on both fundamental and practical issues on legal information processing, with the intention to embrace many disciplines: these include law, social sciences, information processing, logic and philosophy, and the existing conventional "AI and law" area. In alternate years, COLIEE is organized as a workshop of the International Conference on AI and Law (ICAIL), which was the case in 2017, 2019, 2021, and 2023. Until 2017, COLIEE consisted of two tasks: information retrieval (IR) and entailment using Japanese Statute Law (civil law). From COLIEE 2018, we introduced a new and challenging case law IR and entailment tasks based on Canadian case law.

Task 1 is a legal case retrieval task, and it involves reading a query case and extracting supporting cases from the provided case law corpus, hypothesized to be relevant to the query case. Task 2 is the legal case entailment task, which involves the identification of relevant paragraphs or paragraphs from existing cases, which can be confirmed to entail a given fragment of a new case. Tasks 3 and 4 are statute law tasks that use questions from the Japanese Bar exam to judge whether the given statement is true or not. Task 3 is an information retrieval task that identifies relevant articles for the legal entailment (Task 4). Finally, Task 4 is a legal entailment task that judges whether the given statement is true or not. In contrast to COLIEE 2023, COLIEE 2024 introduced 400 new query cases for Task 1 and 100 for Task 2. Furthermore, for the test data of Task 3 and Task 4 in COLIEE 2024, 109 new questions sourced from the 2023 bar exam were used.

The rest of our paper is organized as follows: Sects. 2, 3, 4, and 5 describe each task, presenting their definitions, datasets, list of approaches submitted by the participants, and results attained. Section 6 presents some final remarks.

2   Task 1 - Case Law Retrieval

2.1   Task Definition

This task consists of finding which cases, amongst a set of provided candidate cases, should be "noticed" with respect to a given query case[1]. More formally, given a query case q and a set of candidate cases $C = \{c_1, c_2, ..., c_n\}$, the task is to find the supporting cases $S = \{s_1, s_2, ..., s_n \mid s_i \in C \wedge noticed(s_i, q)\}$ where $noticed(s_i, q)$ denotes a relationship which is true when $s_i \in S$ is a noticed case with respect to q.

2.2   Case Law Dataset

The dataset consists of a total of 7,350 case law files. That dataset contains a labelled training set of 5,616 cases, of which 1,278 are query cases. On average,

---

[1] "Notice" is a legal technical term that denotes a legal case description that is considered to be relevant to a query case.

the training data includes approximately 4.16 noticed cases per query case, which are to be identified among the 5,616 cases. To prevent competitors from merely using existing embedded conventional legal citations in historical cases to identify cited cases, citations are suppressed from all candidate cases and replaced by a "FRAGMENT_SUPPRESSED" tag indicating that a fragment containing a citation was removed from the case contents.

The test set consists of a total of 1,734 cases, with 400 query cases and a total of 1,562 true noticed cases (an average of 3.90 noticed cases per query case). Initially, the golden labels for that test set are not provided to competitors.

2.3 Approaches

We received 26 submissions from 10 different teams for Task 1. In this section, we present an overview of the approaches taken by the teams which submitted papers describing their methods.

- **UMNLP** [2] **(3 runs)** developed a pairwise similarity ranking framework. The authors train a feed-forward neural network to perform a binary classification task based on several features from each query-candidate case pair. Those features include the extraction and similarity matching for a novel feature which the authors call a "proposition" (a short summary of the basis upon which a noticed case has been cited), as well as the name of the judge deciding the case, verbatim quotations from the text, and several other novel features.
- **JNLP** [5] **(3 runs)** proposes a three-phase approach: the first stage performs retrieval after splitting the query document into paragraphs and using a BM25 model with top-k cutout to retrieve candidate documents. Phase two is a re-ranking stage. The last stage is where prediction actually happens: after the re-ranking stage, for each query document, the authors select the top-k candidate documents from the re-ranked list as prediction with k selected, using grid-search on the validation set. They also developed an ensemble strategy by concatenating the prediction results of the re-rankers before selecting the top-k to boost the recall metric of the system.
- **BM24 (1 run)** the authors organize each case into segments summarized by gpt-3.5. Among them, one segment is selected to represent the case. An embedding of that segment is stored in FAISS. A segment of the query case is used to query the FAISS vector store to retrieve similar cases. AnglE is used as the sentence embedding model, trained from SeanLee97/angle-llama-7b-nli-20231027 (from the HuggingFace repository) on the Task 1 training set pre-processed in the same way.
- **CAPTAIN** [6] **(3 runs)** performs some heuristic pre-processing steps, then uses TF-IDF and BM25 to extract keywords and retrieve relevant documents. The team then applies LLMs to summarize the decisions and perform fine-tuning of a retrieval model based on such summaries.
- **NOWJ** [7] **(3 runs)** developed an approach based on a combination of BM25 and a pre-trained Longformer. After an initial pre-processing step, BM25 is

used to calculate the similarity between each pair of query case and candidate case. The result is used as a pre-ranking input to the LongFormer model. Scores from BM25 and LongFormer are then combined, with parameters being defined after a grid search is conducted.

- **MIG (1 run)** chose to offer an informative baseline for Task 1 that does not apply any LLMs. The authors vectorized the cases with a tool on BERT-base and BERT-large. After vectorizing the cases, they compute the cosine similarity between the candidate cases and the given new case using FAISS. Then, for a new case, the authors ranked the candidate cases by their cosine similarity with the new case, and chose 20 candidates that were most similar to the new case. Then the difference between the cosine similarity between the i-th most similar case and the $(i+1)$-th most similar case (d_i) is calculated, and the first i cases are recommended if $d_i > 2d_1$.

- **UBCS (3 runs)** applied TF-IDF to rank cases varying how the model is used. Their first approach is a baseline, with vanilla TF-IDF weighting model being used to retrieve and rank noticed cases for each given query case. The second approach applies summarization only on the query cases before using TF-IDF for retrieval. The third approach applies summarization for both the query and candidate cases.

- **TQM [4] (3 runs)** used lexical matching and dense vector retrieval to generate features (plus some simple features such as case length) that were submitted to a learning to rank method. The authors also applied pre and post processing to avoid irrelevant information. Their method not only applies all of those techniques, but aims at a deeper understanding of the case trying to capture the main facts described in the case.

2.4   Results and Discussion

Table 1 shows the results of all submissions received for Task 1 for COLIEE 2024. A total of 26 submissions from 10 different teams were evaluated. Similar to what happened in recent COLIEE editions, the f1-scores are generally low, which reflects the fact that the task is now more challenging than its previous formulation[2]. However, this year we witnessed a relevant increase of almost 50% in the performance of the winning team, from an f1-score of 0.30 in 2023 to 0.44 in the current edition.

In this edition of COLIEE, we improved our sampling method to provide test data which has similar properties/data distribution to the training data, something we noticed could be improved from the next competition. We have also improved case duplication identification, although some duplicate cases were still present. We intend to further improve our method of duplicate identification in the next competition.

Most of the participating teams applied some form of traditional IR technique such as BM25, transformer based methods such as BERT or more recent

---

[2] For a description of the previous Task 1 formulation, please see the COLIEE 2020 https://sites.ualberta.ca/~rabelo/COLIEE2020/.

Table 1. Task 1 results

Team	F1	Precision	Recall	Team	F1	Precision	Recall
TQM	0.4432	0.5057	0.3944	TQM	0.4342	0.5082	0.3790
UMNLP	0.4134	0.4000	0.4277	UMNLP	0.4097	0.3755	0.4507
UMNLP	0.4046	0.3597	0.4622	YR	0.3605	0.3210	0.4110
TQM	0.3548	0.4196	0.3073	YR	0.3483	0.3245	0.3758
YR	0.3417	0.3184	0.3688	JNLP	0.3246	0.3110	0.3393
JNLP	0.3222	0.3347	0.3105	JNLP	0.3103	0.3017	0.3195
WJY	0.3032	0.2700	0.3457	BM24	0.1878	0.1495	0.2522
CAPTAIN	0.1688	0.1793	0.1594	CAPTAIN	0.1574	0.1586	0.1562
NOWJ	0.1313	0.0895	0.2465	NOWJ	0.1306	0.0957	0.2055
NOWJ	0.1224	0.0813	0.2478	WJY	0.1179	0.0870	0.1831
WJY	0.1174	0.0824	0.2042	MIG	0.0508	0.0516	0.0499
UBCS	0.0276	0.0140	0.7196	UBCS	0.0275	0.0140	0.7177
UBCS	0.0272	0.0139	0.7100	CAPTAIN	0.0019	0.0019	0.0019

LLMs, or a combination of both. Specific error analysis for Task 1 would require manual analysis of the whole dataset, which is not feasible due to the sheer amount of data involved in this task. When it comes to the approaches used in this task, we can see the consolidation of trends observed in recent COLIEE editions, especially the combination of traditional IR methods (usually applied at an initial stage) with LLMs used to perform a more sophisticated (but more computationally intensive) processing on a smaller subset of the data.

3 Task 2 - Case Law Entailment

3.1 Task Definition

Given a base case and a chosen specific text fragment together with a second case relevant to the base case, this task consists in determining which paragraphs of the second case entail that fragment of the base case. More formally, given a base case b and its entailed fragment f, and another case r represented by its paragraphs $P = \{p_1, p_2, ..., p_n\}$ such that $noticed(b, r)$ as defined in Sect. 2 is true. The task consists in finding the set $E = \{p_1, p_2, ..., p_m \mid p_i \in P\}$ where $entails(p_i, f)$ denotes a relationship which is true when $p_i \in P$ entails the fragment f.

3.2 Case Law Dataset

In Task 2, 725 query cases and 25,783 paragraphs were provided for training. There were 100 query cases and 3,651 paragraphs in the testing dataset. On average, there are 35.22 candidate paragraphs for each query case in the training dataset, and 35.58 candidate paragraphs for each query case in the testing dataset. The average number of relevant paragraphs for Task 2 was 1.37 paragraphs for training. The average query length is 35.56 words in the training set and 34.97 in the test set. The average candidate length is 106.86 words in the training set and 105.28 in the test set.

3.3   Approaches

Below are the summaries of the submitted models in Task 2 of COLIEE 2024.

- **AMHR** [8] **(three runs)** proposed two approaches: (1) finetuning a legal-BERT model with triplet loss with labels as positive examples and all other paragraphs as negative examples on the train set provided for task 2. This approach resulted in overfitting. (2) finetuning a monoT5 model pre-trained on the MSMARCO dataset with hard negative mining examples chosen by BM25 and another version of the monoT5 model itself. They choose the top-2 predictions by this model as long as the ratio between their similarity score is less than 6.619 (a hyperparameter found by grid search); otherwise, they choose just the first prediction. The second approach got the best results on task 2, this year.
- **CAPTAIN** [6] **(three runs)** introduces a method that builds upon the state-of-the-art approach used in Task 2 of the 2023 competition. This method incorporates zero-shot and few-shot learning techniques to leverage the knowledge stored in large language models. Initially, they fine-tune a pre-trained monoT5 sequence-to-sequence model using hard negative sampling to produce an output. For each query paragraph, they select the top-k candidates with the highest scores to create zero-shot and few-shot prompting techniques for in-context learning with FlanT5 LLM.
- **JNLP** [5] **(three runs)** fine-tuned MonoT5 on the training set of Task 2 with hard negative sampling. The model MonoT5 is a T5-3B reranker fine-tuned on the MS MARCO passage dataset for 10k steps. They used Flan-T5 and Mixtral for prompting.
- **NOWJ** [7] **(three runs)** proposes two approaches of entailment recognition, using multilingual BERT and monoT5 for the three runs. MonoT5 is a T5-based re-ranking model fine-tuned for the downstream task of classification, while mBERT is a traditional approach for document re-ranker. Multilingual BERT and training the mBERT model with weak labels [10] were our last year's solutions. Therefore, for the first two runs, they fine-tuned the models on this year's dataset.
- **OVGU** [11] **(three runs)** team's proposed approach involves using a chain of pre-trained Custom Legal-BERT models that are fine-tuned on sub-datasets generated using BM25 and a Bi-Encoder to select the top-N candidate paragraphs. To enhance the models' robustness, a binomial test is employed for artifact detection. OpenAI's GPT-3.5-turbo model is used to create adversarial instances for selected training instances with annotation artifacts. The large language model was prompted to switch the previous negative entailment label into a positive one for balancing out the training examples with

annotation artifacts. These instances, along with the top-N candidate paragraph dataset, are further used to fine-tune the models. A chained approach is applied during prediction: If the first model (specialized for high precision) fails to predict a hypothesis with at least one premise as 'Entailed,' the second model is used for that hypothesis. If any hypotheses are missed after using the second model, the BM25 top-ranked premise found for a given hypothesis is labeled as 'Entailed.'

Because last year's winning team used monoT5, in this year, most of the teams utilized monoT5. All the four teams that were ranked from 1st to 4th used monoT5, and achieved promising results.

Table 2. Results attained by all teams on the test dataset of task 2.

Team	run	F1	Prec.	Recall	Team	run	F1	Prec.	Recall
AMHR	mt53bk2r	**0.6512**	0.6364	0.6667	CAPTAIN	fs2	0.6360	0.7281	0.5646
JNLP	07f39	0.6320	0.6967	0.5782	CAPTAIN	zs2	0.6235	0.7700	0.5238
CAPTAIN	zs3	0.6235	0.7700	0.5238	NOWJ	t5	0.6117	0.6181	0.6054
JNLP	join-constr	0.6045	0.6694	0.5510	OVGU	2ovgurun1	0.5962	0.5636	0.6327
NOWJ	weak	0.5946	0.5906	0.5986	JNLP	join	0.5912	0.6378	0.5510
OVGU	2ovgurun2	0.5705	0.5506	0.5918	OVGU	2ovgurun3	0.5532	0.5000	0.6190
NOWJ	bert	0.5197	0.5032	0.5374	MIG	mig1	0.4701	0.5673	0.4014
MIG	mig2	0.4696	0.5800	0.3946	AMHR	lsbk2m42	0.3542	0.3617	0.3469
AMHR	lsbk1.txt	0.3320	0.4100	0.2789	MIG	mig3	0.1364	0.0979	0.2245

3.4 Results and Discussion

The F1-measure is used to assess performance in this task. The actual results of the submitted runs by all participants are shown in Table 2, from which it can be seen that the AMHR team attained the best results. CAPTAIN used last year's winner model, which is based on a fine-tuned monoT5, and their model was ranked second. The first ranked model also used fine-tuned monoT5, but they used a hyperparameter value as a threshold of the similarity score, and got the best result this year.

4 Task 3 - Statute Law Information Retrieval

4.1 Task Definition

Statute law task consists of two different tasks. One is the statute law information retrieval task (Task 3), and the other is the entailment task (Task 4). Statute law information retrieval task is a preprocess of entailment task, which retrieves a subset of Japanese Civil Code articles that can be used to judge whether the given statement can be entailed by the entire Civil Code.

Since this task is a preprocess of the entailment task, it is important to include all necessary articles in the returned results. Therefore, we use the F2 measure, which is a variation of the F1 measure that puts more emphasis on recall. In addition, since we also encourage participants to submit more articles for the difficult queries without reducing the overall results, we use the macro average of the F2 measure as the official evaluation measure.

In the last COLIEE (COLIEE 2023) there was a submission using GPT-4 and we discussed whether to exclude the submission from the official results due to lack of reproducibility and contamination problems (e.g., GPT-4 is frequently updated and one cannot guarantee reproducibility, and models trained with undisclosed data may have contamination problems).

In order to exclude the submission of such closed-source models, we introduce the following rules for the submission of tasks.

> Participants should clearly mention what dataset was used (for example: pretrained by Wikipedia dump data as of 2022xxxx, fine-tuned by...) for reproducibility purposes. Participants can use any external data, but it is assumed that they do not use the test dataset and/or something which could directly contain the correct answers of the test dataset (e.g., published results from Japanese Bar Law Exams).

4.2   Statute Law Dataset

We use the Japanese Civil Code with the official English translation for this task. However, if there is no official English translation for a part of this code, we exclude the articles of these parts. As a result, we used a subset of the Japanese Civil Code with 768 articles. Questions are selected from the Japanese bar exam related to this subset and provided in two languages. Japanese version uses original questions and English translated version are provided by the organizers. For the task training data, we also provide sets of relevant articles for Task 3 and entailment results for Task 4.

The training data was constructed by using previous COLIEE data (1097 questions) and new questions (109 questions) were selected from the 2023 bar exam. Of these 109 questions, 88 questions have one relevant article, and 21 questions require two relevant articles.

4.3   Approaches

There are 20 submitted runs from 8 teams. In these submissions, due to the different interpretations made by the participants, there are three varieties of submissions classified by the use of the Large Language Model (LLM).

1. Submissions using LLM whose model is publicly available, but trained with undisclosed training data.
2. Submissions using LLM trained only on disclosed training data.
3. Submissions without explicit use of LLMs (BERT, LegalBERT, ...).

Some participants assume that the LLM whose model is publicly available is good for reproducibility. However, these models do not meet the requirement of disclosed training data. Some participants assume that the use of LLM is prohibited and submit entries without LLM.

Below is a brief summary of the submissions. To clarify 1 and 2, we add underline to the external resource whose model is publicly available but trained with undisclosed training data or its related resources.

- **AMHR** [8] **runs)** uses BM25 to select the top 50 hits and re-ranks the results using monot5-3b-msmarco (language model tuned with MS MARCO for ranking) fine-tuned for COLIEE task 3 to select the top 5 results. They use 3 variants of LLMs (FLAN-T5 and FLAN-alpaca) to select the final relevant articles.
- **BM24 (one run)** uses AnglE-llama-7b-nli (AnglE embedding calculated by using LLaMA) as the text embedding model for semantic retrieval. They fine-tune the system using COLIEE task data (1 and 3), the Supreme Court of Canada Bulk Decisions dataset, and the Semantic Textual Similarity (STS) dataset. They use GPT3.5 to generate similar sentences for the STS.
- **CAPTAIN** [6] **(three runs)** uses three different settings to ensemble the results. The first system (bjpAll) uses BERT-base-Japanese, which is tuned for COLIEE task 3. 4 best checkpoint models are used to generate ensemble results. The second system (bjpAllMonoP) uses MonoT5 (language model tuned with MS MARCO for ranking) fine-tuned for COLIEE task 3 to generate the results, and filters out the results with prompting technique using LLM (Flan T5). They also ensemble the results obtained by the first system. The third system (bjpAllMonoT5) applies the same prompting technique to the bjpAll results to filter out the results. They ensemble the results from the first and second systems.
- **JNLP** [5] **(three runs)** uses BERT-base-Japanese, which is fine-tuned for COLIEE task 3, and they ensemble the predictions of many checkpoints to produce a ranked list. From the ranked list, they use different LLMs to generate final results. For the first system (Mistral), they use the prompt technique of LLM (Mistral) to select the final results. The second system uses RankLLaMA (language model tuned with MS MARCO for ranking based on LLaMA2) to calculate the score for each paring of legal questions and top 5 relevant articles. The third system (constr-join) uses LLM (Orca and Qwen) to get a more concise list from the ranked list. They also include retrieval results from run Mistral to improve recall.
- **NOWJ** [7] **(three runs)** uses a multitask approach to train the BERT for Sequence Classification model using COLIEE Task 3 and Task 4. The results from this model are ensemble with the corresponding scores from the lexical-based BM25 model.
- **PSI (one run)** does not provide a short description.
- **TQM** [4] **(three runs)** uses MonoT5 (language model tuned with MS MARCO for ranking), fine-tuned for COLIEE task 3 for run1. For run2 and run3 they use LightGBM to integrate the results of different models. Light-

Table 3. Evaluation results of submitted runs (Task 3) showing only best runs from each team.

Submission ID	return	retrieved	F2	Precision	Recall	MAP
JNLP.constr-join *	188	**99**	**0.807**	0.709	**0.870**	0.801
CAPTAIN.bjpAllMonoT5	168	96	0.800	0.732	0.845	**0.815**
TQM-run1 #	140	89	0.782	**0.785**	0.800	0.790
NOWJ-25mulreftask-ensemble #	202	96	0.772	0.690	0.835	0.756
AMHR02	185	95	0.749	0.651	0.825	0.740
UA-anglE	233	91	0.711	0.610	0.800	0.700
BM24-1 *	425	94	0.539	0.282	0.795	-
PSI01 ?	109	9	0.086	0.090	0.085	0.231

Table 4. Number of questions with average F2

Average F2	0–0.2	0.2–0.4	0.4–0.6	0.6–0.8	0.8–1.0
number of questions	15	7	21	14	52

Table 5. Evaluation results for 45 questions with anonymized symbols ("A" and "B")

Submission ID	return	retrieved	F2	Precision	Recall	MAP
AMHR02	87	42	0.669	0.561	0.756	0.726
JNLP.constr-join	83	39	0.662	0.586	0.722	0.735
CAPTAIN.bjpAll	95	42	0.647	0.497	0.756	0.742
TQM-run1	56	33	0.628	0.678	0.633	0.719

GBM is a gradient boosting framework that uses tree-based learning algorithms. For run2, they use BM25, Legal BERT, and MonoT5 for integration. For run3, they apply post-processing to the run2 results.

- **UA [1] (three runs)** uses Universal AnglE Embedding for the text embedding model for semantic retrieval for 2 runs. The first run (anglE) uses whole articles to compute the embedding and the second run (angleE_chunk) uses single sentences for the embeddings. Cosine similarity is used to calculate the scores to find the relevant articles. The third run (mp_net) uses the sentence transformer model MP-net, which is fine-tuned for task 3.

4.4   Results and Discussion

Table 3 shows the evaluation results of all submissions. Submission IDs with "*" use an LLM whose model is publicly available but trained with undisclosed training data. Those with "#" do not use any LLM.

We confirm that the top performance systems achieve higher average F2 compared to the previous COLIEE. The best performance system is JNLP.constr-join, but it uses LLM with undisclosed training data. The best performance system that satisfies the rule condition is CAPTAIN.bjpAllMonoT5. TQM-run1 is the best performance system among the submissions without LLM. This shows that there was room to improve retrieving performance without using LLM. However, since the submission with LLM can better handle the questions that require semantic matching (e.g., questions with anonymized symbols, such as "A" and "B"), the recall is lower than that of the submission with LLM.

Table 4 shows the number of questions with its average F2 score. Almost one half of the questions (52 questions) have an average F2 greater than 0.8. However, we still have 15 questions whose average F2 is lower than 0.2. Out of these 15 questions, 9 questions use anonymized symbols. This ratio is comparatively higher than the overall average (45 questions out of 109 total). However, the recent development of LLM may have improved performance on these questions. Table 5 shows selected evaluation results for 45 questions with anonymized symbols for the best performance results per team. The best performing system is AMHR02, which uses LLM to select articles. It is important to understand the characteristics of the system through such a detailed analysis of question types.

Finally, we discuss the appropriateness of the rules introduced this year as informally discussed with a number of participants. During the discussion, we found that it is difficult to do an in-depth investigation of the training data used in the system. Therefore, for the next time, we would like to allow the use of any LLM whose model is publicly available and is trained before the Japanese Bar Exam. This is a simple rule to guarantee that the model is good for reproducibility, but avoids encoding answers published.

5   Task 4 - Statute Law Textual Entailment and Question Answering

5.1   Task Definition

Task 4 requires the determination of entailment relationships between a given problem sentence and article sentences. Competitor systems should answer "yes" or "no" regarding the given problem sentences and given article sentences. Participants could use any external data, except that they can not use the test dataset and/or something which could directly contain the correct answers of the test dataset to avoid any "contamination" even in the pretraining/fine-tuning datasets of any software they used. This is because this task is intended to be a pure textual entailment task. We also required the participants to make their system reproducible as per an open academic standard, i.e., they should describe which methods and what datasets were used to enable a reproducible result. Note that this contamination/reproducibility issue does not allow the use of black box LLMs like ChatGPT. To encourage deeper analysis, we asked the participants to submit their outputs when using any fragment of the training dataset (H30, R01, and R02), in addition to the formal runs.

5.2 Dataset

Our training dataset and test dataset are the same as for Task 3. Questions related to Japanese civil law were selected from the Japanese bar exam. The organizers provided a data set used for previous campaigns as training data (1097 questions) and new questions selected from the 2024 bar exam as test data (109 questions).

5.3 Approaches

We describe approaches for each team as follows, shown as a header format of **Team Name (number of submitted runs)**. The slash-separated italic names indicate corresponding huggingface IDs.

- **AMHR** [8] **(three runs)** used approximately 80 prompts, all on the *google/ flan-t5-xxl* model, on each question in the training dataset. The best 25 prompts on the training dataset are used to vote on an answer for each question in the test set, where their vote is based on their accuracies on the training dataset, and their accuracies on articles similar (by *sentence-transformers/sentence-t5-x1*, **sentence-transformers/paraphrase-Mini LM -L6-v2**, without fine-tune, and BM25) to the articles used by the test set problem. **AMHR. ensemble0** is the same except the top 50 prompts are used, and the prompts' votes are less based on their previous accuracies. **AMHR.single** is the same except only the best single performing prompt on the train set is selected, without article similarity considered.
- **CAPTAIN** [6] **(three runs)** employs data augmentation that summarizes statute law via *google/flan-t5-xxl* with prompting and filters the good summaries via heuristic rules, generates new pairs of 'Query' and 'Statute Law' by using summary instead of original statute law with various heuristic rules, and fine-tune *google/flan-t5-xxl*. **CAPTAIN2** consists of augmentation and fine-tuning. **CAPTAIN1** uses few shot prompting (using Dense Passage Retrieval for demonstration selection) as input of the model, and then fine-tunes with the augmented data. **CAPTAIN3** generates CoT prompting (by using *google/flan-t5-xxl* for reasoning training data) then ensemble all model.
- **HI (Hybrid Intelligence)** [9] **(three runs)** **HI1** used *declare-lab/flan-alpaca-gpt4-xl* with zero-shot prompting. **HI2** manually crafted Abstract Dialectical Frameworks (ADF) knowledge representations of a small set of legal articles, ascribing factors to these ADFs for each exam question by zero-shot *declare-lab/flan-alpaca-gpt4-xl*, comparing the logical output of the ADF to the claim in the exam question. **HI3** translated articles into additional ADFs for all articles using GPT3.5-turbo.
- **JNLP** [5] **(three runs)** *JNLP1* and *JNLP2* prompted different large language models (Wqen (their original model), Mistral, Flan-Alpaca, and Flan-T5) and ensemble the results with majority voting, **JNLP1** took the top-1 prompt from Flan-Alpaca while **JNLP1** took the top-2; **JNLP3** prompted Flan-T5 and Mistral, and ensemble the results with the Dawid-Skene label model.

- **KIS** [3] **(three runs) KIS1** employed fine-tuning, few shot learning, retrieval-augmented generation, and a novel method that incorporates character count instructions. additionally, the results were ensemble with rule-based methods. **KIS2** is different from **KIS1** in a unique approach where few shot's data were replaced with outputs generated by GPT-4. **KIS3** used fine-tuning only.
- **NOWJ** [7] **(three runs)** leveraged LLMs in inference phase only. **NOWJ. pandap46** utilized *TheBloke/Panda-7B-v0.1-GPTQ*, used the test set of COLIEE 2023 as the validation set to find the best model and legal prompt. **NOWJ.flant5-panda** combined *google/flan-t5-xl* with panda results following bagging approach. **NOWJ.bagging** combined results from 5 different runs (Panda and Flant5 with different prompts) following the major voting approach.
- **OVGU** [11] **(three runs)** used *MoritzLaurer/DeBERTa-v3-base-mnli-fever-anli*. **4OVGUrun1** and **4OVGUrun3** fine-tuned it by the task 4 COLIEE dataset and a specially created dataset designed to address issues of Word Overlap and Contradiction Word Artefacts, while **4OVGUrun2** fine-tuned it solely with the task 4 dataset. **4OVGUrun1** and **4OVGUrun2** were input datasets of a premise, a hypothesis, and a boolean feature that determines if the hypothesis is a complete subsequence of the premise; **4OVGUrun3** used features to assess the word overlap between premise and hypothesis.
- **UA** [1] **(three runs) UA_stack** used zero-shot learning on *google/flan-t5-xxl* with PromptSource[3] for finding potential good prompts, added one positive and one negative example from the training data as part of each prompt and experimented on the rest of the training set (barring the two examples) to find good prompts, chose the top 3 prompts that gave a good performance on the training data, finally performed zero-shot inference with all three prompts and voting between them. **UA_GPT** followed the same process as **UA_stack** but instead of the top 3 prompts chose the top prompt which is a GPT-3 style prompt. **UA_encoder_decoder** fine-tuned the last two layers from both the decoder and decoder of flan-t5-xxl.

5.4 Results and Discussion

Table 6 shows the COLIEE 2024 Task 4 formal run results. The Formal Run (R05) column shows the result of the COLIEE 2024 formal run using the latest Japanese legal bar exam (Year R05). The columns R02, R01, and H30 are the results using the past formal run datasets, which we required participants to submit, in order to compare different datasets for reference due to the smallness of our datasets. Note that these datasets were already made public as part of our training dataset.

The lower part of the table shows runs with "*" as a suffix of the run names, which used external services where its detailed architecture, training datasets, and model weights are not available, resulting in non-reproducible outputs which are prohibited in our participation call.

---

[3] https://github.com/bigscience-workshop/promptsource.

Table 6. Accuracies of Task 4 Results. ∗ indicates runs using not fully disclosed models, + indicates runs with preprocessing by such models.

Team	Formal Run		Past Formal Runs		
	# Correct	R05	R02	R01	H30
BaseLine (Yes to all)	60	0.5505	0.5309	0.5315	0.5143
# Correct /# Total		60/109	43/81	59/111	36/70
CAPTAIN2	90	0.8257	0.7901	0.7568	0.8429
JNLP1 ∗	89	0.8165	0.7901	0.6937	0.7429
UA_slack	87	0.7982	0.7407	0.7117	0.7429
UA_encoder_decoder	87	0.7982	0.8395	0.7207	0.7571
CAPTAIN1	86	0.7890	0.8148	0.7748	0.8286
CAPTAIN3	86	0.7890	0.8395	0.7207	0.7286
JNLP2 ∗	86	0.7890	0.8272	0.7297	0.7857
UA_gpt	85	0.7798	0.7901	0.6847	0.7571
AMHR.ensembleA50	84	0.7706	0.8148	0.3784	0.6571
AMHR.single	84	0.7706	0.7901	0.3874	0.6714
HI1	82	0.7523	0.7284	0.6667	0.7000
NOWJ.pandap46 ∗	82	0.7523	N/A	N/A	N/A
AMHR.ensembleA0	80	0.7339	0.7778	0.4234	0.7000
JNLP3 ∗	80	0.7339	0.7901	0.6126	0.6571
NOWJ.flant5-panda ∗	80	0.7339	N/A	N/A	N/A
NOWJ.bagging ∗	78	0.7156	N/A	N/A	N/A
OVGU1 +	77	0.7064	0.7531	0.6937	0.6714
KIS2 +	76	0.6972	0.6543	0.6036	0.6429
OVGU3 +	76	0.6972	0.7654	0.6306	0.7000
OVGU2 +	70	0.6422	0.6790	0.6396	0.6000
KIS1	67	0.6147	0.6420	0.6847	0.6286
HI3	64	0.5872	0.6296	0.6306	0.6000
HI2	63	0.5780	0.7531	0.6937	0.7143
KIS3	62	0.5688	0.5926	0.6306	0.6429

The best runs by team **CAPTAIN2** used an LLM (flan-T5) with data augmentation and heuristic rules, while all runs in Task 4 used LLMs in some form. Comparing the results of the past test data (R02, R01, and H30), we found that the scores changed but one of the runs of the CAPTAIN team was top ranked.

There is still concern about the usage of LLMs. For example, it is not clear in what way the GPT-based generative AIs could handle logical reasoning. A possibility is that they can apply superficially similar descriptions which include the use of logical reasoning, so they do not directly handle logic but indirectly reflect the use of logic in existing descriptions and their combinations, i.e., their huge stack of similar contents led to providing approximate answers and marginally related evidence. Because Task 4 is intended to be a pure textual entailment task, superficial similarities without logical reasoning would not make much sense, thus we need further investigations about the capability of the generative AIs on logical reasoning. However, as a practical legal application, it can be useful when there are, to some extent, similar contents available as previous existing cases. For our future work, we need new task designs which provide a framework for the explainability of results and to evaluate the explainability of the solvers in more practical task settings.

6   Conclusion

We have summarized the systems and their performance as submitted to the COLIEE 2024 competition. For Task 1, some participants used TF-IDF, BERT, and BM25. In Task 2, many teams used fine-tuned monoT5 and showed similar performances. For Task 3, many teams use BM25 and MS-Marco-based re-ranker. Postprocess using LLM and ensemble technique also improves the performance. Lastly, for Task 4, all runs use LLMs with different ideas to fine-tune them. We intend to further continue to improve dataset quality in future editions of COLIEE so the tasks more accurately represent real-world problems.

This year we introduce the rule to usage of external resources to maintain the reproducibility and avoid the problem of contamination. However, we need to update the rules to improve clarity.

Acknowledgements. This competition would not be possible without the significant support of Colin Lachance from vLex and Compass Law. Our work to create and run the COLIEE competition is also supported by our institutions: the National Institute of Informatics (NII), Shizuoka University and Hokkaido University in Japan, and the University of Alberta and the Alberta Machine Intelligence Institute in Canada. This research is also supported by the Canadian Natural Sciences and Engineering Research Council (NSERC) [including funding reference numbers RGPIN-2022-03469 and DGECR-2022-00369] and Alberta Innovates. This work was also supported by JSPS KAKENHI Grant Numbers, JP22H00543 and JST, AIP Trilateral AI Research, Grant Number JPMJCR20G4. In addition, this research was supported by the Brain Pool program funded by the Ministry of Science and ICT through the National Research Foundation of Korea (RS-2023-00304286).

References

1. Babiker, H., Rahman, M.A., Kim, M.Y., Rabelo, J., Goebel, R.: Legal yes/no question answering through text embedding, fine-tuning, and prompt engineering. In: Proceedings of the Eighteenth International Workshop on Juris-Informatics (JURISIN 2024) (2024)
2. Curran, D., Conwa, M.: Similarity ranking of case law using propositions as features. In: Proceedings of the Eighteenth International Workshop on Juris-Informatics (JURISIN 2024) (2024)

3. Fujita, M., Onaga, T., Kano, Y.: LLM tuning and interpretable CoT: team in COLIEE 2024. In: Proceedings of the Eighteenth International Workshop on Juris-Informatics (JURISIN 2024) (2024)

4. Li, H., Chen, Y., Ge, Z., Ai, Q., Liu, Y., Zhou, Q., Huo, S.: Towards an in-depth comprehension of case relevance for better legal case retrieval. In: Proceedings of the Eighteenth International Workshop on Juris-Informatics (JURISIN 2024) (2024)

5. Nguyen, C., et al.: Pushing the boundaries of legal information processing with integration of large language models. In: Proceedings of the Eighteenth International Workshop on Juris-Informatics (JURISIN 2024) (2024)

6. Nguyen, P., et al.: CAPTAIN at COLIEE 2024: large language model for legal text retrieval and entailment. In: Proceedings of the Eighteenth International Workshop on Juris-Informatics (JURISIN 2024) (2024)

7. Nguyen, T.M., Nguyen, H.L., Nguyen, D.Q., Nguyen, H.T., Vuong, T.H.Y., Nguyen, H.T.: NOWJ@COLIEE 2024: leveraging advanced deep learning techniques for efficient and effective legal information processing. In: Proceedings of the Eighteenth International Workshop on Juris-Informatics (JURISIN 2024) (2024)

8. Nighojkar, A., et al.: AMHR COLIEE 2024 entry: legal entailment and retrieval. In: Proceedings of the Eighteenth International Workshop on Juris-Informatics (JURISIN 2024) (2024)

9. Steging, C., Leeuwen, L.V.: A hybrid approach to legal textual entailment. In: Proceedings of the Eighteenth International Workshop on Juris-Informatics (JURISIN 2024) (2024)

10. Vuong, Y.T.H., et al.: SM-BERT-CR: a deep learning approach for case law retrieval with supporting model. Artif. Intell. Law **31**(3), 601–628 (2023)

11. Wehnert, S., Murugadas, V., Naik, P.V., Luca, E.W.D.: Improving robustness in language models for legal textual entailment through artifact-aware training. In: Proceedings of the Eighteenth International Workshop on Juris-Informatics (JURISIN 2024) (2024)

CAPTAIN at COLIEE 2024: Large Language Model for Legal Text Retrieval and Entailment

Phuong Nguyen[✉], Cong Nguyen, Hiep Nguyen, Minh Nguyen, An Trieu, Dat Nguyen, and Le-Minh Nguyen

Japan Advanced Institute of Science and Technology, Ishikawa, Japan
{phuongnm,congnhm,hiepnkv,minh.nn,antrieu,nguyendt,nguyenml}@jaist.ac.jp

Abstract. Recently, the Large Language Models (LLMs) has made a great contribution to massive Natural Language Processing (NLP) tasks. This year, our team, CAPTAIN, utilizes the power of LLM for legal information extraction tasks of the COLIEE competition. To this end, the LLMs are used to understand the complex meaning of legal documents, summarize the important points of legal statute law articles as well as legal document cases, and find the relations between them and specific legal cases. By using various prompting techniques, we explore the hidden relation between the legal query case and its relevant statute law as supplementary information for testing cases. The experimental results show the promise of our approach, with first place in the task of legal statute law entailment, competitive performance to the State-of-the-Art (SOTA) methods on tasks of legal statute law retrieval, and legal case entailment in the COLIEE 2024 competition. Our source code and experiments are available at https://github.com/phuongnm94/captain-coliee/tree/coliee2024.

Keywords: language model · reasoning prompting · legal text retrieval

1 Introduction

The annual COLIEE competition[1] (Competition on Legal Information Extraction/Entailment) [6] is dedicated to the automated analysis of legal texts. Within a long history of many years, this event incorporates two distinct categories of data, namely case law and statute law. For each data category, two tasks are assigned, specifically focused on legal information retrieval (tasks 1, 3) or entailment (tasks 2, 4). In legal information retrieval tasks, given a query text, a retriever system is tasked with computing the similarity between the query and

---

[1] https://sites.ualberta.ca/~rabelo/COLIEE2024/.

P. Nguyen, C. Nguyen, H. Nguyen, M. Nguyen, A. Trieu and D. Nguyen—Authors contributed equally to the paper.

each instance in a large corpus (e.g., Legal Civil Code or Legal Case documents). To reduce the computation cost, initial filtering involves using simple similarity scores based on overlapped bag-of-words. Examples include BM25 (best matching) [19] or TF-IDF (term frequency and inverse document frequency) scores, effectively eliminating the majority of irrelevant instances from the corpus. The candidates identified in this step then advance to the next component, where semantic meaning similarity is considered. Here, pre-trained language models (LM) like BERT [22] or pre-trained Large Language Models (LLMs) such as Flan-T5 [3] are employed for efficient representation of semantic meaning. Next, to clarify each task, we will introduce the challenge and our approach for each one in this work.

Task 1. Case law is an essential component of legal practice that judges and attorneys use to make decisions. The nature of case law documents is that each document has a great length and typically contains internal writing logic, which can be partitioned into three parts: facts, reasoning, and decision. However, most documents are not partitioned into formal templates, thus presenting considerable challenges. Moreover, the length of one document is on average around 10000 tokens, with the longest one being over 130000 tokens. This is also the reason that existing pre-trained language models (e.g., BERT) find it hard to synthesize the vector representation for the whole document. To overcome this problem, our solution for this task mainly focuses on summarizing the legal case documents using LLMs and then fine-tuning a retriever model based on these summaries.

Task 2. In this task, given a decision along with a relevant case, one or many paragraphs that entail the decision should be retrieved from a set of candidate paragraphs. To tackle this challenge, we propose a method that combines a fine-tuned MonoT5 re-ranking model with the knowledge of Large Language Models. First, a MonoT5 re-ranker is optimized for the pairwise classification task that identifies the binary relation between a candidate paragraph and the given decision. Then, a Large Language Model will apply few-shot and zero-shot learning to re-rank the paragraphs that entail the given decision from top-k candidates retrieved by the fine-tuned MonoT5 re-ranker combined with BM25 scores.

Task 3. In the task of retrieving statute laws, the challenge arises due to both the scarcity of annotated data and the complexity inherent in queries and articles spanning multiple categories. The current state-of-the-art method, as presented by [13], addresses this challenge by employing an ensemble of various sub-models to prevent local optima. However, that method overlooks the relationships among statute law articles within retrieval models. This study extends the current SOTA approach and explores a new method using prompting techniques with LLM to consider both the dependencies between query inputs and articles, as well as among articles simultaneously, for re-ranking purposes.

Task 4. In this task, competitors need to answer the given queries by using the information that lies inside the relevant articles which is given along with the queries. To find correct answers, the conditions inside the queries should be matched with the conditions described in the legal articles. The statement of the relevant articles will be used to determine the answer to the query. However, the complexity of how every query describes the conditions and the shortage of data make the progress of finding the entailment relationship between the queries and the relevant legal articles challenging. To deal with this challenge, we propose an approach of using prompting engineering incorporated with Large Language Models to determine the answer to each query using the relevant legal articles as the input.

2 Related Work

Task 1. Previously, in the 2021 COLIEE, TLIR [12] ranked first using two methods. One is a traditional language model for IR and only utilizes the tag fragment inserted into the text to find potential relevant pieces. The second method is to split the document into paragraphs and rank them using BERT. Later in the 2022 competition, UA [18] used a transformer-based model to generate paragraph embeddings and then calculate the similarity between paragraphs of query and positive and negative cases. [5] explicitly adds external domain knowledge fragments to the case, while JNLP [1] combines term-level matching and semantic relationships on the paragraph level. UA [18] used a transformer-based model to generate paragraph embeddings and then calculate the similarity between paragraphs of query and positive and negative cases. Recently, in the 2023 COLIEE competition, THUIR [10] built a dedicated encoder-decoder model and pre-trained it on legal domain text. JNLP [2], UFAM [16], NOWJ [23], and IITDLI [4] all used a two-phase approach. The first phase utilizes lexical matching models such as BM25 and TF-IDF to create a set of potential candidates. The second phase involves more sophisticated heuristics, models, or even LLMs to classify or re-rank the candidate documents.

Task 2. In the 2021 COLIEE competition, the winning team NM [21] conducted experiments on DeBERTa, MonoT5, and MonoT5-zero-shot models and evaluated an ensemble of MonoT5 and DeBERTa models. The UA team [9] fine-tuned a BERT pre-trained model on the provided training dataset. In the 2022 COLIEE contest, the NM team [20] gained first place by combining the answers from a fine-tuned MonoT5 model and zero-shot method on a MonoT5. The JNLP team [1] gained the second place by 3 runs: combining scores from LegalBERT and BM25, capturing the most important words in the query with corresponding candidate paragraph by AMR (Abstract Meaning Representation) and extracting the relevant paragraphs through the interaction between top candidates of 2 models: LegalBERT and AMR + BM25. In the 2023 COLIEE competition, the CAPTAIN team [13] archived the state-of-the-art performance for task 2 by fine-tuning pre-trained MonoT5 for sequence-to-sequence task with hard negative sampling and ensembling techniques. The THUIR team [10] used 2 lexical models, BM25 and QLD, as baselines and fine-tuned pre-trained models with contrastive learning loss. They also utilized the above features to ensemble the final score.

Task 3. In this task, the challenge is to find the effective method for ranking a large corpus of statute laws (Japanese Civil Code Articles) and choose the most relevant statutes law given query case. The query cases are grouped into two major groups: the question about the cause or result of an article or a specific case is assumed to request the corresponding penalty frame. There have been various approaches to solve this challenge in recent years [6,8]. In 2020, the LLNTU team [22] achieved the highest score with an ensemble of many BERT models. In 2021, the winner team, OvGU [24], also utilized a variety of BERT models and introduced data enrichment techniques based on SentenceBERT. In 2022, team HUKB [26] took first place with a special method augmented legal statute law corpus (original article, articles modified by replacing references, and the article's judicial decision part) to enrich features of articles and reduce the distance with query cases. Last year, our team, CAPTAIN [13], achieved the first prize based on ensemble methods of two pre-trained language models (BERT Japanese and MonoT5 [17]) incorporating various data-filter method supported model learn from various aspects of data. Extended from SOTA results in the NLP area recently, this year, we extend last year's results and investigate the effect of LLM in considering the relationship of candidates' articles via prompting techniques.

Task 4. Later, in the COLIEE 2021 competition, HUKB [25] applied a combination of many BERT-based models and a data augmentation method to give out the answer for the input query. They extracted the judicial decision sentences from the articles and generated positive/negative data on them. OvGU [24] applied a graph neural network to tackle this challenge. With each node of the graph representing an article or a query, each query and article is embedded by BERT-based pre-trained models. In the COLIEE 2022 competition, JNLP [1] compared the performance of ELECTRA, RoBERTa, and LegalBERT, the pre-trained language models on English. They also considered the effect of negation data augmentation. LLNTU [11] restructured given data to a dataset of the disjunctive union strings from training queries and articles and established the longest uncommon subsequence similarity comparison model, without stopwords (*LLNTUdiffSim*), and with stopwords (*LLNTUdeNgram*). In the COLIEE 2023 competition, JNLP [2] proposed to use Large Language Models with a Zeroshot setting to generate the answer for the input query using the input articles. By using prompts that are constructed from both query and relevant articles, they collected and ensemble the answers from Flan-T5 and Alpaca-T5 models to get the final answer for the task. With the appearance of LLMs, the approach of this task seems to change from classifying the input with a Yes/No label to generating the answer with realizable positive/negative meaning.

3   Method

3.1   Task 1

First, we pre-processed all the case law documents and the query. Our pre-processing steps include: (1) splitting lines using heuristics, (2) removing noisy tokens, (3) fixing punctuation, and (4) removing non-English sentences. Then, we used TF-IDF to find keywords for each document and used them as the query for the BM25. We selected the top 25 highest TF-IDF-score keywords with the assumption that these keywords are likely to be the most important terms in each case law document. We then construct a query using the selected TF-IDF keywords and then apply the BM25 algorithm to retrieve the top 50 relevant documents.

We used two methods for summarizing: one direct summary using pre-trained Mistral-7B model[2] and another using Flan-T5-XL[3]. Using the Mistral-7B is quite trivial due to its long context length and sliding window attention mechanism (similar to LSTM). However, using FlanT5 is not as trivial because its context length is only 1024. To tackle this problem, we divided our long case law document into smaller chunks of five sentences and summarized each of them using Flan-T5-XL. After obtaining summaries for each chunk, concatenate these individual summaries to form the final summary for the entire document.

We inherit the work of Nogueira et al. [15], using a pre-trained sequence-to-sequence model (T5) to adapt to the document ranking task. In this model, all target tasks are cast as sequence-to-sequence tasks. For our task, the input sequence is: *"Query: q Document: d Relevant: "* where q and d are the query and summarized document text, respectively. The model is fine-tuned to generate the words "true" or "false" depending on whether the document is relevant to the query. During the training process, we also employed "hard negative sampling" by using the model to re-rank all potentially relevant cases. We marked all the "true" labeled cases as positives and selected the same amount of negative yet similar cases in our model's ranking as negative samples. At inference time, we select the documents according to the probabilities assigned to the "true" token with a threshold.

3.2   Task 2

Drawing intuition from the State-of-the-Art results of this task last year [13], we fine-tuned a MonoT5 re-ranking model to predict the binary relationship between a decision and a candidate paragraph. Then, the scores from the fine-tuned re-ranker are combined with the BM25 scores to rank the candidate paragraphs in each case. Top-k candidates are chosen to re-rank with Large Language Models to obtain the final results.

---

[2] https://huggingface.co/mistralai/Mistral-7B-Instruct-v0.2.

[3] https://huggingface.co/google/flan-t5-xl.

Fine-Tuned MonoT5 Re-ranking Model. Based on the idea of the CAPTAIN team in the COLIEE competition in 2023, we fine-tune the MonoT5 as a sequence-to-sequence pairwise classification problem. Each pair of a query (decision) and a candidate paragraph will be labeled as "true" if the paragraph entails the decision else the pair will be labeled as "false". We resample the set of negative samples, which are the paragraphs not implying the decision, at the end of each epoch to by hard negative mining. In the first epoch, the top 10 negative samples relevant to the decision are chosen from the candidate paragraphs by BM25 scores. Then, in the afterward epochs, the top 10 negative candidates are sampled again using the scores from the MonoT5 model. With negative sample mining, the model can distinguish the difference between positive and negative candidate paragraphs and enhance the performance. The scores from the fine-tuned model are then combined with BM25 scores to provide the final scores for each candidate's paragraph.

Re-ranking with Large Language Models. Pairwise classification in the previous step can learn the relationship between the decision and a candidate paragraph but can not capture the interrelationship between the decision and other candidates. To further enhance the performance of the model with the knowledge from Large Language Models and to capture the interrelationship between candidate paragraphs and between candidate paragraphs and the given decision, we perform zero-shot and few-shot learning on top-k candidates ranked by the final scores from the fine-tuned MonoT5 model with FLAN-T5 language model. The candidates together with the decision, form an input prompt asking the Large Language Models to provide the relevant paragraphs to the given decision as the final predictions. For few-shot learning, we choose the adaptive approach in that the model will find the decisions in the training dataset that are most similar to the given decision using BM25. After choosing similar decisions, we collect the positive paragraphs and randomly select negative paragraphs for each decision to generate the input prompt of few-shot learning.

3.3 Task 3

The primary objective of Task 3 in this competition is to identify a specific subset of Japanese Civil Code Articles (A) that pertain to a provided legal bar exam question (Q). Extended from the success of previous works in this task [13,14], this work focuses on utilizing the power of pre-trained language to score the relevance between question (Q) and articles (A). Our idea for the solution to solve this task is simple and follows three steps (coarse-to-fine) to retrieve the article candidates from a legal corpus:

1. Filter top-k (e.g., $k \in \{50, 100, \mathbf{150}\}$) the relevant articles based on the frequency of overlapped words (using TF-IDF and BM25 scores) [14].
2. Fine-tuning a pre-trained language model (e.g., BERT Japanese, MonoT5) to get the articles to have meaning relevant to the question bar from the output of the previous step [14]. Besides, we also follow the idea of [13] to

ensemble various best checkpoints (setting *Mkcpt*) in the training process based on the development set to reduce the bad effect of the local optima and make the system more generalized. To this end, we fine-tuned two pre-trained language BERT Japanese models[4][5], and for each model, we take the two best checkpoints for the ensemble process. In addition, we also fine-tuned the pre-trained MonoT5 model[6] because this model has proved its effectiveness in text retrieval tasks.

3. This final step leverages the power of a Large Language Model to choose the final answer with high accuracy. Difference from the previous step, a pre-trained language model (LM) only sees a pair of one article and a query to classify the label relevance or not. In this step, through a *re-ranking prompting* technique (Table 1), the LLM receives all the content of articles as input to choose the subset of them. To this end, LLM not only considers the relation between the query and articles but also ranks them to choose the sub-set of articles that is more relevant to the query. Besides, we also consider the *relevance verification prompting* technique (Table 1), which only considers the content of one article and query per time for the comparison.

Table 1. Re-ranking and relevance verification prompting template.

Re-ranking prompting template considering to many articles candidates (A) (e.g., article ids a_id1, a_id2) with a query

In bellow articles: Article a_id1: {content of article a_id1}, Article a_id2: {content of article a_id2}, Question: which articles really relevant to query "{query_content}"?

Relevance verification prompting template for a paired: article (A) and query (Q).

{query_content}, {content of article}, Can the article match the question?

3.4   Task 4

Few-shot Prompting. While Language Models (LLMs) exhibit impressive zero-shot capabilities, they face limitations in handling more intricate tasks within the zero-shot setting. Few-shot prompting serves as a technique to facilitate in-context learning, allowing us to present demonstrations within the prompt to guide the model toward improved performance in complex tasks. For this task, we implement the few-shot technique. We construct a prompt by combining the three training samples with similar premises and storing them as training samples.

---

[4] https://huggingface.co/cl-tohoku/bert-base-japanese-whole-word-masking.
[5] https://huggingface.co/cl-tohoku/bert-base-japanese-v2.
[6] https://huggingface.co/castorini/MonoT5-large-msmarco.

Automatic Chain-of-Thought (Auto-CoT). Inspired by [27], we apply the chain-of-thought prompting with demonstrations from the training samples. Our method follows 4 steps: (1) We leverage the LLM with the "Let's think step by step" prompt to generate reasoning chains for each sample; (2) we employ Dense Passage Retrieval to encode the premise and hypotheses. (3) for every testing instance, we choose the top-k hypotheses with the highest similarity scores according to Dense Passage Retrieval (DPR) and concatenate the corresponding reasoning chains to these selected hypotheses; (4) Using the prompt generated in step 3, we employed the Flan-T5-XXL model to forecast the output.

Data Augmentation. Due to the limited training samples provided by the organizer, we augmented the data by building upon the original samples. To leverage the training data, we utilize the Large Language Model (LLM) to summarize the premise and generate synthetic samples. This process involves manually hand-crafting them to ensure they are effective and diverse. From each training sample, we retain the premise and generate additional hypothesis samples through various methods. In the first approach, we use the summarized sentence as a hypothesis and designate it with a "Y" label. In the second approach, we concatenate the summarized sentence with the original hypothesis, preserving the original label. For the third approach, we combine the summarized sentence with an irrelevant hypothesis and label it as "N".

4   Experiments and Results Analysis

4.1   Dataset and Evaluation Metrics

Dataset. The training set for task 1 in the COLIEE 2024 competition contains 5617 documents in total, which are approximately 4.16 relevant cases per query case. In the test set, a total of 1734 documents were provided, comprising 400 queries with no relevant documents revealed. For the legal case retrieval task, the goal is to find all the relevant documents for each of the 400 queries from the given test set. Task 2 contains 625 cases from the Federal Court of Canada case law, each case includes an entailed fragment that represents the given decision, a base case, and a set of paragraphs of a relevant case. We split 625 cases in the training dataset into the training dataset with 525 cases from 1 to 525 and the evaluating dataset with the last 100 cases as the development set. Task 3 comprises 996 questions, a legal corpus featuring 768 articles from the Civil Code, and a collection of 1272 pairs encompasing questions and corresponding relevant articles designated as positive samples. We use all the queries having id in {R02, R03, R04} as a development set and other queries as a training set. In the training process, the best checkpoints are optimized based on the performance of R02 queries. In Task 4, we use the dataset officially provided by the COLIEE 2024 organization to generate the data for a few shots and "chain of thought" settings. The dataset involves 996 legal query cases and the relevant articles. We used the queries in {R01, R02, R03, R04} as data for testing progress, and for the rest of the queries, we used them to generate the data for few-shot and chain of thought settings, which is 695 queries cases.

Evaluation Metrics. We follow the COLIEE competition's official metrics [6,8] for our evaluation of all developing experiments. Particularly, we used F1 scores for legal case retrieval/entailment tasks (Tasks 1, 2), macro F2 for statute law retrieval task (Task 3), and Accuracy for statute law entailment task (Task 4).

4.2 Experimental Setting

Task 1. We split the training dataset into 3 sets: train, development, and test set. The test set is exclusively selected from the list of query documents of the COLIEE 2023 test set. Then, we randomly split the test of the data into a train set and a development set with ratios of 0.9 and 0.1, respectively. We split the dataset to estimate the effectiveness of our proposed methods based on the result of the development set and compared it with the best result COLIEE 2022. We implement the lexical matching based on BM25 using the Python library pyserini[7]. We experimented with different K: 20, 30, 50, 100, 150. We also changed the number of keywords for the TF-IDF query, and using 25 keywords gave us the best results. We use recall to evaluate the list of return candidates. We want to find K as low as possible while keeping recall above 0.7. We chose $K = 50$, with recall being 0.7160. Our team submitted 3 submission: *captainMSTR*, *captainFT5* and *captainBM25*. The *captainBM25* run only uses BM25 lexical matching with $K = 4$. Both *captainMSTR* and *captainFT5* run have the fine-tuning MonoT5 process, the difference is that *captainMSTR* run uses Mistral-7B model whereas *captainFT5* run uses Flan-T5-XL model for summarization.

Task 2. Our baseline model is the state-of-the-art model in Task 2 in last year's competition [13]. The approach outlined in [13] introduced two key hyper-parameters, namely the *margin hyper-parameter (m)* and *top-k candidates*, to facilitate the selection of the optimal sub-set from MonoT5's candidate output. Specifically, they utilized the *margin hyper-parameter (m)*, defined as the difference in confidence scores between adjacent legal documents sorted by MonoT5 predictions, as a probability threshold. This threshold was employed to discern the relevance of a legal document set based on observations from the development set. Our fine-tuned MonoT5 re-ranker is similar to the baseline model however instead of filtering top-k results with a *margin parameter (m)*, we only collect top-k candidate paragraphs from the fine-tuned MonoT5 model and then filter the results by zero-shot learning to leverage the ability of capturing the information among the candidates of large language models for improving the ranking process. We performed our experiments with 2 different values of top-k: 2, 3. The Large Language Model we used for zero-shot learning is Flan-T5-XXL [3] with 11 billion parameters. We conducted zero-shot learning experiments with the input prompt template (Table 2). For adaptive few-shot learning, we use BM25 to find 2 cases from the training set that have the decisions that are most similar to the given decision, and then we randomly selected 2 negative paragraphs along with all positive paragraphs for each similar decision to generate the input

---

[7] https://github.com/castorini/pyserini.

prompt (Table 2). To this end, we install three settings for the final submission: *captainZs2*, *captainZs3* refer to zero-shot learning with top 2, 3 results from the fine-tuned MonoT5 model, respectively; *captainFs2*: refer to adaptive few-shot learning with top 2 results from the fine-tuned MonoT5 model.

Table 2. Zero-shot and few-shot prompting template.

Zero-shot prompting template from a pair of a base case and candidates.

In the below documents: {`list of candidate cases`}   Question: Which documents are relevant to query {`base case`}?

Few-shot prompting template based on pair of a base case and similar cases found by BM25 scores and its corresponding candidates.

In the below documents: {`list of candidate cases`}   Question: Which documents are relevant to query {`case similar to base case`}?   ...   In the below documents: {`list of candidate cases`}   Question: Which documents are relevant to query {`base case`}?

Task 3. As mentioned in Sect. 3.3, our proposed methods utilize the power of pre-trained LM to coarse-to-fine retrieve the relevant articles. We describe three main settings we used for submissions this year:

– **BERT Japanese Multi-checkpoints**: We follow the setting of *Mkcpt* proposed by [13], where the sub-models are the four best checkpoints found in fine-tuning BERT Japanese models[8][9].
– **BERT Japanese + MonoT5**: In this setting, we also follow the previous work [13] in fine-tuning the MonoT5 model on COLIEE 2024 training dataset and get the top 10 best scores as an output. Then, we refine these outputs with a *relevant verification prompting* (Table 1) and ensemble it with the output of the *Mckpt* setting.
– **BERT Japanese + MonoT5 + Re-ranking by LLM**: In this setting, we refine the output of the *Mckpt* setting with the LLM Flan-T5-XXL[10] via the *re-ranking prompting* technique (Table 1). This output is then combined with the output of two previous settings (with the output of LLM as the primary and obtaining the top 1 of the other settings) to obtain the final result.

Task 4. For the experiments of this task, we utilize LoRA [7] to fine-tune the LLMs model using two approaches. The fine-tuning is conducted with both few-shot data (2) and augmented data (3). The following hyperparameters are

---

[8] https://huggingface.co/cl-tohoku/bert-base-japanese-whole-word-masking.
[9] https://huggingface.co/cl-tohoku/bert-base-japanese-v2.
[10] https://huggingface.co/google/flan-t5-xxl.

applied: r and alpha_lora set to 32, the number of epochs is 30, lora_dropout is 0.85, and the learning rate is 3e-5. We use the Flan-T5-XXL model for whole experiments (including the summarization stage for augmented data). We install three settings for the submissions: *CAPTAIN1* represents the model fine-tuned with few-shot data, the *CAPTAIN2* signifies the model fine-tuned with both raw and augmented data, and the *CAPTAIN3* corresponds to the Auto CoT prediction.

4.3   Results Analysis

4.4   Task 1

Table 3 depicts the result comparison of our method versus other teams in the COLIEE 2023 competition. Among our submissions, the *captainMSTR* run has the highest F-score in the development set. However, in the test set, the *captainFT5* run turns out to have the highest F-score. We have also observed a sharp decrease in the performance from the development set to the test set. The reason is that the development set is sampled randomly from the original labeled set, thus maintaining a similar distribution to the training set. From our observation, there are no overlapping files between training files and testing files, while this is not the case for randomly splitting train and development sets. Overall, our precision results are far lower than the winning solution, indicating our lack of heuristic-based analysis.

Table 3. Experiments of Task 1

	Dev Performance			Test 2023 Performance			Official Test 2024		
Submission	Precision	Recall	F1	Precision	Recall	F1	Precision	Recall	F1
captainFT5	0.3578	0.3492	0.3534	0.1779	0.3558	0.2372	0.1574	0.1586	0.1562
captainMSTR	0.3577	0.3791	0.3681	0.1496	0.3748	0.2138	0.1688	0.1793	0.1594
captainBM25	0.276	0.2524	0.2637	0.1638	0.2515	0.1984	-	-	-
TQM	-	-	-	-	-	-	0.4432	0.5057	0.3944
UMNLP	-	-	-	-	-	-	0.4134	0.4	0.4277
YR	-	-	-	-	-	-	0.3605	0.321	0.411
WJY	-	-	-	-	-	-	0.3032	0.27	0.3457
NOWJ	-	-	-	0.2263	0.3527	0.2757	0.1313	0.0895	0.2465

4.5   Task 2

Table 4 shows the F1-scores of our experiments on evaluating dataset (Dev set) and testing dataset (Test set). As can be seen from the results, despite performing best on the evaluating dataset with **76.36** F1-score, **captainZs2** could not archive the top performance on the testing dataset, which belongs to **captainFs2** with **63.60** F1-score. **captainFs2** provides more paragraphs in the answers comparing with **captainZs2** which mostly extracts one paragraph from top-2 candidates.

Table 4. Results on F1-score of Task 2 Experiments

Run	Dev	Official Test 2024
CAPTAIN [13]	75.45	-
AMHR	-	**65.12**
JNLP	-	63.20
NOWJ	-	61.17
captainZs2	**76.36**	63.35
captainZs3	74.55	62.35
captainFs2	70.13	63.60

4.6   Task 3

Development Results. We present the results of our proposed approach on the development sets in Table 5. Based on these results, we found that each setting is strong in one specific set: MonoT5 is strong in R03 dataset but weak in R04 dataset, which in contrast to the *Mkcpt* setting. In the comparison between two settings: *Mckpt* setting and *LLM-re-ranking*, we can observe the effectiveness of the LLM model with the prompting technique because *LLM-re-ranking* setting refines the output of *Mckpt* setting. To this end, the performance of the system increases the accuracy but reduces the recall score, which hurts the overall F2 score. However, the result of *LLM-re-ranking* setting plays an important role in our ensemble method because our ensemble method chooses one sub-module as the main prediction and takes the top 1 from others that prefer high precision of the main sub-module.

Private Test Results. We show the results of our proposed approach on the private test sets evaluated by the COLIEE 2024 organization in Table 5 last column. Both three submissions of our approach achieved high positions (rank 2, 4, and 5) compared with other methods, which proved the effectiveness of our method. Similar to the development result, the ensemble of *MCkpt, MontoT5,* and the *LLM re-ranking* achieved the highest performance and was competitive with the top 1 performance.

4.7   Task 4

Development Results. The results of our methods on the official test set are shown in Table 6, we also compare them with the results of the other methods in the COLIEE 2023 competition. Compared with the results of the other method in the COLIEE 2023 competition, our methods show stable improvement on the queries in {R01, R02, R04}. When comparing the performance of each of our methods against the others, the difference between them is not too great, and in the three approaches, Auto-CoT seems to be the most stable method. However, because of the small size of the data, so depending on test queries,

Table 5. Results of Task 3 on the development set, the underlined settings play as the main sub-method in the ensemble various methods. The notations * refer to the runs using LLM with undisclosed training data, # refer to the runs do not use LLM.

Run	R02	R03	R04	Private Test (R05)
JNLP.constr-join*	-	-	-	**74.08**
TQM-run1#	-	-	-	71.71
NOWJ-25mulreftask-ensemble#	-	-	-	70.81
DatFlt-q+MonoT5# [13]	**76.36**	85.52	75.69	-
Mckpt#	69.49	78.35	77.54	71.35
MonoT5	71.54	79.83	58.96	55.56
LLM-re-ranking	66.67	78.87	75.44	70.64
LLM-re-ranking+MonoT5	73.87	84.04	77.87	72.68
Mckpt+MonoT5	76.13	85.17	78.23	71.71
Mckpt+MonoT5+LLM-re-ranking	75.04	**85.68**	**79.94**	73.35

the performance of each method could be different. For example, when testing with R02, the approach using a fine-tuned model with a few-shot setting is much better than the other methods while in other cases of R04 and R01, the performance of this approach cannot overcome the approach using Auto-CoT.

Private Test Results. The results of our methods on the private test set are shown in the table 7. The results in the private test dataset are quite close to our results in the official test dataset. However, the result of the approach using the fine-tuned model with mixed data between augmented and raw data is overcome by the other methods, it shows that this approach can adapt to the change of data better than the others.

Table 6. Development results of Task 4.

Team	Submission ID	L	R04	R02	R01
JNLP	JNLP3	E	0.7822	0.8025	0.6486
KIS	KIS2	J	0.6931	0.7160	0.6937
AMHR	AMHR01	E	0.6535	0.8025	0.7117
LLNTU	LLNTUdulcsL	J	0.6238	0.5185	0.4955
UA	UA	?	0.6238	0.7531	0.6036
HUKB	HUKB2	J	0.5941	0.6173	0.5405
Ours	Auto-CoT	E	**0.8415**	**0.8395**	0.7207
Ours	Fine-tuning Few-shot	E	0.8217	0.8148	**0.7748**
Ours	Fine-tuning Data Augmentation	E	**0.8415**	0.7901	0.7568

Table 7. Task 4 official results.

Submission	#correct	Accuracy
Baseline	60/109	0.5505
CAPTAIN2	90	**0.8257**
JNLP1	89	0.8165
UA_slack	87	0.7982
CAPTAIN1	86	**0.7890**
CAPTAIN3	86	**0.7890**
UA_gpt	85	0.7798
AMHR.ensembleA50	84	0.7706
NOWJ.pandap46	82	0.7523
HI1	82	0.7523
OVGU1	77	0.7064
...		

5 Conclusion

In this work, we utilize the power of LLMs on four tasks of the COLIEE competition. We achieved first prize in Task 4 and runner-up in tasks 2 and 3. These experimental results proved that our proposed method of applying LLM in the legal domain is effective, especially for the reasoning or re-ranking of the relevance between query and statute law. We believe that our proposed approach can be widely applied to various legal domain tasks as well as other tasks in NLP.

References

1. Bui, M., Nguyen, C., Do, D., Le, N., Nguyen, D., Nguyen, T.: Using deep learning approaches for tackling legal's challenges (COLIEE 2022). In: Sixteenth International Workshop on Juris-informatics (JURISIN) (2022)
2. Bui, Q.M., et al.: JNLP COLIEE-2023: data argumentation and large language model for legal case retrieval and entailment. In: Workshop of the Tenth Competition on Legal Information Extraction/Entailment (COLIEE'2023) in the 19th International Conference on Artificial Intelligence and Law (ICAIL) (2023)
3. Chung, H.W., et al.: Scaling instruction-finetuned language models. arXiv preprint arXiv:2210.11416 (2022)
4. Debbarma, R., Prawar, P., Chakraborty, A., Bedathur, S.: Iitdli: legal case retrieval based on lexical models. In: Workshop of the Tenth Competition on Legal Information Extraction/Entailment (COLIEE'2023) in the 19th International Conference on Artificial Intelligence and Law (ICAIL) (2023)
5. Fink, T., Recski, G., Kusa, W., Hanbury, A.: Statute-enhanced lexical retrieval of court cases for coliee 2022. arXiv preprint arXiv:2304.08188 (2023)
6. Goebel, R., Kano, Y., Kim, M.Y., Rabelo, J., Satoh, K., Yoshioka, M.: Summary of the competition on legal information, extraction/entailment (COLIEE) 2023. In: Proceedings of the Nineteenth International Conference on Artificial Intelligence and Law, pp. 472–480. ICAIL 2023, Association for Computing Machinery, New York, NY, USA (2023)
7. Hu, E.J., et al.: LoRA: low-rank adaptation of large language models. In: International Conference on Learning Representations (2022). https://openreview.net/forum?id=nZeVKeeFYf9
8. Kim, M.Y., Rabelo, J., Goebel, R., Yoshioka, M., Kano, Y., Satoh, K.: COLIEE 2022 summary: methods for legal document retrieval and entailment. In: Takama, Y., Yada, K., Satoh, K., Arai, S. (eds.) JSAI-isAI 2022. LNCS, pp. 51–67. Springer, Cham (2023). https://doi.org/10.1007/978-3-031-29168-5_4
9. Kim, M., Rabelo, J., Goebel, R.: Bm25 and transformer-based legal information extraction and entailment. In: Proceedings of the COLIEE Workshop in ICAIL (2021)
10. Li, H., Su, W., Wang, C., Wu, Y., Ai, Q., Liu, Y.: Thuir@coliee 2023: Incorporating structural knowledge into pre-trained language models for legal case retrieval (2023)
11. Lin, M., Huang, S., Shao, H.: Rethinking attention: an attempting on revaluing attention weight with disjunctive union of longest uncommon subsequence for legal queries answering. In: Sixteenth International Workshop on Juris-informatics (JURISIN) (2022)

12. Ma, Y., Shao, Y., Liu, B., Liu, Y., Zhang, M., Ma, S.: Retrieving legal cases from a large-scale candidate corpus. In: Proceedings of the Eighth International Competition on Legal Information Extraction/Entailment, COLIEE2021 (2021)
13. Nguyen, C., et al.: Captain at COLIEE 2023: efficient methods for legal information retrieval and entailment tasks. arXiv preprint arXiv:2401.03551 (2024)
14. Nguyen, H.T., et al.: JNLP team: deep learning approaches for legal processing tasks in coliee 2021. arXiv preprint arXiv:2106.13405 (2021)
15. Nogueira, R., Jiang, Z., Lin, J.: Document ranking with a pretrained sequence-to-sequence model. arXiv preprint arXiv:2003.06713 (2020)
16. Novaes, L.P., Vianna, D., da Silva, A.: A topic-based approach for the legal case retrieval task. In: Workshop of the Tenth Competition On Legal Information Extraction/Entailment (COLIEE'2023) in the 19th International Conference on Artificial Intelligence and Law (ICAIL) (2023)
17. Pradeep, R., Nogueira, R., Lin, J.: The expando-mono-duo design pattern for text ranking with pretrained sequence-to-sequence models (2021)
18. Rabelo, J., Kim, M.Y., Goebel, R.: Semantic-based classification of relevant case law. In: Takama, Y., Yada, K., Satoh, K., Arai, S. (eds.) JSAI-isAI 2022. LNCS, vol. 13859, pp. 84–95. Springer, Cham (2022). https://doi.org/10.1007/978-3-031-29168-5_6
19. Robertson, S., Zaragoza, H.: The probabilistic relevance framework: Bm25 and beyond. Found. Trends Inf. Retr. **3**(4), 333–389 (2009). https://doi.org/10.1561/1500000019
20. Rosa, G.M., Bonifacio, L., Jeronymo, V., Abonizio, H., Lotufo, R., Nogueira, R.: Billions of parameters are worth more than in-domain training data: a case study in the legal case entailment task. arXiv preprint arXiv:2205.15172 (2022)
21. Rosa, G.M., Rodrigues, R.C., de Alencar Lotufo, R., Nogueira, R.: To tune or not to tune? zero-shot models for legal case entailment. In: Proceedings of the Eighteenth International Conference on Artificial Intelligence and Law, pp. 295–300 (2021)
22. Shao, H.L., Chen, Y.C., Huang, S.C.: Bert-based ensemble model for statute law retrieval and legal information entailment. In: Okazaki, N., Yada, K., Satoh, K., Mineshima, K. (eds.) JSAI-isAI 2020. LNCS, vol. 12758, pp. 226–239. Springer, Cham (2021). https://doi.org/10.1007/978-3-030-79942-7_15
23. Vuong, T.H.Y., Nguyen, H.L., Nguyen, T.M., Nguyen, H.T., Nguyen, T.B., Nguyen, H.T.: NOWJ at COLIEE 2023–multi-task and ensemble approaches in legal information processing. arXiv preprint arXiv:2306.04903 (2023)
24. Wehnert, S., Sudhi, V., Dureja, S., Kutty, L., Shahania, S., De Luca, E.W.: Legal norm retrieval with variations of the Bert model combined with TF-IDF vectorization. In: Proceedings of the Eighteenth International Conference on Artificial Intelligence and Law, pp. 285–294 (2021)
25. Yoshioka, M., Aoki, Y., Suzuki, Y.: Bert-based ensemble methods with data augmentation for legal textual entailment in COLIEE statute law task. In: Proceedings of the Eighteenth International Conference on Artificial Intelligence and Law, pp. 278–284 (2021)
26. Yoshioka, M., Suzuki, Y., Aoki, Y.: HUKB at the COLIEE 2022 statute law task. In: Takama, Y., Yada, K., Satoh, K., Arai, S. (eds.) JSAI-isAI 2022. LNCS, vol. 13859, pp. 109–124. Springer, Cham (2023). https://doi.org/10.1007/978-3-031-29168-5_8
27. Zhang, Z., Zhang, A., Li, M., Smola, A.: Automatic chain of thought prompting in large language models (2022)

LLM Tuning and Interpretable CoT: KIS Team in COLIEE 2024

Masaki Fujita[ID], Takaaki Onaga[ID], and Yoshinobu Kano[(✉)][ID]

Shizuoka University, Johoku, 3-5-1, Chuo-ku, Hamamatsu-shi,
Shizuoka 432-8011, Japan
{mfujita,tonaga,kano}@kanolab.net

Abstract. Focusing on the recently advanced Large Language Models
(LLMs), we studied two key areas: LLM tuning and Chain-of-Thought
(CoT) interpretability, which are crucial in legal tasks. Regarding LLM
tuning, we conducted experiments comparing multiple models, a variety
of techniques including prompt engineering, and the presence or absence
of fine-tune, thereby identifying the most effective settings. Additionally, we proposed new methods to overcome the shortcomings of models during fine-tune, leading to improved accuracy. In terms of CoT
interpretability, we introduced a format that facilitates guiding the CoT
process, enabling the identification of which parts of the reasoning process significantly influence the inference results. Furthermore, we demonstrated that fine-tune enables any model to produce outputs in this format, and this approach can clearly define the differences in reasoning
capabilities among various models. Using implication reasoning tasks in
the civil law section of the judicial examination as a subject, we achieved
enhanced task performance with large-scale language models.

Keywords: COLIEE · Question Answering · Legal Bar Exam · Legal
Information · Large Language Models · LLM · GPT-4 ·
Chain-of-Thought · Retrieval Augmented Generation

1 Introduction

Recent Large Language Models (LLMs) trained with massive amounts of data
and parameters can enhance performance across various tasks. Among LLMs,
GPT-4 [15] by OpenAI is known for its high performance. Furthermore, performance improves when Prompt Engineering technologies, such as Chain-of-
Thought(CoT) [22] and Retrieval Augmented Generation , are combined with
GPT-4. Chain-of-Thought have enabled stepwise reasoning, reporting performance improvements. CoT is a method that goes beyond having LLMs simply
output answers to problems. Instead, it involves generating the necessary intermediate steps of reasoning before producing the answer. There are variations
of CoT, such as zero-shot CoT, where the model is instructed to reason in a
stepwise manner, and few-shot CoT [1], which involves providing examples of
stepwise reasoning.

© The Author(s), under exclusive license to Springer Nature Singapore Pte Ltd. 2024
T. Suzumura and M. Bono (Eds.): JSAI-isAI 2024, LNAI 14741, pp. 140–155, 2024.
https://doi.org/10.1007/978-981-97-3076-6_10

This paper does not thoroughly investigate the effects of combining the CoT approach with fine-tune. Furthermore, it lacks guidance on how to construct prompts that utilize CoT appropriately for specific tasks, a point we wish to emphasize. Retrieval Augmented Generation (RAG) [12] is a method aimed at improving performance not only by teaching the model with knowledge but also by incorporating necessary knowledge from external sources during inference. By using RAG, it becomes possible to perform inference with any additional data without altering the parameters of the model. However, as the training data of many models, including GPT-4, is not entirely public. Also, it is uncertain whether CoT and RAG are effective in general LLMs.

Regarding CoT, it remains unclear which parts of the reasoning process assist in answering, and LLM outputs sometimes include hallucinations [6], indicating room for improvement in the output methods, including stepwise reasoning. Recent studies on Fine tune and RAG have shown that RAG can outperform in certain contexts [17]. However, these studies also note that results can vary significantly depending on the task and model used. This underscores the importance of identifying the optimal settings for specific conditions in our research. Also, due to the huge number of parameters, the inference process in LLMs tends to become a *black box*, leading to research in eXplainable AI (XAI) [14] and explainability [2].

We summarize our two main contributions, *LLM Tuning* and *CoT Interpretability*, as follows.

LLM Tuning. We verified the accuracy with models whose training data is entirely public and also examined whether employing Prompt Engineering techniques is effective. Subsequently, we proposed model-specific training methods and confirmed improvements in performance. In this process, by comparing various LLMs and techniques, we examined how differences in model size and training data impact inference, and identified the settings that maximize accuracy.

In LLMs, Instruct Tuning [21], referred to as RLHF [16], is typically conducted in three stages: Supervised Fine-Tuning (SFT) using only instruction-based data, creating a reward model (RM), and Reinforcement Learning (RL) utilizing the reward model. Next, we observed changes in the outputs by conducting additional fine-tune on these Instruct Tuned models to teach them task-specific and domain-specific information.

Within this context, we confirmed that effective settings and training configurations vary for each model. By employing proposed methods suited to each model, we verified improvements in accuracy.

CoT Interpretability. We proposed a format suitable for LLMs to output while showing the inference process, and by analyzing the CoT process, we demonstrated the ability to identify specific inference steps that contribute to the model's reasoning, as well as to pinpoint areas of inference that the model struggles with. Furthermore, by performing fine-tune on models with publicly disclosed internal structures in accordance with the proposed format, we confirmed the feasibility of producing outputs aligned with the format. Utilizing datasets from the legal field that require step-by-step reasoning, we revealed that even public models, which generally underperform, can exhibit performance comparable to GPT-4 in certain stages of inference when using the proposed methods.

Our study makes two primary contributions. Firstly, we propose a novelty specialized for specific tasks and models through our comprehensive analysis of existing models, learning methodologies, and the application of prompt engineering. Secondly, we suggest the potential applicability of our methods across various tasks that require stepwise reasoning. This second contribution, in particular, is considered to possess high novelty due to its capacity to efficiently and systematically analyze large volumes of data through prompt adjustments. This method indicates its effectiveness especially in tasks where explainability is important.

We applied these two points to the COLIEE 2024 Task 4, showing the effectiveness of our two contributions. As a workshop focused on natural language processing technologies in the field of law, the Competition on Legal Information Extraction and Entailment (COLIEE) [3,7–11,18–20] has been held annually. This competition involves automatically answering problems from the civil law section of Japanese legal bar examination and competing in terms of performance. Task 4 of COLIEE provides a list of civil law articles and past problems, testing the accuracy of answers to the test problems; participants are given a pair of problem text and its related article(s) necessary to solve the problem, answer whether the problem text is correct or not. We conducted training and inference of the model using the Japanese data for Task 4 of COLIEE.

Following this Introduction, we describe sections of LLM Tuning and CoT Interpretability, each divided into Proposed Method, Experiment, Results, and Discussion. The paper concludes with a final section summarizing the findings.

2   LLM Tuning

We aim to find the optimal configuration for tasks in the civil law section of the judicial examination by utilizing multiple models, learning methods, and prompt engineering techniques to achieve maximum accuracy. Next, based on these experimental results, we identify the types of problems that public models struggle with and propose corresponding methodologies.

As techniques in prompt engineering, we try combinations of CoT, zero/few-shot, and RAG to see how these affect the accuracy and output of the responses.

Chain-of-Thought. Without CoT, instructions are given to output only "True" or "False." With CoT, instructions are modified to require the output of key points, followed by "True" if the problem is correct and "False" if it is not, thus enabling step-by-step reasoning.

Zero/Few-Shot Prompting. Zero-shot gives prompts such as instructions, civil law articles, and problem statements. For few-shot, examples of civil law articles, problems, and answers from training dataset are inserted between the instructions and the civil law articles. When without RAG, as mentioned later, the few shots are manually selected from the explanatory answers by GPT-4.

Retrieval-Augmented Generation (RAG). When using RAG, SentenceLUKE [1] that converts text into vectors is employed to select a pair of the highest similarity for the few shots, a positive and a negative answers for each, from the training problems. We utilize data from past problems, excluding the test data and the problems from the answer year. We compare the vector similarity between the text of the problem to be solved and the texts of past problems. The examples with the highest similarity are selected as one positive and one negative instance each. These instances are then used as data examples for the few shot learning scenario.

2.1 Proposed Method

Prompting Number of Characters. We propose to indicate the number of characters of the entire prompt input in the instruction part in advance. This allows the model, particularly the decoder processing the input sequentially from the beginning, to receive information about the input length at an early stage, suggesting the potential for improved internal processing capabilities. Additionally, LLMs might struggle with precise numerical values, we round off the number of characters to the nearest hundred by rounding the tens place. Figure 1 serves as an example of this.

Standard instructions
Below is a civil law problem from the bar examination. Refer to the related civil law articles mentioned in the part of the civil law articles, and output "True" if the problem is correct, or "False" if it is not.

Instructions with inserted character count
Below is a civil law problem from the bar examination. **The character count is approximately 1800 characters.** Refer to the related civil law articles mentioned in the part of the civil law articles, and output "True" if the problem is correct, or "False" if it is not.

Fig. 1. Example of inserting character count into the instructions (This figure represents the Japanese input and output translated into English)

Prompting Explanatory Answers. We propose replacing the past problem-answer pairs of our few-shot with explanatory answers:

---

[1] https://huggingface.co/oshizo/sbert-jsnli-luke-japanese-base-lite.

1. Generate explanatory answers using GPT-4 for training problems by applying CoT, creating responses comprising four elements: key points of the problem, summary of articles, logical reasoning, and the answer.
2. During the answering process for test problems, utilize RAG to extract training problems with high similarity.
3. Replace the original few shot prompts (the problem, related article, and Yes/No answer) with the explanatory answers extracted by RAG as above.

By following the above process, the length of the few-shot is standardized, while retaining information about the problem and civil law articles in the form of summaries, regardless of the length of the original related articles and problem texts. Figure 2 presents an example problem of H21-19-A, selected for its high similarity to problem H18-1-1. This example contrasts a prompt with standard few-shot data, and a prompt with only answers accompanied by explanations are provided (proposed method).

2.2 Experiment and Result

Three LLMs. In COLIEE 2024, to avoid data leakage, only models with all training datasets publicly declared are permitted. Therefore, we use the weblab-10b-instruction-sft model [2] pretrained by 600B tokens of Japanese and English texts; In addition to pre-training, SFT performed in InstructTuning using RLHF; all of these datasets are publicly available.

For comparison, we use OpenAI's GPT-4 [15], which is currently considered to be one of the best LLMs. To prevent changes in results due to parameter updates, we employ the gpt-4-1106-preview, which does not undergo parameter updates. Unfortunately, GPT-4 has the disadvantage of having its learning data and parameters not publicly disclosed and not allowing arbitrary settings for fine-tune.

Additionally, we test stabilityai/StableBeluga-13B [3]. Although this model cannot be used under the COLIEE's constraints because some of its training data is not public, it has publicly available parameters and allows fine-tune. Furthermore, it can provide more accurate answers than Weblab even without fine-tune, thus being tested as an intermediate model between the two models as another public model.

Fine-Tune. We used Lora [5,13] for fine-tune, which allows only a subset of parameters in LLMs to change during training, aiming for efficient and rapid learning. For evaluation, 255 problems from R01 to R03 datasets (three years) are used. For training data for fine-tune, 629 problems from H18 to H30 datasets are used [4]. In this study, parameter settings were precisely adjusted and determined

---

[2] https://huggingface.co/matsuo-lab/weblab-10b-instruction-sft.
[3] https://huggingface.co/stabilityai/StableBeluga-13B.
[4] We found that the problem numbers for R01 were expressed as either R1 or R01; We only used the problems labeled as R01 (65 out of 111 problems).

Example of a problem text
It is possible to conclude a special agreement to exempt warranty liability; however, even in such cases, if the seller has established rights on the object for a third party, the seller cannot be exempted from liability.

Example of standard few shot prompting
Example of civil law article 1
Article 447 The guarantee obligation includes interest on the principal obligation, penalties, damages, and all other obligations subsidiary to it. The guarantor can stipulate the amount of the penalty or damages only for the guarantee obligation.
Example of Problem Text 1
Even if the obligation to restore to the original condition due to cancellation is understood as a separate obligation distinct from the original obligation, considering that whether the obligation to restore to the original condition due to contract cancellation is included within the scope of the guarantee obligation depends on the interpretation of the parties' intentions in the guarantee contract, it is possible to interpret that a guarantor for the seller in a contract for the sale of specified goods bears responsibility for the obligation to restore to the original condition in the event of contract cancellation due to the seller's non-performance.
Example of Answer 1
True

Example of an answer with explanation via few shot prompting
Reference Information
Key point of the problem: Whether a guarantor for the seller in a contract for the sale of specified goods can be deemed responsible for the obligation to restore to the original condition in the event of contract cancellation due to the seller's non-performance.

According to the civil law articles, the guarantee obligation includes interest on the principal obligation, penalties, damages, and all other obligations subsidiary to it.

Therefore, the obligation to restore to the original condition due to contract cancellation can also be interpreted as subsidiary to the obligation, and can be considered to be included within the scope of the guarantee obligation.

Therefore, the statement in the problem is correct.

Fig. 2. Example of modification for few shot prompting (This figure represents the Japanese input and output translated into English)

based on the validation dataset. Specifically, the parameters for LoRA were set as follows: lora_r to 64, lora_alpha to 16, and lora_dropout to 0.2. The learning rate was normally set to 0.001, with a batch size of 4 and the number of epochs at 10 for the training process. Furthermore, regarding LoRA's target_module, c_proj was targeted in the case of weblab, while for stabilityAI, both q_proj and v_proj were targeted.

Evaluation Results: Comparing Models, Prompting, and Fine-Tune.
Experiments are conducted on five models: the three models mentioned in
Sect. 2.2, and fine-tuned models for StabilityAI and weblab. Regarding prompt
engineering, we performed six patterns: two patterns with and without CoT,
by three patterns of zero-shot, few-shot, and few-shot with data selection using
RAG. Thus, we conducted a total of thirty distinct experiments.

The results are shown in Table 1. The output is regarded as correct if the
output string contains either "True" or "False," and matches the answer to
the problem. If the output string does not include either "True" or "False,"
or includes both, it is considered as unanswered; Unless specifically noted, the
denominator for calculating the accuracy rate is limited to those that could be
answered. Because the original number of the problems is 255, if the denominator
in the table is not 255, e.g. 250, it indicates that 5 out of 255 problems were left
unanswered.

Table 1. Accuracy by model, prompting technique, and fine-tune *ZS* and *FS* respectively indicate the use of zero-shot and few-shot. *FT* denotes a model that has undergone fine-tune. *Stab* refers to a model from StabilityAI.

	ZS	FS	FS+ RAG	CoT+ ZS	CoT+ FS	CoT+ FS+ RAG
Weblab	**0.545** (**138/253**)	0.542 (137/253)	0.534 (132/247)	**0.545** (**138/253**)	0.523 (126/241)	0.534 (117/219)
Weblab+ FT	0.608 (155/255)	0.612 (156/255)	**0.624** (**156/250**)	0.602 (153/254)	0.541 (79/146)	0.602 (124/206)
Stab	0.620 (158/255)	0.609 (154/253)	0.630 (160/254)	0.604 (154/255)	0.597 (151/253)	**0.642** (**158/246**)
Stab+ FT	0.686 (166/242)	0.615 (152/247)	**0.709** (**151/213**)	0.691 (170/246)	0.537 (43/80)	0.648 (151/233)
GPT4	0.773 (197/255)	0.824 (210/255)	0.843 (215/255)	**0.874** (**221/253**)	0.846 (215/254)	0.850 (216/254)

Evaluation Results and Formal Runs: Proposed Prompting Methods.
We fine-tuned with our proposed methods (Sect. 2.1) from H30 to R02 and R05
datasets, submitting these results as our Formal Run. For the H30 to R02 test
cases, we used past problems up to H29 as training data, and for R05, we used
data up to R04. In all submissions, we employed Weblab as the pretrained model,
further enhanced through fine-tune, and did not use the CoT because, as shown
in Table 1, this setting had the highest accuracy in Weblab. Additionally, to
improve accuracy, we utilized our previous rule-based system [4], which parses
sentences into clauses, extracts sets of clauses including subject, predicate, and
object for each clause, and compared these sets. We adopted an ensemble approach where answers that could be solved by the highest accuracy module of the
rule-based system were used, and for all other problems, outputs from the LLM

were employed. Furthermore, for KIS1, we combined few-shot and RAG, adding the proposed method 2.1. For KIS2, we combined few-shot and RAG, changing the data provided for few-shot to the one proposed in Sect. 2.1.

Table 2 presents the results of experiments conducted in accordance with the settings described in Sect. 2.2.

Table 2. Results of the proposed method, formal run

	KIS1+ RuleBase	KIS2+ RuleBase	KIS3+ RuleBase	KIS1	KIS2	KIS3
H30	0.629 (44/70)	**0.643 (45/70)**	**0.643 (45/70)**	**0.643 (45/70)**	**0.643 (45/70)**	0.629 (44/70)
R01	**0.685 (76/111)**	0.604 (67/111)	0.631 (70/111)	0.667 (74/111)	0.568 (63/111)	0.613 (68/111)
R02	0.642 (52/81)	0.654 (53/81)	0.593 (48/81)	0.654 (53/81)	**0.667 (54/81)**	0.605 (49/81)
R05	0.615 (67/109)	**0.697 (76/109)**	0.569 (62/109)	0.587 (64/109)	0.688 (75/109)	0.578 (63/109)
Total	0.644 (239/371)	**0.650 (241/371)**	0.606 (225/371)	0.636 (236/371)	0.639 (237/371)	0.604 (224/371)

2.3 Discussion

Comparison of Models, Techniques, and Fine-Tune. From Table 1, we compare the three types of models without fine-tune. GPT-4 consistently shows high accuracy across all settings, followed by StabilityAI, with Weblab showing the lowest accuracy.

We then examine the results by settings. Weblab shows little change in accuracy regardless of the settings used. On the other hand, when FS or CoT is used, an increase in the number of unanswered problems is observed, as indicated by the reduced denominator. With StabilityAI, using only few-shot slightly decreases accuracy compared to not using it. However, accuracy improves when RAG is added to few-shot. For GPT-4, accuracy significantly drops when neither CoT nor few-shot is used. Additionally, using RAG with few-shot shows higher accuracy than using few-shot alone. The highest accuracy is achieved when CoT is combined with zero-shot. From these observations, it is evident that the techniques for improving accuracy vary depending on the model, and selecting methods suitable for the model is crucial.

Next, we analyze the effects of fine-tune. In Weblab, accuracy improves with fine-tune regardless of the techniques used. For StabilityAI, accuracy improves in 5 out of 6 settings with fine-tune. This suggests that fine-tune is likely effective in many settings for both models.

In the case of GPT-4, a tendency for increased accuracy with the use of CoT or few-shot is observed, but this trend is not seen with Weblab and Stability AI. Additionally, a manual check on the impact of prompt length on accuracy revealed that while GPT-4 showed a small correlation between prompt length and accuracy, StabilityAI and Weblab showed a larger correlation, especially when using CoT or few-shot, which tends to lengthen the prompt. Therefore, public models are likely to struggle with long texts.

Furthermore, as mentioned earlier, since longer prompts can make handling long texts more challenging, we propose the method in Sect. 2.1 to incorporate strategies for dealing with longer text and aim for improved accuracy.

Proposed Method, Formal Run Results. From Table 2, we confirm the effectiveness of the proposed methods based on the results of the Formal Run. The use of the proposed methods in KIS1 and KIS2 showed improved results compared to when they were not used. This suggests that the proposed methods are effective during the training of models that struggle with long strings of text. Additionally, the method of adding character count information allows for handling longer texts without losing information, and the method of adding summary information can reduce the length of long text inputs. Therefore, it is conceivable that selecting a method suited to the task can be beneficial.

3   CoT Interpretability

In this section, we describe our method to analyze the process of CoT by employing a format suitable for LLMs to output while demonstrating the reasoning process.

3.1   Proposed Method

We propose a method that standardizes the output format of CoT to enable the comparison of reasoning processes, and demonstrates the effectiveness of each reasoning step and areas for model improvement depending on the task.

1. Based on the characteristics and challenges of the target task, we establish a task-specific prompt and the corresponding CoT output format for the task's response.
2. We apply few-shot or fine-tune to any generative model to ensure it produces outputs in line with the established format.
3. By analyzing where significant changes occur in the final output during the reasoning steps, and comparing these steps with other models, we clarify the effectiveness of each reasoning step and identify areas for model improvement.

3.2   Experiment

It is often challenging to pinpoint specific capabilities that generative models excel in for individual tasks. For example, in COLIEE, possibilities include finding relevant sections from civil law articles and logical reasoning capabilities.

Therefore, we use a standardized output format and CoT to quantify performance differences between GPT-4 and publicly available models. In this paper, after comparing several models, we chose to use stabilityai/StableBeluga13B[5], which showed high accuracy among publicly available models trainable on our hardware, for comparison with GPT-4.

Prompt and Output Format. After comparing different prompts and few-shot approaches, we decided to use the prompt and format shown in Fig. 3. We set the format with four elements: problem key point, article summary, reasoning section, and answer. We established these four elements for the following reasons. First, in civil law problems of the bar examination, there is often a key point for determining implication. Also, the provided civil law articles are not always minimal, and in real trials, it's necessary to extract relevant sections from extensive articles. Finally, we set the format to output the final answer after a logical reasoning step based on the essence of the problem and a summary of the civil law articles.

Fine-Tune of Public Models and GPT-4's Few-Shot. As stabilityai/ Stable-Beluga13B could not perform stepwise reasoning with CoT using only few-shot, we conducted fine-tune. If this model can learn the format, we believe the proposed method can be realized with many other models.

Identifying Effective Reasoning Steps with GPT-4. We confirmed an improvement in the accuracy of COLIEE tasks by using CoT with GPT-4. To identify which parts of the generated reasoning process influence the model's response, we first performed stepwise reasoning using CoT and then divided the process based on the four elements mentioned in Sect. 3.2. Next, we analyzed which elements significantly influence reasoning by having the model respond to the task based on the reasoning process up to each division point (see Fig. 4).

The output of the problem's key points and the article summary is believed to be more effective when the original articles and problem texts are longer. Therefore, we divided the evaluation data into two groups based on the length of the articles and problem texts, to examine whether the length of the problem and articles affects the change in the accuracy rate.

Performance Comparison Between Two Types of Models. We conducted stepwise output in accordance with the previously mentioned four elements (Fig. 5) using CoT with a publicly available model. Subsequently, after dividing the process by elements, we let GPT-4 continue the reasoning and then calculated the correct answer rate. This allowed us to analyze at which stage of CoT the differences in performance between the models emerge.

---

[5] https://huggingface.co/stabilityai/StableBeluga-13B.

Instructions
Below is a civil law problem from the judicial examination. Refer to the related civil law articles mentioned in the civil law text section and state whether the problem is correct or not. After stating the key point of the problem, output "True" if it is correct, or "False" if it is not.
Civil Law Text
Article 5
When a minor performs a legal act, (omitted)
Problem
A purchase contract made by a minor cannot be annulled when it is related to daily life, even if made without the consent of the parental authority.
Answer
Key Point of the Problem: Whether a purchase contract made by a minor without the consent of the parental authority can be annulled when it relates to daily life. According to the civil law articles, a minor must obtain the consent of their legal representative to perform a legal act. However, this does not apply to legal acts that solely acquire rights or relieve obligations. Furthermore, it is stated that minors can freely dispose of property within the scope defined by their legal representative.
Therefore, if a purchase contract made by a minor is related to daily life, it can be interpreted as falling within the scope that minors can freely dispose of, regardless of whether it was made without the consent of the legal representative. Hence, it is considered that such a contract cannot be annulled.
Answer: True

Fig. 3. Example of prompt and output format (This figure represents the Japanese input and output translated into English.)

3.3 Results

Model Training. The training results of the publicly available model described in Sect. 3.2 are shown in Table 3. Fine-tune led to an improvement in the accuracy of answering problems, along with the ability to produce outputs in line with the designated format.

Table 3. Comparison of results before and after training StableBeluga-13B

	Before Training	After Training
Accuracy Rate	0.597 (151/253)	**0.641 (161/251)**
Outputs Meeting Format	0 (0/255)	**0.953 (243/255)**

Identifying Effective Reasoning Steps with GPT-4. The experimental results for identifying effective reasoning steps with CoT as mentioned in Sect. 3.2 are presented in Table 4. The evaluation data was limited to 240 out of 255 problems from COLIEE R01 to R03, for which both the publicly available model and

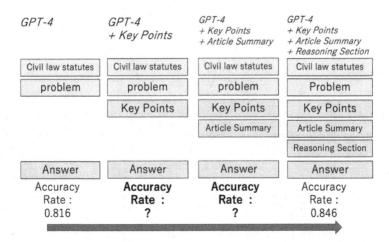

Fig. 4. Quantification of Correct Answer Rates for Each Reasoning Step Using GPT-4

GPT-4 produced outputs aligned with the format. For *Long Problems*, defined as those with a problem text length greater than the median (70 characters) in the evaluation data, accuracy rates for these 121 problems are listed. Similarly, for 119 *Short Problems*, and for civil law articles, we listed the accuracy rates for 120 *Long Articles* and 120 *Short Articles*, based on the median length of 170 characters. In all cases, longer texts showed improved accuracy rates, suggesting the effectiveness of summarization.

Table 4. Changes in correct answer rates at each reasoning step

	GPT-4	GPT-4+ Key Points	GPT-4+ Key Points+ Article Summary	GPT-4+ Key Points+ Article Summary+ Reasoning Section
Accuracy Rate	0.817 (196/240)	0.808 (194/240)	0.838 (201/240)	**0.846 (203/240)**
Long Problems	0.793	0.802	0.843	**0.851**
Short Problems	**0.840**	0.815	0.832	**0.840**
Long Articles	0.842	0.808	0.858	**0.875**
Short Articles	0.792	0.808	**0.817**	**0.817**

Performance Comparison Between Two Types of Models. The accuracy for each step, following the methodology outlined in Sect. 3.2, is presented in Table 5. Each element corresponds to the elements depicted in Fig. 5. That is, the process begins with all steps being executed using the public model. As we move down the table, the share of tasks performed by GPT-4 increases. In the

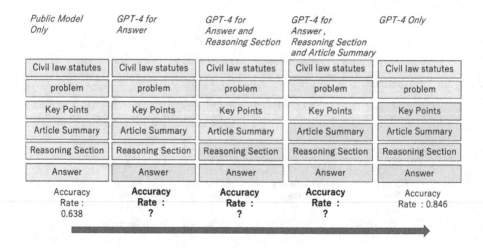

Fig. 5. Method for comparing model performance Red blocks are datasets, green blocks are public models, and blue blocks are GPT-4 (Color figure online)

Table 5. Comparison results of model performance

	Accuracy Rate
Public Model Only	0.638 (153/240)
GPT-4 for Answer	0.771 (185/240)
GPT-4 for Answer and Reasoning Section	0.854 (203/240)
GPT-4 except for Key Points	**0.862 (207/240)**
GPT-4 Only	0.846 (201/240)

lowest part of the table, GPT-4 executes all tasks, showing an improvement in performance as we move downwards. However, beyond the *inference section*, there is little change in performance.

3.4 Discussion

Fine-Tune of Public Models. The results suggest that the possibility of enabling performance comparison of our proposed methods using CoT, by outputting the stepwise format by any LLM.

Identifying Effective Reasoning Steps with GPT-4. Analyzing the results in Table 4, we observe that including the reasoning section improves the overall accuracy rate, regardless of text length. This indicates that embedding a logical reasoning step in text format after summarizing the problem and articles is an effective reasoning step. The use of article summaries leads to improved accuracy rates for both long and short articles, particularly showing a significant improvement in handling long articles, which aligns with the intended effect of summarization. Utilizing key points improves accuracy in long problems, suggesting the effectiveness of summarization. However, the decrease in accuracy for short problems suggests that the format focusing only on key points might lead to reduced accuracy. This indicates that comparing the civil law text in the input section with the key points in the output section is challenging, suggesting that outputting only part of the information necessary for the answer might lead to a decrease in accuracy. In summary, dividing the elements allowed us to quantitatively analyze the contribution of each element to the improvement.

Performance Comparison Between Two Types of Models. From the results in Table 5, we demonstrate the ability to quantitatively analyze which model excels in which aspects when comparing GPT-4 and public models. The lack of significant difference in the results for GPT-4 from Reasoning Section, GPT-4 from Article Summary, and Only GPT-4 (bottom side of Table 5) suggests that there is no significant difference between public models and GPT-4 in extracting key points and summarizing civil law articles. On the other hand, a significant decrease in accuracy when public models handle the reasoning section and answers (top side of Table 5) suggests a substantial difference in performance in understanding implications. The improvement in results for *GPT-4 from Reasoning Section* and *GPT-4 from Article Summary* compared to *GPT-4 Only* suggests that having the public model generate key points and summaries might enable GPT-4 to appropriately utilize these elements, leading to increased accuracy. That is, our CoT method using four elements combining different LLMs performed better than pure GPT-4.

4   Conclusion and Future Works

In this study, we have two main contributions. First, we compared multiple Large Language Models (LLMs) and techniques, identifying the most effective combination of settings for each model. Additionally, we proposed fine-tune methods that proved effective during the training of the models selected in this research. Second, we proposed a method that improves performance by standardizing the output format and reasoning process in CoT. Additionally, this method allows for a stepwise and quantitative analysis of performance differences across various models.

In the analysis method using CoT, using the COLIEE judicial examination for automated answering as a case study, our CoT method using four elements combining different LLMs performed better than pure GPT-4.

In the future, we aim to improve the identified areas of lacking performance through data augmentation and ensemble methods. Additionally, we intend to use the process of template generation, model performance investigation, and improvement to conduct model enhancements based on quantitative analysis, which could be applicable to other tasks.

Acknowledgments. This research was supported by JSPS KAKENHI Grant Numbers JP22H00804, JP21K18115, JP20K20509, and the Secom Science and Technology Foundation's research grant in a specific field.

References

1. Brown, T., et al.: Language models are few-shot learners. In: Larochelle, H., Ranzato, M., Hadsell, R., Balcan, M., Lin, H. (eds.) Advances in Neural Information Processing Systems. vol. 33, pp. 1877–1901. Curran Associates, Inc. (2020). https://proceedings.neurips.cc/paper_files/paper/2020/file/1457c0d6bfcb4967418bfb8ac142f64a-Paper.pdf
2. Doshi-Velez, F., Kim, B.: Towards a rigorous science of interpretable machine learning (2017). https://arxiv.org/abs/1702.08608
3. Goebel, R., Kano, Y., Kim, M.Y., Rabelo, J., Satoh, K., Yoshioka, M.: Summary of the competition on legal information, extraction/entailment (COLIEE) 2023. In: Proceedings of the Nineteenth International Conference on Artificial Intelligence and Law, pp. 472–480 (2023)
4. Hoshino, R., Kiyota, N., Kano, Y.: Question answering system for legal bar examination using predicate argument structures focusing on exceptions. In: Proceedings of the Sixth International Competition on Legal Information Extraction/Entailment (COLIEE 2019), pp. 38–42 (2019)
5. Hu, E.J., et al.: LoRA: low-rank adaptation of large language models. In: International Conference on Learning Representations (2022). https://openreview.net/forum?id=nZeVKeeFYf9
6. Huang, L., et al.: A survey on hallucination in large language models: principles, taxonomy, challenges, and open questions (2023). https://arxiv.org/abs/2311.05232
7. Kano, Y., Kim, M.Y., Goebel, R., Satoh, K.: Overview of COLIEE 2017. In: Satoh, K., Kim, M.Y., Kano, Y., Goebel, R., Oliveira, T. (eds.) COLIEE 2017. 4th Competition on Legal Information Extraction and Entailment. EPiC Series in Computing, vol. 47, pp. 1–8. EasyChair (2017). https://doi.org/10.29007/fm8f, https://easychair.org/publications/paper/Fglr
8. Kano, Y., et al.: COLIEE-2018: evaluation of the competition on legal information extraction and entailment. In: Kojima, K., Sakamoto, M., Mineshima, K., Satoh, K. (eds.) JSAI-isAI 2018. LNCS, pp. 177–192. Springer, Cham (2019). https://doi.org/10.1007/978-3-030-31605-1_14
9. Kim, M.Y., Goebel, R., Kano, Y., Satoh, K.: COLIEE-2016: evaluation of the competition on legal information extraction and entailment. In: International Workshop on Juris-informatics (JURISIN 2016) (2016)
10. Kim, M.Y., Goebel, R., Ken, S.: COLIEE-2015: evaluation of legal question answering. In: Ninth International Workshop on Juris-informatics (JURISIN 2015) (2015)
11. Kim, M.Y., Rabelo, J., Goebel, R., Yoshioka, M., Kano, Y., Satoh, K.: COLIEE 2022 summary: methods for legal document retrieval and entailment. In: Takama, Y., Yada, K., Satoh, K., Arai, S. (eds.) JSAI-isAI 2022. LNCS, vol. 13859, pp. 51–67. Springer, Heidelberg (2023). https://doi.org/10.1007/978-3-031-29168-5_4
12. Lewis, P., et al.: Retrieval-augmented generation for knowledge-intensive NLP tasks. In: Proceedings of the 34th International Conference on Neural Information Processing Systems. NIPS 2020, Curran Associates Inc., Red Hook, NY, USA (2020)

13. Mangrulkar, S., Gugger, S., Debut, L., Belkada, Y., Paul, S., Bossan, B.: PEFT: state-of-the-art parameter-efficient fine-tuning methods. https://github.com/huggingface/peft (2022)
14. Meguro, M.: Research trends in XAI (explainable AI) technology. J. Japan Soc. Secur. Manage. **34**(1), 20–27 (2020). 10.32230/jssmjournal.34.1_20. (in Japanese)
15. OpenAI: GPT-4 technical report (2023). https://arxiv.org/abs/2303.08774
16. Ouyang, L., et al.: Training language models to follow instructions with human feedback (2022). https://arxiv.org/abs/2203.02155
17. Ovadia, O., Brief, M., Mishaeli, M., Elisha, O.: Fine-tuning or retrieval? comparing knowledge injection in llms (2024). https://arxiv.org/abs/2312.05934
18. Rabelo, J., Goebel, R., Kim, M.Y., Kano, Y., Yoshioka, M., Satoh, K.: Overview and discussion of the competition on legal information extraction/entailment (COLIEE) 2021. Rev. Socionetw. Strat. **16**(1), 111–133 (2022). https://doi.org/10.1007/s12626-022-00105-z
19. Rabelo, J., Kim, M.Y., Goebel, R., Yoshioka, M., Kano, Y., Satoh, K.: COLIEE 2020: methods for legal document retrieval and entailment. In: Okazaki, N., Yada, K., Satoh, K., Mineshima, K. (eds.) JSAI-isAI 2020. LNCS, vol. 12758, pp. 196–210. Springer, Cham (2020). https://doi.org/10.1007/978-3-030-79942-7_13
20. Rabelo, J., Kim, M.Y., Goebel, R., Yoshioka, M., Kano, Y., Satoh, K.: A summary of the COLIEE 2019 competition. In: Sakamoto, M., Okazaki, N., Mineshima, K., Satoh, K. (eds.) JSAI-isAI 2019. LNCS, pp. 34–49. Springer, Cham (2020). https://doi.org/10.1007/978-3-030-58790-1_3
21. Wei, J., et al.: Finetuned language models are zero-shot learners. In: International Conference on Learning Representations (2022). https://openreview.net/forum?id=gEZrGCozdqR
22. Wei, J., et al.: Chain-of-thought prompting elicits reasoning in large language models (2023). https://arxiv.org/abs/2201.11903

Similarity Ranking of Case Law Using Propositions as Features

Damian Curran$^{(\boxtimes)}$ ⓘ and Mike Conway ⓘ

School of Computing and Information Systems, University of Melbourne, Parkville, VIC 3010,
Australia
dc.damian.curran@gmail.com, mike.conway@unimelb.edu.au

Abstract. In common law legal systems judges use previous similar cases, known
as *precedent*, to determine how the case they are currently hearing should be
decided. Task 1 of the 2024 *Competition on Legal Information and Extrac-
tion/Entailment (COLIEE)* is designed to emulate the task of retrieving these
similar cases. This paper summarizes the approach of the second placed team,
University of Melbourne Natural Language Processing (UMNLP) in Task 1 of the
2024 COLIEE. We have developed a pairwise similarity ranking framework. We
train a feed forward neural network to perform a binary classification task, based
on a multitude of features from each query-candidate case pair. Those features
include the extraction and similarity matching for a novel feature which we call a
'proposition' (a short summary of the basis upon which a noticed case has been
cited), as well as the name of the judge deciding the case, verbatim quotations
from the text, and several other novel features.

Keywords: Legal case retrieval · pairwise similarity · caselaw feature extraction

1 Introduction

In common law legal systems judges use previous similar cases, known as precedent,
to determine how the case they are currently hearing should be decided. A key skill
of legal researchers and practitioners, therefore, is the ability to retrieve similar cases
based on the facts of a new case. Task 1 of the 2024 *Competition on Legal Information
and Extraction/Entailment (COLIEE)* is designed to emulate those case retrieval tasks.
Participants are required to develop automated methods of identifying, for each 'query'
case, a subset of cases which were 'noticed' in the query case. A case is 'noticed' if it is
referred to by name in the case text by the authoring judge. The noticed cases are selected
from a large set of 'candidate' cases. The task is made challenging by the redaction of
any direct references in the query cases to the corresponding noticed cases, such as case
names or citations.

The same case matching problem (albeit with different datasets) was also posed in
earlier COLIEE competitions. In 2023, the top ranking approach used a structure aware
pre-trained language model, coupled with a learning to rank method with a gradient
boosting machine and other pre- and post- processing techniques [1]. In 2022 the top

T. Suzumura and M. Bono (Eds.): JSAI-isAI 2024, LNAI 14741, pp. 156–166, 2024.
https://doi.org/10.1007/978-981-97-3076-6_11

ranking team trained a binary classifier based on the cosine distances between all pairwise paragraph embeddings, combined with other pre- and post- processing techniques [2]. These recent approaches all utilize forms of transformer based language models (such as SAILER [3] or the all-mpnet-base-v2 model [4]) to encode semantic representations of the case text, followed by a pairwise analysis of each query-candidate case pair. The successful approaches were also supplemented with pre- and post- processing techniques such as the removal of non-English content and heuristic rules relating to the year identified in the case text [2, 5].

In this paper, we have built on these earlier approaches and developed a pairwise similarity ranking framework. Specifically, we trained a feed forward neural network to perform a binary classification task, based on a multitude of features from each query-candidate case pair. Those features include the extraction and similarity matching for a novel feature which we call a 'proposition' (a short summary of the basis upon which a noticed case has been cited), as well as the name of the judge deciding the case, verbatim quotations from the text, and several other features. At inference, we ranked the probability of a positive match for each query-candidate case pair and used simple heuristics to select the set of noticed cases for each query case.

Our team ranked second of the ten teams who made submissions in Tasks 1 (and third of the twenty-six individual submissions), with a maximum F1 score of 0.4134.

2 Methodology

2.1 Overview of Our Approach

We used a pairwise similarity ranking framework. We first extracted statistical and semantic features from each case after performing various pre-processing tasks. We then compared these case-level features to obtain a set of numerical features for each query-candidate case pair. We labelled each query-candidate case pair in which the candidate case was noticed for that query case in the training data with a 1. All other query-candidate case pairs were labelled 0. We trained a fully connected feed forward neural network in binary classification on this dataset. We applied the trained classifier to the test case pairs, ranked each pair in descending order of probability of a positive classification, and applied heuristics to extract the final prediction sets. We set out below the details of each step in this approach.

2.2 Dataset

The 2024 COLIEE Task 1 data was comprised of text files. Each text file was a complete judgment from the Federal Court of Canada, save that certain identifying information such as case names and citations were removed or replaced with placeholders.

The training dataset contained 5,616 unique cases, including 1,278 query cases, and 4,162 cases which were a noticed case in at least one of those query cases. There were 220 cases in the training set which were neither query nor noticed cases. These were ignored.

The test dataset contained 1,734 cases, including 400 query cases. We assumed that all test cases which are not query cases were noticed at least once, and that the query cases were never noticed. Under these assumptions, the task complexity was reduced to matching 400 query cases to 1,334 candidate cases.

As discussed further below, we also developed an additional custom dataset which we used to fine-tuned a t5 transformer model to extract 'propositions' from the query case text.

2.3 Case Feature Extraction

We extracted a variety of statistical and semantic features from each case and then conducted pairwise comparisons to develop a numeric feature set for each query-candidate case pair. Whereas in previous years' competitions, some of these pairwise features had been applied as post-processing logic steps (such as the exclusion of any candidate case which post-dated the query candidate case), we instead incorporate all relevant features into the pair data, often as a binary value, in order that the classifier integrate this implicit knowledge.

A full set of query-candidate case pair features is listed in Table 1. All semantic features are encoded using the HuggingFace *sentence-transformers/all-mpnet-base-v2* model [4], as applied by [2]. The removal of non-English text was conducted using the language identification transformer model *XLM-R* [6]. All word set preprocessing involved the lower-casing, stemming and the removal of English stop words. Sentence tokenization was conducted using the Python spaCy sententizer in the module *en_core_web_sm* [7]. Named entity recognition was conducted using the entity recognition tool in that spaCy module, limited to Event, Geopolitical, Law, Location and Organizational entities. Paragraph segmentation was conducted using regular expressions based on common paragraph numbering formats in the case text. Our full implementation can be found at https://github.com/dc435/COLIEE_2024_Task1. The notable and novel features are discussed in greater detail in the subsections below.

Table 1. Query-Candidate case pair features used to train the neural network

Name	Query feature	Candidate feature	Pair feature
prop_sent_cossim & prop_para_cossim	Proposition embedding	Sentence embedding & Paragraph embeddings	Maximum cosine similarity of all propositions and sentence/paragraph embedding pairs
prop_sent_jaccard & prop_para_jaccard	Proposition word set after preprocessing	Sentences word set & Paragraph word set, after preprocessing	Maximum jaccard similarity of all sets of proposition and sentences/paragraph pairs

(*continued*)

Table 1. (*continued*)

Name	Query feature	Candidate feature	Pair feature
prop_sent_overlap & prop_para_overlap	Proposition word set after preprocessing	Sentences word set & Paragraph word set, after preprocessing	Maximum proportion of proposition word set contained in sentence/paragraph word set of all pairs
prop_max_overall	Proposition embedding	Sentence embeddings	Maximum cosine similarity of all propositions and sentence embedding pairs for *all* candidate cases for that query case, but only if that maximum was found in the candidate case of this pair, else 0
entity_jaccard	Set of named entities in the case text	Set of named entities in the case text	Jaccard similarity between the sets
sent_jaccard	Set of words in the case text, after preprocessing	Set of words in the case text, after preprocessing	Jaccard similarity between the sets
same_case	n/a	n/a	Binary value 1 if the entity_jaccard and sent_jaccard exceed 0.90, else 0
entity_tfidf	String of named entities in the case text	String of named entities in the case text	TFIDF score based on fit of all named entity strings in train query cases
sent_tfidf	String of words in concatenated sentences, after preprocessing	String of words in concatenated sentences, after preprocessing	TFIDF score based on fit of all sentence strings in train query cases
quotes_any	Extracted quotations from case text sections containing a suppressed placeholder	Case text	Binary value 1 if any leading words in any quotation appear in the candidate text, 0 otherwise

(*continued*)

Table 1. (*continued*)

Name	Query feature	Candidate feature	Pair feature
check_year	4-digit year, being highest integer up to 2024 extracted from case text	4-digit year, being highest integer up to 2024 extracted from case text	Binary value 1 if the candidate year is smaller or equal to query year, otherwise 0
judge_pair_ratio	Judge name as string, extracted from first paragraph	Judge name as string, extracted from first paragraph	Decimal proportion of training instance matches in which (judge a, judge b) tuple appears, or mean of those values if no match in train data
judge_match	Judge name as string, extracted from first paragraph	Judge name as string, extracted from first paragraph	Binary value 1 if the judges match, 0 otherwise
hist_bins (x10)	Sentence embeddings	Sentence embeddings	10x histogram bin values between 0.0 and 1.0, representing the proportion of total cosine similarities for the case pair between sentences within that range. Akin to [2], but at sentence level

Propositions. In this section we introduce a novel feature of the query cases that we call a 'proposition.' This concept can be explained by its analogy to academic literature. In, say, a typical computer science conference paper, authors will cite other academic work. Every citation is typically included for the purposes of supporting a specific assertion being made by the author and can be linked back to a sentence or paragraph within the paper via in-line referencing, footnotes or endnotes. This contrasts with, say, a bibliography, which gives broader context to the citing document but may not be directly linked to a specific section of the work.

We hypothesized that, in a similar manner, most noticed cases are relevant to a specific sentence or paragraph within the query case, rather than to the query case as a whole. We presumed that a judge writing a court judgment includes citations to other cases (our 'noticed' cases) for the purpose of providing authority to a specific, pinpoint statement. That statement could be anything from a matter of legal principle, a legal rule, a finding from a previous case or a quotation from a previous case, to name but a few examples. If this observation is true in the cases in the COLIEE dataset, it follows that the reason why a case has been noticed in a query case may be found in the text immediately surrounding a citation (the '*neighborhood text*'), rather than in the balance of the query case text.

To explore this idea, we introduce the *'proposition.'* We define a proposition as the assertion which a citation is supporting. We seek to reduce a proposition to a single sentence summary in a third person, objective tone. For example, given the neighborhood text *"I agree with the Applicant on that matter, as it is well settled law that an appeal against a decision of the Tribunal is reviewable on the reasonableness standard [see Case X]"*, the proposition relevant to the 'Case X' citation is *"An appeal against a decision of the Tribunal is reviewable on the reasonableness standard."* A range of other proposition examples can be found in Table 2, along with the neighborhood text from which they were extracted. We hypothesize that such propositions, or semantically similar statements, will be contained in the text of the matching noticed case and should therefore have significant predictive value, or in any event, greater predictive power than the query case text as a whole.

Table 2. Proposition Examples

Original Neighborhood Text	Extracted Proposition
On this point, the Respondent argues that the Officer's conclusion that there was insufficient evidence cannot be read in isolation and must be considered in the context of the findings and summary of evidence prior to such conclusion. The Respondent states that this Court should not interfere with the Officer's decision unless it is outside the range of acceptable outcomes (citing < FRAGMENT_SUPPRESSED >)	The Court should not interfere with the Officer's decision unless it is outside the range of acceptable outcomes
For example, in < FRAGMENT_SUPPRESSED > Justice Tremblay-Lamer specifically addressed the second of the two conjunctive elements contemplated by paragraph 97(1)(b)(ii), in circumstances in which the first of those elements (personal risk) had been established. In this regard, she observed:	In circumstances where personal risk has been established, the second of the two conjunctive elements contemplated by paragraph 97(1)(b)(ii) can be specifically addressed
In the present circumstances, the adequacy of reasons should be examined in the context of the record before the Delegate. The Delegate accepted the recommendations made in the Reports, thus their content helps to serve as justification for and may constitute part of the reasons for the impugned Decision (<FRAGMENT_SUPPRESSED >)	The content of accepted recommendations can serve as justification for and may constitute part of the reasons for a decision

We extract the propositions from the query case text by first identifying placeholders. As noted in works from earlier COLIEE competitions (such as [8]), the query cases contain placeholder text such as 'FRAGMENT_SUPPRESSED', which are used in lieu of the actual citation in the original case text. Each query case may have none, one or many unique propositions, equal to the number of citation placeholders in the query case.

Because the information that comprises the proposition may variously precede, follow, or bridge the actual placeholder, and may cover several sentences, simple regular expressions may be insufficient to extract the proposition from the neighborhood text. We instead used a custom dataset and sequence-to-sequence transformer to address this challenge. For each placeholder, we generated a new paragraph with the text 'TARGETCASE' in lieu of the target placeholder. We then used a t5 pre-trained sequence-to-sequence transformer capable of, among others, question-answer tasks [9, 10]. We fine-tuned the model on a custom dataset to answer the question *"what is the proposition in TARGETCASE?"* when given the pre-processed neighborhood text as context. Our fine-tuning dataset of input-output pairs was developed by sampling the neighborhood text of placeholders in the training set cases and extracting the propositions from them. An example of the preprocessing and final proposition output is shown in Fig. 1. The full custom dataset and fine-tuning code can be found at https://github.com/dc435/COLIEE_2024_Task1.

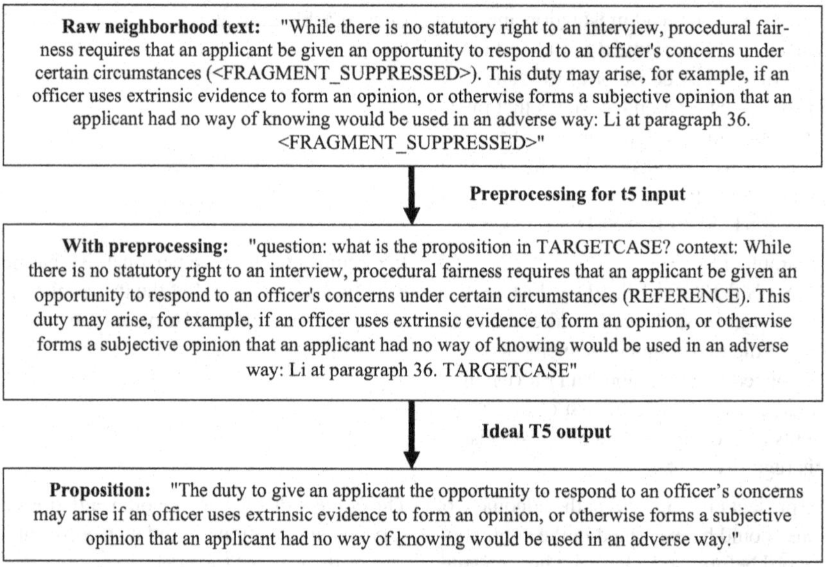

Raw neighborhood text: "While there is no statutory right to an interview, procedural fairness requires that an applicant be given an opportunity to respond to an officer's concerns under certain circumstances (<FRAGMENT_SUPPRESSED>). This duty may arise, for example, if an officer uses extrinsic evidence to form an opinion, or otherwise forms a subjective opinion that an applicant had no way of knowing would be used in an adverse way: Li at paragraph 36.
<FRAGMENT_SUPPRESSED>"

↓ **Preprocessing for t5 input**

With preprocessing: "question: what is the proposition in TARGETCASE? context: While there is no statutory right to an interview, procedural fairness requires that an applicant be given an opportunity to respond to an officer's concerns under certain circumstances (REFERENCE). This duty may arise, for example, if an officer uses extrinsic evidence to form an opinion, or otherwise forms a subjective opinion that an applicant had no way of knowing would be used in an adverse way: Li at paragraph 36. TARGETCASE"

↓ **Ideal T5 output**

Proposition: "The duty to give an applicant the opportunity to respond to an officer's concerns may arise if an officer uses extrinsic evidence to form an opinion, or otherwise forms a subjective opinion that an applicant had no way of knowing would be used in an adverse way."

Fig. 1. Example of the text pipeline to extract propositions using a fine-tuned t5 model

---

Once we had extracted the propositions from the query cases, we were able to apply a variety of similarity measures between each proposition and the full text of the candidate cases. These similarity measures were used as our pairwise features.

Quotations. An examination of the training cases showed that judges would often cite extracts from noticed cases verbatim. This allowed for simple exact string matching, which should have high predictive value for potential query-candidate case pairs. We used regular expressions to extract text within quotation marks and following a citation phrase such as '*who stated:*.' We then performed string matching to identify if the leading words from that quotation are found within the target case. These matches were converted to a binary value of 1 (for any match) or 0 (otherwise).

Judge Names. The name of the judge writing the case judgment was typically noted in the first paragraph of the case text. We extracted the name using regular expressions. For several reasons, we hypothesize that that the links between the judges in query-candidate case pairs may have predictive value. First, the judge may be more likely to cite themselves more than others, either because they have previously written a related case (such as a related procedural hearing) or are already familiar with the subject matter of their own cases. There may also be certain judges who are more commonly cited than others, either because they happen to have written the highly cited case law or happen to sit in the superior courts from where cases are more often cited. We incorporated the judges' names into a pairwise feature by identifying how frequently judge A cites a noticed case from judge B, as a proportion of all query-candidate case pairs in the training set.

2.4 Classifier Training

We trained a fully connected feed forward neural network on a binary classification task. We gave each query-candidate case pair a label of 1 (if the candidate case is noticed by that query case in the training set) or 0 (otherwise). Our training dataset contained over 5 million query-candidate case pairs. We replicated the positive samples in order to achieve an approximately 1:100 ratio of 1:0 labels. We trained our model for 15 epochs using an Adam optimizer with cross entropy loss [11].

2.5 Noticed Cases Selection Heuristics

We applied the trained model to all test query-candidate case pairs. We did not use any of the 400 query cases as candidate cases, as there were very few candidate cases which were also query cases in the training data and this choice greatly reduces the search space. We otherwise included all possible pair combinations. We then ranked the query-candidate case pairs in descending order of probability of a positive classification. We then used two different methods to select the final set. In the first method, we selected a probability threshold, p, (i.e. the probability of positive class 1, as extracted from the neural network model) above which all query-candidate case pairs were selected as a match. In the second method, we selected the top-ranking n pairs for each query case.

In both methods, we further presumed that all candidate cases are noticed at least once, and that all query cases have at least one noticed case. To that end, in both methods we also classified as a match the top ranked (by probability) pair for each candidate case, and the top ranked (by probability) pair for each query case.

2.6 Evaluation

We used cross-validation (4-fold) evaluation techniques on the training set to establish the optimum values of the hyperparameters p (the probability threshold for selection) and n (the number of top-ranking query-candidate case pairs for selection). We sought to optimize the F-score, being the metric used to rank performance in the competition. We found that 0.65 and 2 respectively were optimum values for p and n.

3 Results

There were 26 individual submissions from ten teams in the Task 1 COLIEE competition. The maximum and minimum F1 scores were 0.4432 and 0.0019 respectively, with a mean of 0.2322 and standard deviation of 0.1449. Our team ranked second of the ten teams who made submissions in Tasks 1 (and third of the twenty-six individual submissions), with a maximum F1 score of 0.4134. That submission used the probability threshold method to select the final query-candidate case pairs. Our alternative approach using the top-ranking n-pairs achieved a slightly lower F1 score of 0.4097. Our full results are shown in Table 3.

Direct performance comparisons to earlier COLIEE competitions are not possible, as each year new datasets are used. Nonetheless, the relatively low F1 scores reported in recent years (such as maximum scores from winning submissions of 0.3001 and 0.3715 in 2023 [12] and 2022 [13] respectively) show the difficulty of the task. Our relatively high scores compared to earlier years and relative ranking amongst the 2024 cohort suggest that our approach is robust.

Table 3. Results

Name	Settings	F1	Precision	Recall
Run 1 (using p threshold)	p = 0.65	0.4134	0.4000	0.4277
Run 2 (using n threshold)	n = 2	0.4097	0.3755	0.4507

4 Discussion

Our approach allowed us to use a wide range of metrics as features in our neural network model. Twenty-six numerical features were used for each query-candidate case pair. These different aspects of case similarity could be incorporated into the analysis whilst leaving the implicit feature selection to the neural network model. This approach may also have obviated the need to perform post-processing logic on final case selection, such as the elimination of candidate cases in which the year post-dates the query case.

We used a novel case feature called a 'proposition.' These are extracted from the neighborhood text immediately surrounding pin-point references to noticed cases. Our high ranking in the competition suggests that analysis of the specific reason for the incorporation of the noticed case in the query case, rather than just the similarity of the query and candidate case texts as a whole, has high predictive value.

However, the pairwise approach is computationally expensive. Each feature requires at least qc calculations (with q being the number of query cases, and c the number of candidate cases), as well as a range of pre-processing steps. Therefore, despite good overall performance in the competition rankings, due to time constraints we were unable to conduct any systematic feature improvement or identify which features contributed most to the performance.

Most notably, we did not systematically assess whether the generation of propositions improved system performance. In many cases we observed that the transformed 'proposition' text substantially mirrored the original neighborhood text from which it was derived. Our suspicion is that in many cases, simply using the raw neighborhood text in lieu of the transformed proposition may have resulted in equivalent performance. Nonetheless, we consider the inclusion of the proposition beneficial because it contributes to the explainability of the results. Namely, the propositions may provide a concise, plain language summary of *why* a noticed case was cited in a query case. Such information is itself verifiable by a legally trained person, could supplement legal case citation network analysis and explainable case matching (building on the work of [14]) and more generally be used to increase the interpretability of machine learning output applied to case law (as in [15], which used machine learning methods to extract legal factors from auto stop cases).

Due to time constraints, bar one experimental feature (*'prop_max_overall'*) we were only able to utilize the extracted propositions from each query case as pairwise features by selecting the maximum similarity score between all propositions and the target texts for each query-candidate case pair. This approach did not utilize all of the information extracted from the query case propositions, effectively ignoring any match which did not produce the maximum similarity score for that query-candidate case pair. There are likely to be better approaches available.

Nor were we able to systematically assess the relative performance gain (if any) of incorporating the year checks as model features instead of post-processing logic, or whether our hypotheses regarding the judge-pair features were valid.

These matters may be explored in future work.

5   Conclusion

This paper presents our pairwise similarity ranking framework in the COLIEE 2024 Task 1 competition. We trained a feed forward neural network on a binary classification task, based on a multitude of features from each query-candidate case pair. Those features include the extraction and similarity matching for a novel feature which we call a 'proposition', and several other novel features. Our team ranked second of the ten teams who made submissions in Task 1, with a maximum F1 score of 0.4134.

Acknowledgements. The authors received no specific grant to support this research.

References

1. Li, H., Su, W., Wang, C., et al.: THUIR@COLIEE 2023: incorporating structural knowledge into pre-trained language models for legal case retrieval. Published online first (2023https://doi.org/10.48550/ARXIV.2305.06812

2. Rabelo, J., Kim, M.-Y., Goebel, R.: Semantic-based classification of relevant case law. In: Takama, Y., Yada, K., Satoh, K., et al. (eds.) JSAI-isAI 2022. LNCS, vol. 13859, pp. 84–95. Springer, Cham (2023)
3. Li, H., Ai, Q., Chen, J., et al.: SAILER: structure-aware pre-trained language model for legal case retrieval. In: Proceedings of the 46th International ACM SIGIR Conference on Research and Development in Information Retrieval, pp. 1035–1044 (2023)
4. HuggingFace Sentence Transformers. https://huggingface.co/sentence-transformers/all-mpnet-base-v2
5. Vuong, T-H-Y., Nguyen, H-L., Nguyen, T-M., et al.: NOWJ at COLIEE 2023: multi-task and ensemble approaches in legal information processing. Rev Socionetwork Strat. Published Online First (2024). https://doi.org/10.1007/s12626-024-00157-3
6. Conneau, A., Khandelwal, K., Goyal, N., et al.: Unsupervised cross-lingual representation learning at scale. In: Jurafsky, D., Chai, J., Schluter, N., et al., (eds.) Proceedings of the 58th Annual Meeting of the Association for Computational Linguistics. Online: Association for Computational Linguistics, pp. 8440–8451 (2020). https://doi.org/10.18653/v1/2020.acl-main.747
7. SpaCy Documentation. https://spacy.io/models/en
8. Ma, Y., Shao, Y., Liu, B., et al.: Retrieving legal cases from a large-scale candidate corpus. In: Proceedings of the Eighth International Competition on Legal Information Extraction/Entailment, COLIEE2021 (2021)
9. Raffel, C., Shazeer, N., Roberts, A., et al.: Exploring the limits of transfer learning with a unified text-to-text transformer. J. Mach. Learn. Res. 21, 1–67 (2020)
10. Rajpurkar, P., Zhang, J., Lopyrev, K., et al.: SQuAD: 100,000+ questions for machine comprehension of text. In: Su, J., Duh, K., Carreras, X., (eds.) Proceedings of the 2016 Conference on Empirical Methods in Natural Language Processing. Austin, Texas: Association for Computational Linguistics, pp. 2383–2392 (2016). https://doi.org/10.18653/v1/D16-1264
11. Kingma, D.P., Ba, J.: Adam: a Method for stochastic optimization. Published Online First: (2014). https://doi.org/10.48550/ARXIV.1412.6980
12. Goebel, R., Kano, Y., Kim, M-Y., et al.: Overview and discussion of the competition on legal information, extraction/entailment (COLIEE) 2023. Rev Socionetwork Strat. Published Online First 12 January 2024 (2024). https://doi.org/10.1007/s12626-023-00152-0
13. Kim, M.-Y., Rabelo, J., Goebel, R., et al.: COLIEE 2022 summary: methods for legal document retrieval and entailment. In: Takama, Y., Yada, K., Satoh, K., et al. (eds.) JSAI-isAI 2022. LNCS, vol. 13859, pp. 51–67. Springer, Cham (2023). https://doi.org/10.1007/978-3-031-29168-5_4
14. Sun, Z., Yu, W., Si, Z., et al.: Explainable legal case matching via graph optimal transport. IEEE Trans Knowl Data Eng. 1–14 (2024)
15. Gray, M., Savelka, J., Oliver, W., et al.: Automatic identification and empirical analysis of legally relevant factors. In: Proceedings of the Nineteenth International Conference on Artificial Intelligence and Law, pp. 101–110. ACM Braga Portugal (2023). https://doi.org/10.1145/3594536.3595157

Pushing the Boundaries of Legal Information Processing with Integration of Large Language Models

Chau Nguyen$^{(\boxtimes)}$, Thanh Tran, Khang Le, Hien Nguyen, Truong Do, Trang Pham, Son T. Luu, Trung Vo, and Le-Minh Nguyen

Japan Advanced Institute of Science and Technology, Nomi, Ishikawa, Japan
`chau.nguyen@jaist.ac.jp`

Abstract. The legal domain presents unique challenges in information processing, given the complexity and specificity of legal texts. Addressing these challenges, this work leverages breakthroughs in Large Language Models (LLMs) to push the boundaries in legal information extraction and entailment. Our approaches involve the integration of LLMs in the COLIEE 2024 competition across four tasks: Legal Case Retrieval (Task 1), Legal Case Entailment (Task 2), Statute Law Retrieval (Task 3), and Legal Textual Entailment (Task 4). In Task 1, we employ a two-stage strategy that combines keyword-based retrieval using BM25 with a sophisticated MonoT5 reranker fine-tuned on legal datasets. For Task 2, we further adapt MonoT5, incorporating hard negative sampling. For Task 3, we introduce a novel strategy that utilizes LLMs to enhance the performance of high-recall predictions from smaller language models, an approach we also adapt for Task 2. To address Task 4, we employ an ensemble of LLMs' predictions, adjudicated via majority voting and the Dawid-Skene label model. Our strategies take advantage of the strengths of each model, with prompting techniques and constraints applied to exploit ensemble advantages. Consequently, we have achieved the top-ranked performance in Task 3 and secured promising outcomes in Tasks 1, 2, and 4. This paper describes our methodologies, offering insights into how integrating LLMs into legal information systems can significantly enhance their efficacy in tackling complex legal documents.

Keywords: COLIEE competition · Legal information processing · Large language models

1 Introduction

The intersection of artificial intelligence and the legal domain presents an array of challenges inherent to the nature of legal data - its complexity, formality, and domain-specific nuances [1]. One of the attempts to foster addressing these challenges is the annual COLIEE competition [2], which targets the automated processing of legal documents. The competition contains tasks involving case law and statute law, each with its retrieval and entailment challenges.

© The Author(s), under exclusive license to Springer Nature Singapore Pte Ltd. 2024
T. Suzumura and M. Bono (Eds.): JSAI-isAI 2024, LNAI 14741, pp. 167–182, 2024.
https://doi.org/10.1007/978-981-97-3076-6_12

Task 1 (Legal Case Retrieval) addresses an essential component of legal practice: the retrieval of precedent cases that support a given case law argument. This process is not only instrumental for lawyers in crafting arguments but also pivotal for judges and courts in the judicial decision-making process. Task 2 (Legal Case Entailment) is also about case law but with a distinct challenge: identifying specific paragraphs that entail the decision of a defined case. This task goes beyond retrieval to probe the understanding and logical analysis capabilities of machine learning models in discerning relevant legal arguments.

Tasks 3 (Statute Law Retrieval) and Task 4 (Legal Textual Entailment) challenge the complexities of statute law, a distinct branch of law that encompasses written legislation and statutory codes. These tasks replicate the structure of Tasks 1 and 2, respectively, but within the context of statute law. Task 3 focuses on retrieving relevant statutory provisions, while Task 4 requires models to demonstrate the entailing/contradicting characteristics of such provisions for specific legal statements. It is important to note that while Tasks 1 and 3 are primarily concerned with retrieval and serve as foundational stages for Tasks 2 and 4, respectively, they do not necessarily serve as prerequisites for the entailment tasks. As such, participants have the flexibility to approach each task independently, recognizing the interconnected yet distinct skills required for legal retrieval and entailment.

We tackle the four tasks with the integration of large language models (LLMs) in different ways. In Task 1, we combined keyword-based retrieval using the BM25 algorithm with a fine-tuned MonoT5 reranker to enhance document relevance scoring. For Task 2, we advanced the application of MonoT5 through strategic hard negative sampling. Task 3's methodology featured the utilization of LLMs to refine high-recall predictions from smaller models, with the intention of improving precision-a method also employed in Task 2. Finally, for Task 4, we deployed an approach adjudicating various LLMs' predictions with majority voting or the Dawid-Skene label model [3].

Our methods have resulted in a top performance in Tasks 3, and notable outcomes in Tasks 1, 2 and 4. This paper describes our methods, offering insights into the impact of large-scale language models and how their integration into automated legal systems can significantly improve the processing of complex legal documentation.

2   Related Work

2.1   Case Law

In COLIEE 2023 Task 1, the winning team THUIR [4] introduced a structure-aware language model for comprehending legal cases. They then utilized the fine-tuned models to predict relevant cases. The NOWJ team [5] proposed a two-phase matching approach: mono matching (at the paragraph level) using BM25 and a fine-tuned support model, and panorama matching employing a Longformer model to compare query cases and candidate cases. The JNLP team [6] employed a data augmentation technique to generate additional training data.

They then trained a large language model (LLM) on the augmented dataset to retrieve relevant cases.

For Task 2, the winning team CAPTAIN [7] employed a method based on pre-trained MonoT5 models that fine-tuned with hard negative mining samples. After fine-tuning, they ensemble the checkpoints to determine the final optimal weight. The ensemble model is then used to predict relevant paragraphs. THUIR [8] utilized two lexical matching methods, BM25 and QLD, to ensemble the final score for predicting relevant paragraphs. JNLP [6] used N Transformer models, with each model associated with a specific loss function. The final score combines all N models to predict the final answers.

2.2 Statute Law

In COLIEE 2023 Task 3, LLM-based approaches are commonly employed in the top-performing methods for retrieving relevant legal articles. CAPTAIN [7] used LLM-based ranking models ensembled with fine-tuned Tohoku BERT. JNLP [6] also utilized ensembles of BM25 for Japanese and LLM-based ranking model MonoT5 for English. HUKB [9] employed ensembles of keyword-based IR with different settings and LLM-based ranking models.

For Task 4, in performing the legal textual entailment task, the JNLP team [6] used a zero-shot method with LLMs and 56 different prompts. KIS [10] created the LUKE model, which undergoes data augmentation and ensembles BERT-based models and rule-based models. The trained LUKE model is then used to determine the final answer. UA [11] incorporated semantic information into BERT to enhance pragmatic reasoning and improve natural language inference.

3 Methods

In this section, we describe our methods. Because a part of our method for Task 3 is also applied to Task 2, we will present Task 3 and Task 4 first for the convenience of referring to when we present Task 1 and Task 2.

3.1 Task 3. The Statute Law Retrieval Task

Problem Statement. The goal of Task 3 is to identify a specific set of Japanese Civil Code Articles pertinent to a provided legal bar exam query labeled as Q. Participants must choose articles designated as A_i ($1 \leq i \leq n$), that correspond to the given question Q. Task 3 acts as a preliminary step for Task 4, where participants are tasked with determining the legality of Q by analyzing the pertinent legal articles.

Approaches. We developed three different approaches corresponding to three runs in our submission. The details are as follows:

RankLLaMA-Based Re-ranking. Expanding on the approach employed in prior research studies [12,13], we harness the capabilities of an encoder pre-trained language model and integrate specific negative sampling techniques to refine a model adept at extracting relevant articles from a legal corpus. In the training step, given an input query, we choose the top-k_1 relevant articles (e.g., $k_1 = 150$ as in [13]) using term matching techniques like TfIdf or BM25. Subsequently, these identified articles are paired with the query and fed into a pre-trained language model to identify and retrieve the relevant articles. In the inference step, the fine-tuned model initially retrieves the top-k_2 relevant candidate articles $R = [R_1, R_2, ..., R_{k_2}]$ (e.g., $k_2 = 5, 10, ...$). Subsequently, RankLLaMA [14] is employed to compute scores for each pairing of legal questions and the top-k_2 relevant retrieval articles. The highest-ranking article outputted from RankLLaMA is combined with the top-1 prediction R_1 predicted by the fine-tuned models for the final prediction A.

Few-Shot LLM-Based Re-ranking. Although LLMs have demonstrated robust performance in various NLP tasks [15], their limited context length poses challenges in applying them directly to legal retrieval tasks. To address this, we perform a two-step retrieval process using LLMs. Initially, we retrieve the top-k_2 relevant candidate articles (e.g., $k_2 = 5, 10, ...$) using a fine-tuned encoder language model on the legal dataset. Subsequently, these articles in R are inputted into LLMs to retrieve the final result A.

Similar to the RankLLaMA-based re-ranking approach, we fine-tune an encoder pre-trained language model on the COLIEE dataset. During inference, the fine-tuned model retrieves the top-k_2 relevant candidate articles $R = [R_1, R_2, ..., R_{k_2}]$. In the zero-shot setting, we input the candidate articles R and the query Q to LLMs using a well-designed prompt to generate the relevant articles A. The choice of prompt significantly impacts results, so we experiment with different prompts, evaluate their performance on a small scale, and refine the prompt based on errors to select the best prompt for generating the final answer.

Recognizing that few-shot settings often outperform zero-shot settings with LLMs [16,17], we further enhance our approach by providing demonstrations to LLMs. To achieve this, we extract a set of similar queries from the training set compared to Q using sentence-BERT [18]. We then create an input prompt using these queries along with their relevant articles and the current query Q. LLMs generate the final answer A using this input prompt. By offering demonstration samples to the input prompt, our aim is to enhance the LLMs' understanding of the task and achieve better predictions. Furthermore, through extensive experimentation with different LLMs, we found that Mistral [19] performed well in our legal retrieval tasks and decided to use this model for the run. An example of a few-shot prompt with LLMs is illustrated in Fig. 1.

LLMs to Refine High-Recall Predictions from Smaller Models. In the first step, we apply negative sampling and the fine-tuning strategies in [7] to fine-

---

User: Articles:
Article 424 (1) An obligee may demand the court to rescind an act which the obligor commits ...
Article 425 A final and binding judgment upholding demand for rescission of fraudulent act is ...
...

Statement:
The rescission of a fraudulent act is performed by the court based on the demand of the obligee.

Question:
Which article(s) is needed to clarify the correctness of the statement?

Assistant: The answer(s) is/are: Article 424.

User: Articles:
Article 126 The right to rescind an act is extinguished by the operation of the prescription if it ...
Article 425 The period of the extinctive prescription provided for in Article 166, paragraph (2) ...
...

Statement:
The right to rescind an act induced by fraud is extinguished by prescription, if the obligee does ...

Question:
Which article(s) is needed to clarify the correctness of the statement?

Assistant:

Fig. 1. Example prompt for retrieving statute law. The content enclosed within the dashed box represents demonstrations utilized in the few-shot setting and would be excluded in the zero-shot setting.

tune Tohoku BERT model and ensemble the predictions of top checkpoints to get top-5 relevant legal articles for each legal query. It is noticeable to note that while each query has one or two relevant legal articles, the top retrieval lists have good coverage with a recall of around 90%, which is much better than the other approaches in COLIEE 2023. Based on this observation, we integrate LLMs to process the top-5 retrieval lists as a further filtering step. In particular, we zero-shot prompted with large language models Orca-2 13B (https://huggingface.co/microsoft/Orca-2-13b) and Qwen 14B (https://huggingface.co/Qwen/Qwen-14B-Chat) on the above lists to get a more concise list of retrieval. In detail, we ask the LLMs whether each article in the top-5 list entails the legal query, as well as whether each combination of two legal articles in the top-5 list entails the query; then we ensemble the results with the confidence scores to produce retrieval list of each LLM. Next, we joined the retrieval list of Orca, Qwen, and constrained those lists by the top-2 of the Tohoku BERT predictions. This constraint reduced the recall but kept the precision higher. Finally, we joined the constrained retrieval list with the retrieval list produced by the Mistral model, as we observed that the Mistral model produces quite a different retrieval list than the others, and joining them boosted the F2 score in our validation set.

3.2   Task 4. The Legal Textual Entailment Task

With the robustness of large language models, we decided to employ them in the legal textual entailment task. The inherent attributes of LLMs, including their profound contextual understanding, adept handling of intricate linguistic structures, and discernment of semantic relationships, substantially enhance the precision and efficacy of the textual entailment process within legal domains.

Prompt Collecting. It is proved that prompt can play an essential part in affecting the performance of LLMs in zero-shot settings [20,21]. Therefore, we use all the prompts from the GLUE tasks provided by PromptSource library [22], converting to the JSON format (Listing 1.1) applicable to the chosen models for the legal textual entailment task.

```
[
  {
    "id": 0,
    "label": [
      "True",
      "False"
    ],
    "prompt": "< relevant_articles >
               Question: < query > True or False?"
  },
  ...
]
```

Listing 1.1. Prompt set for Task 4

LLMs Running. Every pair of query Q and relevant articles S, derived from the gold labels of Task 3, is replaced into the $<query>$ and $<relevant\_articles>$ tags in the prompt, respectively. That is the input to the LLM models loaded by the Huggingface library. The models then generate output text. Then, we extract the "True" or "False" from the output text as the predicted answer.

Prompt Selection. To evaluate the effectiveness of prompts for each model, we run the set of prompts on the provided dataset. Based on the performance, we choose the best n prompts as their input prompts. In the experiments, we chose $n = 2$.

Models Ensembling. We have experimented with various combinations of models and prompts. Each model and prompt is evaluated for its potential to complement the others, acknowledging the reciprocal enhancement they may offer. Through this thorough exploration, we aim to discern synergies that result in superior performance. Following rigorous assessment, we designate the most effective combination as the final model for subsequent inference.

3.3   Task 1. Case Law Retrieval Task

The first task of COLIEE is legal case retrieval: Given a query case document as input, the system must retrieve "noticed" legal case documents from a dataset of past legal cases that support the decision of the query case. For evaluating the performance of the retrieval system, this task employs precision, recall, and F1-measure metrics, with precision, are the number of correctly retrieved cases for all queries divided by the number of retrieved cases for all queries, and recall is the number of correctly retrieved cases for all queries divided by the number of relevant cases for all queries. As legal documents are often long and use complex structure and language, this task is particularly challenging, with the participants of past competitions only achieving marginal F1 scores.

To handle the long document retrieval problem in this task, we perform a paragraph-level 2-stage retrieval and re-ranking process. Figure 2 depicts our approach to this task.

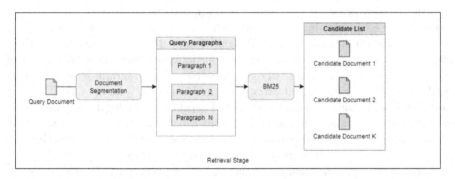

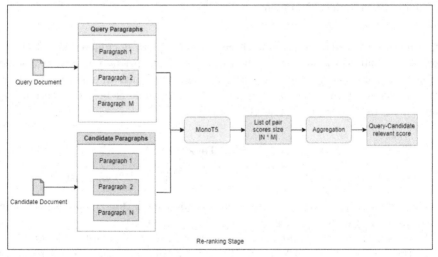

Fig. 2. Our approach for Task 1

Retrieval. In the retrieval stage, for each document in the dataset, we perform segmentation into paragraphs by using regular expressions to capture the paragraph citation indexes [id] that appear at the beginning of each paragraph. We then use the BM25 to index each paragraph. For each query document, we perform sparse retrieval using BM25 on each paragraph of the query with a top-k cutout and merge the result of each paragraph to obtain the candidate set for each query document.

Re-ranking. With each query document now having a corresponding candidate document set with a cardinality much lower than the number of documents in the dataset, we deploy a point-wise re-ranking model for scoring each query-candidate document pair and then sort the candidate set by a score to obtain the refined ranking list for each query. In preliminary experiments, we tested the bi-encoder approach on the full-length document query and candidate pairs with the Legal-domain adapted Longformer models from [23,24]. We extracted the embedding vectors for each document and applied cosine similarity to calculate the score for each pair, but the results were suboptimal. We hypothesized that the complex structure and nuance of legal documents make it difficult for deep-learning models to process and generate meaningful embeddings, so instead of processing the whole document at once, we deployed a paragraph-wise re-ranking strategy. Firstly, we fine-tuned variants of the MonoT5 [25] on the COLIEE 2023 Task 2 dataset for determining the degree of entailment of a legal decision-related paragraph and a candidate paragraph from a past case. After the fine-tuning stage, for each query-candidate document pair, we used the fine-tuned MonoT5 to predict the entailment score of each pair and then we max-aggregated the list of pair scores to get the final score that is used to represent the relevant score of the query-candidate documents.

Prediction. After the re-ranking stage, for each query document, we select the top-k candidate documents from the re-ranked list as prediction with k selected using grid-search on the validation set. We also developed an ensemble strategy by concatenating the prediction results of the re-rankers before selecting the top-k to boost the recall metric of the system.

3.4   Task 2. Case Law Entailment Task

For this task, we submitted 3 runs, "07f39", "join", and "join-constr":

- Run name: "07f39": In this approach, we fine-tuned MonoT5 on the training set of Task 2 with hard negative sampling, following [7].
- Run names: "join", "join-constr": For those runs, we attempted to apply the method we used for Task 3 into Task 2. We obtained the ranked retrieval list from MonoT5 (i.e., Run name "07f39" above). We observed that top-5 retrieval has high recall. Hence, we prompted large language models (with

many prompts) to get the concise retrieval list based on the top-5 candidates. In the Run name "join", we simply joined the predictions of LLMs on high-performance prompts. In the Run name "join-constr", we joined the predictions of LLMs on high-performance prompts, then constrained the ensembled predictions by the MonoT5 predictions (i.e., only predictions which are outputted by MonoT5 and other large language models are kept).

4 Experiments

4.1 Task 3. The Statute Law Retrieval Task

Dataset. The retrieval corpus is the Japanese Civil Code, which comprises 768 legal articles. The test set this year contains 109 legal queries. During the development phase, we selected the test sets of COLIEE 2021, 2022, 2023 to serve as our validation sets.

Submissions. We submitted 3 runs: JNLP.RankLLaMA for the *RankLLaMA-based re-ranking* approach, JNLP.Mistral for the *Few-shot LLM-based re-ranking* approach, and JNLP.constr-join for the *LLMs to refine high-recall predictions from smaller models* approach.

Experimental Results. The results on our validation sets are presented in Table 1. Our approach achieved a higher F2 score than the best system's top performance in the corresponding competition.

Table 1. Task 3: Performance of our approaches on the validation sets.

	JNLP.RankLLaMA			JNLP.Mistral			JNLP.constr-join		
	Precision	Recall	F2 score	Precision	Recall	F2 score	Precision	Recall	F2 score
COLIEE 2021	0.7346	0.7963	**0.7689**	0.6790	0.7901	0.7456	0.6533	0.8148	0.7540
COLIEE 2022	0.8486	0.8378	0.8292	0.7836	0.8396	0.8084	0.7638	0.8827	**0.8311**
COLIEE 2023	0.6931	0.7030	0.6865	0.7756	0.8515	0.8129	0.7642	0.9050	**0.8471**

Official Test Results. Table 2 demonstrates the results of Task 3 of COLIEE 2024. Note that we only keep the best results of other teams due to space reasons. One of our approaches achieved the top F2 score. Besides, our approach also gets top rank on recall and R_5, which meets our expectations for those metrics.

Table 2. Results of Task 3 in COLIEE 2024. Our runs are underlined.

Run name	F2 score	Precision	Recall	MAP	R_5	R_10	R_30
JNLP.constr-join	**0.7408**	0.6502	**0.7982**	0.8010	**0.8769**	0.9154	0.9462
CAPTAIN.bjpAllMonoT5	0.7335	0.6713	0.7752	**0.8149**	0.8615	**0.9308**	0.9538
TQM-run1	0.7171	**0.7202**	0.7339	0.7899	0.8308	0.9000	**0.9615**
JNLP.Mistral	0.7123	0.6682	0.7477	0.7434	0.8308	0.9154	0.9538
NOWJ-25mulreftask-ens	0.7081	0.6334	0.7661	0.7562	0.8231	0.8769	0.9077
AMHR02	0.6876	0.5972	0.7569	0.7405	0.7846	0.8308	0.8462
NOWJ-25multask-ens	0.6654	0.5934	0.7431	0.7180	0.7231	0.8077	0.8692
JNLP.RankLLaMA	0.6555	0.6606	0.6651	0.7400	0.8385	0.9154	0.9538
UA-mp_net	0.6409	0.4908	0.7385	0.7127	0.8000	0.8538	0.9000
BM24-1	0.4945	0.2590	0.7294	–	–	–	–
MIG2	0.1665	0.1604	0.1881	0.2125	0.2615	0.2923	0.3769
PSI01	0.0785	0.0826	0.0780	0.2312	0.3692	0.4769	0.6308

4.2   Task 4. The Legal Textual Entailment Task

Dataset. The dataset we use for experiments in Task 4 is similar to the dataset used for Task 3 but for the task of textual entailment. It contains 996 questions and a legal corpus (Civil Code) with 768 articles. For the validating and testing step, we used the questions in R01 (111 questions), R02 (81 questions), and R03 (106 questions). The remaining questions are used for the training process.

Model Usages. We used Qwen 14B, Mixtral8x7B, Flan-T5, and Flan-Alpaca models.

- *Qwen* (abbreviated as Tongyi Qianwen) is a large language model introduced by Alibaba Cloud. In this experiment, we use the 14B-parameter version. Positioned as a transformer-based large language model, Qwen-14B undergoes pre-training on an extensive corpus, including web texts, literary works, programming codes, and other diverse sources.
- *Mixtral8x7B* is a sparse mixture-of-experts network operating as a decoder-only model, wherein the feedforward block selectively draws from eight distinct parameter groups. Within this architecture, a router network is engaged at each layer and for every token, facilitating the dynamic selection of two expert groups. These chosen groups then process the token, with their outputs amalgamated additively.
- *Flan-T5*, an open-source LLM with unrestricted commercial usability, was introduced by researchers at Google. Functioning as an encoder-decoder model, Flan-T5 has undergone pre-training on a diverse range of language tasks, encompassing both supervised and unsupervised datasets. The primary objective of this training is to acquire a comprehensive understanding of the mappings between sequences of text, a paradigm commonly referred to as text-to-text.

- *Flan-Alpaca* is a version of Flan-T5 fine-tuned on the Stanford Alpaca synthetic instruction dataset.

It is worth noting that the training data of *Flan-T5* and *Flan-Alpaca* are fully disclosed while that of *Qwen* and *Mixtral8x7B* are not fully disclosed.

Submissions. For each of the three runs in Task 4, we prompted different LLM and ensemble their results using majority voting (JNLP1, JNLP2) or the Dawid-Skene label model (JNLP3), following [26]. The LLM used in 3 runs are as follows:

- JNLP1: Qwen + Mixtral + Flan-T5 (top-2 prompt) + Flan-Alpaca (top-1 prompt)
- JNLP2: Qwen + Mixtral + Flan-T5 (top-2 prompt) + Flan-Alpaca (top-2 prompt)
- JNLP3: Mixtral + Flan-T5

Table 3. Performance of LLMs on Task 4 development sets (R01-R04)

Model	R01	R02	R03	R04
Flan-T5	67.57	80.25	74.31	77.23
Flan-Alpaca	64.86	80.25	78.90	76.24
Qwen-72B	71.17	82.72	76.15	72.28
Mixtral 8x7B	70.27	74.07	70.64	67.33
Flan-T5 Ensemble (top-4 prompts)	66.67	81.48	74.31	76.24
Flan-Alpaca Ensemble (top-4 prompts)	65.77	79.01	77.98	76.24
JNLP1	69.37	79.01	78.89	81.18
JNLP2	78.57	72.97	82.72	78.89
JNLP3	63.96	81.48	–	80.20

Experimental Results. Table 3 shows the performance of different LLMs on the development sets (R01-R04). The results show that the performance of the LLMs fluctuates noticeably in different development sets. One model performing well on one set does not guarantee good performance on other sets, suggesting a potential approach of ensembling multiple models. For Flan-T5 and Flan-ALpaca, we also show the performance when ensembling the results of top-4 prompts from PromptSource.

Official Test Results. Table 4 shows the official evaluation results of COLIEE 2024 Task 4. JNLP1 has the best performance among the three runs and achieved the runner-up place in COLIEE 2024.

Table 4. Official Results of Task 4

Run name	Accuracy (%)
CAPTAIN2	**82.57**
JNLP1	81.65
UA_slack	79.82
JNLP2	78.90
AMHR.ensembleA50	77.06
HI1	75.23
NOWJ.pandap46	75.23
JNLP3	73.39
OVGU1	70.64
KIS2	69.72
MIG	63.30

4.3   Task 1. Case Law Retrieval

Dataset. The dataset of Task 1 consists of a training set with gold labels for each query and a test set. In the exploratory data analysis stage, we observed that the training set of this year's competition contains the test set of the previous year's competition so we use the test set of last year's competition as the validation set to develop our approach. Table 5 shows the statistics of the dataset.

Table 5. Dataset statistics of Task 1 data

	Train	Validation	Test
# of queries	959	319	400
# of documents	4398	1216	1734
query/document ratio	4.59	3.81	4.33

Experimental Results. Table 6 and Table 8 shows the validation metrics of the components in our approach. In the retrieval stage, we use the BM25 Lucene implementation in the Pyserini (https://github.com/castorini/pyserini) open-source toolkit with k1=0.9 and b=0.4. We select the cutout top-k=100 in the retrieval stage. In the re-ranking stage, we fine-tuned 3 variants of MonoT5: MonoT5-base (castorini/monot5-base-msmarco-10k), MonoT5-large (castorini/monot5-large-msmarco-10k) and MonoT5-3B (castorini/monot5-3b-msmarco-10k) to use as re-ranker models. In the ensemble stage, we concatenate the re-ranked lists before selecting the top-k predictions.

Submissions. Our submissions are described below:

- MonoT5-3B (Run name: 07f39): BM25 (k=100) retriever with MonoT5-3B re-ranker.

Table 6. Task 1's validation set results

Retrieval	Precision	Recall	F1
BM25 (k=20)	12.11	59.57	20.13
BM25 (k=50)	7.06	71.48	12.85
BM25 (k=100)	4.96	74.25	9.31

Table 7. Task 2's validation set results

Run name	Precision	Recall	F1
07f39	0.8400	0.7500	0.7925
join	0.8246	0.7833	0.8034
join-constr	0.8103	0.7833	0.7966

- Ensemble 1 (Run name: 64b7b-48fe5): BM25 (k=100) retriever with ensemble of MonoT5-base and MonoT5-large re-rankers.
- Ensemble 2 (Run name: 64b7b-07f39): BM25 (k=100) retriever with ensemble of MonoT5-large and MonoT5-3B re-rankers.

Official Test Results. Table 9 shows the official results of Task 1. The evaluation results of our approach on the test set have a significant gap to the validation set, especially on the recall metric. As our approach depends on the first-stage retriever to gather good candidate documents for the second reranking stage, we suspect the performance gap could be due to the difference in the cardinality of the document pools between the validation and test sets. The test set has significantly more documents making it more challenging for the BM25 method to retrieve good candidates, hence impacting the recall of the first-stage retrieval and the overall performance of the system.

4.4 Task 2. Case Law Entailment

Dataset. The provided training data contains 725 samples, of which we split into 625 samples for training and 100 samples for validation. Test data contains 100 samples.

Table 8. Re-ranking results on the validation set

Re-ranking (k=100)	F1@5	Prec@5	Recall@5
MonoT5-base	30.41	27.23	34.42
MonoT5-large	33.67	27.83	42.60
MonoT5-3B (07f39)	37.54	32.65	44.16
Ensemble 1 (64b7b-48fe5)	35.75	29.16	46.21
Ensemble 2 (64b7b-07f39)	37.74	30.62	49.17

Table 9. Results of Task 1 in the competition

Run name	F1 (%)	Precision (%)	Recall (%)
TQM.task1_test_answer_2024_run1	**44.32**	50.57	39.44
UMNLP.task1_umnlp_run1	41.34	40.00	42.77
YR.task1_yr_run1	36.05	32.10	41.10
JNLP.64b7b-07f39	32.46	31.10	33.93
JNLP.07f39	32.22	33.47	31.05
JNLP.64b7b-48fe5	31.03	30.17	31.95
WJY.submit_1	30.32	27.00	34.57
BM24.task1_test_result.txt	18.78	14.95	25.22
CAPTAIN.captain_mstr.txt	16.88	17.93	15.94
NOWJ.nowjtask1run2.txt	13.13	8.95	24.65
MIG.test1_ans.json	5.08	5.16	4.99
UBCS.run3.txt	2.76	1.40	71.96

Submissions. We submitted 3 runs as described in Sect. 3.4.

Experimental Results. Table 7 shows our results on the validation set.

Official Test Results. Table 10 shows the results of Task 2 of COLIEE 2024. Again, we only keep the best results of other teams due to space reasons.

Table 10. Results of Task 2 in COLIEE 2024. Our runs are underlined.

Team	File	F1	Precision	Recall
AMHR	amhr.mt53bk2r.txt	**0.6512**	0.6364	**0.6667**
CAPTAIN	captainfs2.txt	0.6360	**0.7281**	0.5646
JNLP	07f39.txt	0.6320	0.6967	0.5782
NOWJ	t5.txt	0.6117	0.6181	0.6054
JNLP	join-constr.txt	0.6045	0.6694	0.5510
OVGU	2ovgurun1.txt	0.5962	0.5636	0.6327
JNLP	join.txt	0.5912	0.6378	0.5510
NOWJ	bert.txt	0.5197	0.5032	0.5374
MIG	task2.mig1.json	0.4701	0.5673	0.4014
AMHR	amhr.lsbk2m42.txt	0.3542	0.3617	0.3469

5   Conclusions

This paper describes our methods for the four tasks in COLIEE 2024. In this year's competition, although traditional sparse and dense retrieval approaches are still used to reduce the search space efficiently, LLMs and their techniques are actively employed in all tasks to improve performance. We employ various LLM techniques for different tasks, ranging from reranking the retrieval results to prompting directly to obtain entailment predictions. Different LLMs seem effective in different aspects of the data and approaches that ensemble these LLMs are shown to have more improved and robust results. The experimental and official results in COLIEE 2024 show the effectiveness of our proposed methods in all four legal tasks.

References

1. Nguyen, C., Le, N.-K., Nguyen, D.-H., Nguyen, P., Nguyen, L.-M.: A legal information retrieval system for statute law. In: Proceedings of ACIIDS (2022)
2. Goebel, R., Kano, Y., Kim, M.-Y., Rabelo, J., Satoh, K., Yoshioka, M.: Summary of the competition on legal information, extraction/entailment (COLIEE) 2023. In: Proceedings of ICAIL, pp. 472–480 (2023)
3. Dawid, A.P., Skene, A.M.: Maximum likelihood estimation of observer error-rates using the EM algorithm. J. Roy. Stat. Soc.: Ser. C (Appl. Stat.) **28**(1), 20–28 (1979)
4. Li, H., Su, W., Wang, C., Wu, Y., Ai, Q., Liu, Y.: Thuir@ COLIEE 2023: incorporating structural knowledge into pre-trained language models for legal case retrieval. In: COLIEE 2023 (2023)
5. Vuong, T.-H.-Y., Nguyen, H.-L., Nguyen, T.-M., Nguyen, H.-T., Nguyen, T.-B., Nguyen, H.-T.: NOWJ at COLIEE 2023–multi-task and ensemble approaches in legal information processing. In: COLIEE 2023 (2023)
6. Bui, M.Q., et al.: JNLP @COLIEE-2023: data augmentation and large language model for legal case retrieval and entailment. In: COLIEE 2023 (2023)
7. Nguyen, C., et al.: Captain at COLIEE 2023: efficient methods for legal information retrieval and entailment tasks. In: COLIEE 2023 (2024)
8. Li, H., Wang, C., Su, W., Wu, Y., Ai, Q., Liu, Y.: THUIR@ COLIEE 2023: more parameters and legal knowledge for legal case entailment. arXiv preprint arXiv:2305.06817 (2023)
9. Masaharu, Y., Yasuhiro, A.: HUKB at COLIEE 2023: statute law task. In: COLIEE 2023 (2024)
10. Onaga, T., Fujita, M., Kano, Y.: Japanese legal bar problem solver focusing on person names. In: Workshop of the COLIEE 2023 in the 19th International Conference on Artificial Intelligence and Law (ICAIL) (2023)
11. Rabelo, J., Kim, M.-Y., Goebel, R.: HUKB at COLIEE 2023: statute law task. In: COLIEE 2023 (2024)
12. Nguyen, H.-T., et al.: JNLP team: deep learning for legal processing in COLIEE 2020. In: COLIEE 2020 (2020)
13. Nguyen, H.-T., et al.: JNLP team: deep learning approaches for legal processing tasks in COLIEE 2021. arXiv preprint arXiv:2106.13405 (2021)
14. Ma, X., Wang, L., Yang, N., Wei, F., Lin, J.: Fine-tuning llama for multi-stage text retrieval. arXiv preprint arXiv:2310.08319 (2023)

15. Touvron, H., et al.: et al.: Llama 2: open foundation and fine-tuned chat models. arXiv preprint arXiv:2307.09288 (2023)
16. Brown, T.B., et al.: et al.: Language models are few-shot learners. arXiv preprint arXiv:2005.14165 (2020)
17. Liu, P., Yuan, W., Fu, J., Jiang, Z., Hayashi, H., Neubig, G.: Pre-train, prompt, and predict: a systematic survey of prompting methods in natural language processing. ACM Comput. Surv. **55**(9), 1–35 (2023)
18. Reimers, N., Gurevych, I.: Sentence-BERT: sentence embeddings using Siamese BERT-networks. In: Inui, K., Jiang, J., Ng, V., Wan, X. (eds.) Proceedings of EMNLP-IJCNLP, pp. 3982–3992 (2019)
19. Jiang, A.Q., et al.: Mistral 7b. arXiv preprint arXiv:2310.06825 (2023)
20. Kojima, T., Gu, S.S., Reid, M., Matsuo, Y., Iwasawa, Y.: Large language models are zero-shot reasoners. arXiv preprint arXiv:2205.11916 (2022)
21. Reynolds, L., McDonell, K.: Prompt programming for large language models: beyond the few-shot paradigm. In: Extended Abstracts of the 2021 CHI Conference on Human Factors in Computing Systems, pp. 1–7 (2021)
22. Bach, S., et al.: PromptSource: an integrated development environment and repository for natural language prompts. In: ACL: System Demonstrations (2022)
23. Niklaus, J., Matoshi, V., Sturmer, M., Chalkidis, I., Ho, D.E.: MultiLegalPile: a 689GB multilingual legal corpus. arXiv, vol. abs/2306.02069 (2023)
24. Chalkidis, I., Garneau, N., Goanta, C., Katz, D.M., Søgaard, A.: LeXFiles and LegalLAMA: facilitating English multinational legal language model development. In: ACL, Toronto, Canada (2023)
25. Nogueira, R., Jiang, Z., Pradeep, R., Lin, J.: Document ranking with a pretrained sequence-to-sequence model. In: Findings of EMNLP, Online (2020)
26. Nguyen, C., Nguyen, L.-M.: Employing label models on ChatGPT answers improves legal text entailment performance. Lecture Notes in Artificial Intelligence (2023)

NOWJ@COLIEE 2024: Leveraging Advanced Deep Learning Techniques for Efficient and Effective Legal Information Processing

Tan-Minh Nguyen[1], Hai-Long Nguyen[1], Dieu-Quynh Nguyen[1], Hoang-Trung Nguyen[1], Thi-Hai-Yen Vuong[1(✉)], and Ha-Thanh Nguyen[2]

[1] VNU University of Engineering and Technology, Hanoi, Vietnam
yenvth@vnu.edu.vn
[2] National Institute of Informatics, Tokyo, Japan

Abstract. The constantly expanding volume of legal information presents a growing challenge for legal professionals to efficiently handle their workload. COLIEE is an annual competition organized with four tasks about automated legal information processing, which aims to liberate some of the pressures. This paper presents our approaches for all four tasks in the COLIEE 2024, which involve legal case retrieval (task 1), legal case entailment (task 2), statute law retrieval (task 3), and legal textual entailment (task 4). We utilize state-of-the-art deep learning models like BERT, Longformer, large language models, and a joint learning approach. Of a total of 18 submissions in task 2, our best run was ranked sixth on the leaderboard. For tasks 3 and 4, our submissions achieved fourth and fifth places out of nine teams in the overall ranking.

Keywords: Legal information processing · COLIEE · NOWJ team · Joint learning · Large Language Model · Prompt engineering

1 Introduction

Legal AI is a specific field that involves the application of computer and artificial intelligence techniques to make law more effective and efficient. The swift advancement of AI-based tools will liberate legal professionals from the burden of labor-intensive tasks such as document searches and contract reviews. The COLIEE competition [4] is an annual event organized to support the research of legal information processing. The competition covers various challenges, including document retrieval and legal entailment.

This year, as is customary, the competition consists of four tasks, focusing on two different legal systems: case law and statute law. Task 1, case law retrieval, involves reading a legal case from the Federal Court of Canada database and extracting supporting cases for the decision of a given case. Task 1 could be

© The Author(s), under exclusive license to Springer Nature Singapore Pte Ltd. 2024
T. Suzumura and M. Bono (Eds.): JSAI-isAI 2024, LNAI 14741, pp. 183–199, 2024.
https://doi.org/10.1007/978-981-97-3076-6_13

considered the initial phase for task 2, the legal case entailment task. The purpose of task 2 is to identify whether a paragraph from supporting cases entails the decision of a given case. Meanwhile, Tasks 3 and 4 of the competition concentrate on the civil law system, which numerous countries, including Japan, Vietnam, and various European nations have adopted. Task 3, legal information retrieval, requires participants to identify articles that support a given question from the Japanese Bar Exam. After retrieving relevant articles from task 3, task 4 aims to answer "Yes" or "No" as the output for the given query.

COLIEE 2024 is the second year the NOWJ team participated in the competition. We tackle all four tasks by leveraging state-of-the-art models and ensemble techniques. In the first task, BM25 and Longformer are ensembled for an effective retrieval model, which can handle the length of the input sequence. Numerous experiments were conducted for the second task, showcasing the superiority of utilizing monoT5 and multilingual BERT training with weak label data [17]. For task 3, we employed a two-phase pipeline involving a pre-ranking BM25 step and BERT-based re-ranker following the multi-task model proposed in [9]. The weighted ensemble method is utilized to combine scores from different models. Finally, we study the performance of large language models and prompt engineering in the legal textual entailment task. Various experiments are conducted to validate the effectiveness of different prompts in the legal domain.

The paper is structured as follows. Section 2, 3, 4 and 5 describe each of the tasks respectively. Each section is divided into four subsections, which contain the task's problem definition, related works, proposed methods and experimental results. Finally, the conclusion and suggestions for future work are provided in Sect. 6.

2   Task 1: Legal Case Retrieval

2.1   Task Description

The Legal Case Retrieval task consists of identifying the noticed cases of a new case. Noticed cases are the cases that support the decision of a case law. Given a new case Q, this task requires extracting all supporting cases $\{S_1, S_2, \ldots, S_n\}$ of Q. For the first task of the competition, the principle evaluation metrics are precision, recall, and F1-micro. The formula for each measure can be found below.

$$\text{Precision} = \frac{\text{\# correctly retrieved cases for all queries}}{\text{\# retrieved cases for all queries}}$$

$$\text{Recall} = \frac{\text{\# correctly retrieved cases for all queries}}{\text{\# relevant cases for all queries}}$$

$$\text{F1-micro} = \frac{2 \times \text{Precision} \times \text{Recall}}{\text{Precision} + \text{Recall}}$$

In last year's competition, THUIR team [8] utilized pretrained language models to enhance legal case understanding. According to their findings, the summary part of a legal document and sentences containing SUPPRESSED flags are significant. They also reduce data noises by removing unimportant information at the beginning of a case document. With the pre-processing and post-processing techniques, they ranked first place in COLIEE 2023. Whereas, the runner-up in this task - IITDLI team - developed a multi-step approach to tackle task 1, including year, term, and feature extraction [2]. Specially, they use a year filter to refine the results as the support cases cannot be held after the base case.

2.2 Methodology

Before deciding the methods for this task, a short data analysis was conducted. In COLIEE 2024, a train set and a test set are provided by the organizers. The corpus is given as a flat list of files containing all query and noticed cases, for both the training and test datasets. The training dataset is described in a JSON file containing a mapping between the query case and a list of noticed cases.

Table 1. Task 1's data analysis

	Train set	Test set
No. cases in corpus	5616	1734
No. samples	1278	400
Average noticed cases	4.16	–
Paragraph/Case	40.78	44.14
Max Paragraph	1103	653
Word/Case	4490.96	4824.00
Max Word	86504	105472
No. duplicated clusters	823	11
No. duplicated files	1729	24

As seen in Table 1, there is a total of 5616 legal cases in the provided training dataset and 1734 cases in the test set, in which 1278 cases appear as the base cases with labels. The task in this year's competition will be evaluated with the result of predicting the noticed cases for 400 base cases in the test set.

Our proposed method is a combination of BM25 and a pre-trained Longformer. Given the extensive input length and the substantial number of legal cases in the corpus, conventional querying methods are time-consuming. To decrease the retrieving time, NOWJ team has decided to employ the BM25 algorithm from Elasticsearch to optimize the computation time for similarity scores. Besides, there are 33 samples with duplicated noticed cases in the training dataset. Therefore, data cleaning is necessary for any type of usage.

Data Pre-processing: The corpus contains a list of text files. These are raw legal documents retrieved from a predominantly Federal Court of Canada case law database. Most of the documents have a typical structure, divided into sections and paragraphs. Besides, there are a lot of data noises within the corpus such as duplication and line break errors. Therefore, a process of cleaning data was employed. The process includes removing duplicated files, eliminating duplicated labels in the training set, and extracting information from legal documents. Case id, the metadata, the year of the case, and the split paragraphs are extracted for each document in the corpus. The main purpose of this process is to acquire a clearer dataset for other processes without having to deal with redundant texts. This dataset is then utilized for BM25 document ranking and fine-tuning the Longformer model.

Okapi BM25: Okapi BM25 is a lexical-based algorithm for text ranking. This algorithm ranks multiple texts in response to a query based on the frequency of lexical terms. As keywords and specialist terms are often observed in the base case and its supporting documents, BM25 can be utilized to enhance our model's recall and reduce computational costs. The BM25 score of the query case q and candidate case c is calculated with the formula:

$$\text{BM25}(q, c) = \sum \frac{IDF(q) \cdot (k+1) \cdot TF(q, c)}{k \cdot \left(1 - b + b \cdot \left(\frac{len(c)}{avg(len(C))}\right)\right) + TF(q, c)}$$

where C is the legal corpus (e.g. $\{c_1, c_2, \ldots, c_i\}$), k is term frequency saturation, while b controls the impact of candidate case lengths.

In this work, the BM25 algorithm is employed to assess the similarities of each document in the corpus for the query cases. Given the computational intensity associated with the original BM25 in retrieving relevant cases from a corpus of 5616 candidates for 1278 base cases, an Elasticsearch server is utilized. Using Elasticsearch's BM25-based similarity ranking significantly accelerated the process. The outcomes of the BM25 ranking were subsequently utilized as a pre-ranking phase for Longformer.

Longformer: Longformer is a transformer-based model designed for handling lengthy data, as shown in Table 1, where the average document length is 4490.96 words. Unlike other transformer models with a token limit of 512, Longformer can process sequences of up to 4096 tokens thanks to an attention mechanism that scales linearly with input length. Subsequently, a pre-trained legal Longformer was fine-tuned using the cleaned dataset for document ranking.

The scores from BM25 and Longformer model are obtained and ensembled with the formula as follows. A grid search was conducted to find the optimal parameter α and threshold θ.

$$score_{final} = \alpha \times score_{bm25} + (1 - \alpha) \times score_{longformer}$$

2.3   Experiments and Results

Various experiments were conducted to find the optimal number of top cases retrieved by Elasticsearch BM25. Table 2 demonstrates the recall score of top-k noticed cases retrieved by BM25, evaluated on the training set. In our final submission, the top 200 cases were used to infer and ensemble with the results from Longformer model. The Longformer model is trained with the provided training data for three epochs with a label ratio of 1:2 and a train - test ratio of 8:2.

Table 2. Evaluation of each Top-k of BM25

Top-k	**200**	150	100	50	20
Recall	**0.6496**	0.5952	0.5289	0.4302	0.3254

The three runs are the ensemble results with different weights and thresholds for each run. Specifically, after a grid search was conducted, the optimal weights α are 0.7, 0.55, 0.15 and the optimal thresholds θ are 0.63, 0.71, 0.92 respectively. The detailed results are shown in Table 3. As recall takes precedence, the precision scores for all three of our runs are not notably high. The best run of our team ranks eighth in the overall leaderboard of each team's best runs based on the F1 score. Enhancements in precision are recommended for future endeavors to achieve a more favorable harmonic score.

Table 3. Task 1's final results on private test set (**bold** represents the highest score, underlined denotes our result)

Team	F1	Precision	Recall
TQM	**0.4432**	**0.5057**	0.3944
UMNLP	0.4134	0.4000	**0.4277**
YR	0.3605	0.3210	0.4110
JNLP	0.3246	0.3110	0.3393
WJY	0.3032	0.2700	0.3457
BM24	0.1878	0.1495	0.2522
CAPTAIN	0.1688	0.1793	0.1594
NOWJ (Run 2)	0.1313	0.0895	0.2465
NOWJ (Run 3)	0.1306	0.0957	0.2055
NOWJ (Run 1)	0.1224	0.0813	0.2478
MIG	0.0508	0.0516	0.0499
UBCS	0.0276	0.0140	0.7196

3   Task 2: Legal Case Entailment

3.1   Task Description

Given a decision Q of a new case and a relevant case R, a specific paragraph that entails the decision Q needs to be identified. We confirmed that the answer paragraph cannot be identified merely by information retrieval techniques using some examples. Because case R is relevant to Q, many paragraphs in R can be relevant to Q regardless of the entailment. This task aims to identify which paragraph entails the decision of Q. Task 2 will be evaluated with the same measures as the first task, with paragraphs instead of cases.

Having understood the task at hand, CAPTAIN (3 runs) [10] proposes an approach based on the pre-trained monoT5 sequence-to-sequence model, which is fine-tuned with hard negative mining and ensembling techniques. The ensembling stage involves hyperparameter searching to find the optimal weight for each checkpoint. The approach achieved state-of-the-art performance in task 2 that year, demonstrating the effectiveness of their proposed techniques. Similarly, THUIR team sets BM25 and a QLD model as baselines and also experimented with monoT5 [8]. Their run with monoT5 acquires second place in the competition.

3.2   Methodology

Common approaches to the legal case entailment task often involve using natural language processing (NLP) techniques to analyze and compare textual content. These approaches may include using pre-trained language models, such as BERT, or designing task-specific architectures to capture the entailment between cases. Additionally, incorporating attention mechanisms and fine-tuning strategies are also considered to enhance the model's understanding of the legal context. In this work, two approaches are experimented: multilingual BERT classification with weak labeling and monoT5 document ranking.

Multilingual BERT with Weak Labeling: The application of Multilingual BERT (Bidirectional Encoder Representations from Transformers) to address the challenges of multilingual NLP tasks is introduced. Multilingual BERT, a pre-trained language model, demonstrates its versatility by providing a framework for understanding and processing text across multiple languages. In COLIEE 2023, this method of utilizing multilingual BERT has produced promising results [16]. We decided to use this as the baseline and explored the potential of using weak labeling to enhance its performance. Weak labeling in NLP refers to the process of assigning labels to data instances using imperfect or noisy sources, such as heuristics, distant supervision, or rule-based methods, rather than relying on manually annotated ground truth labels. In [17], Vuong et al. applied a heuristics method to automatically extract supporting text-pairs from training dataset in COLIEE 2020 legal case retrieval task and created a "weak-labeling" dataset. Their dataset is employed in our method to enrich the training data for the Multilingual BERT model.

monoT5: monoT5 is a T5-based sequence-to-sequence model that is fine-tuned with the MS MARCO dataset for the task of document ranking. This model was first introduced by the authors in [13], and utilized for the legal case entailment task in COLIEE 2023 [10] demonstrating excellent results.

3.3 Experiments and Results

As shown in Table 4, three runs were submitted, corresponding to three different models: original mBERT, mBERT trained with weak labels, and the monoT5 model. The results from the original mBERT are expected to be lower than those of the other two. Weak labeling proves its contribution as it has improved the F1-score significantly by roughly 7.5%, from 0.5197 to 0.5946. The best run is produced by the monoT5 model and settles in fourth place on the final ranking. Future work would consider applying the weak labeling approach with state-of-the-art language models.

Table 4. Task 2's final results on private test set (**bold** represents the highest score, underlined denotes our result)

Team	F1	Precision	Recall
AMHR	**0.6512**	0.6364	**0.6667**
CAPTAIN	0.6360	**0.7281**	0.5646
JNLP	0.6320	0.6967	0.5782
NOWJ (monoT5)	0.6117	0.6181	0.6054
OVGU	0.5962	0.5636	0.6327
NOWJ (weak_label)	0.5946	0.5906	0.5986
NOWJ (BERT)	0.5197	0.5032	0.5374
MIG	0.4701	0.5673	0.4014

4 Task 3: Statute Law Retrieval

4.1 Task Description

Given a legal question Q selected from the Japanese Exam Bar, participating teams are required to retrieve relevant articles $A1, A_2, \ldots, A_n$ from the Japanese Civil Code. The organizer also provides an English translation of both legal question Q and Japanese civil law corpus.

Metrics used for evaluation in this task are the macro average of F2, precision, and recall. In addition, ordinary retrieval measures such as Mean Average Precision and R-precision are provided for better investigation of teams' performances. Each measure is calculated as follows:

$$\text{Precision} = \text{average of } \frac{\# \text{ correctly retrieved articles for each query}}{\# \text{ retrieved articles for each query}}$$

$$\text{Recall} = \text{average of } \frac{\text{\# correctly retrieved articles for each query}}{\text{\# relevant articles for each query}}$$

$$\text{F2} = \text{average of } \frac{5 \times \text{Precision} \times \text{Recall}}{4 \times \text{Precision} + \text{Recall}}$$

CAPTAIN team [10] developed an effective approach based on the hypothesis of *data diversity* that questions and articles from the Japanese Civil Code contain many categories. Particularly, they constructed sub-models that are assumed to be biased to some categories, training on different datasets to enhance the robustness of models. Finally, they employed the *main-auxiliary ensemble method* to combine all sub-model articles without decreasing the precision. As a result, the CAPTAIN team achieved the first rank with two runs leading the leaderboard.

4.2 Methodology

A statute law retrieval system often involves two main phases: a pre-ranking step based on term matching (e.g. TF-IDF or BM25) and a re-ranking step constructed on deep learning models like BERT and monoT5. The pre-ranking phase serves as a filter to identify candidate articles that are lexically related to the given query. This filter would reduce the retrieving time of the overall system while maintaining a relatively good recall score. Finally, a re-ranking phase based on state-of-the-art models and ensemble techniques is employed to produce final outputs to improve the precision of the previous step.

Our method for the statute law retrieval task study and ensemble the following types of approaches:

Lexical-Based Retrieval Approach: BM25 is a simple yet effective retrieval method based on the frequency and occurrence of query terms on a set of documents to estimate the relevance score between them. This method has computational and time complexity strength and is easy to implement in various real-world scenarios. Furthermore, BM25 has great performance on large datasets with high scalability, which is suitable for search engines and industrial applications. However, as BM25 computes relevance scores based on term matching, its precision may not be as good as other contextual matching retrieval methods.

Dense Retrieval Approach: The dense retrieval approach involves encoding input documents as dense vectors in high-dimensional space to represent the semantic information of documents. This representation enables dense retrieval models to capture complex relationships between queries and documents, making them effective when tackling synonyms or antonyms compared to the lexical-based retrieval models. These advantages of the dense retrieval approach allow efficient relevance search and ranking of documents. However, large amounts of labeled data and resources are required to construct a dense vector representation.

Joint Learning Approach for Legal Text Retrieval and Textual Entailment: Long et al. [9] proposed a multi-task learning architecture to exploit the supportive relationship between *relevancy* (article retrieval) and *affirmation* (textual entailment) for enhancing the performance of the retrieval task. Particularly, the multi-task model adopts a backbone of BERT with two different output heads and loss functions for article retrieval and textual entailment tasks. The two loss functions are combined with a ratio of 1 : 1, which reflects the equal contribution of both tasks in the overall performance.

Ranking Strategy: We employed a weighted ensemble approach to combine scores from different retrieval models. Each model is assigned a weight w_i present its contribution to the overall performance. A threshold $\mathcal{K}$ determines the most relevant articles as the final output. The optimal weight set $\mathcal{W}$ and threshold $\mathcal{K}$ are determined using the grid search method on the validation set.

4.3 Experiments and Results

As described in Sect. 4.2, the retrieval problem will be addressed through two steps: pre-ranking using the BM25 model and the first re-ranking phase using a BERT-based model with the multi-task design. We used 20% of the training set as the validation set to optimize parameters and weights. The specific implementation and deployment details of these phases will be thoroughly outlined in the following sections.

BM25 Pre-ranking Model BM25 is a lexical-based model with fast retrieval–time. Therefore, it is utilized in the initial phase with the task of filtering out lexically relevant articles, aiming to maximize recall. After obtaining the relevance scores from the BM25 model for all articles in the validation set, the top–k articles with the highest relevance scores are selected for subsequent re-ranking phases. The value of top–k is crucial as it directly influences the recall score of the entire retrieval system. To assess the impact of different top-k values, a statistical analysis has been conducted, and Table 5 presents the recall scores achieved with various top-k thresholds on the validation set.

Table 5. Recall score of each top-k using BM25 model

Top-k	**500**	400	300	200	100	50	**30**	10	5
Recall	**0.9498**	0.9362	0.9242	0.8993	0.8579	0.8130	**0.7847**	0.7149	0.6493

Table 5 demonstrates that $top-k = 500$ has achieved sufficiently high recall, indicating that the predicted candidate set encompasses nearly all truly relevant texts. Consequently, during the inference of the multi-task BERT model, $top-k = 500$ is utilized. Meanwhile, to ensure both speed and accuracy, as well as data-balancing, $top-k = 30$ is employed during training. The multi-task BERT models are trained for 3 epochs to prevent overfitting to the training set.

Multi-task Re-ranking Model. The BM25 model performed well in pre-ranking by effectively reducing a considerable number of candidate articles while maintaining a relatively high recall score. However, relying solely on lexical similarity can only achieve a high recall score (around 0.9498 with top-k = 500), which is not sufficient to improve precision. Therefore, a model based on the BERT architecture with multi-task design as described in the Sect. 4.2 is utilized as a re-ranking step to extract semantically relevant texts to the query, based on the candidates obtained from the pre-ranking step.

The training of the multi-task re-ranking model requires each training sample to be a pair (query-article) with a label of 0 or 1, corresponding to unrelated or related. In practice, during the inference on the test set, the multi-task re-ranking model also needs to select among the output candidates of BM25, which candidates are most semantically relevant to the query. Consequently, the articles chosen to form (query-article) pairs are extracted from the top-k most relevant documents according to the perspective of the BM25 model. To ensure a balanced distribution of labels and prevent the model from overfitting excessively, the top–30 documents with the highest BM25 relevance scores are selected to form the training set for the multi-task re-ranking model.

Due to the original language of the dataset being Japanese, Japanese is chosen as the language for training. The Multilingual BERT model, a pre-trained model trained on a multilingual dataset, including Japanese, is utilized to initialize parameters for the multi-task model. The model undergoes training for 3 epochs using the Adam Optimizer [7] with a learning rate of $1e-4$.

Inference Results Using the Weighted Ensemble Method. The experiments reveal that while the BM25 model excels in increasing recall, the re-ranking model performs admirably in narrowing down candidates based on semantic similarity and improving the precision of the predicted result set. To leverage the strengths of both models, the inference process uses the relevance scores from both the BM25 model and the multi-task model through the weighted ensemble method. To select the best set of weights for the model, a validation set was used to conduct the grid-search method, searching for the optimal ensemble weights. The best set of parameters will be utilized for inference on the test dataset. The optimized weights and threshold $\mathcal{K}$ in each run are as follows:

- Run 1 (multi-task + BM25): $W_{multi-task-en} = 0.3$, $W_{multi-task-jp} = 0.1$, $W_{BM25} = 0.6$, $\mathcal{K} = 0.3$
- Run 2 (mBERT-based + BM25): $W_{mBERT-en} = 0.3$, $W_{mBERT-jp} = 0.5$, $W_{BM25} = 0.2$, $\mathcal{K} = 0.1$
- Run 3 (multi-task + mBERT-based + BM25): $W_{mBERT-en} = 0.1$, $W_{mBERT-jp} = 0.2$, $W_{multi-task-en} = 0.1$, $W_{multi-task-jp} = 0.2$, $W_{BM25} = 0.4$, $\mathcal{K} = 0.3$

Table 6 presents the official evaluation of participants in the Statute Law Retrieval task. We submitted three runs with different approaches: combining relevance scores from the multi-task model and BM25, mBERT-based and BM25, and finally, all three models. By leveraging the advantages of all three models,

Table 6. Results of Statute Law Retrieval task in COLIEE 2024

	F2	Precision	Recall
Best run of other teams			
JNLP.constr-join	**0.7408**	0.6502	**0.7982**
CAPTAIN.bjpAllMonoT5	0.7335	**0.6713**	0.7752
TQM-run1	0.7171	0.7202	0.7339
AMHR02	0.6876	0.5972	0.7569
UA-anglE	0.6526	0.5596	0.7339
BM24-1	0.4945	0.2590	0.7294
MIG2	0.1665	0.1604	0.1881
PSI01	0.0785	0.0826	0.0780
Our runs			
Run 3	0.7081	0.6334	0.7661
Run 1	0.6654	0.5934	0.7431
Run 2	0.6649	0.5916	0.7202

this run achieved the highest score among the three runs, with an F2 score of 0.7081, which ranks fourth on the leaderboard. One significant aspect worth mentioning is that, despite not employing LLMs in any phase of our methodology, we still managed to attain highly competitive results, securing the fourth position on the leaderboard. Indeed, these results emphasize the potential of our approaches when competing with LLMs-based methods from other teams. However, there is room for improvement in precision, suggesting adding a step for further re-ranking. Future work could consider other ensemble and retrieval techniques, such as LLM-based re-ranker.

5   Task 4: Legal Textual Entailment

5.1   Task Description

In this task, participants are required to answer "Yes/No" bar exam questions based on retrieved articles from the previous task. The Legal Textual Entailment task could be described as follows: given a legal question Q and a set of relevant articles $A_1, A_2, \ldots . A_n$, a system must respond to an answer of "Yes" or "No" for each question. Therefore, the accuracy metric is used as the official evaluation measure for this task.

In COLIEE 2023, the JNLP team decided to leverage the performance of LLMs in a zero-shot approach for the legal textual entailment task. Their method consists of three main steps: Prompt Collecting, LLMs Deployment, and Answer Extracting. They experimented with various LLMs, ranging from 7B to 20B parameter models. JNLP team also emphasized the effect of different prompts when there was a 23% gap between the best-performing prompt and the worst-performing prompt. Consequently, they secured the top position in the competition, emphasizing the effectiveness and potential of LLMs in handling legal entailment tasks.

5.2 Methodology

The development of pre-trained language models such as BERT [3] and T5 [14] have dominant various domains in NLP, including the legal domain [11,17]. These models have great scalability based on pre-train and fine-tune processes, which helps them learn domain knowledge for specific tasks such as textual entailment [12,18].

In recent years, many researchers have focused their interest on large language models, which are language models with billions of parameters and are pre-trained on enormous amounts of data. Large language models like GPT-3 [1], and LLaMA [15] have shown their powerful performance in various downstream tasks and fields. Researchers have explored and implemented large language models within the legal domain through various studies. A study shows that large language models could learn a special kind of legal logic to perform the judgment prediction task [6].

In this work, we assess the performance of large language models in a zero-shot prompting setting for the Legal Textual Entailment task. Our method involves three steps: prompt collection, LLMs deployment, and answer extraction.

Prompt Collection. We construct the prompt collection following both zero-shot and chain-of-thought prompting. Legal reasoning techniques such as IRAC (issue, reasoning, application, conclusion) are applied to further improve the performance of LLMs [5,19]. Finally, we obtained a set of 50 prompts that could be used as instructions for LLMs.

LLMs Deployment. We experiment with some 3B and 7B parameters models (Panda-7B-v0.1[1] which is based on Mistral-7B-Instruct-v0.2 and FlanT5-xl[2]) using Huggingface slibrary. The phrases {premise} and {hypothesis} in the prompt template are replaced with the content of the question and article. If there is more than one relevant article, we concatenate them to form one hypothesis base. Finally, LLMs generate outputs for the given query, which could contain simple binary answers, or with explanations.

Answer Extraction. We constructed a scanning function that scans negative and positive patterns (e.g. "false", "true", etc.) in the generated answers. If the scanning function detects one of the negative patterns, it returns "N". If it meets positive patterns, it returns "Y", otherwise it returns "E". The reason is

---

[1] https://huggingface.co/TheBloke/Panda-7B-v0.1-GPTQ.
[2] https://huggingface.co/google/flan-t5-xl.

that some prompts may instruct models to generate neutral answers (e.g. "It's impossible to say", "What is the answer to this question?") instead of only binary answers. These neutral answers are considered inaccurate when evaluating the models' output. In addition, as depicted in Table 7, Panda-7B always generates explanations even when we instruct the model to answer only Yes/No.

After evaluating the performance of our models on a sub-set divided from the training set, the prompts with the highest accuracy are chosen as the ones used in the inference phase.

Table 7. Illustration of two models' outputs.

Model	Size	Output
FlanT5-xl	3B	True
Panda-v0.1	7B	True. The reasoning behind this is that, according to the given legal grounds, a contract of sales concluded by an adult ward is voidable, with the exception of contracts related to daily necessities or to any other act involved in day-to-day life. This means that the adult ward's consent, even if obtained with the consent of the guardian, may be rescinded except in cases related to daily life

5.3   Experiments and Results

This section presents our experiments with zero-shot learning and different prompting strategies. We also analyzed the performance of models with different sizes and pre-trained data. We validate models on 100 samples split from the training set. Each experiment is run 3 times to ensure the consistency of the results. The parameters for text generation are set as default.

Tables 8 and 9 present the accuracy of FlanT5-xl with different prompts on the validation set. The legal reasoning prompt (id 46) achieves a higher accuracy than other simple prompts. Table 9 presents top-3 lowest results on the validation set. Overall, the model could perform better with instructive prompts.

Table 8. Top-5 highest results of FlanT5-xl with zero-shot learning on the validation set. The phrases {premise} and {hypothesis} in the prompt template are replaced with the content of the question and articles.

Id	Prompt	Accuracy
4	Please determine if the following {hypothesis} is True or False based on the legal grounds:{premise}. Therefore, the hypothesis (True or False) is	0.6733
14	Assume it is true that {premise}. Therefore, {hypothesis} is guaranteed or impossible?	0.6733
10	{premise} Keeping in mind the above text, consider: {hypothesis} Is this always or never correct?,	0.6533
37	Exercise: read the text and answer the question by True or False. Text: {premise} Question: {hypothesis} ?	0.6467
46	Please analyze if the hypothesis is True or False according to the given legal reasoning approach. Approach: Issue, general rule, precedent, application, conclusion. Premise: {premise} Hypothesis: {hypothesis} True or False?	0.6467

Table 9. Top-3 lowest results of FlanT5-xl with zero-shot learning on the validation set. The phrases {premise} and {hypothesis} in the prompt template are replaced with the content of the question and articles.

Id	Prompt	Accuracy
26	Given {premise} Is it guaranteed true that {hypothesis}? Yes or no?	0.4967
30	{premise} Question: {hypothesis} Answer:	0.4933
33	Based on the following passage, {hypothesis}? {premise}	0.3467

Table 10 shows the results of 9 participants in the Legal Textual Entailment task in COLIEE 2024. We submitted 3 runs using Panda-7b, and FlanT5-xl with legal reasoning prompt, and combined outputs from different prompts. The runs using the Panda-7b model achieved the highest accuracy among the three runs, ranked fifth on the leaderboard. It suggests that appropriate instructions for LLMs could lead to better performance than combining results from different prompts. Future work would involve studies to leverage the advantages of LLMs, such as data augmentation and fine-tuning, instead of simple prompt engineering.

Table 10. Results of Legal Textual Entailment task in COLIEE 2024

	Accuracy
Best run of other teams	
CAPTAIN2	**0.8257**
JNLP1	0.8165
UA_slack	0.7982
AMHR.ensembleA50	0.7706
HI1	0.7523
OVGU1	0.7064
KIS2	0.6972
MIG	0.6330
Our runs	
NOWJ.pandap46	0.7523
NOWJ.flant5-panda	0.7339
NOWJ.bagging	0.7156

6   Conclusion

COLIEE 2024 competition provided a valuable opportunity for our team to explore and experiment with various techniques addressing legal NLP tasks. Despite the simplicity of our proposed methods, they demonstrated promising results across all tasks. Areas that could be further explored for improvement in case law tasks include developing techniques for managing long sequence data more efficiently and implementing more advanced ensemble methods, especially for task 2. Additionally, focusing on utilizing information more effectively from case documents may lead to better performance in both case law and statute law retrieval tasks. We look forward to employing the lessons learned throughout this competition to develop innovative approaches and solutions that advance the field of Legal AI.

Acknowledgement. Hai-Long Nguyen was funded by the Master, PhD Scholarship Programme of Vingroup Innovation Foundation (VINIF), code VINIF.2023.ThS.075. Additionally, this research was partly supported by the AIP Challenge Funding in relation to JST, AIP Trilateral AI Research, under Grant Number JPMJCR20G4.

References

1. Brown, T., et al.: Language models are few-shot learners. In: Advances in Neural Information Processing Systems, vol. 33, pp. 1877–1901 (2020)
2. Debbarma, R., Prawar, P., Chakraborty, A., Bedathur, S.: IITDLI: legal case retrieval based on lexical models. In: Workshop of the Tenth Competition on Legal Information Extraction/Entailment (COLIEE 2023) in the 19th International Conference on Artificial Intelligence and Law (ICAIL) (2023)
3. Devlin, J., Chang, M.W., Lee, K., Toutanova, K.: BERT: pre-training of deep bidirectional transformers for language understanding. arXiv preprint arXiv:1810.04805 (2018)
4. Goebel, R., Kano, Y., Kim, M.Y., Rabelo, J., Satoh, K., Yoshioka, M.: Summary of the competition on legal information, extraction/entailment (COLIEE) 2023. In: Proceedings of the Nineteenth International Conference on Artificial Intelligence and Law, ICAIL 2023, pp. 472–480. Association for Computing Machinery, New York (2023). https://doi.org/10.1145/3594536.3595176
5. Hoang, L., Bui, T., Nguyen, C., Nguyen, L.M.: AIEPU at ALQAC 2023: deep learning methods for legal information retrieval and question answering. In: 2023 15th International Conference on Knowledge and Systems Engineering (KSE), pp. 1–6 (2023). https://doi.org/10.1109/KSE59128.2023.10299426
6. Jiang, C., Yang, X.: Legal syllogism prompting: teaching large language models for legal judgment prediction. In: Proceedings of the Nineteenth International Conference on Artificial Intelligence and Law, ICAIL 2023, pp. 417–421. Association for Computing Machinery, New York (2023). https://doi.org/10.1145/3594536.3595170
7. Kingma, D.P., Ba, J.: Adam: a method for stochastic optimization. arXiv preprint arXiv:1412.6980 (2014)
8. Li, H., Su, W., Wang, C., Wu, Y., Ai, Q., Liu, Y.: THUIR@COLIEE 2023: incorporating structural knowledge into pre-trained language models for legal case retrieval (2023)
9. Long, N.H., Vuong, T.H.Y., Nguyen, H.T., Phan, X.H.: Joint learning for legal text retrieval and textual entailment: leveraging the relationship between relevancy and affirmation. In: Proceedings of the Natural Legal Language Processing Workshop 2023, pp. 192–201 (2023)
10. Nguyen, C., et al.: Captain at COLIEE 2023: efficient methods for legal information retrieval and entailment tasks. arXiv preprint arXiv:2401.03551 (2024)
11. Nguyen, H.T., et al.: Transformer-based approaches for legal text processing: JNLP team-COLIEE 2021. Rev. Socionetwork Strat. **16**(1), 135–155 (2022)
12. Nguyen, H.T., et al.: JNLP team: deep learning approaches for legal processing tasks in COLIEE 2021. arXiv preprint arXiv:2106.13405 (2021)
13. Nogueira, R., Jiang, Z., Pradeep, R., Lin, J.: Document ranking with a pretrained sequence-to-sequence model. In: Cohn, T., He, Y., Liu, Y. (eds.) Findings of the Association for Computational Linguistics: EMNLP 2020, pp. 708–718. Association for Computational Linguistics, Online (2020). https://doi.org/10.18653/v1/2020.findings-emnlp.63. https://aclanthology.org/2020.findings-emnlp.63
14. Raffel, C., et al.: Exploring the limits of transfer learning with a unified text-to-text transformer. J. Mach. Learn. Res. **21**(140), 1–67 (2020). http://jmlr.org/papers/v21/20-074.html
15. Touvron, H., et al.: Llama: open and efficient foundation language models. arXiv preprint arXiv:2302.13971 (2023)

16. Vuong, T.H.Y., Nguyen, H.L., Nguyen, T.M., Nguyen, H.T., Nguyen, T.B., Nguyen, H.T.: NOWJ at COLIEE 2023 – multi-task and ensemble approaches in legal information processing (2023)
17. Vuong, Y.T.H., et al.: SM-BERT-CR: a deep learning approach for case law retrieval with supporting model. Artif. Intell. Law **31**(3), 601–628 (2023)
18. Yoshioka, M., Suzuki, Y., Aoki, Y.: HUKB at the COLIEE 2022 statute law task. In: Takama, Y., Yada, K., Satoh, K., Arai, S. (eds.) JSAI-isAI 2022. LNCS, vol. 13859, pp. 109–124. Springer, Cham (2023). https://doi.org/10.1007/978-3-031-29168-5_8
19. Yu, F., Quartey, L., Schilder, F.: Legal prompting: teaching a language model to think like a lawyer. arXiv preprint arXiv:2212.01326 (2022)

AMHR COLIEE 2024 Entry: Legal Entailment and Retrieval

Animesh Nighojkar[✉], Kenneth Jiang, Logan Fields, Onur Bilgin,
Stephen Steinle, Yernar Sadybekov, Zaid Marji, and John Licato

Advancing Machine and Human Reasoning (AMHR) Lab, Department of Computer
Science and Engineering, University of South Florida, Tampa, USA
`anighojkar@usf.edu`

Abstract. This paper presents the methodologies and results of the participation of the Advanced Machine Human Reasoning (AMHR) group in the 2024 Conference on Legal Information and Information Technology (COLIEE). Our team participated in Tasks 2, 3, and 4, which focused on the legal case entailment, the retrieval of statute laws, and the legal textual entailment, respectively. In Task 2, we explore two approaches to identify paragraphs from older cases relevant to a given case fragment. The first approach used a fine-tuned legalBERT model, which resulted in overfitting, while the second approach employed a fine-tuned monoT5 model, augmented with hard negative mining, which won the competition for Task 2. In Task 3, our strategy involved sorting Civil Code articles using a fine-tuned MonoT5 model, followed by a large language model with post-processing for article selection, prioritizing the F2-score. Task 4 involved various prompting strategies using Google's flan-T5-xxl model, with a focus on ranked preference voting for top prompts to identify the entailment of legal queries from legal articles. Our methodologies used advanced deep learning techniques, tailored to the specific legal domain, and were supported by solid engineering practices, enabling competitive outcomes in the COLIEE 2024 competition. This paper details our approaches, providing information on the challenges and innovations in the field of legal AI.

Keywords: legal retrieval · legal entailment · natural language processing · monoT5 · hard negative mining · flan-T5

1 Introduction

COLIEE is an academic competition focused on developing algorithms for legal case retrieval and textual entailment. COLIEE features four main tasks: Legal Case Retrieval (find the relevant case(s) to a query case), Legal Case Entailment (determine cases that support the query case), Statute Law Retrieval (find relevant statute(s) for a legal query), and Legal Textual Entailment (determine statutes that support the query). Teams use natural language processing, machine learning, knowledge representation, and other techniques to develop

T. Suzumura and M. Bono (Eds.): JSAI-isAI 2024, LNAI 14741, pp. 200–211, 2024.
https://doi.org/10.1007/978-981-97-3076-6_14

systems that can effectively search, analyze, and draw inferences from legal documents and case data. The COLIEE competition uses a variety of datasets in its four tasks. The Task 1 dataset contains more than 5,700 files, with a training set of 4,400 cases (959 queries) and a test set of 1,335 cases (319 queries). The Task 2 dataset provides 625 training queries with 22,018 paragraphs and 100 test queries with 3,765 paragraphs. Datasets for tasks 3 and 4 are derived from questions from the Japanese bar exam linked to a subset of the Japanese Civil Code, with 996 training questions and 101 test questions from the 2022 exam [17].

In 2024, our team (the (AMHR) group) demonstrated notable success in Tasks 2, 3 and 4 of the competition.

- Task 2 is legal textual entailment, whose objective is to identify specific paragraphs from existing cases that entail the decision of the new case. We propose two approaches: (1) fine-tuning a legalBERT [11] model with triplet loss [32] on the train set provided for task 2, and (2) fine-tuning a monoT5 model [26] pre-trained on the MSMARCO dataset [5] with hard negative mining examples chosen by BM25 and another version of the monoT5 model. We choose the top-2 predictions of this model as long as the ratio between their similarity scores is less than 6.619 (a hyperparameter found by grid search); otherwise, just the first prediction. Our second approach got the best results on task 2 this year.
- Task 3 is the statute-law retrieval task. The objective is to query the retrieval of relevant articles from a set of Civil-Code articles. The evaluation metric is the F2 score, which prioritizes recall. For this task, we used a fine-tuned MonoT5 model to sort the articles according to their probabilities and reduce the pool of candidate articles. Then we used a large language model (LLM) with the following post-processing to select the final articles.
- Task 4 is the textual entailment task, in which the objective is to determine whether a set of relevant articles entails a given legal query. The evaluation metric is accuracy, with respect to whether the entailment or non-entailment was correctly identified. For this task, we attempted a battery of prompting strategies using Google's flan-T5-xxl LLM and ranked preference voting for the top prompts, based on their performance on similar articles. We also tested different thresholds for lack of consensus among the prompts.

2 Related Work

2.1 Legal Retrieval

Legal proceedings worldwide often rely on the results of previous cases to guide decisions in new situations, particularly when existing laws do not directly address the issue at hand. This practice, known as case law [33], is integral to many judicial systems. However, the sheer volume of cases to consider is a significant challenge in applying case law. For example, in 2021, Canada recorded

215,113 criminal cases [2]. A judge overseeing a case does not have time to manually search through each of the millions of cases across Canadian history, so they must reduce the number of cases to be considered.

The evolution of case retrieval in the legal profession began with the development of reference documents to catalog legal precedents. Legal professionals reviewed summaries of cases and compared them with their current case to determine whether the summarized case was worth reviewing. The advent of digital search engines and databases, such as the US Supreme Court Database [1], streamlined this process, transitioning the workspace from reference books to digital catalogs (although many professionals still use reference books). The task is unsuitable for conventional search engines, as the entire query case must be weighed against all other cases. More recently, the integration of machine learning and artificial intelligence algorithms has further improved retrieval by finding ways to reduce the amount of information needed to perform a query-target comparison.

The main problem with performing searches naively is the enormous processing time required. Performing searches on raw text is highly inefficient, as documents contain many strings that must be compared, and often the volume of documents makes this prohibitive [22]. Modern search algorithms rely on extracting the optimal amount of information required to identify a document as relevant, thus reducing the overall search space. The "term frequency inverse document frequency" (TF-IDF) is an algorithm commonly used for the extraction of keywords or keyphrases. It assigns weighted scores to words in a document based on their frequency within that document compared to their frequency in other documents in the collection [35]. Longer documents are more likely to generate additional terms, giving them more weight in TF-IDF. The BM25 algorithm uses TF-IDF and accounts for the length of the document [31]. BM25 downweights these documents by averaging their word frequencies by the length of the document. TF-IDF and BM25 are used to rank a list of target files based on the query file, but BM25 is favored for the above reasons.

One weakness of these methods is the lack of consideration for context. This weakness is something that Semantic Textual Similarity (STS) directly addresses [30]. STS utilizes cosine similarity to determine how similar two texts are. The data can be generated into an embedding that captures the whole meaning of the text, including the order of words and their relationship to each other ("I told him the item I saw was a steal" vs. "I saw him steal the item"). The target documents are usually ranked in order of similarity, and then the most similar document is chosen as the answer to the query. In practice, it is not enough to find the similarity between two documents, as token limits for the models used to compute the embeddings used for similarities do not accept more than a few hundred words. The most effective solutions combine BM25 and STS, with BM25 performing an efficient first pass to reduce the decision space and STS comparing the documents with each other section by section to refine the results. Additionally, case text can be provided to LLMs directly for comparison, but due to the extreme limitations on token size, each algorithm must have a different approach to data prepossessing.

During the 2023 COLIEE competition, the first three tasks involved comparing case law with a corpus of material and finding some relevance between them. The first task involved determining which case documents are relevant to a query case (legal case retrieval), the second task involved determining which paragraphs of a document entail a query paragraph (legal case entailment), and the third task involved retrieving relevant paragraphs necessary to answer a query question (statute law retrieval) [17]. Two of the top three participants for task 1, IITDLI and NOWJ, used BM25 to filter down the potential case results as part of their algorithms. NOWJ followed this with an STS model, which ranked the cases for selection. IITDLI applied a round of TF-IDF before BM25, followed by data-specific filters. The first-place team, THUIR, trained three separate models to handle cases broken down into facts, holdings, and decisions [17]. THUIR then used ensembles of transformer models to compare case text via semantic similarity. One of the teams used BM25 to rank the text before finding similarity, while the other two relied on mono-T5 voting. The best performing algorithms for task 3 used approaches similar to task 2, ranking the target text and choosing the highest result. Two teams used BM25 to rank the text and LLMs to rank the highest results. The other team used LLMs for ranking but split the models by language.

2.2   Legal Entailment

Legal case entailment involves determining the logical relationship between legal cases, wherein one case logically follows—or is entailed from—another. This is crucial for legal research and practice, as it is the basis for identifying precedents and determining the implications of one case on another [20]. This is essential for lawyers, judges, and legal scholars to understand the legal reasoning behind decisions and to predict the potential outcomes of similar cases based on existing precedents [15]. Additionally, legal case entailment aids in retrieving prior cases, a fundamental aspect of legal research. By determining the entailment relationships between cases, legal professionals can effectively navigate vast amounts of legal information to find relevant precedents and make informed arguments [34]. It is a complex task that involves using various techniques, such as transformer-based approaches, information retrieval methods, and natural language inference mechanisms [20].

Legal case entailment has significantly impacted all areas of legal reasoning. The ability of legal authorities to obtain immediate and long-term compliance with their decisions from the public is crucial in legal practice [36]. In judicial decision making, the severity of the offense is a key legal factor that impacts the process [9]. Furthermore, the influence of technology on legal practices and education cannot be overlooked. In legal education, technology has played a role in shaping the learning process and preparing students for real-world legal scenarios [23]. Furthermore, the influence of non-legal factors on judicial decisions has been extensively debated, highlighting the complexity of decision-making processes [8]. The role of legal policy in organizing legal practice and subordinating it to specific goals and objectives has also been highlighted [29]. This under-scores the broader impact of legal frameworks on the shaping of legal practices and ensuring their alignment with overarching policy objectives.

Legal case entailment has evolved significantly, transitioning from traditional methods to digital and AI-based approaches. Different social, political, and eco-nomic outcomes influence traditional legal methods and the role of litigation and case selection in sociolegal change [7,16]. The evolution of laws and the role of historical facts in judicial decisions have been key in understanding legal changes [3,25]. Furthermore, the use of background knowledge in case-based legal reasoning has been a significant aspect of traditional legal methods [4]. Recently, there has been a shift toward digital and AI-based approaches in legal case entailment. Research has explored various approaches to apply BERT models to downstream legal tasks [12]. In addition, methodologies have been developed to address the challenges of retrieval and entailment of legal cases using semantic understanding, exact matching, and Transformer methods [20,28,34]. Artificial intelligence algorithms and legal background knowledge have also been used to predict the outcome of legal cases [18]. The digitization of the legal space has also caused significant changes in ideas about law, its regulatory opportunities, and the status of its subjects [6]. Recognizing Textual Entailment (RTE) has been recognized as a benchmark for methods adapted to legal texts [10]. More-over, the use of lexical morphological modeling for the analysis of legal texts has gained prominence in the digital era [10].

3   Task 2: Legal Case Entailment

Task 2 focuses on legal case entailment in the context of legal information pro-cessing. The objective is to predict the decision of a new legal case by automati-cally identifying a specific paragraph from existing cases that entails the decision of the new case. Training data includes triples consisting of a query (new case), a noticed case, and a paragraph number from the noticed case that entailed the decision of the query. Participants are required to develop systems that compare the meanings of paragraphs in the noticed case with the decision expressed in the query. The evaluation for task 2 measures the accuracy of identifying the correct paragraph that entails the decision for a given query. The process is carried out automatically without human intervention.

We tried two primary approaches for this task. The first was fine-tuning a legalBERT [11] model to create an SBERT model. SBERT is a Siamese archi-tecture that generates embeddings for two pieces of text and then calculates a similarity score between them. The SBERT model can be trained in many ways, but considering the nature of the task, we deemed the triplet loss [32] with labels as positive examples and all other paragraphs as negative examples to be the best. We created triplets consisting of an anchor, a positive sentence (semantically similar to the anchor), and a negative sentence (semantically dif-ferent from the anchor). This technique is crucial in training models on semantic relationships. By evaluating the model's ability to distinguish between similar and dissimilar sentences, we enhance its understanding of nuanced semantic differences. The triplet loss function ensures that the model learns to minimize the distance between semantically similar sentences while maximizing the distance between dissimilar ones. Upon training, the model demonstrated a robust ability to identify paraphrases and understand semantic similarities between sentences. However, this approach performed poorly on the test set, likely due to overfitting. This can be seen in Table 1 where `lsbK1` and `lsbK2M42` are submissions based on this approach.

For our second approach, we took some inspiration from last years' winner CAPTAIN [24], and used pygaggle's reranker[1] with the MonoT5 3 billion parameters model trained on the MSMARCO passages dataset[2]. We used the hard negative mining approach to fine-tune the model for the task at hand. In the first step, we create the fine-tuning set using the BM25 model to rank all articles associated with a query based on their relevance to the query. We selected the top 10 matching articles that are not labeled as relevant (i.e. hard negatives) for each query and maintained a balanced dataset by including 10 relevant articles with repetition as necessary. We fine-tuned the MonoT5 model using the fine-tuning dataset. For the second step, we create another fine-tuning dataset, this time selecting the top 10 matching articles using the fine-tuned model from the first step and fine-tuning the original model using the second dataset.

After fine-tuning MonoT5, we experimented with various strategies to optimize for the best F1 score. A notable method involved using the standard deviation of the model's scores for each potential answer. This technique used a dynamic threshold for the selection of answers, where we include a paragraph p_i with a score s_i in our list of guesses only if $s_i \geq s_1 - q\sigma$, where q is a hyperparameter whose best value is found by grid search and σ is the standard deviation of the list of scores generated by the monoT5 model. This approach allowed for a flexible selection of answers, balancing precision and recall effectively. By an iterative adjustment of q, we adapted the selection criteria to the variability in the scores, improving the model's ability to accurately identify relevant answers across different queries. Although insightful, this method was not the best performing one. Our more successful approach involved a refined strategy that focused on a combination of selection of K top answers and margin adjustment. In this new method, we evaluated the predictions of the MonoT5 model considering the top K answers for each query, adjusted by a specific margin, including a paragraph only if $s_i \geq s_1 - margin$. For each combination of K and margin, we calculate the precision, recall, and F1 scores to evaluate the effectiveness of each configuration. Finally, we changed the margin to ratio including a paragraph only if $s_i \leq s_1 * ratio$ (all scores are negative, hence the sign $\leq$. This combined approach of top-K selection and ratio adjustment proved to be more precise and effective. It enhanced the MonoT5 model's output, ensuring that the selected answers were not just among the highest scoring, but also surpassed a relative ratio threshold. This led to more accurate and relevant results. Our

---

[1] https://github.com/castorini/pygaggle.

[2] https://huggingface.co/castorini/monot5-3b-msmarco.

analysis showed that the best configurations significantly improved the model's performance, marking this method as the most accurate in our experiments. We call this method mT53bK2r in Table 1.

Table 1. Precision, recall, and F1 scores for our submitted approaches. The winning approach has the performance on the test set in brackets. The values for *margin* and *ratio* are chosen based on a grid search on the last 100 items in the train set.

Submission	Top-K	Criteria	Precision	Recall	F1-score
lsbK1	1		0.850	0.780	0.813
lsbK2M42	2	$margin = 0.042$	0.839	0.849	0.844
mT53bK2r	2	$ratio = 6.619$	0.760 (0.636)	0.825 (0.667)	0.791 (0.651)

4   Task 3: Statute Law Retrieval

Task 3 focuses on retrieving legal documents in the domain of the Japanese civil code. The goal is to assess the performance of systems in searching a static set of civil code articles using previously unseen queries. The task requires participants to return relevant articles in the collection to a query, with relevance determined by the query sentence being answerable (Yes/No) based on the meaning of the article. The training dataset includes pairs of queries and relevant articles, and the process of executing queries on the articles and generating experimental runs is performed entirely automatically. Evaluation metrics, including precision, recall, and the F2 measure, emphasize the importance of recall in the information retrieval process.

The first stage used BM25 to rank all available articles according to their relevance to a given query. We selected the top 50 matches for each query and proceeded to the second step, which used pygaggle's re-ranker with the MonoT5 3 billion parameter model trained on the MSMARCO passages dataset. However, we didn't use the original model; rather, we fine-tuned it with negative hard mining in a manner similar to Task 2. We first chose the top 10 matches using BM25 that were not labeled as relevant and an equal number of relevant articles with repetition as needed to create a balanced dataset. A second dataset was generated using the ranking generated by the aforementioned fine-tuned model to fine-tune the original model. With the fine-tuned model at hand, the reranker scored and ordered the 50 articles selected by the BM25 model using the fine-tuned model's outputs.

Next, the probability values from the previous step are scaled to 0–1 to increase the distance between the matches for the following post-processing. The five most relevant candidates are selected for further processing with LLMs to eliminate irrelevant candidates. For submission AMHR01, we used a 0-shot Flan-T5. For submission AMHR02, a 1-shot Flan-T5[3] [14], and for submission AMHR03, a

---

[3] https://huggingface.co/google/flan-t5-xxl.

1-shot Flan-Alpaca[4] [13]. Here, we applied the chain-of-thought (CoT) prompting approach [21,37]. After eliminating irrelevant candidates using LLMs, we postprocessed the selected candidate set to filter out matches with a probability value of 0.89 or less and included the top match from the MonoT5 step in case LLM did not select this match. Our results on the test set are shown in Table 2.

Table 2. Precision, recall, and F2 scores for our submitted approaches for task 3.

Submission	Model	Shots	Threshold	Precision	Recall	F2-score
AMHR01	Flan-T5	0	0.89	0.654	0.802	0.767
AMHR02	Flan-T5	1	0.89	0.695	0.817	**0.789**
AMHR03	Flan-Alpaca	1	0.89	0.759	0.772	0.770

5   Task 4: Legal Textual Entailment

Task 4 aims to construct Yes/No question answering systems for legal queries through entailment from relevant Civil Law articles. Given a 'Yes/No' legal bar exam question, participants are required to develop legal information retrieval systems that retrieve relevant Civil Law articles. The task involves evaluating the system's performance in answering 'Yes' or 'No' to previously unseen queries by comparing the meanings between the queries and the retrieved Civil Law articles. The training data consists of triples comprising a query, relevant article(s), and a correct answer ('Y' or 'N'). The test data includes only queries and relevant articles, without Y/N labels. The evaluation measure is accuracy, indicating the correct confirmation of 'true' or 'false' for the Yes/No questions.

Inspired by recent work showing that the mixture of expert models (MoE) can produce significant improvements over single models trained on a complex task [19], we set out to determine whether different types of questions in the Task 4 dataset were better answered by different experts. However, the number of questions in the Task 4 training set is not large enough to split into subgroups that individually would be enough to fine-tune a large language model. Instead, we explored an approach built on the following assumptions:

1. A prompt to an LLM can act as an "expert", in the sense that different prompts may do better on different types of problems.
2. A domain of expertise in Task 4 will be reflected in the similarity between articles. In other words, if an expert does well on problems containing article A, then it should also do well on problems containing articles highly similar to A.

---

[4] https://huggingface.co/declare-lab/flan-alpaca-xxl.

To construct our prompts, we manually wrote five headers (templates that provided the articles and query) and combined them with 16 footers (templates that provided instructions on how to solve the problem). The footers were manually written combinations of simple questions ("Is this query correct? Answer 'Y' for yes or 'N' for no."), chain-of-thought prompts [37], self-ask prompts [27], and other prompting tricks that have previously been shown to be successful [38,39]. Some of these prompts were specifically structured to specialize in certain topics (e.g., "Is this query correct? Solve by breaking the problem into steps. First, discuss what the articles say about contracts, agreements, or obligations. Then reason about whether the query is correct.").

All resulting experts (we will refer to each constructed prompt as an "expert") were run for every problem in the train set on `flan-t5-xxl`. Because the generated text was often much more than could be parsed with a simple string search, we then used a separate prompt to extract the answer from the generated text: "*Consider the following, which was an evaluation of a legal query: {response} According to that reasoning, was the legal query allowed (Y) not allowed (N)? Answer just Y or N, and DO NOT say anything else.*" If the extraction prompt still failed to produce a 'Y' or 'N' response, we defaulted to 'N'.

Given a problem $(\mathbf{A}, q)$ consisting of articles $\mathbf{A} = a_1, ..., a_n$ and a query q, we used a combination of measures to determine how much each expert should be allowed to vote on the correct answer. First, for all articles a we calculate $sim_5(a)$ = the set of five articles that are most similar to a, along with their similarity scores, using SBERT [30]. For each expert prompt e, and for each $a' \in sim_5(a)$, we calculate $num(a')$ = the amount of problems in the train set $train$ that had a' and $corr(e, a')$ = the number of problems that e got correct. We then define $pr_{a'}^e$ as the likelihood that e would have earned this score or better through random guessing:

$$pr_{a'}^e = \binom{num(a')}{corr(e, a')} 0.5^{num(a')}$$

The raw voting power of an expert on a problem is then:

$$\sum_{a' \in \{a_1, ..., a_n\}} \frac{sim(a, a')corr(e, a')}{num(a')pr_{a'}^e}$$

To obtain the actual voting power of each expert, we first softmax all of the raw voting powers to normalize them. We then add an additional voting power based on the softmaxed accuracies of all expert articles across all articles, multiplied by a hyperparameter α. This helps us prefer expert prompts that have good all-around performance (and penalize those that do not).

Before the votes are combined, we make two more adjustments. First, we keep only experts with the highest λ voting power scores, in order to avoid a situation where the most qualified expert is outvoted by a large number of low-quality experts. After all the votes are tabulated for 'Y' and 'N', if the amount of votes for the highest scoring option multiplied by a "fudge factor" η does not exceed the amount of votes for the second highest option, then we consider the vote to be too close to call, and simply defer to the vote suggested by whichever expert had the highest accuracy overall on all problems in the training set.

We performed a grid search over the hyperparameters α, λ, η and chose the following three submissions based on their averaged performance across all dev sets (when using older problems as train sets):

- **AMHR.ensembleA50** - $\alpha = 50, \lambda = 25, \eta = 0.5$
- **AMHR.ensembleA0** - $\alpha = 0, \lambda = 50, \eta = 0.9$
- **AMHR.single** - This is simply the single prompt that performed best overall on the train set.

The results of these three submissions are listed in Table 3.

Table 3. Summary of results for the Task 4 submitted models.

Model	η	λ	α	H30	R01	R02	R03	R04	Average	Weighted
ensembleA50	0.5	25	50	70.00%	70.77%	77.78%	77.06%	75.25%	74.17%	74.65%
ensembleA0	0.9	50	0	65.71%	64.62%	81.48%	75.23%	77.23%	72.85%	73.71%
single	n/a	1	n/a	67.14%	66.15%	79.01%	77.06%	76.24%	73.12%	73.94%

6 Conclusion

We described our approaches to solving tasks 2, 3, and 4 in COLIEE 2024. We used deep learning techniques and machine learning engineering practices, resulting in successful results in these tasks. In the future, we plan to study the datasets more closely to develop stronger and more robust strategies for the subsequent editions of COLIEE, as well as for the larger field of legal reasoning using NLP.

Acknowledgments. We would like to thank the following students who contributed their time to helping us in this competition: Ba Nguyen, Boburjon Usmonov, and Alexander Ambrioso.

This material is based upon work supported by the National Science Foundation under Grant No. 2311286.

Disclosure of Interests. The authors have no competing interests to declare that are relevant to the content of this article.

References

1. The supreme court database
2. Table 35-10-0027-01 adult criminal courts, number of cases and charges by type of decision
3. Ahamat, H., Basir, S.M., Aziz, S.N.A., Kamal, M.H.M.: China's south china sea claims, the historic rights debate and the middle approach of Islamic international law. J. Int. Stud. **19** (2023). https://doi.org/10.32890/jis2023.19.1.10

4. Aleven, V.: Using background knowledge in case-based legal reasoning: a computational model and an intelligent learning environment. Artif. Intell. **150**, 183–237 (2003). https://doi.org/10.1016/s0004-3702(03)00105-x

5. Bajaj, P., et al.: MS MARCO: a human generated machine reading comprehension dataset (2018)

6. Baranov, P.P., Mamychev, A.Y., Dremliuga, R.I., Miroshnichenko, O.I.: Legal consciousness and legal culture in the era of total digitalization. Linguist. Cult. Rev. **5**, 899–910 (2021). https://doi.org/10.21744/lingcure.v5ns3.1665

7. Bork, K.: An evolutionary theory of administrative law. SSRN Electron. J. (2018). https://doi.org/10.2139/ssrn.3170158

8. Cahill-O'Callaghan, R.J.: The influence of personal values on legal judgments. J. Law Soc. **40**, 596–623 (2013). https://doi.org/10.1111/j.1467-6478.2013.00642.x

9. Carvacho, P., Droppelmann, C., Mateo, M.: The effect of extralegal factors in decision-making about juvenile offenders in Chile: a quasi-experimental study. Int. J. Offender Ther. Comp. Criminol. **67**, 398–419 (2022). https://doi.org/10.1177/0306624x211066839

10. Carvalho, D., Nguyen, M.T., Tran, C.X., Nguyen, M.L.: Lexical-morphological modeling for legal text analysis. In: Otake, M., Kurahashi, S., Ota, Y., Satoh, K., Bekki, D. (eds.) JSAI-isAI 2015. LNCS, vol. 10091, pp. 295–311. Springer, Cham (2017). https://doi.org/10.1007/978-3-319-50953-2_21

11. Chalkidis, I., Fergadiotis, M., Malakasiotis, P., Aletras, N., Androutsopoulos, I.: LEGAL-BERT: The muppets straight out of law school. In: Cohn, T., He, Y., Liu, Y. (eds.) Findings of the Association for Computational Linguistics: EMNLP 2020, pp. 2898–2904. Association for Computational Linguistics, Online (2020). https://doi.org/10.18653/v1/2020.findings-emnlp.261, https://aclanthology.org/2020.findings-emnlp.261

12. Chalkidis, I., Fergadiotis, M., Malakasiotis, P., Aletras, N., Androutsopoulos, I.: LEGAL-BERT: the muppets straight out of law school, pp. 2898–2904 (2020). https://doi.org/10.18653/v1/2020.findings-emnlp.261

13. Chia, Y.K., Hong, P., Bing, L., Poria, S.: INSTRUCTEVAL: towards holistic evaluation of instruction-tuned large language models. arXiv preprint arXiv:2306.04757 (2023)

14. Chung, H.W., et al.: Scaling instruction-finetuned language models. arXiv preprint arXiv:2210.11416 (2022)

15. Danziger, S., Levav, J., Avnaim-Pesso, L.: Extraneous factors in judicial decisions. Proc. Natl. Acad. Sci. **108**, 6889–6892 (2011). https://doi.org/10.1073/pnas.1018033108

16. Fon, V., Parisi, F., Depoorter, B.: Litigation, judicial path-dependence, and legal change. Eur. J. Law Econ. **20**, 43–56 (2005). https://doi.org/10.1007/s10657-005-1014-0

17. Goebel, R., Kano, Y., Kim, M.Y., Rabelo, J., Satoh, K., Yoshioka, M.: Summary of the competition on legal information, extraction/entailment (COLIEE) 2023. In: Proceedings of the Nineteenth International Conference on Artificial Intelligence and Law, pp. 472–480 (2023)

18. Guo, X., Zhang, H., Li, S.: RnRTD: intelligent approach based on the relationship-driven neural network and restricted tensor decomposition for multiple accusation judgment in legal cases. Comput. Intell. Neurosci. **2019**, 1–18 (2019). https://doi.org/10.1155/2019/6705405

19. Jiang, A.Q., et al.: Mixtral of experts. arXiv preprint arXiv:2401.04088 (2024)

20. Kim, M.Y., Rabelo, J., Okeke, K., Goebel, R.: Legal information retrieval and entailment based on BM25, transformer and semantic thesaurus methods. Rev. Socionetwork Strategies **16**, 157–174 (2022). https://doi.org/10.1007/s12626-022-00103-1

21. Kojima, T., Gu, S.S., Reid, M., Matsuo, Y., Iwasawa, Y.: Large language models are zero-shot reasoners. In: Advances in Neural Information Processing Systems, vol. 35, pp. 22199–22213 (2022)

22. Manning, C., Raghavan, P., Schütze, H.: Introduction to Information Retrieval. Cambridge University Press, Cambridge (2008)

23. Maranga, K.M.: The role and impact of technology in legal education. SSRN Electron. J. (2010). https://doi.org/10.2139/ssrn.1520831

24. Nguyen, C., et al.: Captain at COLIEE 2023: efficient methods for legal information retrieval and entailment tasks (2024)

25. Niblett, A., Posner, R.A., Shleifer, A.: The evolution of a legal rule. J. Legal Stud. **39**(2), 325–358 (2010)

26. Nogueira, R., Jiang, Z., Lin, J.: Document ranking with a pretrained sequence-to-sequence model (2020)

27. Press, O., Zhang, M., Min, S., Schmidt, L., Smith, N.A., Lewis, M.: Measuring and narrowing the compositionality gap in language models. arXiv preprint arXiv:2210.03350 (2022)

28. Rabelo, J., Kim, M.Y., Goebel, R.: Combining similarity and transformer methods for case law entailment. In: Proceedings of the Seventeenth International Conference on Artificial Intelligence and Law (2019). https://doi.org/10.1145/3322640.3326741

29. Rastoropov, S.V., Korobova, A.P., Karev, D.A.: On legal policy and legal practice relations in the era of digitalization. In: Global Challenges and Prospects of the Modern Economic Development (2021). https://doi.org/10.15405/epsbs.2021.04.02.136

30. Reimers, N., Gurevych, I.: Sentence-BERT: sentence embeddings using Siamese BERT-networks. arXiv preprint arXiv:1908.10084 (2019)

31. Robertson, S., Zaragoza, H., Taylor, M.: Simple BM25 extension to multiple weighted fields. In: Proceedings of the Thirteenth ACM International Conference on Information and Knowledge Management, pp. 42–49 (2004)

32. Schultz, M., Joachims, T.: Learning a distance metric from relative comparisons. In: Thrun, S., Saul, L., Schölkopf, B. (eds.) Advances in Neural Information Processing Systems, vol. 16. MIT Press (2003)

33. Team, W.D.: case law

34. Tran, V., Nguyen, M.L., Satoh, K.: Building legal case retrieval systems with lexical matching and summarization using a pre-trained phrase scoring model. In: Proceedings of the Seventeenth International Conference on Artificial Intelligence and Law (2019). https://doi.org/10.1145/3322640.3326740

35. Turtle, H., Flood, J.: Query evaluation: strategies and optimizations. Inf. Process. Manage. **31**(6), 831–850 (1995)

36. Tyler, T.R.: Procedural justice, legitimacy, and the effective rule of law. Crime Just. **30**, 283–357 (2003). https://doi.org/10.1086/652233

37. Wei, J., et al.: Chain-of-thought prompting elicits reasoning in large language models. In: Advances in Neural Information Processing Systems, vol. 35, pp. 24824–24837 (2022)

38. Yang, C., et al.: Large language models as optimizers. arXiv preprint arXiv:2309.03409 (2023)

39. Zhou, Y., et al.: Large language models are human-level prompt engineers. arXiv preprint arXiv:2211.01910 (2022)

Towards an In-Depth Comprehension of Case Relevance for Better Legal Retrieval

Haitao Li[1,2], You Chen[1,2], Zhekai Ge[3], Qingyao Ai[1,2],
Yiqun Liu[1,2]([✉]), Quan Zhou[2,4], and Shuai Huo[2,4]

[1] DCST, Tsinghua University, Beijing, China
liht22@mails.tsinghua.edu.cn, yiqunliu@tsinghua.edu.cn
[2] Quan Cheng Laboratory, Shenzhen, China
[3] Columbia University, New York, USA
[4] MegaTech.AI, Zhaoqing, China

Abstract. Legal retrieval techniques play an important role in preserving the fairness and equality of the judicial system. As an annually well-known international competition, COLIEE aims to advance the development of state-of-the-art retrieval models for legal texts. This paper elaborates on the methodology employed by the TQM team in COLIEE2024. Specifically, we explored various lexical matching and semantic retrieval models, with a focus on enhancing the understanding of case relevance. Additionally, we endeavor to integrate various features using the learning-to-rank technique. Furthermore, fine heuristic pre-processing and post-processing methods have been proposed to mitigate irrelevant information. Consequently, our methodology achieved remarkable performance in COLIEE2024, securing first place in Task 1 and third place in Task 3. We anticipate that our proposed approach can contribute valuable insights to the advancement of legal retrieval technology.

Keywords: Legal case retrieval · Dense retrieval · Pre-training

1 Introduction

Efficient legal retrieval is essential in the judicial process. It supports lawyers in argumentation, guides judges in decision-making, and aids scholars in analyzing legal trends. With the evolution of the legal field into the digital age, the ability to efficiently navigate vast legal databases with advanced search techniques is essential for the maintenance of justice ensuring the judicial fairness [1,2,14,18,19,26,33].

The Competition on Legal Information Extraction/Entailment (COLIEE) has emerged as a significant platform for advancing the state-of-the-art in legal information processing and retrieval. The competition consists of several tasks focusing on two categories: legal retrieval and legal entailment.

ⓒ The Author(s), under exclusive license to Springer Nature Singapore Pte Ltd. 2024
T. Suzumura and M. Bono (Eds.): JSAI-isAI 2024, LNAI 14741, pp. 212–227, 2024.
https://doi.org/10.1007/978-981-97-3076-6_15

This year, our team TQM primarily focused on participating in the legal retrieval tasks, i.e. Task 1 and Task 3. Task 1 involves retrieving relevant documents to support a given query case within the case law system. Task 3 involves retrieving civil law related to Japanese Legal Bar exam questions under the statutory law system. Through a thorough comprehension of case relevance, the TQM team achieved commendable results in COLIEE2024.

In legal practice, case relevance is complex and differs from that of conventional web search [17,21,25]. In the context of legal retrieval, relevance transcends mere lexical matches or semantic similarities. The relevance of legal cases usually involves an in-depth analysis of the facts of the case, legal principles, and prior jurisprudence. This requires the retrieval system to understand not only the words and concepts in the text, but also to gain insight into their interactions within a particular legal framework. Traditional methods often prove inadequate in capturing the nuanced aspects that determine case relevance, including the construction of legal arguments, key legal facts, and the particular nature of applicable laws.

Therefore, during COLIEE2024, our team, TQM, not only investigated the effectiveness of established methods in legal retrieval but also explored new strategies to improve the model's understanding of case relevance. Specifically, within the traditional lexical matching approach, we employed BM25_ngram to underscore the significance of law-specific terms in determining relevance. Additionally, in the semantic similarity approach, we utilized the translation process between different structures of legal cases to deepen the understanding of key facts. Subsequently, we employed learning-to-rank techniques to integrate different features. In addition, we design delicate heuristic pre-processing and post-processing methods to mitigate the impact of irrelevant information. In conclusion, the official results reveal our team's remarkable achievement, attaining first place in Task 1 and third place in Task 3. This shows the effectiveness of our design approach.

The paper is structured as follows: Sect. 2 offers an overview of foundational concepts in legal case retrieval and dense retrieval. Section 3 elaborates on the COLIEE2024 legal case retrieval task, encompassing its description, datasets, and evaluation metrics. Section 4 delves into the technical aspects of the study. Following this, Sect. 5 presents the results of our experiments. The paper concludes with Sect. 6, summarizing key findings and outlining directions for future research.

2   Related Work

2.1   Legal Retrieval

In the area of legal retrieval, the integration of deep learning techniques has become foundational, giving rise to a plethora of methodologies such as CNN-based models [27], BiDAF [24], and SMASH-RNN [10], among others. Generative transformers have emerged as the preferred architecture in this domain, notably powering innovations like LEGAL-BERT [3] and Lawformer [29]. Besides, Jiang et al. [11] demonstrated improvements in cross-lingual retrieval, by using Multilingual BERT to handle the linguistic space in legal documentation. Recent contributions further enriched this field. By focusing on context-aware citation recommendations [9] and graph-based legal reasoning [35], we can significantly enhance relevance and semantic richness of case retrieval methods. Also, Li et al. proposed SAILER [14], which utilizes the structure of legal documents for pretraining and achieves the best results on some legal benchmarks. These developments highlights the potential of transformative strides in AI and machine learning to legal information retrieval.

2.2   Dense Retrieval

A radical departure from traditional retrieval has emerged through dense retrieval, which leverages dual encoders to map the queries and documents into dense embeddings and capture intricate contextual nuances [7,30]. This method has been progressively improved through a series of innovative works: Zhan et al. [15] introduced dynamic negative sampling to refine the matching process and Chen et al. [5] unveiled ARES that incorporates retrieval axioms during pretraining, which substantially improved performance. Similarly, Karpukhin et al. [12] introduced DPR (Dense Passage Retrieval) which surpassed traditional IR methods by a large margin in large-scale open-domain question-answering tasks, and Xiong et al. [31] introduced ANCE (Approximate Nearest Neighbor Negative Contrastive Learning), which dynamically updated the negative samples and further optimized the retrieval process. These studies, demonstrate the potential of dense retrieval to revolutionize IR technologies, providing more accurate results across various applications.

3   Task Overview

3.1   Task1. The Case Law Retrieval Task

Task Description. The Competition on Legal Information Extraction/Entailment (COLIEE), an annual international contest, is committed to advancing state-of-the-art methodologies in legal text processing. In COLIEE2024, four tasks are presented, with our exclusive focus directed towards the legal retrieval task.

Task 1, referred to as the Case Law Retrieval task, involves the identification of supporting cases that substantiate the decisions of query cases within an extensive corpus. Formally, for a given query case denoted as q and a set of candidate cases represented by S, the objective is to identify all supporting cases, designated as $S_q^* = \{S_1, S_2, ..., S_n\}$ from the extensive candidate pool. Participants are allowed to submit any number of supporting cases for each individual query in this task. Hence, it is also crucial to identify the conditions fulfilled by the relevant cases.

The data corpus utilized for Task 1 comprises a collection of case law documents from the Federal Court of Canada, provided by Compass Law. Detailed

Table 1. Dataset statistics of COLIEE Task 1.

	COLIEE2021		COLIEE2022		COLIEE2023		COLIEE2024	
	Train	Test	Train	Test	Train	Test	Train	Test
# of queries	650	250	898	300	959	319	1278	400
# of candidate case per query	4415	4415	3531	1263	4400	1335	5616	1734
avg # of relevant candidates/paragraphs	5.17	3.60	4.68	4.21	4.68	2.69	4.16	–

statistics of this dataset are presented in Table 1. Through our analysis, we find that there is a significant difference in the average number of relevant documents per query between the COLIEE2023 training and test sets. Therefore, we similarly consider possible bias for effective post-processing in COLIEE2024. We employ the test set of COLIEE2023 as the validation set and apply the best parameters in COLIEE2023 to COLIEE2024.

Metrics. For COLIEE 2024 Task 1, the evaluation metrics will include precision, recall, and the F1-measure:

$$\text{Precision} = \frac{\#TP}{\#TP + \#FP} \tag{1}$$

$$\text{Recall} = \frac{\#TP}{\#TP + \#FN} \tag{2}$$

$$F - \text{measure} = \frac{2 \times \text{Precision} \times \text{Recall}}{\text{Precision} + \text{Recall}} \tag{3}$$

where $\#TP$ represents the total number of accurately retrieved candidate cases across all queries, $\#FP$ denotes the number of incorrectly retrieved candidate cases for all queries, and $\#FN$ signifies the count of overlooked noticed candidate paragraphs in all queries. Notably, the evaluation process employed a micro-average approach, where the evaluation measure is computed based on the collective results of all queries. This differs from a macro-average approach, which calculates the evaluation measure for each query individually before averaging these values.

3.2 Task3. The Statute Law Retrieval Task

Task Description. This task focuses on retrieving civil law articles relevant to a given "Yes/No" question. For a legal bar exam question denoted as Q Q and a set of Japanese Civil Code Articles represented as $S = S_1, ..., S_n$, the objective is to compile a subset E from S that aids in answering Q. The questions for this task are sourced from Japanese Legal Bar Exams and are translated into English, along with the entire corpus of Japanese Civil Law articles.

The dataset of this task consists of 1097 pairs, a legal corpus (Civil Code) with 768 articles, and 109 test queries. Participants need to find the relevant

Article	**Article 398-12** (1) Before the principal is crystallized, a revolving mortgagee may assign a revolving mortgage, with the approval of the mortgagor of the revolving mortgage. (2) A revolving mortgagee may divide the revolving mortgage into two revolving mortgages and assign either of the same pursuant to the provisions of the preceding paragraph.In this case, the rights for which that revolving mortgage is the subject matter is extinguished with respect to the revolving mortgage that was assigned. (3) In order to effect an assignment under the provisions of the preceding paragraph, the approval of the person that holds the rights for which that revolving mortgage is the subject matter must be obtained. **Article 398-13** Before the principal is crystallized, a revolving mortgagee may, with the approval of the mortgagor of the revolving mortgage, effect a partial assignment of the revolving mortgage (meaning assignments of revolving mortgages that the assignor effects without dividing the revolving mortgage in order to co-own the same with the assignee; hereinafter the same applies in this Section).
Text	Since a revolving mortgage before the fixing of principal can be described as a right which dominates the value of the maximum amount detached from the secured claim, it can be transferred in whole or in part, but since the obligor and the secured claim may change, approval must be obtained from the revolving mortgagor.

Fig. 1. Example of task3 in COLIEE2024. The label is Yes, which means that the text is relevant to the articles.

articles for the test query. The examples of this dataset are shown in Fig. 1. More accurately, this task is more like a ranking task, since the candidate set has only 768 legal entries. We selected questions with IDs beginning with R04 with 101 questions to form a validation set. This subset was utilized to conduct evaluations of various models and settings.

Metrics. For COLIEE 2024 Task 3, the evaluation criteria include macro-average precision, recall, and F2-measure, diverging from the micro-average measures traditionally used in Task 1.

$$\text{Precision} = \text{Average of} \frac{|\text{Correctly articles for each query}|}{|\text{Retrieved articles for each query}|} \tag{4}$$

$$\text{Recall} = \text{Average of} \frac{|\text{Correctly retrieved articles for each query}|}{|\text{Correct articles for each query}|} \tag{5}$$

$$F - \text{measure} = \frac{5 \times \text{Precision} \times \text{Recall}}{4 \times \text{Precision} + \text{Recall}} \tag{6}$$

4   Method

In this section, we present our approach and motivation for the legal case retrieval task in COLIEE2024.

4.1   Task1. The Case Law Retrieval Task

In this section, we present our solution in detail for Task 1 of COLIEE2024. Overall, we followed the framework of last year's first place team THUIR [19]. We first pre-process the data to eliminate noisy information. After that, we implemented the classical lexical matching method and the state-of-the-art semantic retrieval model. The difference is that we improve both approaches from the perspective of case relevance. Following this, we use learning to rank to fuse features from different perspectives for better modeling of case relevance. Finally, we propose heuristic post-processing strategies by observing common properties of relevant cases.

Pre-processing. Following li et al [19], we perform the fine data pre-processing before training. To be specific, our initial step involved the removal of text before the "[1]" character in each case document, which typically includes procedural details such as time and court. Subsequently, we eliminated all placeholders, notably "FRAGMENT_SUPPRESSED", to avoid interference in similarity computations. Additionally, in cases where legal documents contained French text, we utilized the Langdetect tool to identify and remove French passages. Documents predominantly in French were translated into English to retain their essential information. In the process of summary extraction, we selectively extracted sections under "summary" subheadings, which generally encapsulate key case elements, and integrated these at the beginning of the processed text. Through preprocessing, Through this pre-processing, we aimed to reduce as much noisy information in the case documents as possible, which does not contribute to the relevance judgment.

Lexical Matching Models. In previous competitions, many participants have discovered that traditional lexical matching models can produce competitive results. This phenomenon can be attributed to two primary factors. Firstly, bag-of-words models do not impose limitations on the text length, rendering them well-suited for handling legal case documents with lengthy texts. Secondly, the legal domain encompasses numerous specialized terms, where relevance is often discernible through word matching. Therefore, in this section, we experimented with the following methods:

- **BM25** [23] a probabilistic relevance model grounded in the bag-of-words concept, calculates relevance between a query q and a document d. The formulation of BM25 is presented as follows:

$$BM25(d,q) = \sum_{i=1}^{M} \frac{IDF(t_i) \cdot TF(t_i,d) \cdot (k_1 + 1)}{TF(t_i,d) + k_1 \cdot \left(1 - b + b \cdot \dfrac{len(d)}{avgdl}\right)} \tag{7}$$

where k_1, b are free hyperparameters. TF denotes term frequency and IDF signifies inverse document frequency. The term $avgdl$ is the represents the average document length across the dataset.
- **QLD** [34] is an efficient probabilistic statistical model, assesses relevance scores by evaluating the likelihood of query generation. The computation of the QLD score is outlined as follows:

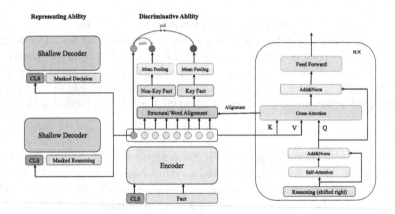

Fig. 2. Pre-training designs of DELTA.

$$\log p(q|d) = \sum_{i:c(q_i;d)>0} \log \frac{p_s(q_i|d)}{\alpha_d p(q_i|\mathcal{C})} + n \log \alpha_d + \sum_i \log p(q_i|\mathcal{C}) \quad (8)$$

For more information, please refer to Zhai et al.'s work [34].

– **BM25_ngram** is a modified version of BM25 in order to better determine relevance through lexical matching. Given the abundance of uncommon specialized terms in legal case documents, which hold unique meanings in specific contexts, specific combinations of terms can offer fresh insights into relevance identification. Therefore, we implemented Bm25_ngram by adapting the ngram_range parameter of the TfidfVectorizer. The ngram_range parameter specifies the lower and upper boundaries for the range of n-values corresponding to different n-grams to be extracted.

Semantic Retrieval Models. Semantic retrieval models can effectively avoid the problem of lexical mismatch and have been widely used in legal retrieval. However, pre-trained language models often perform unsatisfactory due to the limited input length and the difficulty of effectively understanding legal structures. Recently, a series of work has achieved state-of-the-art results by designing specific pre-training objectives for legal case retrieval. In this section, we implement SAILER and optimize it for better identification of legal case relevance.

– **SAILER** [14] is a structure-aware pre-trained model. It fully utilizes the structure of legal documents to construct information bottlenecks and achieves state-of-the-art results on legal case retrieval tasks. We continued to fine-tune SAILER with the training sets of COLIEE2023 and COLIEE2022.
– **DELTA** is an improved version of SAILER, which enhances the understanding of key facts in the legal cases and improves the discriminatory ability. To be specific, DELTA introduces a deep decoder which implements the translation of Fact section to Reasoning section. Afterwards, the word alignment

Table 2. Features employed in our learning-to-rank approach for COLIEE2024 Task1. The placeholder contains "FRAGMENT_SUPPRESSED", "REFERENCE_ SUPPRESSED", "CITATION_SUPPRESSED".

Feature ID	Feature Name	Description
1	query_length	Length of the query
2	candidate_length	Length of the candidate paragraph
3	query_ref_num	Number of placeholders in the query case
4	doc_ref_num	Number of placeholders in the candidate case
5	BM25	Query-candidate scores with BM25 ($k\_1 = 3.0$, $b = 1.0$)
6	BM25_rank	Rank of documents in the search list of the query by BM25 score
7	QLD	Query-candidate scores with QLD
8	QLD_rank	Rank of documents in the search list of the query by QLD score
9	BM25_ngram	Query-candidate scores with BM25_ngram
10	BM25_ngram_rank	Rank of documents in the search list of the query by BM25_ngram score
11	SAILER	Inner product of query and candidate vectors generated by SAILER
12	SAILER_rank	Rank of documents in the search list of the query by SAILER score
13	DELTA	Inner product of query and candidate vectors generated by DELTA
14	DELTA_rank	Rank of documents in the search list of the query by DELTA score

mechanism is employed to determine key facts. Following this, the representation of the case in the vector space is pulled closer to the key facts and pushed away from the non-key facts. The framework of DELTA is shown as Fig. 2.

Learning to Rank. Following previous work [4,8,16,28,32], lWe utilize Lightgbm to integrate all feature scores. Table 2 shows the details of all the features. A total of 14 features were used to integrate the final score. For optimizing ranking, we employ the Normalized Discounted Cumulative Gain (NDCG) as our objective. The model demonstrating the highest performance on the validation set is selected for subsequent testing.

Post-processing. Finally, we post-processed the ranking scores from the relevance perspective to remove irrelevant documents. Apart from Filtering by trial date, Filtering query cases and Dynamic cut-off proposed in previous li et al. work [19], we add Filtering duplicate cases as a post-processing strategy. The specific details are as follows:

- **Filtering by trial date.** Considering that a query case typically cites cases preceding its trial date, it is logical to filter the candidate set based on this criterion. By extracting all dates mentioned within each case, we determine the latest date as the trial date, thereby minimizing erroneous exclusions. In instances where dates cannot be extracted from query cases, we retain all cases in the candidate set.
- **Filtering query cases.** We find that query cases hardly become noticed case for other queries. Therefore we remove all query cases from the search results.
- **Filtering duplicate cases.** We find that all the noticed cases are not repeating in the COLIEE2021, COLIEE2022 and COLIEE2023 query cases respectively, indicating that deleting duplicate cases might be effective. Kim et

al. [13] also used removing repeating cases in the previous retrieval task, utilizing maximum duplicate cases as the hyper-parameter. By noticing that removing duplicate cases may delete all the candidate cases for some query cases, we define t as the maximum numbers of duplicate cases and then supplement s cases with higher score for those query cases without candidate case. Grid search in the validation set is utilized to find optimal t and s.

- **Dynamic cut-off** To accommodate the variability in the number of supporting cases associated with different query cases, we implement a dynamic-cutoff mechanism for each query case. This involves defining three hyperparameters: h, l, and p, respectively. Here, h represents the maximum, and l the minimum number of supporting cases to be retrieved per query case. Additionally, if the highest score achieved by supporting cases for a specific query case is denoted as S, then only those supporting cases scoring above $p \times S$ are selected. A grid search technique is employed to ascertain the optimal values for these hyperparameters h, l and p.

4.2   Task3. The Statute Law Retrieval Task

In this section, we follow the framework of Task 1 to implement Task 3. Specifically, we design heuristic pre-processing and post-processing strategies and implement advanced retrievers and rankers. Finally, we use learning to rank to integrate all scores.

Pre-processing. In Task 3, we primarily pre-process the retrieval pool, i.e., the legal articles. Specifically, we started by removing the lead-in information from the Civil Code. For example: "Part I General Provisions", "Chapter I Common Provisions". We consider that this information does not contribute to the relevance judgment. Subsequently, we deleted all explanatory descriptions in brackets, such as (Standards for Construction). We consider that these are too general and do not facilitate the differentiation of legal articles. Finally, we obtain a mapping of article IDs and specific content to form the retrieval set.

Retriever. We implemented the following retriever to get the most relevant legal articles from the full set:

- **BM25** [23] is a robust lexical matching method. In Task 3, we set k_1 to 0.99 and b to 0.75.
- **QLD** [34] is another effective probabilistic lexical model. The detailed description can be found in Sect. 4.1.

Reranker. After getting the retrieved *top*200 relevant legal articles, we use reranker to further rank them. The detailed model is as follows:

- **BERT** [6] is the classic pre-trained language model, which employs a multi-layer bidirectional Transformer encoder architecture, BERT leverages both the Masked Language Model (MLM) and Next Sentence Prediction (NSP) as its pre-training tasks.

Table 3. Features that we used for learning to rank in COLIEE2024 Task 3.

Feature ID	Feature Name	Description
1	query_length	Length of the query
2	article_length	Length of the candidate article
3	BM25	Query-article scores with BM25
4	QLD	Query-article scores with QLD
5	BERT	Query-article scores with BERT
6	RoBERTa	Query-article scores with RoBERTa
7	LEGALBERT	Query-article scores with LEGAL-BERT-base
8	monoT5_large	Query-article scores with monoT5_large
9	monoT5_3B	Query-article scores with monoT5_3B

- **RoBERTa** [20] represents an advancement over BERT, utilizing a more extensive dataset for pre-training. Unlike BERT, RoBERTa is exclusively pre-trained using the Masked Language Model (MLM) task.
- [3] has been pre-trained on an extensive English legal database and has demonstrated state-of-the-art performance across a variety of legal tasks.
- **monoT5** [22] adopts an encoder-decoder architecture. It operates by generating a "true" or "false" token, reflecting the relevance between queries and candidates. The model then considers the probability of generating "true" as the ultimate relevance score.

For BERT, RoBERTa, and LEGALBERT, we train them with the cross-encoder architecture. Specifically, the query and legal articles are spliced together and fed into the encoder, and the vector of $[CLS]$ token is passed through the MLP layer to get the final score. The loss function for training is as follows:

$$L(q, d^+, d_1^-, ..., d_n^-) = -\log \frac{exp(s(q, d^+))}{exp(s(q, d^+)) + \sum_{j=1}^{n} exp(s(q, d_j^-))} \qquad (9)$$

where d^+ and d^- are relevant and negative articles. We employ irrelevant articles from the *top*200 articles retrieved by BM25 as negative examples. For monoT5, we trained three versions of monoT5_base, monoT5_large, and monoT5_3B.

Learning to Rank. Similar to Task 1, we integrate all the features using Lightgbm. The features utilized in Task 3 are displayed in Table 3. A total of 9 features were employed to integrate the final score. We adopt *Precision*@1 as the optimization objective and select the best model based on performance on the validation set for testing purposes.

Post-processing. Finally we performed the heuristic post-processing on the ranking scores. Upon analysis, it was observed that the majority of queries are associated with no more than two relevant legal articles. Therefore, we define the maximum score for one query to be S. Only articles that exceed the $S \times p$

Table 4. Performance and optimal hyperparameter on COLIEE2024 validation set.

Model	F1 score	Precision	Recall	p	h	l	t	s
TQM_run1	0.3824	0.3708	0.3046	0.7	5	4	1	2
TQM_run2	0.4294	0.4064	0.4552	0.3	7	4	1	2
TQM_run3	0.4592	0.4530	0.4656	0.46	7	1	1	2

score are considered relevant. The hyperparameter p is finely tuned to maintain consistency in the proportion of queries with two relevant laws across both the training and validation sets.

Table 5. Results on the official test of COLIEE2024 Task 1. Best results are marked bold.

Team	Submission	F1	Precision	Recall
TQM	task1_test_answer_2024_run1	**0.4432**	**0.5057**	0.3944
TQM	task1_test_answer_2024_run3	0.4342	0.5082	0.3790
UMNLP	task1_umnlp_run1	0.4134	0.4000	0.4277
UMNLP	task1_umnlp_run2	0.4097	0.3755	0.4507
UMNLP	task1_umnlp_runs_combined	0.4046	0.3597	0.4622
YR	task1_yr_run1	0.3605	0.3210	0.4110
TQM	task1_test_answer_2024_run2	0.3548	0.4196	0.3073
YR	task1_yr_run2	0.3483	0.3245	0.3758
YR	task1_yr_run3	0.3417	0.3184	0.3688
JNLP	64b7b-07f39	0.3246	0.3110	0.3393
JNLP	07f39	0.3222	0.3347	0.3105
JNLP	64b7b-48fe5	0.3103	0.3017	0.3195
WJY	submit_1	0.3032	0.2700	0.3457
BM24	task1_test_result	0.1878	0.1495	0.2522
CAPTAIN	captain_mstr	0.1688	0.1793	0.1594
CAPTAIN	captain_ft5	0.1574	0.1586	0.1562
NOWJ	nowjtask1run2	0.1313	0.0895	0.2465
NOWJ	nowjtask1run3	0.1306	0.0957	0.2055
NOWJ	nowjtask1run1	0.1224	0.0813	0.2478
WJY	submit_3	0.1179	0.0870	0.1831
WJY	submit_2	0.1174	0.0824	0.2042
MIG	test1_ans	0.0508	0.0516	0.0499
UBCS	run3	0.0276	0.0140	**0.7196**
UBCS	run2	0.0275	0.0140	0.7177
UBCS	run1	0.0272	0.0139	0.7100
CAPTAIN	captain_bm25	0.0019	0.0019	0.0019

5   Experiment Result

In this section, we present the results of our experiments and the corresponding analysis.

5.1   Task1. The Case Law Retrieval Task

Submissions. For COLIEE2024 Task 1, we submitted 3 runs with the following details

- **task1_test_answer_2024_run1:** We implemented the lexical matching model QLD and searched for the best parameters t, s, h, l, p on the validation set based on the QLD scores in the post-processing stage and applied them to the test set.
- **task1_test_answer_2024_run2:** The improved lexical matching model BM25_ngram was implemented, and an optimal set of parameters t, s, h, l, p was identified through a search on the validation set, guided by the BM25_ngram scores during the post-processing stage. These parameters were subsequently applied to the test set.
- **task1_test_answer_2024_run3:** The lightgbm integrates all the features to get the final score, after which the best post-processing parameters are obtained based on this score and applied to the test set.

Table 6. The performance of various model on COLIEE2024 task3 validation set. Best results are marked bold.

Model	F2	Precision	Recall
BM25	0.5267	0.6039	0.5181
QLD	0.3888	0.4257	0.3844
BERT	0.6698	0.7524	0.6600
RoBERTa	0.6637	0.7524	0.6534
LEGALBERT	0.6929	0.7920	0.6815
monoT5_base	0.6951	0.7821	0.6848
monoT5_large	0.7072	0.8019	0.6963
monoT5_3B	**0.7171**	**0.8118**	**0.7062**

Results. Table 4 shows the effectiveness and optimal parameters of submission runs on the validation set. Table 5 shows the final official evaluation results. From the experimental results, we can draw the following conclusions:

- From the results of the validation set, the lexical matching model Bm25_ngram achieved competitive results. Learning to rank effectively combines the perspectives of lexical matching model and semantic retrieval model to achieve the best results.

Table 7. Results on the official test of COLIEE2024 Task 3.Best results are marked bold. * indicates runs that use LLMs with undiscolsed training data. · indicates runs that use LLMs with discolsed training data. # is runs without LLM.

Submission_id	F2	Precision	Recall	MAP	R_5	R_10	R_30
JNLP.constr-join*	**0.7408**	0.6502	**0.7982**	0.8010	**0.8769**	**0.9154**	0.9462
CAPTAIN.bjpAllMonoT5·	0.7335	0.6713	0.7752	**0.8149**	0.8615	0.9308	0.9538
TQM-run1#	0.7171	**0.7202**	0.7339	0.7899	0.8308	0.9000	**0.9615**
CAPTAIN.bjpAllMonoP·	0.7171	0.6743	0.7477	0.7731	0.8538	0.9308	0.9538
CAPTAIN.bjpAll#	0.7135	0.6227	0.7844	0.8149	0.8615	0.9308	0.9538
JNLP.Mistral*	0.7123	0.6682	0.7477	0.7434	0.8308	0.9154	0.9538
NOWJ-25mulreftask-ensemble#	0.7081	0.6334	0.7661	0.7562	0.8231	0.8769	0.9077
AMHR02·	0.6876	0.5972	0.7569	0.7405	0.7846	0.8308	0.8462
AMHR03·	0.6825	0.6456	0.7202	0.7405	0.7846	0.8308	0.8462
AMHR01·	0.6749	0.5734	0.7569	0.7405	0.7846	0.8308	0.8462
NOWJ-25multask-ensemble#	0.6654	0.5934	0.7431	0.7180	0.7231	0.8077	0.8692
NOWJ-25mulref-ensemble#	0.6649	0.5916	0.7202	0.7315	0.8154	0.8462	0.8923
TQM-run2#	0.6621	0.5734	0.7110	0.7082	0.7769	0.8077	0.8077
JNLP.RankLLaMA*	0.6555	0.6606	0.6651	0.7400	0.8385	0.9154	0.9538
UA-mp_net#	0.6409	0.4908	0.7385	0.7127	0.8000	0.8538	0.9000
UA-anglE#	0.6399	0.4679	0.7477	0.6935	0.7538	0.8077	0.8769
TQM-run3#	0.6330	0.5963	0.6606	0.7492	0.8154	0.8692	0.9308
BM24-1*	0.4945	0.2590	0.7294	–	–	–	–
MIG2#	0.1665	0.1604	0.1881	0.2125	0.2615	0.2923	0.3769
MIG1#	0.1637	0.1187	0.2064	0.2049	0.2385	0.2923	0.3846
MIG3#	0.1629	0.1631	0.1789	0.2049	0.2385	0.2923	0.3846
PSI01	0.0785	0.0826	0.0780	0.2312	0.3692	0.4769	0.6308

- However, the official test results showed different performance. BM25_ngram had the worst results and QLD achieved the best performance. We speculate this is due to the bias in the distribution of terms on the test sets of COLIEE2023 and COLIEE2024. Since the distribution of the BM25_ngram scores is different on the two datasets, it results slightly lower performance of learning to rank than the single model.
- Overall, our approach achieves championship in the legal case retrieval task and shows sufficient robustness, which is crucial in legal scenarios where large-scale annotation data is lacking.

5.2   Task3. The Statute Law Retrieval Task

Submissions. In Task 3, we submit 3 runs as follows:

- **TQM_run1:** We fine-tuned monoT5_3B using the training data and performed post-processing.
- **TQM_run2:** Lightgbm was employed to integrate all features and use Precision@1 as the optimization objective.
- **TQM_run3:** Lightgbm was employed to integrate all features and use Precision@2 as the optimization objective.

Results. Table 6 shows the performance of various models on the validation set. Table 7 shows the official evaluation results. We derive the fol- lowing observations from the experiment results.

- From the Table 6, it can be observed that Ranker performs better than the Retriever. The best single model result was achieved by mono_T5.
- However, the performance drops significantly after learning to rank on the test set. We think this is due to overfitting caused by too little training data. How to effectively integrate each feature deserves further research.
- Overall, our submission had the best performance among all the runs without LLMs, and ranked third among all the submissions. This suggests that LLMs can be effective in enhancing the understanding of the law thus improving the performance.

6 Conclusion

This paper presents TQM Team's approaches to the legal case retrieval task in the COLIEE 2024 competition. We try to enhance the understanding of the model for case relevance from multiple perspectives and achieve some progress. We obtained the best performance in Task 1 among all submissions, and the third place in Task 3. In the future we will continue to explore infusing legal knowledge into the model to better understand case relevance.

References

1. Althammer, S., Askari, A., Verberne, S., Hanbury, A.: DoSSIER@ COLIEE 2021: leveraging dense retrieval and summarization-based re-ranking for case law retrieval. arXiv preprint arXiv:2108.03937 (2021)
2. Bench-Capon, T., et al.: A history of AI and law in 50 papers: 25 years of the international conference on AI and law. Artif. Intell. Law **20**(3), 215–319 (2012)
3. Chalkidis, I., Fergadiotis, M., Malakasiotis, P., Aletras, N., Androutsopou- los, I.: Legal-BERT: the muppets straight out of law school. arXiv preprint arXiv:2010.02559 (2020)
4. Chen, J., Li, H., Su, W., Ai, Q., Liu, Y.: THUIR at WSDM cup 2023 task 1: unbiased learning to rank (2023)
5. Chen, J., et al.: Axiomatically regularized pre-training for ad hoc search. In: Pro- ceedings of the 45th International ACM SIGIR Conference on Research and Devel- opment in Information Retrieval, pp. 1524–1534 (2022)
6. Devlin, J., Chang, M.W., Lee, K., Toutanova, K.: BERT: pre-training of deep bidirectional transformers for language understanding. arXiv preprint arXiv:1810.04805 (2018)
7. Dong, Q., et al.: I3 retriever: incorporating implicit interaction in pre-trained lan- guage models for passage retrieval. In: Proceedings of the 32nd ACM International Conference on Information and Knowledge Management, pp. 441–451 (2023)
8. Han, X., Tu, Y., Li, H., Ai, Q., Liu, Y.: THUIR_SS at the NTCIR-17 session search (SS) task. (No Title) (2023)

9. Huang, Z., et al.: Context-aware legal citation recommendation using deep learning. In: Proceedings of the Eighteenth International Conference on Artificial Intelligence and Law, pp. 79–88 (2021)

10. Jiang, J.Y., Zhang, M., Li, C., Bendersky, M., Golbandi, N., Najork, M.: Semantic text matching for long-form documents. In: The World Wide Web Conference, pp. 795–806 (2019)

11. Jiang, Z., El-Jaroudi, A., Hartmann, W., Karakos, D., Zhao, L.: Cross-lingual information retrieval with BERT. arXiv preprint arXiv:2004.13005 (2020)

12. Karpukhin, V., et al.: Dense passage retrieval for open-domain question answering. arXiv preprint arXiv:2004.04906 (2020)

13. Kim, M.Y., Rabelo, J., Babiker, H.K.B., Rahman, M.A., Goebel, R.: Legal information retrieval and entailment using transformer-based approaches. Rev. Socionetwork Strategies 1–21 (2024)

14. Li, H., et al.: SAILER: structure-aware pre-trained language model for legal case retrieval (2023)

15. Li, H., et al.: Constructing tree-based index for efficient and effective dense retrieval (2023)

16. Li, H., Chen, J., Su, W., Ai, Q., Liu, Y.: Towards better web search performance: pre-training, fine-tuning and learning to rank. arXiv preprint arXiv:2303.04710 (2023)

17. Li, H., Shao, Y., Wu, Y., Ai, Q., Ma, Y., Liu, Y.: LeCaRDv2: a large-scale Chinese legal case retrieval dataset (2023)

18. Li, H., Su, W., Wang, C., Wu, Y., Ai, Q., Liu, Y.: THUIR@COLIEE 2023: incorporating structural knowledge into pre-trained language models for legal case retrieval (2023)

19. Li, H., Wang, C., Su, W., Wu, Y., Ai, Q., Liu, Y.: THUIR@COLIEE 2023: More parameters and legal knowledge for legal case entailment (2023)

20. Liu, Y., et al.: RoBERTa: a robustly optimized BERT pretraining approach. arXiv preprint arXiv:1907.11692 (2019)

21. Ma, Y., et al.: LeCaRD: a legal case retrieval dataset for Chinese law system. In: Proceedings of the 44th International ACM SIGIR Conference on Research and Development in Information Retrieval, pp. 2342–2348 (2021)

22. Nogueira, R., Jiang, Z., Lin, J.: Document ranking with a pretrained sequence-to-sequence model. arXiv preprint arXiv:2003.06713 (2020)

23. Robertson, S., Zaragoza, H., et al.: The probabilistic relevance framework: BM25 and beyond. Found. Trends® Inf. Retrieval **3**(4), 333–389 (2009)

24. Seo, M., Kembhavi, A., Farhadi, A., Hajishirzi, H.: Bidirectional attention flow for machine comprehension. arXiv preprint arXiv:1611.01603 (2016)

25. Shao, Y., et al.: An intent taxonomy of legal case retrieval. ACM Trans. Inf. Syst. **42**(2) (2023). https://doi.org/10.1145/3626093

26. Shao, Y., et al.: BERT-PLI: modeling paragraph-level interactions for legal case retrieval. In: IJCAI, pp. 3501–3507 (2020)

27. Tran, V., Nguyen, M.L., Satoh, K.: Building legal case retrieval systems with lexical matching and summarization using a pre-trained phrase scoring model. In: Proceedings of the Seventeenth International Conference on Artificial Intelligence and Law, pp. 275–282 (2019)

28. Tu, Y., Li, H., Chu, Z., Ai, Q., Liu, Y.: THUIR at the NTCIR-17 FairWeb-1 task: an initial exploration of the relationship between relevance and fairness. In: Proceedings of NTCIR-17 (2023). https://doi.org/10.20736/0002001317

29. Xiao, C., Hu, X., Liu, Z., Tu, C., Sun, M.: Lawformer: a pre-trained language model for Chinese legal long documents. AI Open **2**, 79–84 (2021)

30. Xie, X., et al.: T2Ranking: a large-scale Chinese benchmark for passage ranking. arXiv preprint arXiv:2304.03679 (2023)
31. Xiong, L., et al.: Approximate nearest neighbor negative contrastive learning for dense text retrieval. arXiv preprint arXiv:2007.00808 (2020)
32. Yang, S., et al.: THUIR at the NTCIR-16 WWW-4 task. In: Proceedings of NTCIR-16 (2022)
33. Yu, W., et al.: Explainable legal case matching via inverse optimal transport-based rationale extraction. In: Proceedings of the 45th International ACM SIGIR Conference on Research and Development in Information Retrieval, pp. 657–668 (2022)
34. Zhai, C.: Statistical language models for information retrieval. Synthesis Lect. Hum. Lang. Technol. 1(1), 1–141 (2008)
35. Zhang, K., Chen, C., Wang, Y., Tian, Q., Bai, L.: CFGL-LCR: a counterfactual graph learning framework for legal case retrieval. In: Proceedings of the 29th ACM SIGKDD Conference on Knowledge Discovery and Data Mining, pp. 3332–3341 (2023)

Improving Robustness in Language Models for Legal Textual Entailment Through Artifact-Aware Training

Sabine Wehnert[1,2]([envelope]) [ORCID], Venkatesh Murugadas[1], Preetam Vinod Naik[1], and Ernesto William De Luca[1,2] [ORCID]

[1] Otto von Guericke University Magdeburg, Magdeburg, Germany
[2] Leibniz Institute for Educational Media | Georg Eckert Institute, Braunschweig, Germany
`sabine.wehnert@gei.de`

Abstract. In this paper, we describe our participation in COLIEE 2024, focusing on legal textual entailment (Tasks 2 and 4). Our goal is to address language artifacts during language model training for improved robustness. Limited domain-specific datasets pose challenges, leading us to apply language artifact detection and mitigation methods tailored to legal textual entailment tasks. For Task 2, involving identifying relevant paragraphs in previous cases, we address annotation artifacts in premises. In Task 4, predicting if statute law articles entail or contradict legal bar exam questions, we identify and mitigate various artifact types in hypotheses. We caution against relying on specific language artifacts and advocate for data profiling and measures to balance these implicit biases, enhancing overall model robustness.

Keywords: entailment classification · language artifacts · data augmentation

1 Introduction

In our contribution to the 2024 Competition on Legal Information Extraction/Entailment (COLIEE), the OVGU team participated in Tasks 2 and 4, focusing on legal textual entailment classification. Our aim for this COLIEE edition was to show that language artifacts are an issue to consider when training language models, as well as how to overcome this issue and make models more robust. In domain-specific datasets, we often face the challenge that they are limited in size. Therefore models that are trained on an unrepresentative or limited number of samples may be prone to develop biases and exhibit poor generalization capabilities. In order to make language models more robust and to understand their behavior better, it is worthwhile to detect potential language artifacts in the datasets that the models are trained on. Knowing the pitfalls leads the way to avoid them via several strategies which we employed in this paper. To the best of our knowledge, we are the first work that employs language artifact detection and mitigation methods on legal textual entailment tasks.

T. Suzumura and M. Bono (Eds.): JSAI-isAI 2024, LNAI 14741, pp. 228–244, 2024.
https://doi.org/10.1007/978-981-97-3076-6_16

The competition tasks themselves are on two different datasets: Task 2 on case law, and Task 4 on statute law. The objective of the second task is to locate a paragraph within previous cases that involves the decision relevant to a new case. When provided with a query or fragment from an old case, there could be several premises or paragraphs from a new case (P = P1, P2, P3,... Pn) that entail it. The objective of this task is to identify the particular paragraph P that corresponds to query Q. The data is linked to a database primarily consisting of case laws from the Federal Court of Canada, supplied by Compass Law.

The objective of Task 4, "Statute Law Textual Entailment", is to develop a system to predict if a set of relevant statute law articles either entails ("YES") or contradicts ("NO") a given legal bar examination question (Q). The Task 4 corpus of legal questions is drawn from Japanese Legal Bar exams, and all the Japanese statute law articles are also provided. The training data consists of a pair id, query, relevant article(s) and a correct answer "Y" or "N". The test data will include only pair id, queries and relevant articles, but no "Y/N" label. The relevant statute articles are considered as the premise and the legal bar exam questions are considered as the hypothesis in this paper.

On these tasks, our contributions are the following:

- We detect and mitigate annotation artifacts in the premises of Task 2.
- We detect several artifact types in the hypotheses of Task 4: sentence length, word overlap, contradition word, and subsequence heuristic.
- We mitigate word overlap and contradiction word artifacts for Task 4.

This paper's remainder is organized as follows: Sect. 2 covers artifact detection and mitigation concepts, referencing related work. In Sect. 3, we detail our approaches for Tasks 2 and 4. Section 4 includes the evaluation setup, results, and discussion. Finally, Sect. 5 concludes the work.

2 Background and Related Work

This section introduces basic concepts and approaches for language artifact detection and mitigation. There is no prior work specifically addressing artifacts in legal textual entailment use cases, leading us to works on artifacts in general Natural Language Inference (NLI) tasks.

In supervised learning, neural network models may generalize from weak features, termed language artifacts, introducing biases in dataset labels and affecting model predictions' reliability. These dataset biases are distinct from societal biases, being implicit and unintentional. Recognizing and addressing these subtle, yet influential, characteristics is crucial for improving the validity and performance of neural network models in supervised learning environments.

Artifact Detection. In Natural Language Processing (NLP), language artifacts are subtle biases within a language dataset that models often rely on for predictions. While achieving high performance on a specific dataset, these models may fail in real settings or on different datasets, as they rely on non-generalizable "shortcuts" instead of capturing essential task features. The term "language artifacts" is used to encompass various biases in language datasets. These artifacts can arise from lexical and/or syntactic features, with this study specifically addressing both types.

Annotation Artifacts occur when annotators consistently follow patterns while labeling sentences, leading to implicit biases across a dataset [7]. For instance, a strong correlation between a unigram feature "A" and a label "X" may cause the model to predict "X" whenever it encounters "A", overlooking other relevant features. This type of bias is referred to as an annotation artifact. Also, this strong correlation between a unigram feature and a class label is described as a spurious correlation/competency problem [5]. Similarly, this phenomenon is also labeled as lexical co-occurrence [17]. For detection of annotation artifacts, Pointwise Mutual Information (PMI) [7], Z-statistic scores [5] and also Binomial tests can be used to identify statistically significant strong correlations between single-word features in hypothesis and class label pairs.

Sentence Length Artifacts are characterized by an unequal length distribution in the hypothesis for each class label. In common Natural Language Inference (NLI) datasets, such as SNLI [3] and MNLI [22], the sentence length was detected as a syntactic artifact, potentially causing a bias in a statistical learner [7]. It is evident that the mere length of an input text shall not be indicative for a language model to predict a specific class label when performing an NLI task.

Word Overlap Artifacts in NLI occur when there is a significant overlap of words between the premise and the hypothesis. The guiding presumption behind these artifacts is that "Entailed" instances typically exhibit greater overlaps than "Not Entailed" classes. Word overlap artifacts are present in the SNLI and MNLI datasets, influencing the models trained on these datasets [13,25].

Contradiction Word Artifacts occur when a strong correlation exists between the presence of negation words in a training instance and the "Not Entailed" class label. There were studies conducted to scrutinise how contradiction words correlate with the contradiction label across different datasets [25].

Subsequence Heuristic Artifacts in Natural Language Inference (NLI) assume that the hypothesis is entirely derived from a subset of the premise, representing a special case of word overlap artifacts. Each segment of the hypothesis is considered a continuous subsequence of the premise [13]. These artifacts are commonly associated with "Entailed" instances.

Artifact Mitigation. For addressing language artifacts in NLI, researchers have employed both data-centric and model-centric approaches.

Data-Centric Strategies involve modifying datasets to reduce biases. Edit-based data augmentation [5] and sensitivity-based models [9] were proposed to minimize artifacts. Various data augmentation and adversarial filtering techniques were suggested [1,7,25], including premise swapping and adversarial systems to evenly distribute artifacts and improve generalization [21]. Studies also recommended to employ diverse annotators and separation of training and test set annotators [5,6].

Model-Centric Approaches focus on adapting NLI models. Adversarial classifiers can be used to mitigate hypothesis-only biases [1]. An ensemble method combining a naive and a robust model can be implemented to improve generalization [4]. Likewise, end-to-end learning strategies such as Products of Experts [12] and Debiased Focal Loss [16] concentrate on challenging examples. Various techniques for generalization in BERT-based models, including Siamese networks, HEX projections, and increasing the model size were also explored [2]. Techniques to fine-tune language models on difficult datasets [19], and to apply regularization for prompt-based fine-tuning in BERT-based models [20] can also be used for mitigation. These approaches collectively aim to reduce the influence of artifacts in NLI, thereby enhancing the robustness and accuracy of NLI systems.

3 Methodology

3.1 Task 2: Legal Case Entailment Classification

We discuss our approaches used for identifying and mitigating annotation artifacts for the COLIEE legal case entailment task. Overall, our artifact mitigation approach improved model robustness. For Task 2, we use BM25 [8] and a Bi-Encoder in the initial phase to select the best instances for a specific hypothesis. The data obtained from BM25 and the Bi-Encoder is then analyzed using a Binomial test to detect any annotation artifacts. Subsequently, we use the GPT-3.5-turbo[1] model from OpenAI because of its low costs and high performance to augment the COLIEE training dataset using predefined prompts to modify the artifact-containing premise slightly to switch the entailment label. This modified premise is added to the dataset to partially even out the label-respective co-occurrence with an annotation artifact to overcome these biases. A detailed explanation of these steps is presented in the following.

Candidate Selection Using BM25 and Bi-Encoder. The training dataset is heavily imbalanced towards the "Not Entailed" label, with 24,929 instances of "Not Entailed" and only 854 instances of "Entailed". If a model was to be trained on this data, it would focus primarily on "Not Entailed" examples and not learn enough about "Entailed" examples. To address this issue, BM25 from

---

[1] https://platform.openai.com/docs/models/gpt-3-5.

`rank-bm25`[2] was used to rank similar premises for a given hypothesis. We also used a Bi-Encoder from SentenceTransformer (`multi-qa-MiniLm-16-cos-v1`[3]) to find the most semantically similar premises for a given hypothesis. Our method involved two approaches to gather premises. Firstly, we used BM25 to find the top 5 premises. Secondly, we utilized a Bi-Encoder to obtain another set of top 5 premises. If there is any overlap between these two sets and the total number of premises is less than 10, we fill the remaining premises by selecting the next top-ranked result from BM25 for a given hypothesis. This process generates a dataset named the "Top 10". We also apply the same strategy to obtain the "Top 30" dataset, which consists of the top 30 similar instances for a given hypothesis. These datasets will be referred to as the "Top10" and "Top30" datasets in our paper. To address the issue of imbalanced data, we created a new dataset named "EquallyNotEntailed". This dataset comprises all "Entailed" premises for a specific hypothesis, along with an equal number of "Not Entailed" premises from the "Top 10" dataset. We will use the "EquallyNotEntailed" dataset, "Top 10" dataset, and "Top 30" dataset to fine-tune the model as explained in Sect. 3.1.

Artifact Detection. The training data significantly impacts model performance, and to ensure its quality, we apply the Binomial test for artifact detection on the "Top 10" dataset. Artifacts are detected in premises, since one hypothesis is compared to multiple premises, some containing relevant information influencing entailment classification.

Initially, we noted token occurrences in both "Not Entailed" and "Entailed" labels and conducted statistical analysis to identify biases toward a specific label. To identify the tokens that are more likely to be associated with the labels "Entailed" and "Not Entailed", the conditional probability was calculated between a token and a label. Then, to make sure that the observed association between tokens and labels is not just by chance, a statistical method known as a binomial significance test was applied with a significance level set at 0.1. For the "Not Entailed" label, we specifically consider tokens that have a conditional probability greater than 0.5 in texts labeled as "Not Entailed" and a p-value (a measure of significance) lower than 0.1 in the binomial significance test. Then, these tokens were considered as biased towards the "Not Entailed" label as their association with this label is strong and statistically significant. Later, similar steps were followed to find the "Entailed" bias tokens.

Upon analyzing the model's predictions on the validation set, we discovered that the model made incorrect predictions for "Not Entailed" bias tokens, classifying them as "Not Entailed" when they were in fact "Entailed". This led us to select "Not Entailed" bias tokens as a priority in our bias mitigation efforts, as this suggested that the model may be biased towards "Not Entailed" labels. In Table 1, we observe an excerpt of bias tokens that co-occur with the "Not Entailed" label. The word "applicant" was the most frequently occurring word in the "Not Entailed" list of labels, with a count of 3030 (see "N_Count"), while it only appeared 619 times in an "Entailed" label (see "Y_Count").

---

[2] https://pypi.org/project/rank-bm25/.

[3] https://huggingface.co/sentence-transformers/multi-qa-MiniLM-L6-cos-v1.

Table 1. "Not Entailed" annotation artifacts (top 5 and bottom 5 tokens).

Token	Count	N_Count	N_Prob	Y_Count	Y_Prob
applicant	3649	3030	0.83	619	0.17
evidence	3039	2378	0.78	661	0.22
canada	3042	2347	0.77	695	0.23
decision	2852	2286	0.80	566	0.20
court	2768	2145	0.77	623	0.23
...	...	...	...	...	...
routinely	4	4	1.00	0	0.00
knee	4	4	1.00	0	0.00
dual	4	4	1.00	0	0.00
valuing	4	4	1.00	0	0.00
gets	4	4	1.00	0	0.00

Artifact Mitigation. After identifying the annotation artifacts, we take steps to correct them by concentrating on the biases present in the top 40 and bottom 40 tokens. We focus on these subsets due to constraints on time and resources, which made it impractical to create new premises for every token identified. Instead, we generate 30 instances for each artifact token from both the top 30 and bottom 30 subsets using OpenAI's `GPT-3.5-turbo`[4] model, with a predefined prompt for a given "Not Entailed" bias token. The prompt instructs the GPT model to act as an NLP researcher with expertise in understanding complex legal texts. The model is given an example input consisting of a premise, hypothesis, and label. An example output is then provided in the prompt to demonstrate how to modify the premise to achieve an "Entailed" label. The modification involves incorporating a bias token, negation words, and antonyms of the specified token while retaining most of the original premise's wording. The prompt includes the following requirements for generating a new premise.

1. The token should be present in the new premise that is being created.
2. The original text should be preserved while adding negation and antonyms to switch the label from "Not Entailed" to "Entailed".

We illustrate the effect of artifact mitigation for the token *"Applicant"*, highlighting previous words in the premise in purple and replacements in yellow:

Before Mitigation: In summary, I am unable to agree with the Applicant that the Officer breached the rules of procedural fairness by cloaking adverse credibility findings in findings of insufficient evidence and then not according the Applicant an opportunity to respond to the Officer's concerns. The opportunity for the Applicant to put her best foot forward by providing

---

[4] https://platform.openai.com/docs/models/gpt-3-5.

full written representations in relation to all aspects of her application was ▮ accorded. This satisfied the participatory rights required by the duty of fairness in this case [...]

After   Mitigation: In summary, I am   able   to agree with the Applicant that the Officer breached the rules of procedural fairness by   revealing   adverse credibility findings in findings of sufficient   evidence and then   according the Applicant an opportunity to respond to the Officer's concerns. The opportunity for the Applicant to put her worst foot forward by not providing any   written representations in relation to   any aspect   of her application was not accorded. This did not satisfy the participatory rights required by the duty of fairness in this case [...]

We initially generated new premise instances for only the top 20 and bottom 20 bias tokens using the GPT-3.5-Turbo model. The new premises generated by this model were validated by using a validation prompt before they could be used for augmentation. If the validation failed (the newly created premise from the model did not entail the given hypothesis), we made three attempts before settling on the last generated premise. The instances created using the top 20 and bottom 20 bias tokens with this process were incorporated in the "Top 10" dataset, which we named the "Top10Adv20" dataset. Eventually, we generated further premises. This list was then added to the "Top 10" dataset to finally create the "Top10Adv40" dataset.

Model Fine-Tuning. Table 2 presents the model name and the corresponding data used to fine-tune the model. While tuning the model, we used the hyper-parameters as stated in the Sect. 4.1. For the remainder of this paper, we will refer to the models using the names provided in the table. We employed Custom Legal-BERT [24], which was trained on the Harvard law case corpus from 1965. This corpus includes 3,446,187 judicial decisions from federal and state courts.

Model Inference. During model inference, a chained approach was employed to leverage the strengths of the models. For the second task, we submitted three runs. In every run, we first checked for any instances in which the entire hypothesis corresponded exactly to a part of the premise which could be exploited as a subsequence heuristic. If any subsequences were found in an instance, we would have labeled that instance as "Entailed" and excluded it from further predictions, however, this case did not occur in the 2024 test data. For the *first run*, initial predictions for the hypotheses were made using Model 1, a model which had high precision scores on our validation data. However, for a few hypotheses all premises were predicted as "Not Entailed". Since each hypothesis must have at least one premise that entails it, the top 10 candidates for these hypotheses from the top 10 datasets were selected. Next, we forwarded these hypotheses to Model 4. The results generated were reviewed, and two additional hypotheses were still found to not have a single "Entailed" label. For these hypotheses, the top-ranked candidate from the BM25 result was used to label them as "Entailed". Finally, the results from all three techniques were combined to obtain the final result. During the *second run*, Model 2 was applied to the "Top 10" dataset to test the hypotheses. In case any hypotheses were missed, Model 3 was employed. However, after analyzing the results, three hypotheses were still found to be missing. The issue was resolved by using the same technique as in run 1, using BM25. In the *third run*, Model 5 was initially used on the "Top 10" dataset. For any hypotheses missed, Model 3 was used, and the same procedure from earlier was used. Table 3 contains results from a Vanilla Model trained on entire Task 2 data, showing high precision, but low recall performance.

Table 2. Table illustrating the dataset employed for model fine-tuning.

Model Name	Data Used
Model 1	"Top10" dataset
Model 2	"Top30" dataset
Model 3	"EquallyNotEntailed" dataset
Model 4	"Top10Adv20" dataset
Model 5	"Top10Adv40" dataset

3.2   Task 4: Statutory Law Entailment Classification

Artifact Detection. In Task 4, the following language artifacts were identified:

Sentence Length Artifact. To identify irregularities in hypothesis sentence lengths, we examined instances with lengths surpassing the average within both entailment and non-entailment labels. In the training dataset, 247 instances labeled as "Entailed" and 217 instances labeled as "Not Entailed" had sentence lengths exceeding the average of 39 words. Thereof, the higher number of "Entailed"-labeled instances suggests sentence length artifacts in the dataset.

Word Overlap Artifact. To identify these artifacts, we calculated the extent of word overlap between the premises and hypotheses. In the training dataset we observed that there are 203 "Entailed" instances and 140 "Not Entailed" instances with above 75% word overlap. This higher frequency of word overlaps in "Entailed" instances, indicates the presence of a word overlap artifact.

Contradiction Word Artifact. Similarly, we examined the correlation between the presence of negation words in the hypothesis and the assigned class labels. The negation words used to identify the contradiction word artifacts are: "not", "no", "n't", "none", "neither", "never", "nobody", "nothing", "nowhere", "hardly", "scarcely", "barely", "rarely", "seldom". In the training set, based on the listed negation words there are 277 "Not Entailed" instances and 246 "Entailed" instances with negation words. This indicates that instances with "Not Entailed" labels contain more negation words compared to those with "Entailed" labels, suggesting the presence of a contradiction word artifact.

Subsequence Heuristic Artifact. Regarding these artifacts, we explored instances where the entire hypothesis appeared as a subsequence within the premise. In the training set there were 14 such instances with an "Entailed" label and zero instances with a "Not Entailed" label. This points to the presence of subsequence heuristic artifacts in entailment instances. These identified language artifacts were used as features in the BERT-based textual entailment model to understand the impact of these artifacts on the performance of the model.

Model Fine-Tuning. This study examined the impact of language artifacts on BERT-based models, using the DeBERTa (Decoding-enhanced BERT with Disentangled Attention) [10] architecture. DeBERTa, an encoder model based on BERT and RoBERTa, incorporates a disentangled attention mechanism and an improved mask decoder. Pretraining involves a 78GB text corpus with a primary focus on Masked Language Modeling. For fine-tuning, a novel virtual adversarial training method is employed to enhance robustness and performance by normalizing word embeddings and introducing small perturbations. Due to the limited size of the statute law entailment dataset, the base model was fine-tuned on larger Natural Language Inference datasets. The chosen model `nli-deberta-v3-base`[5] [11] with 184 million parameters was fine-tuned on large Natural Language Inference (NLI) datasets such as Multi-NLI [22], Fact Extraction and VERification (FEVER) [18] and Adversarial NLI (ANLI) [23]. The base model is fine-tuned using the statute law entailment dataset. To evaluate the influence of language artifacts on the model's performance, these artifacts were integrated directly into the model inputs. The model's input comprises three elements: the premise, hypothesis, and language artifact features, each separated by a "SEP" token.

Artifact Mitigation. This study aimed to address two language artifacts: word overlap and contradiction word artifacts. Data augmentation was chosen to mitigate these issues in the training dataset. Instances requiring augmentation were identified based on high word overlap between premise and hypothesis with the class label "Y" (entailment) for word overlap artifacts, and instances with negation words in the hypothesis and a class label "N" for contradiction word artifacts. Per selected artifact token 30 counter-artifact instances, without artifacts, were created to balance the training dataset through a series of steps.

Step 1 Identify and filter existing counter-artifact instances in the training dataset for word overlap and contradiction word artifacts. The required number of counter-artifact instances is the difference between artifact and existing counter-artifact instances.

---

[5] https://huggingface.co/MoritzLaurer/DeBERTa-v3-base-mnli-fever-anli

Step 2 Paraphrase the hypothesis from the filtered instances using GPT-4 [14] to generate synthetic counter-artifact instances. Paraphrasing criteria include at least 1 negation word for a contradiction word artifact and 60% word overlap between the paraphrased hypothesis and the premise for a word overlap artifact. *Step 3* Validate the paraphrased hypothesis through a 3-fold process: 1) GPT-4 model comparison for checking if the meaning of the original and the paraphrased hypothesis are equal, 2) Cosine similarity calculation using a sentence transformer [15] with a 75% threshold, and 3) Manual validation for similarity to the original hypothesis. If any validation fails, repeat steps 2 and 3 until a valid paraphrased hypothesis is generated. Once the necessary number of instances without artifacts is generated they are then appended to the original training dataset to balance out the effect of artifacts. This new augmented dataset is then used to fine-tune the DeBERTa v3 model. The model inputs, hyperparameters of the model fine-tuning, and the criteria for choosing the best model remain the same as in the implementation of model fine-tuning without artifact mitigation.

Model Inference. We have defined three runs for assessing the performance of the models on the current (R05) and previous years' (H30, R01, R02) test data. The first two approaches, labeled as 4OVGUrun1 and 4OVGUrun3, incorporated an extra step of fine-tuning the DeBERTa model. This fine-tuning used the augmented dataset. Conversely, the approach denoted as 4OVGUrun2 involved fine-tuning the DeBERTa model exclusively with the Task 4 COLIEE dataset. For the 4OVGUrun1 and 4OVGUrun2 approaches, the input data comprised a "Premise", a "Hypothesis", and a Boolean feature determining if the hypothesis is a complete subsequence of the premise. In the case of 4OVGUrun3, inputs included "Premise", "Hypothesis", and additional features (a number and a boolean value) assessing word overlap between the premise and hypothesis.

4 Evaluation

4.1 Evaluation Setup

Task 2. The case law entailment task training dataset was divided with 80% for training and 20% for validation. The models underwent fine-tuning using various sub-datasets explained in the methodology section. They were further trained for 5 epochs during fine-tuning. The learning rate was set to 2e-5, and the maximum token length was configured as 512. A batch size of 8 was used for both the training and validation sets. For models 4 and 5, we used the same hyper-parameters with different random seeds: 100 for model 4 and 200 for model 5, while keeping the seed as 42 for the remaining models. The second task is evaluated using precision, recall, and F1 score.

Task 4. The statute law entailment dataset provided was divided, allocating 90% for training and 10% for validation. The training process involved fine-tuning the model under different conditions: without any artifact features, with

Table 3. Individual model performance on the Task 2 validation data.

Model	Precision	Recall	F1 Score
Vanilla Model	0.77	0.24	0.36
Model 1	0.62	0.48	0.54
Model 2	0.68	0.46	0.55
Model 3	0.23	0.75	0.36
Model 4	0.41	0.54	0.47
Model 5	0.59	0.44	0.50

Table 4. Performance across various runs on the Task 2 validation data.

Run Name	Models	Precision	Recall	F1 Score
2OVGUrun1	1&4	0.57	0.55	0.56
2OVGUrun2	2&3	0.51	0.67	0.58
2OVGUrun3	5&3	0.5	0.65	0.57

a combination of all artifact features, and with each artifact feature independently. The models underwent a fine-tuning process that spanned 15 epochs, using a learning rate of 3e−05. In addition, a weight decay of 0.06 was implemented for regularization purposes. Recognizing the stochastic nature of neural networks, the fine-tuning was conducted with three distinct seed values to ensure robustness. Each model's performance was evaluated on the validation dataset, with the best validation accuracy serving as the criterion for model selection. In Task 4, the metric used to assess performance is accuracy, determined by the rate of correctly validated yes/no questions.

4.2 Results

Task 2. The performance comparisons of different models on the validation set are shown in Table 3. Based on the results, Model 2 demonstrated the highest precision among all models on the validation set. On the other hand, Model 3 showed the highest recall, indicating that it was able to accurately identify the actual positives. Model 5 exhibited a balance between precision and recall. We chained multiple models, as discussed in Sect. 3.1, to achieve the best precision,

Table 5. Task 2 official runs on the COLIEE 2024 test data.

Run Name	Precision	Recall	F1 Score
2OVGUrun1	**0.5636**	**0.6327**	**0.5962**
2OVGUrun2	0.5506	0.5918	0.5705
2OVGUrun3	0.5000	0.6190	0.5532

recall, and F1 score. Table 4 shows the performance comparison of different runs on the validation set. For "2OVGUrun1", there was a balanced precision and recall, which resulted in an F1 Score of 0.56. In the second run, the recall was higher at 0.67, but the precision was slightly lower at 0.51, leading to an F1 Score of 0.58. Additionally, the third run exhibited a balanced precision-recall trade-off, which produced an F1 Score of 0.57. Table 5 displays the performance of different runs submitted for the competition on the test data. The combination of the high-precision "Model 1" and the model trained on the top-20 and bottom-20 bias tokens augmented data "Model 4" in "2OVGUrun1" yielded the best performance. We could not fully assess the overall impact of using the augmentation method due to the lack of previous year comparisons for Task 2 models with and without artifact mitigation, particularly in the context of chained models. However, preliminary experiments showed a performance boost across various seeds, suggesting enhanced stability. Our data augmentation methodology, while effective, had limitations such as not considering stopwords as bias tokens, which could have improved model performance. Additionally, ensuring validity of newly generated premises is crucial; our approach allows for three attempts, reverting to the last validated premise as "Not Entailed" if unsuccessful, potentially resulting in some tokens remaining unmitigated. After training on the augmented data, we inspected several instances to perform an error analysis and found the following activation profile for one of them using `transformers-interpret`[6]:

Wrongly Predicted Instance after Mitigation:
"[CLS] mr [UNK] justice gibson held breach procedural fairness visa officer fail consider use discretion subsection 76 [UNK] 3 [UNK] requested so [UNK] [SEP] singh v minister citizenship immigration see footnote colleague justice bla ##is noted paragraph reasons well estab lished law decision visa officer whether grant permanent resident visa discretionary decision based essentially factual assessment goes however paragraph reasons note ##how ##ever concerns raised alleged breach procedural fairness proper standard review correctness court determines breach procedural fairness occurred must return deci sion first instance decisionmaker redetermination citation omitted ##i satisfied allegation officer failed consider exercise positive discretion substituted evaluation specifically requested applicants application permanent residence allegation breach procedural fairness therefore review allegation standard review correctness ##fa ##il ##ure consider exercise positive discretion substituted evaluation [SEP]"

---

[6] https://github.com/cdpierse/transformers-interpret.

After mitigation, this instance was wrongly classified as "Not Entailed" instead of "Entailed". We highlight the attribution towards the "Not Entailed" label, i.e., green highlights show the tendency of the model towards this label, while red highlights indicate negative attribution against the label "Not Entailed". Although we see that the influence of the artifact "decision" is still strong after mitigation, not every occurrence of it is attributed anymore. Considering Table 1, we see that the difference between "Entailed" and "Not Entailed" instances for the artifact "decision" is still 1690 instances, even after augmenting 30 instances during mitigation. Also, the artifact "court" is still attributed. Although the mitigation has improved model performance, future work shall consider creating more adversarial instances to balance out the strongly biased artifacts. Visualizing attention in transformer models can aid in understanding their behavior, but limitations arise due to tokens marked as unknown ("UNK"), leading to potential new language artifacts.

Task 4. The analysis of the DeBERTa model's performance, is documented in Table 6, both before and after the mitigation of language artifacts. This analysis, focusing on average scores, reveals a slight enhancement in certain features, notably "NO FEATURE", "WORD_OVERLAP", and "CONTRADICTION_WORD", following the mitigation process. The post-mitigation increase in average scores for the "NO FEATURE" category signifies improved overall model robustness, achieved without targeting specific language artifact features. Notably, the model showed enhanced performance in mitigating "WORD_OVERLAP" and "CONTRADICTION_WORD" features, which were the focus of mitigation efforts. Performance consistency across different seeds underscores the necessity of targeted mitigation strategies. Also, mitigating word overlap and contradiction word artifacts decreased model accuracy when using the "SENTENCE_LENGTH" feature. This likely stems from a bias introduced during augmentation: hypotheses with the "Not Entailed" label were lengthened in word overlap augmented instances, while "Entailed" hypothesis sentences were shortened in contradiction word augmented instances. This artificial correlation may have hindered the model's ability to generalize beyond the "SENTENCE_LENGTH" feature, leading it to rely on this bias and reducing post-mitigation accuracy. Results on the COLIEE test data (Table 7) demonstrate the effectiveness of artifact mitigation. Notably, "4OVGUrun1" and "4OVGUrun3", both using data augmentation, outperformed "4OVGUrun2". "4OVGUrun1" displayed higher recall than "4OVGUrun2", however, it is crucial to also acknowledge the study's limitations. The DeBERTa model was fine-tuned on large Natural Language Inference (NLI) datasets, potentially containing inherent language artifacts not explicitly addressed here. This shows the necessity for a comprehensive approach to artifact mitigation in language models, encompassing both downstream task interventions and inherent training data characteristics. We conducted error analysis on the COLIEE 2024 Task 4 test set, examining the impact of mitigating word overlap and contradiction word artifacts on model performance, and provided illustrative examples. In instance "R05-12-U" containing contradiction word artifacts with the "Entailed" label, the mitigated model runs ("4OVGUrun1" and "4OVGUrun3") outperformed the unmitigated run ("4OVGUrun2"). The instance "R05-09-E" was a case where mitigation improved performance in instances with high word overlap with a "Not Entailed" label. However, instances such as "R05-18-E" (see Table 8) were correctly predicted by the unmitigated run, while they were misclassified by the mitigated models. This might suggest that where high word overlap and contradiction words occur in the hypothesis, the model may still depend on the word overlap artifact. Augmenting the dataset with instances exhibiting high word overlap and contradiction terms with the "Entailed" label could potentially reduce these errors. Similarly, the instance "R05-18-U" with high word overlap and a "Not Entailed" label demonstrated poorer performance after mitigation, indicating the strategy's limitations. This indicates that future work should incorporate additional augmented data to address word overlap artifacts and further improve model robustness.

Table 6. Validation performance before and after mitigation: average accuracy scores with corresponding Standard Errors (SE) across different seed values.

Feature Name	Avg Accuracy Before Mitigation ($\pm$SE)	Avg Accuracy After Mitigation ($\pm$SE)
NO FEATURE	0.6667 $\pm$ 0.018	0.6757 $\pm$ 0.003
ALL	0.6606 $\pm$ 0.011	0.6606 $\pm$ 0.003
SENTENCE_LENGTH	0.7030 $\pm$ 0.011	0.6545 $\pm$ 0.005
WORD_OVERLAP	0.6727 $\pm$ 0.019	0.6909 $\pm$ 0.0000
CONTRADICTION_WORD	0.6757 $\pm$ 0.013	0.6788 $\pm$ 0.008
SUBSEQUENCE	0.6725 $\pm$ 0.005	0.6727 $\pm$ 0.019

Table 7. Task 4 official runs on the current (R05) and previous test data.

Run name	R05	R02	R01	H30
4OVGUrun1	**0.7064**	0.7531	**0.6937**	0.6714
4OVGUrun2	0.6422	0.6790	0.6396	0.6000
4OVGUrun3	0.6972	**0.7654**	0.6306	**0.7000**

Table 8. Task 4 "R05-18-E" inspection for overlaps and contradiction words.

Premise	Hypothesis
Article 424 (1) An obligee may demand the court to rescind an act which the obligor commits knowing that it will prejudice the obligee; provided, however, that this does not apply if a person that benefits from that act (hereinafter referred to as the "beneficiary" in this Subsection) does not know, at the time of the act, that the obligee will be prejudiced. (2) [...] (3) [...] (4) The obligee may not make demand for rescission of fraudulent act if the obligee's claim is not enforceable by compulsory execution.	Assume that A has a claim against B for 20 million yen based on a contract for sale with B and that B is insolvent and knows that each act is prejudicial to the obligee. A and B has agreed not to carry out compulsory execution regarding said claim. In this case, even if B has given land owned by B to G and G knew that such gift was prejudicial to the obligee, A cannot make a demand for rescission of the fraudulent act with respect to such gift

5   Conclusion

In this work, we employed language artifact detection and mitigation strategies on the legal textual entailment tasks of the COLIEE competition. We found that artifact-aware training can increase language model robustness. Future research can employ the proposed methods on further language models. Generating adversarial test datasets, especially in the legal domain, is an effective method to detect model susceptibilities and to overcome them. Further work can be done on more extensive model introspection (e.g., visualizing attention scores) to potentially prove if a language model indeed attends to artifacts for predictions.

Disclosure of Interests. The authors have no competing interests to declare that are relevant to the content of this article.

References

1. Belinkov, Y., et al.: On adversarial removal of hypothesis-only bias in natural language inference. In: Mihalcea, R., et al. (eds.) Proceedings of the Eighth Joint Conference on Lexical and Computational Semantics, *SEM@NAACL-HLT 2019, Minneapolis, MN, USA, 6–7 June 2019, pp. 256–262. Association for Computational Linguistics (2019). https://doi.org/10.18653/V1/S19-1028
2. Bhargava, P., et al.: Generalization in NLI: ways (not) to go beyond simple heuristics (2021). http://arxiv.org/abs/2110.01518
3. Bowman, S.R., et al.: A large annotated corpus for learning natural language inference. In: Màrquez, L., Callison-Burch, C., Su, J. (eds.) Proceedings of the EMNLP 2015, pp. 632–642. Association for Computational Linguistics, Lisbon (2015). https://doi.org/10.18653/v1/D15-1075

4. Clark, C., et al.: Don't take the easy way out: ensemble based methods for avoiding known dataset biases. In: Inui, K., et al. (eds.) Proceedings of the EMNLP-IJCNLP 2019, Hong Kong, China, 3–7 November 2019, pp. 4067–4080. Association for Computational Linguistics (2019). https://doi.org/10.18653/V1/D19-1418

5. Gardner, M., et al.: Competency problems: on finding and removing artifacts in language data (2021). http://arxiv.org/abs/2104.08646

6. Geva, M., et al.: Are we modeling the task or the annotator? An investigation of annotator bias in natural language understanding datasets (2019). http://arxiv.org/abs/1908.07898

7. Gururangan, S., et al.: Annotation artifacts in natural language inference data (2018). http://arxiv.org/abs/1803.02324

8. Gururangan, S., et al.: Annotation artifacts in natural language inference data. CoRR abs/1803.02324 (2018). http://arxiv.org/abs/1803.02324

9. Hahn, M., et al.: Sensitivity as a complexity measure for sequence classification tasks. Trans. ACL **9**, 891–908 (2021)

10. He, P., et al.: DeBERTav3: improving DEBERta using ELECTRA-style pre-training with gradient-disentangled embedding sharing (2023)

11. Laurer, M., et al.: Less annotating, more classifying – addressing the data scarcity issue of supervised machine learning with deep transfer learning and BERT - NLI. Preprint (2022). https://osf.io/74b8k

12. Mahabadi, R.K., et al.: End-to-end bias mitigation by modelling biases in corpora. In: Jurafsky, D., et al. (eds.) Proceedings of the ACL 2020, Online, 5–10 July 2020, pp. 8706–8716. Association for Computational Linguistics (2020). https://doi.org/10.18653/V1/2020.ACL-MAIN.769

13. McCoy, T., et al.: Right for the wrong reasons: diagnosing syntactic heuristics in natural language inference. In: Korhonen, A., Traum, D.R., Màrquez, L. (eds.) Proceedings of the 57th Conference of the Association for Computational Linguistics, ACL 2019, Florence, Italy, 28 July–2 August 2019, Volume 1: Long Papers, pp. 3428–3448. Association for Computational Linguistics (2019). https://doi.org/10.18653/v1/p19-1334

14. OpenAI: GPT-4 technical report. ArXiv abs/2303.08774 (2023). https://arxiv.org/abs/2303.08774

15. Reimers, N., Gurevych, I.: Sentence-BERT: sentence embeddings using Siamese BERT-networks. In: Proceedings of the 2019 Conference on Empirical Methods in Natural Language Processing. Association for Computational Linguistics (2019). http://arxiv.org/abs/1908.10084

16. Sanh, V., et al.: Learning from others' mistakes: avoiding dataset biases without modeling them (2020). http://arxiv.org/abs/2012.01300

17. Tan, S., et al.: Investigating biases in textual entailment datasets (2019). http://arxiv.org/abs/1906.09635

18. Thorne, J., et al.: FEVER: a large-scale dataset for fact extraction and VERification. In: Walker, M., et al. (eds.) Proceedings of the 2018 Conference of the North American Chapter of the Association for Computational Linguistics: Human Language Technologies, Volume 1 (Long Papers), pp. 809–819. Association for Computational Linguistics, New Orleans (2018). https://doi.org/10.18653/v1/N18-1074

19. Tu, L., et al.: An empirical study on robustness to spurious correlations using pre-trained language models. Trans. Assoc. Comput. Linguistics **8**, 621–633 (2020). https://doi.org/10.1162/TACL_A_00335

20. Utama, P.A., et al.: Avoiding inference heuristics in few-shot prompt-based fine-tuning. arXiv preprint arXiv:2109.04144 (2021)

21. Wang, H., et al.: What if we simply swap the two text fragments? A straightforward yet effective way to test the robustness of methods to confounding signals in nature language inference tasks. In: AAAI 2019, IAAI 2019, EAAI 2019, Honolulu, Hawaii, USA, 27 January–1 February 2019, pp. 7136–7143. AAAI Press (2019). https://doi.org/10.1609/AAAI.V33I01.33017136
22. Williams, A., et al.: A broad-coverage challenge corpus for sentence understanding through inference. In: Walker, M.A., et al. (eds.) Proceedings of the NAACL-HLT 2018, New Orleans, Louisiana, USA, 1–6 June 2018, Volume 1 (Long Papers), pp. 1112–1122. Association for Computational Linguistics (2018). https://doi.org/10.18653/V1/N18-1101
23. Williams, A., et al.: ANLIzing the adversarial natural language inference dataset (2020)
24. Zheng, L., et al.: When does pretraining help?: assessing self-supervised learning for law and the casehold dataset of 53, 000+ legal holdings. In: Maranhão, J., Wyner, A.Z. (eds.) ICAIL 2021: Eighteenth International Conference for Artificial Intelligence and Law, São Paulo Brazil, 21–25 June 2021, pp. 159–168. ACM (2021). https://doi.org/10.1145/3462757.3466088
25. Zhou, X., Bansal, M.: Towards robustifying NLI models against lexical dataset biases (2020). http://arxiv.org/abs/2005.04732

Eighth International Workshop on SCIentific DOCument Analysis (SCIDOCA 2024)

SCIDOCA is an annual international workshop focusing on various aspects and perspectives of scientific document analysis for their efficient use and exploration. Recent proliferation of scientific papers and technical documents has become an obstacle to efficient information acquisition of new information in various fields. It is almost impossible for individual researchers to check and read all related documents. Even retrieving relevant documents is becoming harder and harder. This workshop gathers all the researchers and experts who are aiming at scientific document analysis from various perspectives, and invite technical paper presentations and system demonstrations that cover any aspects of scientific document analysis. The Eighth International Workshop on SCIentific DOCument Analysis (SCIDOCA 2024) associated with JSAI International Symposia on AI 2024 (IsAI-2024).

Relevant topics include, but are not limited to, the following:

– Text analysis
– Document structure analysis
– Logical structure analysis
– Figure and table analysis
– Citation analysis of scientific and technical documents
– Scientific information assimilation
– Summarization and visualization
– Knowledge discovery/mining from scientific papers and data
– Similar document retrieval
– Entity and relation linking between documents and knowledge base
– Survey generation
– Resources for scientific documents analysis
– Document understanding in general
– NLP systems aiming for scientific documents including tagging, parsing, coreference, etc.

Among all submitted papers reviewed by experts in the field, we discussed intensively nominating the best of them with sufficiently high quality for inclusion in the LNAI proceedings.

We thank all the Steering Committee, Advisory Committee, and Program Committee of SCIDOCA 2024, all authors who submitted papers, and all the members of the Organizing Committee of JSAI-isAI.

May 2024

Minh Le Nguyen
Vu Tran
Yuji Matsumoto

A Framework for Enhancing Statute Law Retrieval Using Large Language Models

Trang Ngoc Anh Pham$^{(\boxtimes)}$, Dinh-Truong Do, and Minh Le Nguyen

Japan Advanced Institute of Science and Technology, Nomi, Japan
{trangpna,truongdo,nguyenml}@jaist.ac.jp

Abstract. Large language models (LLMs) have proven effective across a range of natural language processing tasks, yet their application in the legal domain, particularly for legal retrieval tasks, remains largely unexplored. This paper introduces a novel framework aiming to harness the capabilities of LLMs for statute law retrieval. Initially, we employed a legal-data-fine-tuned encoder language model to retrieve candidate articles. Subsequently, we incorporated LLMs to refine high-recall predictions from the candidate articles, aiming to enhance precision through in-context learning and self-generated explanations. Our experiments on the statute law retrieval task of COLIEE 2023 showcase the effectiveness of our framework, achieving a new state-of-the-art result with a 2.9% higher F2 score.

Keywords: Statue Law Retrieval · Legal information processing · Large language models

1 Introduction

Along with our increasingly complex society, the increasing in complexity and volume of legal information requires advanced retrieval systems that can efficiently and accurately extract relevant legal documents [1]. This growing need reflects the demand for efficient legal retrieval solutions as legal practitioners contend with extensive databases housing diverse documents, from statutes to case law. Recent advances in digitization have greatly expanded lawyers' access to online legal resources. However, the proliferation of legal documents has made it increasingly challenging to locate the most pertinent legal information crucial for lawyers' court preparation. Thus, developing an automated law retrieval system is significant in improving the lawyer's workflow. It can be seen that the use of automatic systems in finding and retrieving documents that match the needs of users is a mandatory requirement. Because of the importance of correctness in the legal field, the performance of these systems holds significant importance for their real-world applicability. As a result, research on legal information retrieval systems has received attention from both legal and information retrieval communities [2,3].

T. Suzumura and M. Bono (Eds.): JSAI-isAI 2024, LNAI 14741, pp. 247–259, 2024.
https://doi.org/10.1007/978-981-97-3076-6_17

In the context of statute law retrieval, the objective is to develop a system that effectively curates a subset of articles directly relevant to a specified legal question (Fig. 1). The task involves the selection of articles, denoted as A_i, that directly and comprehensively address the nuances of the given question Q. A_i is considered "relevant" to Q if that question can be answered Yes/No, entailed from the meaning of the article. If multiple articles collectively provide an answer to a query sentence, all relevant articles are considered. Consider the following illustrative scenario, given the Question (Q): "Explain the legal implications of 'force majeure' in Japanese contract law", the system is expected to select a subset of legal articles that provide a detailed and relevant discussion on the legal concept of 'force majeure' within the context of Japanese contract law.

Addressing the challenge of statute law retrieval, prior studies [4,5] have demonstrated the effectiveness of fine-tuning an encoder language model on legal datasets. Moreover, large language models (LLMs) have proven their efficacy across various natural language processing tasks (NLP) [6,7], including legal retrieval [2]. However, prior approaches employing LLMs for statute law retrieval tasks could only use LLMs pre-fine-tuned on retrieval datasets like MS-MACRO [8]. This limitation hinders generalizability to other LLMs, and if application to other models is desired, retraining on retrieval data becomes an expensive necessity.

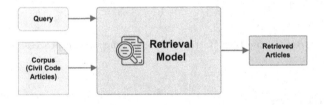

Fig. 1. A standard flow of statute law retrieval system.

This paper introduces a framework designed to address the challenge of statute law retrieval, comprising two key phases: *BERT-based retrieval* and *LLM-based re-ranking* (Fig. 2). In the initial phase, aligning with a previous approach [4,5], we fine-tune an encoder language model on a legal dataset using the TfIdf term matching technique as negative sampling method, with the top-k_1 relevant articles (e.g., $k_1 = 150$) as negative samples. During inference, the fine-tuned model retrieves the top-k_2 articles $R = [R_1, R_2, ..., R_{k_2}]$ (e.g., $k_2 = 5$). In the second phase, utilizing the top-k_2 articles, we leverage LLMs to refine high-recall predictions, aiming to enhance precision. To achieve this, we propose three prompting methods that input into LLMs, harnessing the power of in-context learning and self-generated explanations. The output of this second phase constitutes the final answer. Unlike previous works [2,4], our approach is versatile and can be applied to any human-instruction fine-tuned LLMs. In summary, our contributions to this paper can be outlined as follows:

- First, we present a novel framework harnessing the capabilities of LLMs for statute law retrieval.
- Second, we conduct a comprehensive experiment showcasing the effectiveness of our framework, achieving new state-of-the-art results on the COLIEE 2023 dataset [9].
- Third, we undertake a thorough analysis to deepen our understanding of the proposed framework.

2 Related Work

Information retrieval stands as a fundamental task within natural language processing (NLP). In the legal domain, retrieval systems play a crucial role in delivering relevant and valuable legal content to users. A variety of approaches have been proposed to address the challenges of legal retrieval, particularly in the context of statute law retrieval. Nguyen et al. [5] employed a bert-base-japanese-whole-word-masking model, augmented with TfIdf-based data enhancement, and introduced innovative strategies like Next Foreign Sentence Prediction and Neighbor Multilingual Sentence Prediction. Kim et al. [10] focused on traditional information retrieval methods, achieving optimal results with the BM25 algorithm. Yoshioka et al. [11] developed a BERT-based information retrieval system complemented by Indri and a newly curated article database. Bui et al. [12] devised two specialized deep-learning models to address ordinal and use-case inquiries. Additionally, Yoshioka et al. [13] applied diverse information retrieval models, each distinguished by unique features in terms of document databases and sentence embeddings.

With the rise of Large Language Models (LLMs), powered by the Transformer architecture [14], ranging from models like T5 [15] with tens of billions of parameters to GPT-3 [16] with hundreds of billions, a new era in NLP has unfolded. LLMs exhibit the ability to generate fluent text and excel in various NLP tasks [6,7]. They can interpret natural language instructions to perform tasks in a zero-shot setting or generalize tasks with minimal annotated data in a few-shot setting [17], relying on in-context learning [18]. Notable LLMs like Llama-2 [6], GPT-4 [19], and Mistral [20] have garnered attention for their impressive results. While previous research showcases LLMs' effectiveness across various NLP tasks, their direct application to information retrieval, particularly in the legal domain, remains largely unexplored. Legal articles are typically lengthy, surpassing the context length limitations of LLMs, which are constrained to thousands of tokens. In this study, we propose a method to leverage the capabilities of LLMs for statute law retrieval.

3 Method

3.1 Overview

In this paper, we employ a two-step retrieval process utilizing LLMs. Our proposed framework, illustrated in Fig. 2, comprises two phases: BERT-based retrieval and LLM-based re-ranking. Initially, we fine-tune a BERT-based encoder model on the annotated dataset. Following fine-tuning, during the inference phase, we obtain the top-k_2 relevant retrievals. In the second phase, we leverage high-performance prompts in tandem with LLMs to achieve the final prediction. In the context of the few-shot setting, LLMs are presented with a set of examples extracted from similar cases within the training dataset, enhancing their comprehension of the designated task and resulting in improved predictions. Additionally, we employ LLMs to generate explanations using the few-shot with explanation method, aiming for a thoughtful approach where LLMs think first and then provide answers.

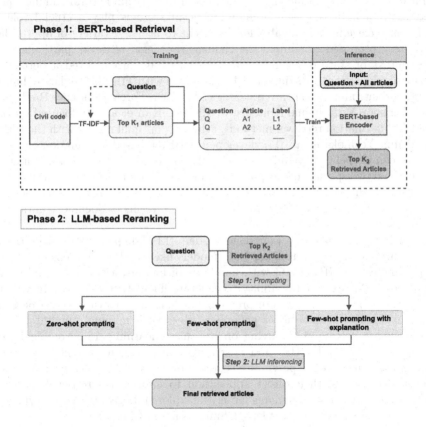

Fig. 2. An overview of our proposed method.

3.2 BERT-Based Retrieval

During this phase, our objective is to assemble a set of candidate articles with the expectation that this set exhibits high recall. This set is then utilized as a seed to input into LLMs to enhance precision. Building upon strategies employed in previous research [5], we leverage the capabilities of a pre-trained encoder language model and incorporate specific negative sampling techniques to refine a model adept at extracting relevant articles from a legal corpus. In the training process, given an input query, we select the top-k_1 relevant articles (e.g., $k_1 = 150$ as in [5]) using term matching techniques like TfIdf. Subsequently, these identified articles are paired with the query and input into a pre-trained language model to identify and retrieve the relevant articles. During the inference step, the fine-tuned model initially retrieves the top-k_2 relevant candidate articles $R = [R_1, R_2, ..., R_{k_2}]$ (e.g., $k_2 = 5, 10, ...$).

3.3 LLMs-Based Re-ranking

Building upon top-k_2 relevant candidate articles retrieved from the previous phase, our framework employs LLMs to produce the final result through three distinct prompting strategies: *zero-shot prompting, few-shot prompting*, and *few-show with explanation prompting*.

Zero-Shot Prompting. In the zero-shot prompting approach, we feed the LLMs with candidate articles $R = [R_1, R_2, ..., R_{k2}]$ and the query Q (Fig. 3). Various prompts are meticulously designed to elicit responses from the LLMs, significantly influencing the obtained results. To assess these prompts' performance, we conduct experiments and analyze their outcomes on a small scale. The essence of our strategy lies in the continuous refinement of prompts based on observed mistakes during experimentation. Through analyzing LLM-generated responses, we pinpoint common errors or inconsistencies in the final answers. This iterative refinement process allows us to improve prompts, address identified errors, and enhance the quality and relevance of the generated final responses.

After thorough studies and repeated refinement, we have identified the optimal prompt design that consistently produces the most accurate and relevant final answers from the LLMs, as illustrated in Fig. 3. Our experiments underscore the critical importance of controlling information provided to LLMs to ensure the generation of precise responses. Particularly in the zero-shot setting, we have found that prefixing the Assistant's response with "The answer(s) is/are: Article" efficiently manages information flow, directing LLMs to focus on providing relevant article selections. This strategic approach improves the interpretability and relevance of generated final answers, ultimately enhancing the overall efficacy of our zero-shot LLM-based prediction methodology.

Few-Shot Prompting. Prior studies have acknowledged that few-shot settings tend to outperform zero-shot settings with LLMs [16,21]. Therefore, we further refine this strategy by incorporating demonstrations for LLMs with a few-shot prompting. To implement this, we utilize sentence-BERT [22] to extract a set of similar queries from the training set in comparison to the current query Q. These similar queries capture semantic similarities, offering examples for LLMs to base from. Leveraging sentence-BERT allows us to efficiently identify relevant queries,

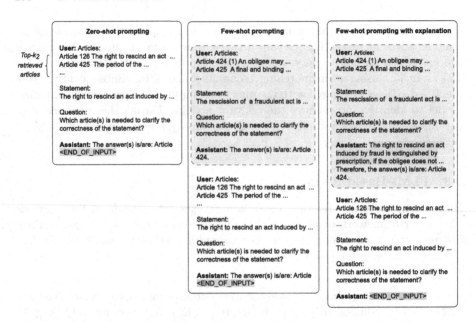

Fig. 3. Three different prompting approaches in our method. The content enclosed within the dashed box represents demonstrations utilized in the few-shot setting and would be excluded in the zero-shot setting. The explanation of the result text is highlighted in green (Color figure online).

serving as effective demonstrations to guide LLMs in generating accurate and pertinent final answers.

Once we have identified these similar queries, we construct an input prompt for the few-shot prompting. This prompt includes the similar queries, along with their relevant articles and the responses generated for each query, preceding the current query Q and articles R. Essentially, we provide LLMs with instructional examples demonstrating the desired behavior when responding to queries akin to Q. These demonstration examples are incorporated into the conversation history of LLMs before posing the actual query Q, ensuring they are easy to handle and influential in guiding the model's understanding. Subsequently, LLMs generate the final answer using this input prompt. By offering demonstration samples within the input prompt, our objective is to enhance LLMs' understanding of the task, achieving improved predictions, and thereby advancing the effectiveness of our legal document retrieval methodology. An example of a few-shot prompt with LLMs is depicted in Fig. 3.

Furthermore, when prompting demonstration examples to LLMs, we faced challenges associated with managing lengthy text inputs, particularly when incorporating multiple demonstration examples and relevant articles into the input prompt. Acknowledging the constraints imposed by the maximum length limitations of LLMs, we introduced a threshold for the maximum length of the input prompt. If the combined length of demonstration examples, relevant

Prompt to create explanation

User: Articles:
Article 424 (1) An obligee may demand the court to rescind an act which the obligor commits ...
Article 425 A final and binding judgment upholding demand for rescission of fraudulent act is ...
...

Statement:
The rescission of a fraudulent act is performed by the court based on the demand of the obligee.

Question:
Which article(s) is needed to clarify the correctness of the statement?

Assistant: The answer(s) is/are: Article 424.

User: Explain shortly the reason why you gave that answer.

Assistant: <END_OF_INPUT>

Fig. 4. Illustration of employing LLMs to generate explanations for answers.

articles, and the current query surpasses this threshold, we dynamically adjust the input prompt by reducing the number of examples and relevant articles. Through experimentation with various configurations, including 1-shot, 2-shot, 3-shot, and different quantities of related articles, we observed that only a small number of prompts exceeded the memory limit. This technique ensures the integrity of the input prompt while also facilitating experimentation with larger settings.

Few-Shot Prompting with Explanation. As a further extension of the few-shot approach, we introduce the incorporation of explanations into the input prompt, fostering a step-by-step thinking process for LLMs. Previous studies [23,24] have suggested that prompting LLMs to articulate their reasoning steps can improve the quality of their responses, potentially leading to more logical and human-like outcomes. Our objective is to enhance the model's understanding of the task and improve the coherence and accuracy of its answers by guiding it through a series of reasoned steps. To implement this method, we initiate by retrieving a set of similar queries from the training dataset using sentence-BERT, as detailed in the previous section. These queries act as reference points for the current query Q, capturing semantic similarities that aid in contextual understanding. Building on this foundation, we prompt the LLMs to provide explanations for why each relevant article is pertinent to the given query. This prompts the model to engage in a logical reasoning process, articulating the rationale behind its selection of relevant articles and elucidating the thought process underlying its decision-making.

The resulting set of examples, which includes queries paired with their corresponding explanations and final answers, forms the basis of our input prompt for the few-shot with explanation setting. An illustration of this prompting method is demonstrated in Fig. 3. By incorporating these explanations into the prompt, we provide the LLMs with a rich context for understanding the task and generating informed responses. This approach not only enhances the model's ability to navigate complex legal documents but also facilitates a more human-like reasoning process, ultimately advancing the effectiveness of our legal document retrieval methodology.

4   Experiments

4.1   Datasets

The experiments utilized datasets from COLIEE 2023, which included 996 questions, a legal corpus (Civil Code) consisting of 768 articles, and 1272 pairs of questions and relevant articles (positive samples). The dataset is originally in Japanese, and an English-translated version was also provided by the organizers. Both versions of the datasets were utilized in this study.

In addition to adhering to the official competition's train/test division, questions with IDs starting with R02 and R03 were specifically allocated for validation, with model and settings evaluations conducted on this subset. Our experimental assessment aims to gauge the effectiveness of our proposed methods, comparing the results with the best outcome from COLIEE 2023 based on the development set. To ensure a fair comparison with COLIEE 2023's best result, we optimized model hyperparameters using the R02 and R03 subsets and evaluated performance on the R04 subset.

4.2   Evaluation Metrics

In this research, we utilize evaluation metrics such as precision, recall, and the F2-measure. Among these, recall is given priority due to the primary emphasis on information retrieval in the task, specifically, the selection of candidate articles relevant to the given query. The definitions of these metrics are as follows:

$$\text{Precision} = \text{average of } \frac{\text{the number of correctly retrieved articles for each query}}{\text{the number of retrieved articles for each query}} \quad (1)$$

$$\text{Recall} = \text{average of } \frac{\text{the number of correctly retrieved articles for each query}}{\text{the number of relevant articles for each query}} \quad (2)$$

$$\text{F2-measure} = \frac{5 \times \text{Precision} \times \text{Recall}}{4 \times \text{Precision} + \text{Recall}} \quad (3)$$

4.3   Experiments Configurations

The experiments were carried out on the COLIEE 2023 test set, and the following models and configurations were employed to generate the results in the experimental section:

- **BERT-based Retrieval:** We followed the method of previous work [5] to retrieve the set of candidate articles. We keep the hyperamter same as the original paper that employed the BERT-Tohoku for Japanese[1] with specific

---

[1] https://huggingface.co/cl-tohoku/bert-base-japanese.

settings, including five training epochs, a learning rate of $2e-5$, a batch size of 16, and top-k_1 tfidf set to 150.

- **LLM-based Re-ranking:** We explored Mistral [20], Llama-2-7B [6], and Qwen-7B Chat [25] in a zero-shot setting to identify the most suitable LLMs, ultimately selecting Mistral for the remaining zero-shot and few-shot runs. For reproducibility, the temperature was set to 0, and the maximum sequence length was set to 7000.

As baselines, we present the outcomes of the top two performing approaches in the COLIEE 2023 competition. The highest ranking team [4] employed outputs from MonoT5 model [26] combined with BERT-Tohoku fine-tuned on COLIEE data. The second best method [2] also utilized ensembles, incorporating BM25 for Japanese and the ranking model MonoT5 for English.

4.4 Main Results

Table 1 displays the results of our proposed framework compared with previous works on the COLIEE test set. We can see that our best proposed method outperforms current SOTA results by a margin of 2.9 F2 score [4]. Moreover, upon comparing different prompting methods, we observe that the few-shot with explanation method yields higher results than pure few-shot prompting, and pure few-shot prompting achieves higher results compared to zero-shot prompting. This highlights the effectiveness of in-context learning and self-generated explanations. Additionally, we noted that BERT-base retrieval exhibited exceptionally high recall results, especially when considering the top-5 articles. This is the reason we incorporate the BERT-based retrieval phase to obtain candidates for inputting into LLMs.

Table 1. Main results of our methods with previous works on COLIEE 2023 test set.

Method	Precision (%)	Recall (%)	F2 (%)
Best method at COLIEE 2023 [4]	72.60	79.20	75.70
2nd best method at COLIEE 2023 [2]	64.5	78.20	74.50
(Our methods)			
BERT-based retrieval (Top-5 articles)	22.77	**91.58**	55.64
Zero-shot prompting	66.09	82.18	76.08
Few-shot prompting	**72.61**	81.68	77.63
Few-shot with explanation prompting	68.22	85.15	**78.66**

4.5 Analysis

In this section, we perform a thorough analysis to gain deeper insights into our framework and the rationale behind selecting key hyperparameters. The experiments in this section are assessed using the development set.

Impact of Varying the Number of Candidate Articles (R) Values. In this analysis, our goal is to determine an appropriate value for the number of candidate articles (R) (refer to Sect. 3.2). Specifically, we select the top-k_2 = {5,7,10,15,20} articles as candidate articles R from the initial BERT-based retrieval phase and employ zero-shot prompting with the candidate set R. The results for different k_2 values are presented in Table 2. It is observed that the performance achieves the highest results at $k_2 = 10$, there seems to be a balance point between precision and recall when working with LLMs.

Table 2. Impact of varying the number of candidate articles (R) values.

Method	Evaluate on R02			Evaluate on R03			Avg F2
	P (%)	R (%)	F2 (%)	P (%)	R (%)	F2 (%)	
Zero-shot Prompting k_2=5	61.32	74.69	69.88	69.57	81.56	76.59	73.23
Zero-shot Prompting k_2=7	60.08	73.46	68.74	72.32	83.39	78.87	73.80
Zero-shot Prompting k_2=10	63.17	78.4	72.77	74.08	84.31	79.61	**76.19**
Zero-shot Prompting k_2=15	57.61	72.22	57.61	73.55	83.93	79.00	68.30
Zero-shot Prompting k_2=20	59.36	70.37	66.03	72.94	80.72	76.57	71.30

Impact of Different LLMs Models. Table 3 presents the results of our framework achieved with three distinct LLMs: Mistral-7B [20], Llama2-7B-chat [6], and Qwen-7B-chat [25]. It is evident that the Mistral model outperforms the other models, showcasing its superior performance in the statute law retrieval task. The experimental findings highlight the potential effectiveness of the Mistral model for this specific task.

Impact of Number Demonstrations in Few-Shot Prompting. In our experimentation with the Mistral model, where we had previously established top-k_2 = 10 as yielding the highest results on F2, we decided to investigate the impact of varying values for the number of demonstrations, which represents the number of similar examples provided to the few-shot setting. Starting with using 1 demonstration, we progressively increased the number of examples to assess its influence on model performance. The results started quite unfavorably for small examples but continued to improve, and until we expanded this number up to 4, we achieved the best results. However, we observed a decrease in performance

Table 3. Performance of our framework among various LLMs with the same number of parameters.

Method	Evaluate on R02			Evaluate on R03			Avg F2
	P (%)	R (%)	F2 (%)	P (%)	R (%)	F2 (%)	
Mistral-7B	63.17	78.4	72.77	74.08	84.31	79.61	**76.19**
Llama2-7B-chat	35.26	71.91	55.5	36.01	81.61	61.13	58.31
Qwen-7B-chat	39.59	69.75	50.40	50.46	75.23	61.20	55.80

when we increase this further than 5. While an increase in giving LLMs top similar queries benefits up to a certain point, providing 4 demonstration appears to yield the best results.

Table 4. Effect of a number of demonstrations on overall system performance.

Method	Evaluate on R02			Evaluate on R03			Avg F2
	P (%)	R (%)	F2 (%)	P (%)	R (%)	F2 (%)	
Few-shot - demonstrations=1	60.49	75.31	69.34	71.25	81.33	76.52	72.93
Few-shot - demonstrations=2	62.14	75.93	70.55	73.85	81.02	77.69	74.12
Few-shot - demonstrations=3	63.79	77.78	72.12	72.94	79.42	76.09	74.10
Few-shot - demonstrations=4	67.9	81.17	75.97	76.3	83.78	80.21	**78.09**
Few-shot - demonstrations=5	67.9	80.56	75.2	72.32	79.19	76.03	75.61

5   Conclusions

In conclusion, our study addresses the escalating challenges posed by the burgeoning complexity and volume of legal information in today's intricate society through the introduction of a law retrieval framework. Our proposed automated law retrieval framework, particularly tailored for statute law retrieval, offers a strategic two-phase framework-BERT-based retrieval and LLM-based re-ranking. This approach not only demonstrates versatility by outperforming previous methods but also showcases significant advancements. Our comprehensive experiments on the COLIEE 2023 dataset yield state-of-the-art results, confirming the efficacy of our framework. Furthermore, our in-depth analysis contributes to a deeper understanding of our proposed methodology, marking a substantial step forward in the realm of legal information retrieval systems.

References

1. Anh, D.H., Do, D.-T., Tran, V., Le Minh, N.: The impact of large language modeling on natural language processing in legal texts: a comprehensive survey. In: 2023 15th International Conference on Knowledge and Systems Engineering (KSE), pp. 1–7. IEEE (2023)

2. Bui, M.Q., et al.: Jnlp @coliee-2023: Data augmentation and large language model for legal case retrieval and entailment. In: COLIEE 2023 (2023)

3. Kim, M.Y., Rabelo, J., Goebel, R., Yoshioka, M., Kano, Y., Satoh, K.: COLIEE 2022 summary: methods for legal document retrieval and entailment. In: Takama, Y., Yada, K., Satoh, K., Arai, S. (eds.) JSAI-isAI 2022. LNCS, vol. 13859, pp. 51–67. Springer, Cham (2022). https://doi.org/10.1007/978-3-031-29168-5_4

4. Nguyen, C., et al.: Captain at COLIEE 2023: efficient methods for legal information retrieval and entailment tasks. In: COLIEE 2023 (2024)

5. Nguyen, H.-T., et al.: JNLP team: deep learning approaches for legal processing tasks in COLIEE 2021. arXiv preprint arXiv:2106.13405 (2021)

6. Touvron, H., et al.: Llama 2: open foundation and fine-tuned chat models. arXiv preprint arXiv:2307.09288 (2023)

7. Zhao, W.X., et al.: A survey of large language models. arXiv preprint arXiv:2303.18223 (2023)

8. Nguyen, T., et al.: MS MARCO: a human generated machine reading comprehension dataset. CoRR, vol. abs/1611.09268 (2016)

9. Goebel, R., Kano, Y., Kim, M.-Y., Rabelo, J., Satoh, K., Yoshioka, M.: Summary of the competition on legal information, extraction/entailment (COLIEE) 2023. In: Proceedings of the Nineteenth International Conference on Artificial Intelligence and Law, pp. 472–480 (2023)

10. Kim, M., Rabelo, J., Goebel, R.: Bm25 and transformer-based legal information extraction and entailment. In: Proceedings of the COLIEE Workshop in ICAIL (2021)

11. Yoshioka, M., Suzuki, Y., Aoki, Y.: BERT-based ensemble methods for information retrieval and legal textual entailment in COLIEE statute law task. In: Proceedings of the Eight International Competition on Legal Information Extraction/Entailment (COLIEE 2021), pp. 78–83 (2021)

12. Bui, Q.M., et al.: JNLP team: deep learning approaches for tackling long and ambiguous legal documents in COLIEE 2022. In: Takama, Y., Yada, K., Satoh, K., Arai, S. (eds.) JSAI-isAI 2022. LNCS, vol. 13859, pp. 68–83. Springer, Cham (2022). https://doi.org/10.1007/978-3-031-29168-5_5

13. Yoshioka, M., Suzuki, Y., Aoki, Y.: HUKB at the COLIEE 2022 statute law task. In: Takama, Y., Yada, K., Satoh, K., Arai, S. (eds.) JSAI-isAI 2022. LNCS, vol. 13859, pp. 109–124. Springer, Cham (2022). https://doi.org/10.1007/978-3-031-29168-5_8

14. Vaswani, A., et al.: Attention is all you need. In: Advances in Neural Information Processing Systems, vol. 30 (2017)

15. Raffel, C., et al.: Exploring the limits of transfer learning with a unified text-to-text transformer. J. Mach. Learn. Res. **21**(1), 5485–5551 (2020)

16. Brown, T., et al.: Language models are few-shot learners. In: Advances in Neural Information Processing Systems, vol. 33, pp. 1877–1901 (2020)

17. Kojima, T., Gu, S.S., Reid, M., Matsuo, Y., Iwasawa, Y.: Large language models are zero-shot reasoners. In: Advances in Neural Information Processing Systems, vol. 35, pp. 22199–22213 (2022)

18. Xie, S.M., Raghunathan, A., Liang, P., Ma, T.: An explanation of in-context learning as implicit Bayesian inference. arXiv preprint arXiv:2111.02080 (2021)

19. Achiam, J., et al.: GPT-4 technical report. arXiv preprint arXiv:2303.08774 (2023)

20. Jiang, A.Q., et al.: Mistral 7B. arXiv preprint arXiv:2310.06825 (2023)

21. Liu, P., Yuan, W., Fu, J., Jiang, Z., Hayashi, H., Neubig, G.: Pre-train, prompt, and predict: a systematic survey of prompting methods in natural language processing. ACM Comput. Surv. **55**(9), 1–35 (2023)

22. Reimers, N., Gurevych, I.: Sentence-BERT: sentence embeddings using Siamese BERT-networks. In: Inui, K., Jiang, J., Ng, V., Wan, X., (eds.) Proceedings of EMNLP-IJCNLP, pp. 3982–3992 (2019)
23. Wei, J., et al.: Chain-of-thought prompting elicits reasoning in large language models. In: Advances in Neural Information Processing Systems, vol. 35, pp. 24824–24837 (2022)
24. Yao, S., et al.: Tree of thoughts: deliberate problem solving with large language models. arXiv preprint arXiv:2305.10601 (2023)
25. Bai, J., et al.: Qwen technical report. arXiv preprint arXiv:2309.16609 (2023)
26. Nogueira, R., Jiang, Z., Pradeep, R., Lin, J.: Document ranking with a pretrained sequence-to-sequence model. In: Cohn, T., He, Y., Liu, Y., (eds.) Findings of the Association for Computational Linguistics: EMNLP 2020, pp. 708–718, Association for Computational Linguistics (2020)

Vietnamese Elementary Math Reasoning Using Large Language Model with Refined Translation and Dense-Retrieved Chain-of-Thought

Nguyen-Khang Le[(✉)], Dieu-Hien Nguyen, Dinh-Truong Do, Chau Nguyen, and Minh Le Nguyen

Japan Advanced Institute of Science and Technology, Nomi, Ishikawa, Japan
{lnkhang,ndhien,truongdo,chau.nguyen,nguyenml}@jaist.ac.jp

Abstract. State-of-the-art large language models (LLMs) have succeeded in various tasks but still show limitations in solving math reasoning problems. Although this problem is actively studied in the English language, a scarcity of work has been conducted to explore LLMs in math reasoning in low-resource languages. Recent advances in LLMs show their ability to obtain cross-lingual knowledge. However, a systematical approach to bridge the language gap and employ these LLMs to math reasoning in low-resource language has yet to be studied. This study proposes a pipeline to solve math problems in Vietnamese by integrating the chain-of-thought technique with high-quality in-context learning exemplars obtained by multilingual dense retrieval. The pipeline is model-agnostic and capable of adapting to any language without fine-tuning. Empirical results show that the proposed pipeline obtains remarkable performance gains compared to competitive baseline LLMs, paving the way for future research on employing English-focus LLMs to solve complex reasoning tasks in low-resource languages.

Keywords: Large language model · Low-resource language · Mathematics reasoning

1 Introduction

Large language models (LLMs) have achieved significant results in many tasks in the last few years [5, 24, 26]. It is believed that the larger the model's size, the better the model performs [11]. However, in math problem-solving, even recent LLMs with hundreds of billions of parameters show limitations in solving this task. Even instruction fine-tuned LLMs still need to improve multi-step reasoning and logical thinking, which are essential to solving math problems. Many math problem datasets have been introduced. For example, ASDiv [20], GSM8K [6], and MATH [8] datasets are grade-school math problems. Their problems require a few steps to solve and are written in English. Some other mathematic datasets with symbolic data [14] and logical reasoning [16] are also provided

T. Suzumura and M. Bono (Eds.): JSAI-isAI 2024, LNAI 14741, pp. 260–268, 2024.
https://doi.org/10.1007/978-981-97-3076-6_18

in English. Although LogiQA [16] and a few other datasets [30, 31] are in Chinese, most well-known datasets are in English. Few works have been conducted in mathematics reasoning in low-resource languages. This study focuses on elementary mathematics reasoning in Vietnamese, a language spoken by more than a hundred million people worldwide.

Recently, the tasks of solving Vietnamese elementary mathematics problems has been proposed in ZaloAI Challenge[1] a popular annual AI competition in Vietnam. The large-scale dataset provided in this challenge is in alignment with the Vietnamese Education Program and contains multiple-choice elementary-level math questions. Table 1 shows some examples of the Vietnamese mathematics problems in the challenge. The input is a multiple-choice math question with four possible choices and only one is the correct answer. The output is the correct choice for the given math question. Our preliminary tests show that multilingual LLMs have the potential to solve the problems in Vietnamese despite having little knowledge of the language. We find that bridging the language gap can exploit their ability in another language.

Table 1. Examples of elementary-level multiple choices math question

Input	Output
Example 1 Số "bảy triệu hai trăm nghìn"có: A. Ba chữ số 0 B. Bốn chữ số 0 C. Năm chữ số 0 D. Sáu chữ số 0	C. Năm chữ số 0
Translation: The number "seven million two hundred thousand" has: A. Three digits 0 B. Four digits 0 C. Five digits 0 D. Six digits 0	C. Five digits 0
Example 2 Mẫu số của một phân số thập phân có thể là những số nào? A. Các số chẵn B. Các số 10; 100; 1000; ... C. Các số lẻ D. Mọi số tự nhiên khác 0	B. Các số 10; 100; 1000; ...
Translation: What numbers can the denominator of a decimal fraction be? A. Even numbers B. Numbers 10; 100; 1000; ... C. Odd numbers D. All natural numbers other than 0	B. Numbers 10; 100; 1000; ...

Motivated by these problems, we introduce a pipeline capable of answering math questions in Vietnamese. This method is also applicable to other low-resource languages. Our contributions are as follows:

---

[1] Competition website: https://challenge.zalo.ai.

- By integrating chain-of-thought with high-quality in-context learning exemplars obtained by multilingual dense retrieval, we proposed a novel pipeline employing pretrained state-of-the-art LLMs to perform translation and elementary mathematics reasoning in Vietnamese language. The pipeline also guides the model to perform multiple-choice questions and includes a reprompt step to ensure the answer is among the choices.
- The proposed pipeline requires no fine-tuning, can be adapted to any LLMs and dense retrieval architectures. Our proposed system wins the **first prize** in the Zalo AI Challenge 2023 competition.

2   Related Works

The math-solving task aims to answer mathematical problems automatically according to the text description. Initially, the idea was to use rule-based methods [7,34]. These methods typically process a restricted range of well-formatted input sentences, mapping them into predefined structures through pattern matching. They are primarily focused on basic mathematical operations like addition or subtraction.

Some other methods use statistical machine learning [13,35]. Generally, they aim to identify the optimal solution equation by training a probabilistic model. However, they may struggle to generalize unseen mathematical problems. They also require a large amount of labeled data to achieve satisfactory performance. Besides, many researchers make use of the semantic parsing method [10,22]. However, it is heavily essential that the natural language is parsed into mathematical expressions correctly, which may lead to a lack of flexibility. Deep learning methods were also used to solve the problems. For example, the works of Wang et al. [28] and Huang et al. [9] are based on recurrent Sequence2Sequence models. Although they have achieved promising performances, they have some weaknesses, such as generating spurious numbers or equation duplication problems.

With the appearance of the transformer [25], there are various studies with encouraging results relying on this method [4,12,15]. While transformers offer potent capabilities for natural language understanding, their application to math-solving tasks has several limitations related to mathematical reasoning, contextual understanding, and numerical manipulation. Recently, applying LLMs to the math-solving task has been an active subject. Many works have been proposed, including prompting frozen LLMs [3,17,32] or fine-tuning LLMs [1,18,33]. Our work also employs the LLM, though we enhance it in several aspects, notably its reasoning and dealing with low computational resources.

3   Methods

Overall. Figure 1 presents the overview of the proposed system. The system consists of two main phases: offline data preparation and question answering. The question-answering phase can be divided into two subtasks: translation and math-solving. In the data preparation phase, we prepare the chain-of-thought

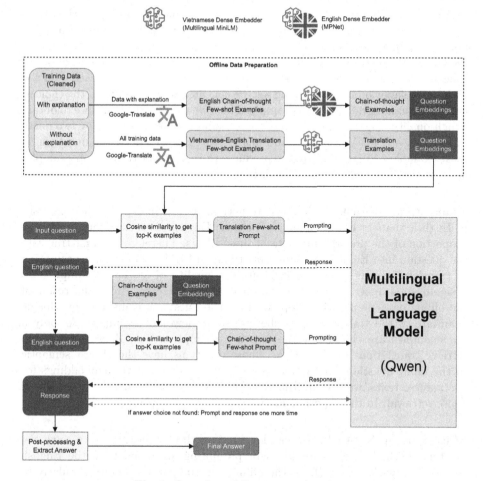

Fig. 1. Overview of the proposed system

[29] and translation examples by employing Google Translate[2] and two dense embedders, one for Vietnamese and one for English. The English dense embedder is based on the MPNet [23]; the Vietnamese dense embedded is based on multilingual MiniLM [27]; both embedded are pretrained following the SBERT architecture [21]. In the question-answering phase, for each input question, we first use dense retrieval to obtain top-K translation examples to form the few-shot prompt. Then, we prompt the LLM and get the translation of the question. Once again, we use dense retrieval to get top-K chain-of-thought examples to form the few-shot prompt for the math-solving. We then prompt the LLM again to solve the math problem. The response is then post-processed to extract the final answer. If the model gives answers other than candidates, we prompt the model again to solve the math problem.

---

[2] https://translate.google.com.

Offline Data Preparation. The purpose of this phase is to prepare the chain-of-thought and translation examples, along with their question embeddings. We use all training data for translation examples and data with explanations for the chain-of-thought examples. First, for each question in all training data, we concatenate the question and the choices to form an example. For each question with an explanation in the training set, we concatenate the question, the choices, and the explanation to form an example. Then, we use Google Translate to obtain a high-quality English translation of these examples. Next, we employ two dense embedders, one for Vietnamese and one for English, to embed the questions in these examples. Finally, this phase produces the corpus for translation examples and few-shot CoT examples in English.

Translation Subtask. LLMs tend to perform better in-depth reasoning tasks in English than in other languages because English data account for a large proportion of the pre-training data of these LLMs. Therefore, we first translate the question into English. We use a multilingual LLM with few-shot prompting to translate the question into English. The quality of few-shot examples has a significant impact on the translation quality. Therefore, from the result of the offline data preparation step, we take the questions translated by Google Translate in the training set as the corpus for few-shot examples. As only a few examples are chosen for the few-shot prompt, we use dense retrieval to retrieve translations in the corpus whose questions have the closest semantic to the input question (in Vietnamese). As we need to get the embeddings for Vietnamese texts, we use Multilingual MiniLM [27] as the dense embedder for dense retrieval. In the experiments, we use 5-shot prompting.

Math-Solving Subtask. We employ LLMs with CoT in English to solve elementary math. Examples for few-shot prompting are taken from the English corpus for few-shot CoT (from the offline data preparation step). Similarly to choosing examples in the translation subtask, we use dense retrieval to retrieve examples in the corpus with the closest semantic to the input question (in English) to get the best performance. Because we need to get the embeddings of the English questions, we use MPNet as the dense embedder for dense retrieval. In the experiments, we use 5-shot prompting. We prompt the LLM with the few-shot prompt to get the response. This response typically follows the template of the few-shot examples. Therefore, we can extract the answer choice from the response using the same template as the few-shot examples. We also have a rule-based post-processing step to deal with edge cases. Sometimes, the model may respond that the answer is outside the candidate's choices. In such cases, we prompt the model again to make it solve the math problem again.

4   Experiments and Results

Dataset. We experimented on the Zalo AI Challenge 2023's dataset. We use the training set, which contains approximately 1200 examples, to construct the offline data corpus. We evaluate the methods on the public test set, which includes 200 math problems. Each test data sample consists of id, question, and choices; where "id" is the id of the problem, "question" is the math problem required solving, "choices" is a list of candidate answers. Below is a sample of training data:

Baselines. We conduct experiments to compare our pipeline with competitive LLMs. The baselines include WizardMath [19], Vicuna v1.5 [5], LLaMA-2 [24], and Qwen-Chat [2]. These LLMs have been proven to have high performance and robustness on a wide range of popular benchmarks. Although a significant proportion of their training data is in English, a small portion is in other languages. Our preliminary experiments show that they perform well in Vietnamese. In the experiments, we use these LLMs in zero-shot, chain-of-thought, and fine-tuned fashions. The training set, in Vietnamese or English translation, is used for fine-tuning these LLMs.

Evaluation. We evaluate the participating system by using the accuracy, which is based on the number of correct answers:

$$Accuracy = \frac{\text{Number of correct answers}}{\text{Total number of questions}}$$

Results. Table 2 shows the results of the experiments with chosen LLMs on the dataset with different settings. The models were fine-tuned with Vietnamese or English-translated training data. With chain-of-thought settings, we used few-shot prompting with examples and explanations. Our proposed pipeline uses Qwen-Chat as the core LLMs. The results suggest that our proposed pipeline outperforms other baselines and the original Qwen-Chat model.

Table 2. Experimental results

Model	Model size	Language	Fine-tuned	CoT	Accuracy (%)
WizardMath	13B	Vietnamese	–	–	47.594
Vicuna v1.5	13B	Vietnamese	–	–	13.369
Vicuna v1.5	13B	Vietnamese	✓	–	23.529
Vicuna v1.5	13B	Vietnamese	–	✓	49.198
LLaMA 2	13B	Vietnamese	✓	–	54.545
LLaMA 2	13B	English	✓	–	54.011
LLaMA 2	13B	Vietnamese	–	✓	45.989
LLaMA 2	13B	Vietnamese	✓	✓	57.219
Qwen-Chat	14B	Vietnamese	–	–	62.032
Qwen-Chat	14B	English	–	–	70.053
Qwen-Chat	14B	English	–	✓	70.053
Qwen-Chat (Our Pipeline)	14B	English	–	✓	**77.540**

5   Conclusion

This study proposed a novel pipeline employing pretrained state-of-the-art LLMs to solve elementary mathematics problems in the Vietnamese language by integrating chain-of-thought with high-quality in-context learning exemplars obtained by multilingual dense retrieval. The study focus on improving the two main phases, namely refined translation and chain-of-thought reasoning, with dense-retrieved in-context exemplars. In the translation step, a corresponding dense embedder is used to retrieve relevant translations from the pre-processed training data to form the few-shot prompt. We prompt the model with the few-shot prompt to get the English translation of the question. In the math-solving step, a corresponding dense embedder is used to retrieve CoT examples from the pre-processed training data. These examples are used as the few-shot prompt to obtain the response from the LLM. Empirical results show that the proposed pipeline is effective in solving elementary mathematics problems in Vietnamese and outperforms competitive baseline LLMs, laying a foundation for employing state-of-the-art English-focus LLMs to solve complex reasoning tasks in low-resource languages.

References

1. An, S., Ma, Z., Lin, Z., Zheng, N., Lou, J.G., Chen, W.: Learning from mistakes makes LLM better reasoner (2024)
2. Bai, J., et al.: QWEN technical report. arXiv preprint arXiv:2309.16609 (2023)
3. Chen, W., Ma, X., Wang, X., Cohen, W.W.: Program of thoughts prompting: disentangling computation from reasoning for numerical reasoning tasks. Trans. Mach. Learn. Res. (2023)
4. Chiang, T.R., Chen, Y.N.: Semantically-aligned equation generation for solving and reasoning math word problems. In: Burstein, J., Doran, C., Solorio, T. (eds.) Proceedings of the 2019 Conference of the North American Chapter of the Association for Computational Linguistics: Human Language Technologies (Volume 1: Long and Short Papers), Minneapolis, Minnesota, pp. 2656–2668. Association for Computational Linguistics (2019). https://doi.org/10.18653/v1/N19-1272. https://aclanthology.org/N19-1272
5. Chiang, W.L., et al.: Vicuna: an open-source chatbot impressing GPT-4 with 90%* ChatGPT quality (2023). https://lmsys.org/blog/2023-03-30-vicuna/
6. Cobbe, K., et al.: Training verifiers to solve math word problems. arXiv preprint arXiv:2110.14168 (2021)
7. Fletcher, C.: Understanding and solving arithmetic word problems: a computer simulation. Behav. Res. Methods Instrum. Comput. 17(5), 565–571 (1985). https://doi.org/10.3758/BF03207654
8. Hendrycks, D., et al.: Measuring mathematical problem solving with the math dataset. In: Vanschoren, J., Yeung, S. (eds.) Proceedings of the Neural Information Processing Systems Track on Datasets and Benchmarks, vol. 1. Curran (2021)
9. Huang, D., Liu, J., Lin, C.Y., Yin, J.: Neural math word problem solver with reinforcement learning. In: Bender, E.M., Derczynski, L., Isabelle, P. (eds.) Proceedings of the 27th International Conference on Computational Linguistics, Santa Fe, New Mexico, USA, pp. 213–223. Association for Computational Linguistics (2018). https://aclanthology.org/C18-1018

10. Huang, D., Shi, S., Lin, C.Y., Yin, J.: Learning fine-grained expressions to solve math word problems. In: Palmer, M., Hwa, R., Riedel, S. (eds.) Proceedings of the 2017 Conference on Empirical Methods in Natural Language Processing, Copenhagen, Denmark, pp. 805–814. Association for Computational Linguistics (2017). https://doi.org/10.18653/v1/D17-1084. https://aclanthology.org/D17-1084

11. Kaplan, J., et al.: Scaling laws for neural language models (2020)

12. Kim, B., Ki, K.S., Lee, D., Gweon, G.: Point to the expression: solving algebraic word problems using the expression-pointer transformer model. In: Webber, B., Cohn, T., He, Y., Liu, Y. (eds.) Proceedings of the 2020 Conference on Empirical Methods in Natural Language Processing (EMNLP), pp. 3768–3779. Association for Computational Linguistics, Online (2020). https://doi.org/10.18653/v1/2020. emnlp-main.308. https://aclanthology.org/2020.emnlp-main.308

13. Kushman, N., Artzi, Y., Zettlemoyer, L., Barzilay, R.: Learning to automatically solve algebra word problems. In: Toutanova, K., Wu, H. (eds.) Proceedings of the 52nd Annual Meeting of the Association for Computational Linguistics, Baltimore, Maryland (Volume 1: Long Papers), pp. 271–281. Association for Computational Linguistics (2014). https://doi.org/10.3115/v1/P14-1026. https:// aclanthology.org/P14-1026

14. Lample, G., Charton, F.: Deep learning for symbolic mathematics (2019)

15. Liang, Z., et al.: MWP-BERT: numeracy-augmented pre-training for math word problem solving. In: Carpuat, M., de Marneffe, M.C., Meza Ruiz, I.V. (eds.) Findings of the Association for Computational Linguistics: NAACL 2022, Seattle, USA, pp. 997–1009. Association for Computational Linguistics (2022). https://doi.org/ 10.18653/v1/2022.findings-naacl.74. https://aclanthology.org/2022.findings-naacl. 74

16. Liu, J., Cui, L., Liu, H., Huang, D., Wang, Y., Zhang, Y.: LogiQA: a challenge dataset for machine reading comprehension with logical reasoning. In: Proceedings of the Twenty-Ninth International Joint Conference on Artificial Intelligence, IJCAI 2020 (2021)

17. Lu, P., et al.: MathVista: evaluating mathematical reasoning of foundation models in visual contexts. In: International Conference on Learning Representations (ICLR) (2024)

18. Lu, P., et al.: Dynamic prompt learning via policy gradient for semi-structured mathematical reasoning. In: International Conference on Learning Representations (ICLR) (2023)

19. Luo, H., et al.: Wizardmath: Empowering mathematical reasoning for large language models via reinforced evol-instruct. arXiv preprint arXiv:2308.09583 (2023)

20. Miao, S., Liang, C.C., Su, K.Y.: A diverse corpus for evaluating and developing English math word problem solvers. In: Jurafsky, D., Chai, J., Schluter, N., Tetreault, J. (eds.) Proceedings of the 58th Annual Meeting of the Association for Computational Linguistics, pp. 975–984. Association for Computational Linguistics, Online (2020). https://doi.org/10.18653/v1/2020.acl-main.92. https:// aclanthology.org/2020.acl-main.92

21. Reimers, N., Gurevych, I.: Sentence-BERT: sentence embeddings using siamese BERT-networks. In: EMNLP-IJCNLP 2019 - 2019 Conference on Empirical Methods in Natural Language Processing and 9th International Joint Conference on Natural Language Processing, Proceedings of the Conference, pp. 3982–3992 (2019). https://doi.org/10.18653/v1/d19-1410. https://arxiv.org/abs/1908.10084v1

22. Shi, S., Wang, Y., Lin, C.Y., Liu, X., Rui, Y.: Automatically solving number word problems by semantic parsing and reasoning. In: Màrquez, L., Callison-Burch, C., Su, J. (eds.) Proceedings of the 2015 Conference on Empirical Methods in Natural Language Processing, Lisbon, Portugal, pp. 1132–1142. Association for Computational Linguistics (2015). https://doi.org/10.18653/v1/D15-1135. https://aclanthology.org/D15-1135
23. Song, K., Tan, X., Qin, T., Lu, J., Liu, T.Y.: MPNet: masked and permuted pre-training for language understanding. In: Advances in Neural Information Processing Systems **2020-December** (2020). https://arxiv.org/abs/2004.09297v2
24. Touvron, H., et al.: Llama 2: Open Foundation and Fine-Tuned Chat Models (2023). https://arxiv.org/abs/2307.09288v2
25. Vaswani, A., et al.: Attention is all you need. In: Advances in Neural Information Processing Systems, vol. 30 (2017)
26. Wang, A., et al.: SuperGLUE: A Stickier Benchmark for General-Purpose Language Understanding Systems. Curran Associates Inc., Red Hook (2019)
27. Wang, W., Wei, F., Dong, L., Bao, H., Yang, N., Zhou, M.: MiniLM: deep self-attention distillation for task-agnostic compression of pre-trained transformers. In: Advances in Neural Information Processing Systems, vol. 33, pp. 5776–5788 (2020). https://aka.ms/minilm
28. Wang, Y., Liu, X., Shi, S.: Deep neural solver for math word problems. In: Palmer, M., Hwa, R., Riedel, S. (eds.) Proceedings of the 2017 Conference on Empirical Methods in Natural Language Processing, Copenhagen, Denmark, pp. 845–854. Association for Computational Linguistics (2017). https://doi.org/10.18653/v1/D17-1088. https://aclanthology.org/D17-1088
29. Wei, J., et al.: Chain-of-Thought Prompting Elicits Reasoning in Large Language Models Chain-of-Thought Prompting
30. Wei, T., Luan, J., Liu, W., Dong, S., Wang, B.: Cmath: can your language model pass Chinese elementary school math test? (2023)
31. Wu, H., Hui, W., Chen, Y., Wu, W., Tu, K., Zhou, Y.: Conic10K: a challenging math problem understanding and reasoning dataset. In: Bouamor, H., Pino, J., Bali, K. (eds.) Findings of the Association for Computational Linguistics: EMNLP 2023, Singapore, pp. 6444–6458. Association for Computational Linguistics (2023). https://doi.org/10.18653/v1/2023.findings-emnlp.427. https://aclanthology.org/2023.findings-emnlp.427
32. Wu, Y., et al.: An empirical study on challenging math problem solving with GPT-4 (2023)
33. Yang, Z., et al.: GPT can solve mathematical problems without a calculator (2023)
34. Yuhui, M., Ying, Z., Guangzuo, C., Yun, R., Ronghuai, H.: Frame-based calculus of solving arithmetic multi-step addition and subtraction word problems. In: 2010 Second International Workshop on Education Technology and Computer Science, vol. 2, pp. 476–479 (2010). https://doi.org/10.1109/ETCS.2010.316
35. Zhou, L., Dai, S., Chen, L.: Learn to solve algebra word problems using quadratic programming. In: Màrquez, L., Callison-Burch, C., Su, J. (eds.) Proceedings of the 2015 Conference on Empirical Methods in Natural Language Processing, Lisbon, Portugal, pp. 817–822. Association for Computational Linguistics (2015). https://doi.org/10.18653/v1/D15-1096. https://aclanthology.org/D15-1096

Texylon: Dataset of Log-to-Description and Description-to-Log Generation for Text Analytics Tools

Masato Nakata[✉], Kosuke Morita, Hirotaka Kameko, and Shinsuke Mori

Kyoto University, Yoshida-honmachi, Sakyo-ku, Kyoto 606-8501, Japan
nakata.masato.26m@st.kyoto-u.ac.jp

Abstract. We propose two tasks for text analytics tools, description generation and log estimation, and a dataset to solve them. Text analytics tools, popular in the digital humanities, provide researchers with various functions for texts based on natural language processing (NLP). Our first task, description generation from operational logs, helps these researchers write papers easily and accurately. Our second task, log estimation given a paper, is just the opposite and helps readers reproduce the analyses in the paper. For those tasks, we created a dataset consisting of descriptions and logs in text analytics experiments. Because our dataset is not large enough, we also propose some methods for data augmentation: swapping a value of each configuration with another value, pseudo-labeling using BERT and NER, pseudo-labeling using BERT and T5, and a combination of them. The highest BLEU score for that model in the description generation task is 36.98, and F1 score in the log generation task is around 0.7.

Keywords: Data-to-text · Text-to-data · Text analytics · Natural language processing · Digital humanities

1 Introduction

The uses of informatics have been getting more and more common for the humanities in these decades [3, *inter alia*]. Among them one of the most typical and classical usage is statistical analysis of texts, such as term frequencies/document frequencies of words, co-occurrence network, correspondence analysis for word distribution, and cluster analysis. A text analytics tool, Voyant Tools[1], has recently been awarded by Alliance of Digital Humanities Organizations, for example. In addition to such web-based tools, installation type tools are also available. Famous one is KH Coder [7,8], which provides many powerful functions to analyze texts in various domains, including literature, historical documents, questionnaires, etc.

---

[1] https://voyant-tools.org/ accessed on 2023/Oct/20.

T. Suzumura and M. Bono (Eds.): JSAI-isAI 2024, LNAI 14741, pp. 269–283, 2024.
https://doi.org/10.1007/978-981-97-3076-6_19

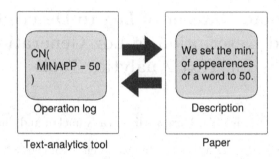

Operation log   Description

Text-analytics tool   Paper

Fig. 1. Bidirectional conversion between operation logs and descriptions.

One of the faults in many analytics tools is that configurations are a bit complicated for non-specialists in statistics, so that describing what the configurations are appropriately can be hard work. Such a difficulty implies another problem: inappropriate descriptions result in the low reproducibility for readers. A proper description for a general-purpose text analytics tool needs authors/readers to have statistical knowledge (Fig. 1).

In this background, we aim to build a model that

1. generates an appropriate description given a set of configurations to lighten the burden on the authors' side, and
2. estimates underlying configurations given a description to help readers reproduce the results;

however, no proceeding datasets have been constructed for those tasks, so this time we announce the first dataset, Texylon, which can be used for description/log generation tasks. The precise definitions of a "description" and a "log" are given in Sect. 3, but roughly speaking, a description is a part of a paper where the authors explain which operation they conducted and with which configurations. A log corresponds to the configurations for that operation.

One drawback of our dataset is the modest size nevertheless, as it is the first dataset in this domain. To relieve that problem, the second subject of our paper has appeared now — we had better augment the dataset in order to predict descriptions/logs more precisely and stably. The augmentation algorithms, as well as the original dataset Texylon, will be publicly available on the Internet, but now please contact us via an e-mail when you would like to utilize them.

In this paper, first we define the tasks because we use confusing terms to name similar concepts, then introduce our dataset. We also present several methods for augmenting the data. In particular, some methods require specific language models, so we will also describe the construction of such models. Then, we will go on to the evaluation of the augmentation methods by proposing a baseline model for the log-to-description and description-to-log tasks.

2   Related Work

He et al. studied effective and efficient usages of software logs in a statistical or machine learning way [6]. They presented a survey on some topics, including the design of logging systems, log compression and parsing logs into structured data. In their paper, the definition of a log is closer to ours of a "description" (see Sect. 3), and structured data means our "logs."

They aimed for more reliable engineering. Although their approaches looked good for engineering, where a log is always formatted and well-structured, they do not work for natural language tasks.

Nivikova et al. published E2E, a dataset for natural language generation in the restaurant domain [12]. It contains a large amount of meaning representations (MRs) of restaurants and reference texts that explain about the restaurants in natural language.

Kale et al. proposed a method which can be applied to general data-to-text generation tasks [9]. They used pre-trained T5 models [15], the large language models (LLMs) of a wide range of application, and then fine-tuned them on a few shot data representing the structured data. For example, they tried ToTTo [14], which consists of Wikipedia tables paired with natural language descriptions, as a fine-tuning dataset.

3   Task Definitions

The tasks we introduce in this paper are the following two:

1. **Log-to-description**: description generation from operational logs, which helps text analytics researchers write papers easily and accurately,
2. **Description-to-log**: operational log estimation from descriptions, which helps paper readers reproduce the analyses.

Here, by an "operational log" we mean a pair composed of the following data:

- a function name — which function(s) is used in a research;
- configurations — key-value pairs that represent the parameters to this function(s).

To formulate the two tasks in a stricter manner, we define a few sets as follows. Let $\mathcal{F}_T$ be a set of all the functions in a text analytics tool T. For each function $f \in \mathcal{F}_T$, we have a set of *keys* of its configurations, denoted by $\mathcal{K}_T(f)$, and a set of possible *values* for a key $k \in \mathcal{K}_T(f)$, denoted by $\mathcal{V}_T(f, k)$. Then, a *configuration* of f is no more than an ordered pair (k, v), where $k \in \mathcal{K}_T(f)$ and $v \in \mathcal{V}_T(f, k)$.

Before we describe about configuration*s*, remember that the symbol $\coprod$ represents a disjoint union of a family of sets:

$$\coprod_{\lambda \in \Lambda} X_\lambda := \{(\lambda, x) \mid \lambda \in \Lambda, x \in X_\lambda\} \tag{1}$$

for a family of sets X_λ indexed by $\lambda \in \Lambda$. Using this symbol, the disjoint union of $\mathcal{V}_T(f, k)$ running $k \in \mathcal{K}_T(f)$ is a set

$$\mathcal{V}_T(f) := \coprod_{k \in \mathcal{K}_T(f)} \mathcal{V}_T(f, k) = \{(k, v) \mid k \in \mathcal{K}_T(f), v \in \mathcal{V}_T(f, k)\}. \qquad (2)$$

Now we can define *configurations* of f as a map $c : K \to \mathcal{V}_T(f)$ for some subset $K \subset \mathcal{K}_T(f)$ with a property $c(k) \in \{k\} \times \mathcal{V}_T(f, k)$. A condition for a key $k \in \mathcal{K}_T(f)$ being *not* contained in K implies that the key k is not mentioned in a paper and its value appears set to the default value. We denote the set of configurations of f by

$$\mathcal{C}_T(f) := \{\text{configurations of } f\}, \qquad (3)$$

and an *operational log*, or simply a *log*, is an element of the set

$$\mathcal{L}_T := \coprod_{f \in \mathcal{F}_T} \mathcal{C}_T(f) = \{(f, c) \mid f \in \mathcal{F}_T, c \in \mathcal{C}_T(f)\}. \qquad (4)$$

Let us provide an example situation here. KH Coder [7,8] has a function "co-occurrence network," which is useful for the visual analysis of the word statistics. We denote it by $\mathsf{CN} \in \mathcal{F}_{\mathsf{KC}}$ (KC stands for "**KH Coder**"). For this function CN, the key set $\mathcal{K}_{\mathsf{KC}}(\mathsf{CN})$ contains, for example, $\mathsf{Pos} := $ "target parts of speech" and $\mathsf{MinApp} := $ "the minimum number of appearances of a word." The value sets may include these instances:

$$\text{"noun and verb"} \in \mathcal{V}_{\mathsf{KC}}(\mathsf{CN}, \mathsf{Pos}), \qquad (5)$$

$$50 \in \mathcal{V}_{\mathsf{KC}}(\mathsf{CN}, \mathsf{MinApp}). \qquad (6)$$

If we define a map $c : \{\mathsf{Pos}, \mathsf{MinApp}\} \to \mathcal{V}_{\mathsf{KC}}(\mathsf{CN})$ by $\mathsf{Pos} \mapsto$ "noun and verb," $\mathsf{MinApp} \mapsto 50$, we obtain configurations $c \in \mathcal{C}_{\mathsf{KC}}(\mathsf{CN})$. Suppose that we have conducted an experiment expressed by the above operational log (CN, c), and that we are about to write a paper. In this case, the "description" may be fully descriptive sentences like "We calculated the co-occurrence network by KH Coder. To this end, we set the target parts of speech to 'noun and verb', and the minimum number of appearances of a word to 50."

With these notations, our tasks can be formulated in this way:

1. **Log-to-description.** Given an operation log $\ell \in \mathcal{L}_T$, output a description d which maximizes the probability $p(d \mid \ell)$;
2. **Description-to-log.** Given a description d, output an operational log $\ell \in \mathcal{L}_T$ which maximizes the probability $p(\ell \mid d)$.

4   Dataset

To evaluate methods for the tasks and even train methods based on machine learning techniques, we constructed a dataset, which we call Texylon. Texylon

Table 1. Dataset size of the manual annotation and the data augmentations.

Dataset Type	# of logs	# of newly added
Texylon	253	–
Swapping	1,873	(+1,620)
BERT-NER	3,592	(+3,339)
BERT-T5	14,375	(+14,122)
Hybrid	5,212	(+4,959)

consists of manually annotated description-log pairs (d, ℓ)'s, where d is a description fetched from a real-world paper and ℓ is its operational log $\in \mathcal{L}_T$ for some text-anatytics tool T.

In this section we explain our dataset, Texylon, and then we propose four augmentation methods. Table 1 summarizes the specifications of Texylon and the augmentation results.

4.1 Data Construction

We took KH Coder [7,8] as the example of text analytics tools. We first collected papers written in Japanese published in 2021 in the list of its official web page[2]. Then annotators located the descriptions about the operations of the tool, and, given such descriptions, the annotators created their operational logs manually. Of course, there can be a potential bias to focus on the only *one* text analytics tool; however, descriptions obtained should be similar among all the tools, so our data augmentation methods (Sect. 4.2) and a model (Sect. 5.1) are applicable beyond KH Coder.

The format of the logs is in a python style like `FUNCTION(KEY1=VALUE1, ...)`. The following is an example.

```
CN(Pos="noun and verb", MinApp=50)
```

Here, `Pos` and `MinApp` $\in \mathcal{K}_{KC}(CN)$, represent the keys defined in Sect. 3.

Since almost all the researches in the selected papers focused on co-occurrence network or correspondence analysis, we selected only the papers which conducted co-occurrence network or correspondence analysis as our first attempt.

The possible configurations $\mathcal{C}_{KC}(f)$ of each function $f \in \mathcal{F}_{KC}$ were known in advance at the annotation time, so it had little cost for determining the rigorous annotation standard.

Note that the above annotation is not ambiguous for human, we did not ask multiple annotators to work on the same part in order to calculate inter-annotator agreement.

---

[2] https://khcoder.net/bib.html accessed on 2023/Oct/19.

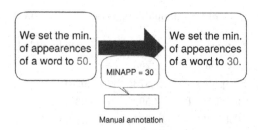

Fig. 2. Swapping, replacement of a value with another in a manually annotated dataset.

4.2 Data Augmentation

Since our task is novel and hence the size of our dataset is not large enough for machine learning, we propose four methods for augmenting the data. In the subsequent part, we explain these one by one.

Swapping. The first method of data augmentation is swapping [4]. Swapping is a simple algorithm that replaces values in configurations by different existing values (Fig. 2).

More precisely, we created first the list of all the configurations obtained from Texylon (Sect. 4.1) for a function f (co-occurrence network or correspondence analysis). Call this list $L_{\mathrm{ann}}(f) \subset C_{\mathsf{KC}}(f)$. Next, for each paper and each function f that is used there, let its configurations be $c : K \to V_{\mathsf{KC}}(f)$ for some $K \subset \mathcal{K}_{\mathsf{KC}}(f)$. For each key $k \in K$, we randomly selected a new value $v'_k \in V_{\mathsf{KC}}(f, k)$ from the list $L_{\mathrm{ann}}(f)$ which belonged to the same key k. Then we collected the new key-value pairs $\{(k, v'_k)\}_{k \in K}$, and we got the new configurations $c' : k \mapsto (k, v'_k)$. We repeated this operation 1,000 times per configurations c, until we add 20 new configurations.

We made new corresponding descriptions as well by simple pattern matching. Because different keys have different values ($V_{\mathsf{KC}}(f, k) \cap V_{\mathsf{KC}}(f, k') = \emptyset$) in Texylon, a simple replacement was enough to produce the new descriptions unambiguously.

Pseudo-labeling. Pseudo-labeling is the second method to enlarge our dataset. Here we suggest two ways for pseudo-labeling: BERT-NER and BERT-T5, as discussed below.

We prepared target texts to pseudo-label by downloading all the papers of KH Coder experiments found in the official list (as mentioned in Sect. 4.1) on October 11th, 2022. Note that Texylon was made from the papers in 2021; therefore we excluded the year 2021 from those target texts.

BERT-NER BERT is a transformer-based language representation model proposed by Devlin et al. [5] We used BERT to classify functions ($\in \mathcal{F}_{\mathsf{KC}}$) used in papers: i) co-occurrence network, ii) correspondence analysis, and iii) others (see

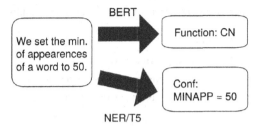

Fig. 3. Pseudo-labeling: BERT classifies functions and NER or T5 extract configurations.

Fig. 3). We adopted a BERT model pre-trained on Japanese Wikipedia articles[3], and then it was fine-tuned on Texylon, so that it can predict the function given a description.

On the other hand, we predicted configurations by named entity recognition (NER). Before applying NER, we tokenized the descriptions in Texylon into words with a Japanese morphological analyzer, MeCab [11]. For annotating NER labels, we preset 19 types of named entity (NE) specially for this task, each of which corresponds to each *key* in the possible configurations (Table 2). Then, we annotated the *values* word-by-word in the IOB2 (inside-outside-beginning) format. For example, a label B-PART means the "beginning of a value" for the configuration 分析対象の品詞 (*bunseki taishou no hinshi*, target parts of speech), and a label I-MINAPP indicates that a word is "inside a value" for the configuration 最小出現数 (*go no saishou shutsugen suu*, the minimum number of appearances of a word).

After annotating, the NER model was trained via the Flair framework [1]. We utilized the Japanese word embeddings provided with Flair by default. Furthermore, we eliminated the NE entries whose confidence scores are less than 0.5 to decrease noisy data.

BERT-T5. As in BERT-NER, we classified the target papers by BERT into three classes of functions ($\in \mathcal{F}_{KC}$), namely i) co-occurrence network, ii) correspondence analysis, and iii) others (see Fig. 3 again). We discarded the "others" class, and, for the classes i) and ii), we produced logs given the descriptions by a T5 model. T5 is a language model first introduced by Raffel et al. [15], with the great focus on transfer learning.

---

[3] https://huggingface.co/cl-tohoku/bert-base-japanese-whole-word-masking accessed on 2023/Oct/19.

Table 2. NE tags of co-occurrence network and correspondence analysis.

NE tag	Meaning	Freq.
MINAPP	Min. # of appearances of a word	79
MET	Method of calculation of co-occurrence relations	79
TOP	Display the top N co-occurrence relations	73
EXT	External variables	41
METNUM	Threshold for co-occurrence	34
BOLD	Bolder line for stronger co-occurrence relations	25
BUBBLE	Bubble chart	25
SUBG	Type of community detection	21
PART	Target parts of speech	13
UNIT	Unit of analysis	10
TYPE	Type of co-occurrence relations	10
TREE	Display only MST	8
MINDOC	Min. document frequency	8
DIF	Analyze only words with prominent differences	6
ORI	Display only word labels far from the origin	3
MAXAPP	Max. # of appearances of a word	3
STAN	Standardize coefficients	3
BUBSIZE	Size of a bubble chart	1
MAXDOC	Max. document frequency	1
Total		443

Our model was pre-trained on Japanese Wikipedia articles[4], and the pre-trained model was transferred to our dataset Texylon.

Hybrid. The final method of data augmentation, the hybrid dataset, is just the conjunction of the datasets of swapping and BERT-NER.

5 Evaluations

We evaluated our dataset Texylon and the data augmentation methods for the log-to-description task and the description-to-log task separately, to find out how our augmentation methods are useful for the tasks.

---

[4] https://huggingface.co/sonoisa/t5-base-japanese accessed on 2023/Oct/19.

5.1 Multi-task Generation Model

As a baseline model for our tasks (Sect. 3), we adopted one proposed by Kale et al. [9], which was based on T5 [15]. Here our task was defined as "translation" between descriptions and logs; hence we regarded the datasets as collections of correct translations from one language (namely "log") to another ("description"), and vice versa. We distinguished the two tasks from each other by prepending prefixes like "`Translate A to B:`," as it is suggested for a multi-task mixture [15].

To be precise, to each description-log pair (d, ℓ), we associated two data as follows that represent inputs and outputs for training the model. The first data has as an input "`Translate log to text:` ℓ" and its output is d. On the other hand, the second data is a pair of an input "`Translate text to log:` d" with an output ℓ. We passed to the model all the data which were constructed in that way.

5.2 Experiment Settings

Unless otherwise specified below, all the hyperparameters were set to the default values, or values suggested by inventors/implementers of models.

BERT-NER. For the Flair framework, we set an initial learning rate to 0.5, with a batch size 8. For a BERT model, we used Adam [10] as an optimizer with a learning rate 1e-5 and the maximum number of input tokens 256. We trained a model for 20 epochs.

BERT-T5. The hyperparameters to BERT are the same as BERT-NER. For a T5 model, we adopted another optimizer, Adafactor [16], with a learning rate 1e-3, a batch size 8 and the number of steps 100,000.

Multi-task Generation Model. We passed the same hyperparameters as BERT-T5 to a T5 model.

5.3 Cross Validation

As the tasks are novel, the datasets are not large enough. Thus we followed the 5-fold cross validation to have more reliable results. First we split our dataset, Texylon, randomly into five equal-sized subsets. Then for each fold, we took one subset for the test and executed the following procedures:

1. form the training-validation subsets from the four subsets other than the test set,
2. split the training-validation subset into training/validation data with a ratio of 4/1 randomly,

3. augment the training data using the methods explained in Sect. 4.2 to have additional data,
4. train the generative model (Sect. 5.1) on the concatenation of the training data and the additional data, and
5. measure the performance of the model on the test subset.

Finally we calculated the averages of evaluation metrics.

5.4   Metrics

Log-to-Description Task. We adopted the following metrics, which are widely used for natural language generation tasks, to calculate to what extent generated descriptions and reference texts coincide:

1. BLEU-N [13] — weighted geometric mean of p_n $(1 \leqslant n \leqslant N)$ with the brevity penalty, where p_n is the n-gram precision,
2. METEOR [2] — weighted harmonic mean of the uni-gram precision and the uni-gram recall with penalty on adjacent uni-grams,
3. BERTScore [17] — the precision/recall/F1 scores of similarities of token embeddings.

Description-to-Log Task. The metric for the description-to-log task is F1 scores, since a log is the well-structured data and it does not need any metrics for natural language evaluations, contrary to the log-to-description task. Thus we calculated the F1 scores for two components, namely for functions and for configurations. In the calculation, if an output is not in the right format (see Sect. 4.1), we ignored it; hence the F1 scores are calculated only among well-formatted logs.

5.5   Results

You can see example outputs for both the tasks in the Tables 3 and 4 respectively.

The results for log-to-description are shown in Table 5. Texylon alone achieved the highest scores for most of the metrics, and the hybrid was the second best (or higher) for all the metrics. It implies that the data augmentations may lower the accuracy in our case. We guess that the main reason is noises in the augmented data.

Table 6 shows the results for description-to-log. As we see in the table the model successfully predicted functions with a high accuracy, and there were no remarkable differences among the datasets. Moreover, the model produced few errors for most of the datasets.

To sum up, the data augmentations did not enhance the accuracy for both tasks. We find the reasons of the drawbacks be in the datasets themselves and in the models. Because the augmented data can contain a certain amount of noises, it results in errors for generated texts. The format of logs (Sect. 4.1) causes the low accuracy as well when the language models used for the data augmentation did not have a plenty of examples in the same format. Therefore, the models can have failed to recognize them.

Table 3. Examples of description generation from an input log. The rightmost column represents the English translation. We preserved grammatical or orthographic errors in English translation as much as possible.

Input	共起ネットワーク (語の最小出現数＝25, 上位＝60)	CN(MinApp=25, Top=60)
Texylon	共起ネットワーク分析では，最小出現数を 25 に設定し，描画する共起関係の絞り込みにおいては描画数を 60 に設定した．	For co-occurrence network, we set the min. # of appearances to 25, and set the # of renderings to 60 in the filter of rendered co-occurrence relations.
Swapping	次に，頻出語の最小出現数を 24 回に設定し，描画する共起関係の絞り込みにおいては，描画数を 60 に設定して，関連が特に強い語同士を線で結んだ共起ネットワーク注 2) を作成した．	Next, we set the min. # of appearances of frequent words to 24, set the # of renderings to 60 in the filter of rendered co-occurrence relations, and created a co-occurrence network (Notion 2) that links words of particularly strong relations with lines.
BERT-NER	図 12012 年版『小学校学習指導要領解説社会編』における頻出語の共起ネットワーク図 (出現回数 25 回以上・共起関係上位 60) (kh coder3 より，筆者作成)	Figure 1 figure of a co-occurrence network for frequent words (# of appearances ≥ 25, top 60 co-occurrence relations) in 2012 ver. "Course of Study for Elementary School: Social Studies" (From kh coder3, the author created)
BERT-T5	表 4 は，これらの抽出語のうち，出現頻度が高い上位 60 語を表 4 に，共起ネットワークを図 1 に示す．	For Table 4, among these extracted words, we show the top 60 words of highest frequency in Table 4, and a co-occurrence network in Figure 1.
Hybrid	図-24 は共起ネットワークを表す．出現数による単語の取捨選択では最小出現数 24 に設定し，描画する共起関係の絞り込みでは描画数を 60 に設定した．	Figure-24 shows a co-occurrence network. We set the min. # of appearances to 24 in the word filter by the # of appearances, and set the # of renderings to 60 in the filter of rendered co-occurrence relations.

Table 4. Examples of log generation from an input description. The rightmost column represents the English translation.

Input	「失敗経験」の内容について khcoder(樋口,2014) の共起ネットワーク分析を行なった. 解釈可能性の観点から分析設定は, ひらがなのみの名詞・動詞・形容詞・副詞・否定助動詞・形容詞 (非自立) は削除, 出現数は 10 以上の語を分析対象とし, jaccard 係数が上位 50 の共起関係を描画した.	We conducted co-occurrence network analysis of khcoder (Higuchi, 2014) about "failure experience." From a point of view of interpretability, for analysis configurations, we deleted hiragana nouns, verbs, adjectives, adverbs, negative auxiliary verbs, adjectives (ancillary). The target of analysis is words with the # of appearances $\geqslant$ 10, and we rendered co-occurrence relations of top 50 Jaccard coefficient.
Texylon	共起ネットワーク (語の最小出現数=10, 描画する共起関係の選択=jaccard 係数, 上位=50)	`CN(MinApp=10, Select=jaccard coefficient, Top=50)`
Swapping	共起ネットワーク (語の最小出現数=10, 描画する共起関係の選択=jaccard 係数, 上位=50)	`CN(MinApp=10,Select=jaccard coefficient, Top=50)`
BERT-NER	共起ネットワーク (品詞による語の取捨選択=名詞・動詞・形容詞・副詞・否定助動詞・形容詞 (非自立) に削除, 語の最小出現数=10, 描画する共起関係の選択=jaccard 係数, 上位=50)	`CN(SelectByPos=delete with nouns ... adjectives (ancillary), MinApp=10, Select=jaccard coefficient, Top=50)`
BERT-T5	共起ネットワーク (語の最小出現数=10, 描画する共起関係の選択=jaccard 係数, 上位=50)	`CN(MinApp=10,Select=jaccard coefficient, Top=50)`
Hybrid	共起ネットワーク (品詞による語の取捨選択=名詞・動詞・形容詞・副詞・否定助動詞・形容詞 (非自立) に, 語の最小出現数=10, 描画する共起関係の選択=jaccard 係数, 上位=50)	`CN(SelectByPos=with nouns ... adjectives (ancillary), MinApp=10, Select=jaccard coefficient, Top=50)`

Table 5. Results for the log-to-description task.

Dataset Type	BLEU-1	BLEU-2	BLEU-3	BLEU-4	METEOR	BERT-P	BERT-R	BERT-F1
Texylon	**36.98**	**24.47**	**18.20**	**14.64**	**30.35**	0.73	**0.74**	**0.74**
Swapping	34.06	22.24	16.20	12.85	29.39	0.72	0.73	0.73
BERT-NER	33.07	21.33	15.32	11.89	27.81	0.73	0.73	0.73
BERT-T5	24.88	15.70	10.90	8.13	23.94	**0.75**	0.71	0.72
Hybrid	35.84	23.85	17.43	13.74	29.40	0.74	**0.74**	**0.74**

Table 6. Results for the description-to-log task. F1-func for the classification of functions, and F1-conf for generating configurations. The errors are the total numbers of ill-formatted logs.

Dataset Type	F1-func	F1-conf	Errors
Texylon	0.962	0.711	3
Swapping	0.960	0.698	4
BERT-NER	0.943	**0.717**	0
BERT-T5	0.947	0.692	12
Hybrid	**0.967**	0.704	1

6 Conclusion

We introduced Texylon, the dataset of description-log pairs, and proposed four types of data augmentation of that dataset. Then we considered the multi-task generative model that converts logs to descriptions and vice versa as a baseline model to evaluate the data augmentation methods. Although Texylon itself exhibited the highest scores for log-to-description, the data augmentation methods equally high scores for description-to-log. The reasons is that the augmented data contain noises, or that the baseline model was not suitable for our dataset(s).

Our next plan is to invent a generative model more sensible to the format. Then, we should employ a new method for data augmentation which makes better data than Texylon. We would like to build a "general" model as well in a sense that it is applicable to other text-anatytics tools than KH Coder.

Disclosure of Interests. The authors have no competing interests to declare that are relevant to the content of this article.

References

1. Akbik, A., Bergmann, T., Blythe, D., Rasul, K., Schweter, S., Vollgraf, R.: FLAIR: an easy-to-use framework for state-of-the-art NLP. In: Proceedings of the 2019 Conference of the North American Chapter of the Association for Computational Linguistics (Demonstrations), pp. 54–59. Association for Computational Linguistics, Minneapolis, Minnesota (2019). https://doi.org/10.18653/v1/N19-4010, https://aclanthology.org/N19-4010
2. Banerjee, S., Lavie, A.: METEOR: an automatic metric for MT evaluation with improved correlation with human judgments. In: Proceedings of the ACL Workshop on Intrinsic and Extrinsic Evaluation Measures for Machine Translation and/or Summarization, pp. 65–72. Association for Computational Linguistics, Ann Arbor, Michigan (2005). https://aclanthology.org/W05-0909
3. Berry, D.M.: Introduction: understanding the digital humanities, pp. 1–20. Palgrave Macmillan UK, London (2012). https://doi.org/10.1057/9780230371934_1
4. Chang, E., Shen, X., Zhu, D., Demberg, V., Su, H.: Neural data-to-text generation with LM-based text augmentation. In: Proceedings of the 16th Conference of the European Chapter of the Association for Computational Linguistics: Main Volume, pp. 758–768. Association for Computational Linguistics, Online (2021).https://doi.org/10.18653/v1/2021.eacl-main.64
5. Devlin, J., Chang, M.W., Lee, K., Toutanova, K.: BERT: pre-training of deep bidirectional transformers for language understanding. In: Proceedings of the 2019 Conference of the North American Chapter of the Association for Computational Linguistics: Human Language Technologies, Volume 1 (Long and Short Papers), pp. 4171–4186. Association for Computational Linguistics, Minneapolis, Minnesota (2019).https://doi.org/10.18653/v1/N19-1423
6. He, S., He, P., Chen, Z., Yang, T., Su, Y., Lyu, M.R.: A survey on automated log analysis for reliability engineering. ACM Comput. Surv. 54(6), 1–37 (2021). https://doi.org/10.1145/3460345
7. Higuchi, K.: A two-step approach to quantitative content analysis: KH Coder tutorial using Anne of green gables (Part I). Ritsumeikan Soc. Sci. Rev. 52, 77–91 (2016). http://hdl.handle.net/10367/8013
8. Higuchi, K.: A two-step approach to quantitative content analysis: KH Coder tutorial using Anne of green gables (Part II). Ritsumeikan Soc. Sci. Rev. 53, 137–147 (2017). http://hdl.handle.net/10367/8610
9. Kale, M., Rastogi, A.: Text-to-text pre-training for data-to-text tasks. In: Proceedings of the 13th International Conference on Natural Language Generation, pp. 97–102. Association for Computational Linguistics, Dublin, Ireland (2020). https://aclanthology.org/2020.inlg-1.14
10. Kingma, D.P., Ba, J.: Adam: a method for stochastic optimization. arXiv preprint: arXiv:1412.6980 (2017). https://arxiv.org/abs/1412.6980
11. Kudo, T., Yamamoto, K., Matsumoto, Y.: Applying conditional random fields to Japanese morphological analysis. In: Proceedings of the 2004 Conference on Empirical Methods in Natural Language Processing, pp. 230–237. Association for Computational Linguistics, Barcelona, Spain (2004). https://aclanthology.org/W04-3230
12. Novikova, J., Dušek, O., Rieser, V.: The E2E dataset: new challenges for end-to-end generation. In: Proceedings of the 18th Annual SIGdial Meeting on Discourse and Dialogue, pp. 201–206. Association for Computational Linguistics, Saarbrücken, Germany (2017).https://doi.org/10.18653/v1/W17-5525

13. Papineni, K., Roukos, S., Ward, T., Zhu, W.J.: BLEU: a method for automatic evaluation of machine translation. In: Proceedings of the 40th Annual Meeting of the Association for Computational Linguistics, pp. 311–318. Association for Computational Linguistics, Philadelphia, Pennsylvania, USA (2002).https://doi.org/10.3115/1073083.1073135, https://aclanthology.org/P02-1040
14. Parikh, A., et al.: ToTTo: a controlled table-to-text generation dataset. In: Proceedings of the 2020 Conference on Empirical Methods in Natural Language Processing (EMNLP), pp. 1173–1186. Association for Computational Linguistics, Online (2020).https://doi.org/10.18653/v1/2020.emnlp-main.89
15. Raffel, C., et al.: Exploring the limits of transfer learning with a unified text-to-text transformer. J. Mach. Learn. Res. **21**(140), 1–67 (2020). http://jmlr.org/papers/v21/20-074.html
16. Shazeer, N., Stern, M.: Adafactor: adaptive learning rates with sublinear memory cost. In: Dy, J., Krause, A. (eds.) Proceedings of the 35th International Conference on Machine Learning. Proceedings of Machine Learning Research, vol. 80, pp. 4596–4604. PMLR (2018). https://proceedings.mlr.press/v80/shazeer18a.html
17. Zhang, T., Kishore, V., Wu, F., Weinberger, K.Q., Artzi, Y.: BERTscore: evaluating text generation with BERT. In: International Conference on Learning Representations (2020). https://arxiv.org/abs/1904.09675

Semantic Parsing for Question and Answering over Scholarly Knowledge Graph with Large Language Models

Le-Minh Nguyen[✉], Le-Nguyen Khang, Kieu Que Anh, Nguyen Dieu Hien, and Yukari Nagai

Japan Advanced Institute of Science and Technology, Nomi, Japan
{nguyenml,khangln,queanh,ynagai}@jaist.ac.jp

Abstract. This paper presents a study to answer the question of how to map a natural language (NL) sentence to a semantic representation and its application to question answering over the DBLP database. We investigate the deep learning approach using pre-trained models and their fine-tuning on training data for semantic parsing tasks. Experimental results on standard datasets show the effectiveness of pre-trained models in mapping an NL sentence to SPARQL, a query language for semantic databases. The results also show that the T5 and Flan-T5 models outperform other models in terms of translation accuracy. In addition to the empirical results on pre-trained models, we also consider the problem of examining large language models (LLMs) such as Llama and Mistras, or Qwen models for answering questions on the DBLP database. Experimental results showed the potentiality of using LLMs with chain-of-thought prompting methods. The results indicated that without using training data, we were able to obtain promising results for some types of questions when translating them to SPARQL.

Keywords: Relation search · Semantic Representation · Semantic parsing · Question Answering · Knowledge Graph · Mapping NL to SPARQL

1 Introduction

Over the past decade, knowledge graphs (KGs) such as Freebase [5,16], and Wikidata [25] have become significant sources of general information. They use a linked data architecture to store facts about the world in a "subject predicate object" triple format. These triples can be visually represented as node-edge-node molecules in a graph structure. There has been considerable interest in finding methods for extracting information from these KGs.

Question Answering over Knowledge Graphs (KGQA) is the primary approach for achieving this objective. The primary method used in KGQA is a translation method that converts a natural language question into a formal logical form. Previously, rule-based systems were used for this purpose. However,

© The Author(s), under exclusive license to Springer Nature Singapore Pte Ltd. 2024
T. Suzumura and M. Bono (Eds.): JSAI-isAI 2024, LNAI 14741, pp. 284–298, 2024.
https://doi.org/10.1007/978-981-97-3076-6_20

machine learning-based methods and neural networks have become more popular for this task in recent years. With the development of neural approaches (such as transformer models), KGQA can achieve significant results compared to conventional methods.

A scholarly knowledge graph (KG) is a type of KG that includes bibliographic details. The Microsoft Academic Graph, OpenAlex, ORKG, and DBLP are well-known examples of scholarly KGs. DBLP is designed to serve the bibliography needs of the computer science field and is, therefore, smaller than other scholarly KGs. DBLP is an online reference for bibliographic information on major computer science publications, with over 4.4 million publications published by more than 2.2 million authors.

This paper proposes a study investigating question-answering baselines over the DBLP-QuAD dataset, the most significant scholarly question-answering dataset. The DBLP-QuAD dataset consists of 10,000 question-answer pairs with corresponding SPARQL queries that can be executed over the DBLP KG to fetch the correct answer. DBLP-QuAD can be considered the largest scholarly question-answering dataset.

ChatGPT [6], a typical large language model (LLM), has recently shown its influence and is considered the most significant breakthrough in natural language processing (NLP). It has fundamentally transformed research and development in the field. ChatGPT is one of the most exciting LLM systems that have been developed recently, showcasing impressive skills for language generation and attracting a great deal of public attention. In this work, we also want to verify the performance of ChatGPT on difficult tasks such as semantic parsing for mapping a query to SPARL semantic representation. The limitation of ChatGPT is that it is not fully open, and we cannot see what is inside the model. The information of questions is also sent to ChatGPT. Therefore, the privacy issue is violated. However, it is very good that Meta has recently released LLama2 [23], which is a large and open-source language model. Following LLama2 models, many open models have been recently released, such as the Qwen and Mistral models. In this paper, we would like to show how we used Large Language Models for parsing a query to SPARL semantic representation.

To understand the full impacts of pre-trained models on this task, this paper compares various pre-trained models for semantic representation that map a natural language sentence to a SPARQL representation in the context of question answering over the DBLP-QuAD dataset. We also propose comparing the performance of LLMs with other pre-trained models in this task. Our experimental evaluation demonstrates the potential of applying semantic parsing to convert a question to SPARQL for question answering over the DBLP-QuAD dataset. The paper consists of three main sections: The first section reviews related works on the DBLP-QuAD dataset. The second section evaluates the performance of LLMs models, including LLama2, Qwen, and Mistral, and our baseline methods for the question-answering task on DBLP-QuAD.

2   Related Work

Knowledge graph-based question answering is a suitable approach for dealing with QA in a specific domain, and there are various methods deployed to generate KGQA datasets such as the works [3,15,24], and [7]. Semantic parsing is a challenging task in natural language processing, and many attempts have been made to exploit semantic parsing in question-answering over knowledge graphs. Many databases are built to contribute to developing questions and answering over the database, such as Freebase [5].

Question and answering systems for scholarly knowledge graphs have been strongly relying on semantic parsing. Many standard scholar knowledge graphs have been constructed from this task, including ORKG-QA benchmark [12] LC-QuAD 2.0 an extension of LC-QuAD 1.0 [24], KQA Pro [8].

The above datasets have attempted to introduce semantic parsing for converting an NL sentence to a semantic representation [9], as well as semantic parsing over the database [14], with leaderboards on the QA tasks [20].

The most recent work for semantic parsing over the database is developed by [2]. The authors developed a question-answering dataset using the DBLP scholarly knowledge graph (KG), containing over 4.4 million publications authored by more than 2.2 million authors. The dataset comprises 10,000 pairs of questions and answers and exploits the use of pre-trained models such as T5 for the semantic parsing task of mapping a question to a SPARQL representation. Another work to utilize a pre-trained model and ChatGPT for mapping NL to a SPARQL representation is presented in [18].

3   Method

This section presents our investigation into mapping natural language sentences to semantic representations using deep learning approaches. We explore using pre-trained models and fine-tuning them based on training data consisting of natural language sentences and their corresponding semantic representations. Additionally, we utilize ChatGPT and LLama2 models to map sentences to SQL representations. We consider various forms of LLaMa2 models to examine how they can contribute to mapping NL sentences to semantic representations such as (SPARQL).

Figure 1 showed the proposed Knowledge Graph-based Question-answering framework (KBQA), which consists of the major component that converts a question to a semantic representation (i.e., logical form). This is the general framework for question and answering problems over the database. The NL query will be mapped to a logical form representation using a semantic parsing component. Then, it is retrieved from the DBLP database to find subset candidates and obtain the answer. Therefore, semantic parsing can be considered a main component of the proposed system.

Figure 1 showed the proposed framework for semantic parsing that translates an NL sentence to a logical form representation. In this case, we would like to map an NL sentence to a SPARQL representation. We design the model based on sequence to sequence model that we can utilize various pre-trained models, including T5 and BART models.

The major components are pre-trained models and the use of how to represent the input sentence to a sequence for encoder models. The pre-trained models are typically transformer models, which were trained on large-scale text documents.

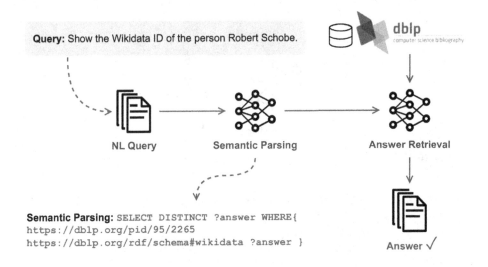

Query: Show the Wikidata ID of the person Robert Schobe.

NL Query   Semantic Parsing   Answer Retrieval

Semantic Parsing: SELECT DISTINCT ?answer WHERE{
https://dblp.org/pid/95/2265
https://dblp.org/rdf/schema#wikidata ?answer }

Answer √

Fig. 1. The proposed KGQA framework

3.1 Semantic Parsing with Pre-trained Models

Figure 2 illustrates our proposed framework using pre-trained models. Intuitively, the system's input is an NL sentence, and then semantic parsing will be applied to transform an NL sentence to a logical form - SPARQL. After that, a query representation will be performed over the database to obtain the answer.

The following models are considered in our framework as follows:

- BART [17]: Sequence-to-sequence BERT variant: permute/make/delete tokens, then predict full sequence autoregressively using the transformer encoder- decoder
- T5 [21] uses an Encoder-Decoder: several downstream tasks (including machine translation, question answering, and classification) are cast as seq2seq tasks.
- Flan-T5 [10] works as follows: Pre-train, then fine-tune on a bunch of tasks, generalize to unseen tasks, scale the number of tasks, models size (Flan-T5, Flan-Palm), and fine-tune on chain-of-thought data.

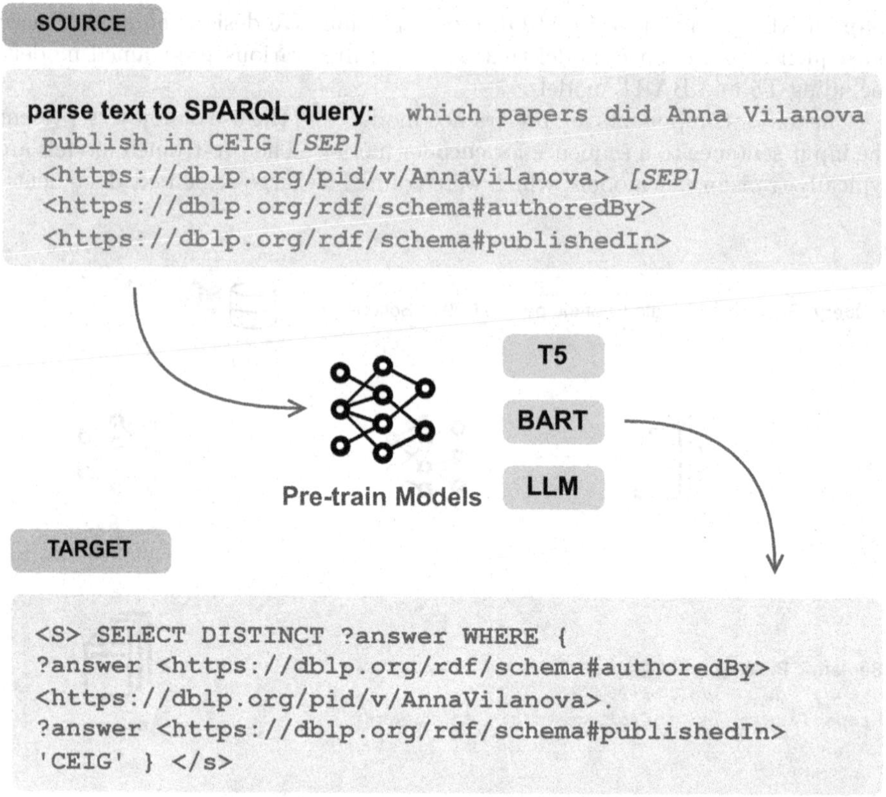

SOURCE

parse text to SPARQL query: which papers did Anna Vilanova
publish in CEIG *[SEP]*
<https://dblp.org/pid/v/AnnaVilanova> *[SEP]*
<https://dblp.org/rdf/schema#authoredBy>
<https://dblp.org/rdf/schema#publishedIn>

T5

BART

LLM

Pre-train Models

TARGET

<S> SELECT DISTINCT ?answer WHERE {
?answer <https://dblp.org/rdf/schema#authoredBy>
<https://dblp.org/pid/v/AnnaVilanova>.
?answer <https://dblp.org/rdf/schema#publishedIn>
'CEIG' } </s>

Fig. 2. An example of translation from query to SPARQL

Our method investigates a list of pre-trained models for translating an NL
sentence to a SPARQL representation, including the works by Banerjee et al.
[3].

Following Banerjee et al. [3] and [2], we assume the entities and the relations
are linked and only focus on query building. We formulate the source as shown
in Fig. 2, where the prefix "parse text to SPARQL query:" is added for each
natural language question. The entity URIs are joined with the source string,
and relation schema URIs are separated by a special token [SEP]. We also use
the sentinel tokens provided by T5 to represent the DBLP prefixes to support
the T5-tokenizer in fragmenting the target text in the inference process.

We follow the work described in [2] for fine-tuning T5-Base and T5-Small
on the DBLP-QuAD train set with the same parameters. We also conduct a
fine-turning on BART pre-trained models to compare our results.

3.2   Using LLMs for Semantic Parsing

This subsection will describe how we adapt large language models (LLMs) for semantic parsing, which maps a natural language (NL) sentence to a SPARQL query. Figure 3 depicts our semantic parsing framework using LLMs and prompting techniques. We consider the chain-of-thought (CoT) method for this purpose. We recognize that depending on the type of questions, we should design appropriate prompt methods. Then, we will perform LLM inferring to obtain the SPARQL representation.

Our main areas of investigation are (1) choosing LLMs, (2) developing prompting techniques, and (3) fine-tuning techniques. We will describe these areas in detail below.

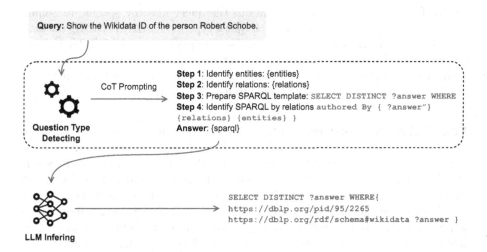

Fig. 3. Semantic Parsing using LLM

Choosing LLM. Large language models (LLMs) have made significant progress recently, and we have developed an approach to apply them to semantic parsing in DBLP-QuAD. One of the state-of-the-art foundational LLMs that is open-source for research is LLaMA [22]. LLaMA models are available in various sizes, ranging from 7 billion to 65 billion parameters. Building on the success of LLaMA, the subsequent work LLaMA-2 [23] was developed, with model sizes ranging from 7 billion to 70 billion parameters. In this work, we employ LLaMA-2 for semantic parsing. To facilitate the reproducibility of our experiments, we used the 7 billion parameter version of LLaMA-2. In addition to LLaMa-2, we also consider the recent models, including Qwen-Chat [1] and Mistral models [13].

Prompting Techniques. Various prompting techniques were proposed to exploit the strength of LLMs. In the simplest form, an LLM is provided with a natural text prompt and will continuously predict the next tokens to generate the response. Few-shot learning [19], referring to the technique of learning the data pattern with just a few exemplars, is another prompting technique that shows robust performance on various benchmarks. More sophisticated techniques, such as Chain-of-thought (CoT) [26], Graph-of-thought (GoT) [4], and Tree-of-thought (ToT) [27], were also proposed. CoT prompting guides the models in performing complicated reasoning by supplying a sequence of intermediate reasoning steps. In this work, we conduct experiments on few-shot prompting and CoT techniques. For few-shot prompting, the prompt includes five examples (5-shot) for each query type in the DBLP-QuAD. Each example contains the query, the entities, the relations, and the target SPARQL. For CoT prompting in DBLP-QuAD, a CoT prompt contains the query and the specific reasoning steps to arrive at the answer. For each query type in the DBLP-QuAD dataset, we design a CoT template and use it as the prompts for the LLM. Table 1 shows the CoT templates used in our experiments. Based on query types, we design a chain of thought templates. Those templates may not be optimal, but they effectively map an NL sentence to SPARQL using LLMs.

Fine-Tuning Approaches. Another line of work focuses on adapting LLMs to downstream tasks by only fine-tuning a subset of their parameters. In this line of work, LoRA [11] is one of the most robust and efficient techniques to fine-tune an LLM. In this work, we also experiment with the fine-tuning of the LLaMA-2 model using LoRA on the DBLP-QuAD dataset. In the experiments, we use LoRA with the rank of the update matrices as $r = 8$. The target modules to apply the LoRA update matrices are the query-projection and value-projection matrices in the attention layers. We fine-tuned the LLaMA-2 model for five epochs; the optimizer is Adafactor, and the learning rate is 2e−5.

Table 1. Chain-of-though templates for each query type in DBLP-QuAD

Query type	Chain-of-thought template
SINGLE_FACT	**Template 1** (When the relation is authored by) Answer the following query. Query: {question} Given entities are {entities}. Given relations are {relations} ### Step 1: Identify entities: {entities} ### Step 2: Identify relations: {relations} ### Step 3: Prepare SPARQL template: SELECT DISTINCT ?answer WHERE" ### Step 4: Identify SPARQL by relations: authoredBy { ?answer"} {relations} {entities} } ### Answer: {sparql} **Template 2** (When the relation is other than authored by (wikidata, webpage, primary affiliation, ...)) Answer the following query. Query: {question} Given entities are {entities}. Given relations are {relations} ### Step 1: Identify entities: {entities} ### Step 2: Identify relations: {relations} ### Step 3: Prepare SPARQL template: SELECT DISTINCT ?answer WHERE ..." ### Step 4: Identify SPARQL by relations: wikidata { ?answer"} {entities} {relations} } ### Answer: {sparql}
MULTI_FACT	Answer the following query. Query: {question} Given entities are {entities}. Given relations are {relations} ### Step 1: Identify entities: {entities} ### Step 2: Identify relations: {relations} ### Step 3: Prepare SPARQL template: SELECT DISTINCT ?answer WHERE ... " ### Answer: {sparql}
DOUBLE_INTENT	Answer the following query. Query: {question} Given entities are {entities}. Given relations are {relations} ### Step 1: Identify entities: {entities} ### Step 2: Identify relations: {relations} ### Step 3: Prepare SPARQL template: SELECT DISTINCT ?firstanswer ?secondanswer WHERE ..." ### Answer: {sparql}
BOOLEAN	Answer the following query. Query: {question} Given entities are {entities}. Given relations are {relations} ### Step 1: Identify entities: {entities} ### Step 2: Identify relations: {relations} ### Step 3: Prepare SPARQL template: Prepare SPARQL template: ASK ..." ### Answer: {sparql}
NEGATION	Answer the following query. Query: {question} Given entities are {entities}. Given relations are {relations} ### Step 1: Identify entities: {entities} ### Step 2: Identify relations: {relations} ### Step 3: Prepare SPARQL template: ASK ..." ### Answer: {sparql}
DOUBLE_NEGATION	Answer the following query. Query: {question} Given entities are {entities}. Given relations are {relations} ### Step 1: Identify entities: {entities} ### Step 2: Identify relations: {relations} ### Step 3: Prepare SPARQL template: Prepare SPARQL template: ASK ..." ### Answer: {sparql}
UNION	Answer the following query. Query: {question} Given entities are {entities}. Given relations are {relations} ### Step 1: Identify entities: {entities} ### Step 2: Identify relations: {relations} ### Step 3: Prepare SPARQL template: SELECT DISTINCT ?answer WHERE ... UNION ..." ### Answer: {sparql}
DISAMBIGUATION	Answer the following query. Query: {question} Given entities are {entities}. Given relations are {relations} ### Step 1: Identify entities: {entities} ### Step 2: Identify relations: {relations} ### Step 3: Prepare SPARQL template: SELECT DISTINCT ?answer WHERE ..." ### Answer: {sparql}
COUNT	**Template 1** (When the question is about counting) Answer the following query. Query: {question} Given entities are {entities}. Given relations are {relations} ### Step 1: Identify entities: {entities} ### Step 2: Identify relations: {relations} ### Step 3: Prepare SPARQL template: SELECT (COUNT(DISTINCT ?answer) AS ?count) WHERE " ### Answer: {sparql} **Template 2** (When the question is about the average number) Answer the following query. Query: {question} Given entities are {entities}. Given relations are {relations} ### Step 1: Identify entities: {entities} ### Step 2: Identify relations: {relations} ### Step 3: Prepare SPARQL template: SELECT (AVG(?count) AS ?answer) { SELECT (COUNT(?y) AS ?count) WHERE " ### Answer: {sparql}
SUPERLATIVE + COMPARATIVE	Answer the following query. Query: {question} Given entities are {entities}. Given relations are {relations} ### Step 1: Identify entities: {entities} ### Step 2: Identify relations: {relations} ### Step 3: Prepare SPARQL template: SELECT ... " ### Answer: {sparql}

4 Experimental Results

4.1 Corpus

To conduct our experiments, we chose the DBLP-QuAD dataset to compare various pre-trained models, LLaMa2 and ChatGPT. DBLP stands for Digital Bibliography & Library Project. It was established in 1993 and has since evolved into a prominent service for hosting bibliographic databases of research papers in the field of computer science. Over the years, DBLP has significantly expanded in its size and coverage, now encompassing bibliographic information spanning a wide array of topics within computer science.

DBLP primarily comprises two key entities: "Person" and "Publication". While additional metadata, such as the affiliations of authors with journals and conferences, currently exist as string literals, the RDF dump itself encompasses nearly 3 million entities, including over 6 million publication entries, and boasts more than 255,573,199 RDF triples. DBLP does not offer a SPARQL endpoint; however, interested users can access and download the RDF dump. For those desiring to execute SPARQL queries against the DBLP knowledge graph, the utilization of a local SPARQL endpoint, such as the Virtuoso Server, is used.

The live RDF data model on DBLP follows the schema shown in Fig. 4.

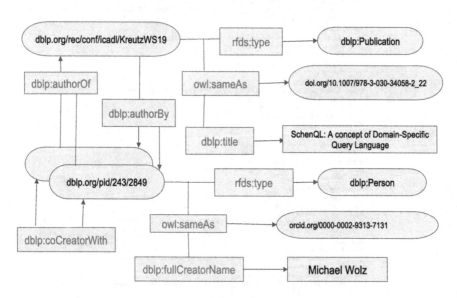

Fig. 4. Example of entries in the DBLP-KG with its schema [3]

The statistical information of the dataset is shown in Table 2.

The dataset information is sketched in Table 3. This information showed that the query and SPARQL representation are challenging enough for semantic parsing tasks. In addition, the dataset contains different types of questions, and the number of question-query pairs is 10,000 pairs of questions and queries.

Table 2. Statistics for DBLP-QuAD

Metric	Value
Number of question-query pairs	10,000
Train set size	7,000
Validation set size	1,000
Test set size	2,000
Number of creators and publications	13,348
Number of predicates	11

Table 3. Statistics for DBLP-QuAD

Metric	Average	Standard Deviation
Question word length	17.32	- -
Question character length	114.2	- -
SPARQL query vocab length	12.65	–
SPARQL query character length	249.48	–
Unigram Jaccard similarity	0.62	0.22
Bigram Jaccard similarity	0.47	0.24
Levenshtein edit distance	32.99	23.12

DBLP-QuAD presents challenging entity linking with data augmentation on literals for a more natural representation of entity surface forms. In the valid and test sets, 18.9% % and 19.3% % of instances, respectively, were generated using unique SPARQL query templates and natural language question templates.

4.2 Evaluation Settings and Results

To demonstrate the effectiveness of semantic parsing representation, we compare the performance of the following methods: T5-base, T5-small, T5-large, BART-base, and BART-large. We also experimented with Flan-T5-small, Flan-T5-base, Flan-T5-large models [10] and Efficient-T5-small, Efficient-T5-base, Efficient-T5-large models [21]. Table 4 shows the detailed evaluation results. We discovered that the proposed framework uses T5 methods to attain a better result than BART pre-trained models. The Flan-T5-large model obtained the best performance.

We compared the accuracy of different pretrained models on various questions and selected three models-Flan-T5-base, T5-base, and Efficient-T5-base-because they performed the best among the models we tested. Figure 5 shows our results using pre-trained models when tested on different types of questions.

Our analysis revealed that Flan-T5-base and T5-base achieved higher accuracy than Efficient-T5-base across all questions. Specifically, Flan-T5-base performed well on negation, boolean, and comparative questions, while T5-base out-

294   L.-M. Nguyen et al.

Table 4. Evaluation results on systems

Methods	Extract Match (EM:5)	Extract Match (EM: 10)
T5-small	63.80	
T5-base	81.30	
Our methods:		
T5-small	50.40	59.35
T5-base	79.50	83.15
T5-large	77.25	70.9
Flan-T5-small	38.10	76.44
Flan-T5-base	80.50	81.6
Flan-T5-large	81.96	84.5
Efficient-T5-small	25.50	62.45
Efficient-T5-base	68.25	75.9
Efficient-T5-large	72.45	73.15
BART-base	23.60	24.3
BART-large	26.55	20.5

performed Flan-T5-base on all other types of questions. These results suggest that choosing an appropriate pre-trained model for semantic parsing is essential based on the type of questions being asked. We also test the KBQA system using the query generated by our semantic parsing. We first parse a query to a SPARQL and then retrieve the results in our DBLP database. The results were evaluated as F1 score. Table 5 shows the detailed evaluation results. We discovered that the Flan-T5-large model obtained the best performance.

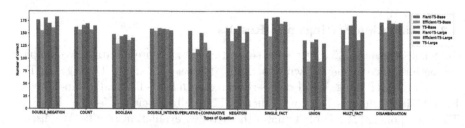

Fig. 5. Performance with different types of questions

To illustrate the performance of our work, we built a question-answering system that uses the semantic parsing representation and then retrieves results from the database to obtain the answer. Figure 6 demonstrates our system.

As mentioned in the introduction, we also tested our system using Llama2 and other available LLMs with designing prompts, few-short, fine-turning, and chain-of-thought. Table 6 showed our comparison using different configurations of LLaMa2 and other models:

Table 5. Evaluation results on systems testing on Database

Methods using pre-trained models	Exact Match (EM)	F1	Exact Match (EM:10)	F1:10
T5-small	63.80	72.1		
T5-base	81.30	86.8		
Our methods:				
T5-base	79.50	85.91	78.85	86.19
T5-large	77.25	85.27	83.15	89.73
Flan-T5-base	80.50	87.39	81.6	89.81
Flan-T5-large	81.96	89.18	**84.5**	**89.79**
Efficient-T5-base	68.25	78.13	75.79	83.77
Efficient-T5-large	72.45	82.97	73.15	82.55

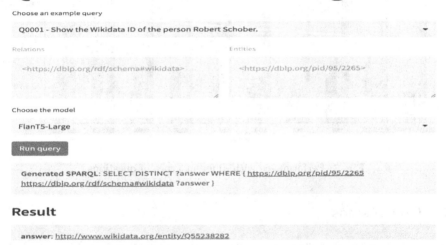

Fig. 6. An illustration of the proposed system

We compared the accuracy of LLMs, including LLama-2, Mistral, and Qwen models on various questions and selected three models-Flan-T5-base, T5-base, and Efficient-T5-base-because they performed the best among the models we tested. Figure 7 shows our results using pre-trained models when tested on different types of questions.

In the results, CoT is higher than few-shot in single-fact, count, and double-negation question types; the rest is equivalent to few-shot, especially in single-fact type, the CoT is higher than T5 models. CoT results also depend on the design of CoT prompts.

Table 6. Evaluation results on systems

Methods using LLMs	Exact Match (EM)	F1
Our methods:		
LLaMA 2 7b (5 shot)	31.20	58.00
LLaMA 2 7b - LoRA	16.75	45.60
LLaMA 2 7b (CoT)	35.80	58.00
Qwen 14b (CoT)	39.45	57.25
Mistral 7b (CoT)	30.6	51.75

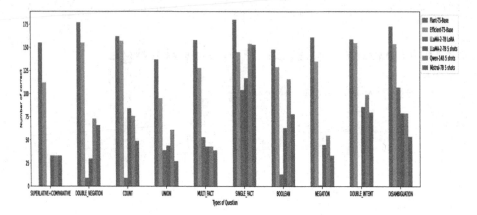

Fig. 7. Performance with different types of questions

5   Conclusions

This paper investigates using pre-trained models for mapping an NL sentence to a SPARQL representation. We found that an appropriate pre-trained model can help to obtain a good result. Further investigation on using LLama2, Mistral, and Qwen models, we found that designing suitable prompts with a chain of thought would help to obtain promising results.

In addition, this work demonstrates an investigation of a difficult task of questions and answers over a large knowledge graph. Through experiments, we showed that LLMs could not overcome the fine-turning approach for given questions in this dataset. This was because of some ambiguity issues in question, making it difficult to find reliable answers. In some context situations, if we provide suitable prompts - LLMs with prompting can generate results.

In future work, we would like to directly apply our semantic representation for question-answering on the DBLP database.

References

1. Bai, J., et al.: Qwen technical report. arXiv preprint: arXiv:2309.16609 (2023)
2. Banerjee, D., Awale, S., Usbeck, R., Biemann, C.: DBLP-QUaD: a question answering dataset over the DBLP scholarly knowledge graph. CoRR **abs/2303.13351** (2023). https://doi.org/10.48550/arXiv.2303.13351
3. Banerjee, D., Nair, P.A., Kaur, J.N., Usbeck, R., Biemann, C.: Modern baselines for SPARQL semantic parsing. In: Proceedings of the 45th International ACM SIGIR Conference on Research and Development in Information Retrieval, SIGIR '22, pp. 2260-2265. Association for Computing Machinery, New York, NY, USA (2022) https://doi.org/10.1145/3477495.3531841
4. Besta, M., et al.: Graph of thoughts: solving elaborate problems with large language models (2023)
5. Bollacker, K.D., Evans, C., Paritosh, P.K., Sturge, T., Taylor, J.: Freebase: a collaboratively created graph database for structuring human knowledge. In: SIGMOD Conference (2008)
6. Brown, T.B., et al..: Language models are few-shot learners (2020)
7. Cai, Q., Yates, A.: Large-scale semantic parsing via schema matching and lexicon extension. In: Annual Meeting of the Association for Computational Linguistics (2013)
8. Cao, S., et al.: KQA pro: a dataset with explicit compositional programs for complex question answering over knowledge base. In: Proceedings of the 60th Annual Meeting of the Association for Computational Linguistics (Volume 1: Long Papers), pp. 6101–6119. Association for Computational Linguistics, Dublin, Ireland (2022) https://doi.org/10.18653/v1/2022.acl-long.422
9. Chakraborty, N., Lukovnikov, D., Maheshwari, G., Trivedi, P., Lehmann, J., Fischer, A.: Introduction to neural network-based question answering over knowledge graphs. Wiley Interdisc. Rev.: Data Mining Knowl. Discov. **11**, e1389 (2021)
10. Chung, H.W., et al.: Scaling instruction-finetuned language models (2022)
11. Hu, E.J., et al.: LoRA: low-rank adaptation of large language models. In: International Conference on Learning Representations (2022). https://openreview.net/forum?id=nZeVKeeFYf9
12. Jaradeh, M.Y., Stocker, M., Auer, S.: Question answering on scholarly knowledge graphs. In: International Conference on Theory and Practice of Digital Libraries (2020)
13. Jiang, A.Q., et al.: Mistral 7b (2023)
14. Kwiatkowski, T., et al.: Natural questions: a benchmark for question answering research. Trans. Assoc. Comput. Linguist. **7**, 452–466 (2019). https://doi.org/10.1162/tacl_a_00276
15. Lan, Y., He, G., Jiang, J., Jiang, J., Zhao, W.X., Rong Wen, J.: A survey on complex knowledge base question answering: methods, challenges and solutions (2021). arXiv:abs/2105.11644
16. Lehmann, J., et al.: DBpedia - a large-scale, multilingual knowledge base extracted from Wikipedia. Semant. Web **6**, 167–195 (2015)
17. Lewis, M., et al.: BART: denoising sequence-to-sequence pre-training for natural language generation, translation, and comprehension. In: Proceedings of the 58th Annual Meeting of the Association for Computational Linguistics, pp. 7871–7880. Association for Computational Linguistics, Online (2020). https://doi.org/10.18653/v1/2020.acl-main.703

18. Nguyen, M., Khang Le, A.K., Nagai, Y.: Semantic parsing for questions and answering over DBLP database. presented in SCIDOCA 2023 (2023)
19. Parnami, A., Lee, M.: Learning from few examples: a summary of approaches to few-shot learning (2022)
20. Perevalov, A., Yan, X., Kovriguina, L., Jiang, L., Both, A., Usbeck, R.: Knowledge graph question answering leaderboard: a community resource to prevent a replication crisis. In: Proceedings of the Thirteenth Language Resources and Evaluation Conference, pp. 2998–3007. European Language Resources Association, Marseille, France (2022). https://aclanthology.org/2022.lrec-1.321
21. Tay, Y., et al.: Scale efficiently: insights from pre-training and fine-tuning transformers. CoRR **abs/2109.10686** (2021). https://arxiv.org/abs/2109.10686
22. Touvron, H., et al.: LLaMA: open and efficient foundation language models (2023)
23. Touvron, H., et al.: LLaMA 2: open foundation and fine-tuned chat models (2023)
24. Trivedi, P., Maheshwari, G., Dubey, M., Lehmann, J.: LC-QuAD: a corpus for complex question answering over knowledge graphs. In: International Workshop on the Semantic Web (2017)
25. Vrandečić, D., Krötzsch, M.: Wikidata: a free collaborative knowledgebase. Commun. ACM **57**, 78–85 (2014)
26. Wei, J., et al.: Chain-of-thought prompting elicits reasoning in large language models (2023)
27. Yao, S., et al.: Tree of thoughts: deliberate problem solving with large language models (2023)

Improving LLM Prompting with Ensemble of Instructions: A Case Study on Sentiment Analysis

Vu Tran$^{(\boxtimes)}$ and Tomoko Matsui

The Institute of Statistical Mathematics, Tachikawa, Japan
{vutran,tmatsui}@ism.ac.jp

Abstract. In the era of large language models, exploring the capability of a large language model is a trending research direction where one is prompt engineering aiming at drafting the best instructions to ask a large language model. We assume that a selected large language model has a certain knowledge and capability of a given task, and the way to ask is strongly related to the task's performance. This is certainly useful when we don't have sufficient resource for finetuning or aligning the large language model. Following that direction, we present our approach towards improving the effectiveness of prompting a large language model by finding an optimal ensemble of instructions by using the large language model's self-generated instructions and labeled data. A case study on sentiment analysis is carried out in a preliminary experiment. The positive results of our case study shows that the approach is promising.

Keywords: Large Language Model (LLM) · Prompt Engineering · Zero-Shot Learning · Ensemble · Self-Generated Data · Sentiment Analysis

1 Introduction

Large language models are now everywhere. The emergent ability comes as we observed the increment of LLM parameter size comes with the discovery of new or better ability at solving tasks that were not explicitly trained for [2,6,9].

Prompt engineering is an ongoing research trend with a lot of attention due to the need to effectively operate LLMs, which is a different approach than finetuning parameters for downstream tasks. In the work [3], they discover a magic prompt "Let's think step by step." which evidently improve LLM performance. Though it is quite simple, and ready to be used in any task, there was no optimization process to discover such magic prompt. Another example of this approach is assigning an expert identity [4], for example "Suppose you are an expert in ...". In the work [11], they proposed a prompt engineering framework to find the optimal prompt by iteratively generating new prompts and selecting the ones with high task performance. Their optimization algorithm, however,

T. Suzumura and M. Bono (Eds.): JSAI-isAI 2024, LNAI 14741, pp. 299–305, 2024.
https://doi.org/10.1007/978-981-97-3076-6_21

relies on a scoring method for which they employed task performance metric which in turn requires annotated data. In another perspective, say generate knowledge prompt, additional knowledge about the task can helps improve task performance and such knowledge can actually be generated by the same LLM [5,7]. To this end, we believe that a well pretrained LLM may potentially have a good knowledge about a natural language process (NLP) task, so materializing such knowledge is beneficial for improving task performance.

We dwell into the direction of exploring the potential of improving LLM prompting without a direct training dataset. The idea here is that instead of using ground-truth data, we can use the data generated by the selected LLM to generate plausible instructions. Since we will obtain a set of plausible instructions, it would be beneficial if we can find an optimal way of aggregating the generated instructions into one system, i.e., making an optimal ensemble. We will develop the approach into finding a connection between close-test results on the LLM's own generated data and open-test results on the real datasets. We will conduct our experiments with sentiment analysis, an interesting NLP task and important for understanding public trend which can drive the directions of social behavioral changes or economic evolution.

2 Method

2.1 Overview

Under the assumption that the selected LLM have some understanding of the task, the following is feasible:

- The LLM can generate examples of the task.
- The LLM can generate instructions of the task.

With that, we design our framework with the following procedure:

1. Generation: Generate examples and instructions.
2. Close-Test: Evaluate the outputs of the LLM when prompting it with the examples and the instructions.
3. Ensemble-Construction: Select the best ensemble setting based on the results of the close-test. An ensemble is a collection of LLM executions defined by two parameters: N^p (the number of different prompts because of different inserted instructions) $\times$ N^r (the number of runs of the same prompts). The final output of an ensemble is selected via majority voting. Throughout this paper, we name a base ensemble setting whose parameters are $(N^p, N^r) = (1, 20)$.

We, then, evaluate our approach on the two real datasets: TweetSemEval [8] and Sentiment140 [1].

In this preliminary study, we utilized Mixtral[1] and obtained the weights from Huggingface[2]. The LLM achieved superior performance compared to LLaMA-2 [10] at the majority of compared tasks.

---

[1] https://mistral.ai/news/mixtral-of-experts/.

[2] https://huggingface.co/mistralai/Mixtral-8x7B-Instruct-v0.1.

2.2 Data Self-generation

We sample data including labeled sentences, and task instructions by prompting the LLM in a conversation as following:

- User: Prompt the LLM to give examples of sentences with positive, negative, neutral sentiments.
- LLM: Responded sentences.
- User: Prompt the LLM to give instructions of sentiment analysis based on the generated examples.
- LLM: Responded instructions.

We prompt the LLM to give examples of sentences with the following three settings:

- Easy: *"Give a sentence with positive sentiment, a sentence with negative sentiment, and a sentence with neutral sentiment"*.
- Hard: *"Give a sentence with positive sentiment, a sentence with negative sentiment, and a sentence with neutral sentiment. Make the examples **hard** to distinguish their sentiment"*.
- Extreme: *"Give a sentence with positive sentiment, a sentence with negative sentiment, and a sentence with neutral sentiment. Make the examples **extremely hard** or extremely confusable to distinguish their sentiment"*.

Then we prompt the LLM to give instructions with the prompt: *"Based on the examples, in less than 100 words, write instructions to classify a sentence into positive, negative, or neutral"*.

For each setting, we collected 99 sentences and 33 instruction sets. Examples are shown in Table 1. We can observe that easy sentences are simple and contains words belonging to one sentiment category, and harder sentences are more complex and contains words belonging to more than one sentiment categories.

Now, we perform a close test on the examples the LLM generates. For that, two prompting settings are used:

- Simple prompt: "Classify the sentiment of the following text into positive, negative, or neutral".
- Enriched prompt: "Instructions: [PLACEHOLDER]. Based on the above instructions, classify the sentiment of the following text into positive, negative, or neutral". For the "PLACEHOLDER", we insert each of the $3 \times 33 = 99$ instruction sets to enrich the prompt.

For each prompt, we repeat the call to the LLM 20 times, and take majority voting on the 20 outputs. This is, we call, the base ensemble setting.

We observed from the close test results (Table 2) that 1) the LLM is able to follow our instructions to generate examples that are even hard for it to distinguish and 2) the prompting with enriched prompt improve the LLM performance even on this close test.

As the accuracy of the "easy" set is 100%, we discard this set when constructing an ensemble.

Table 1. Examples of generated sentences and instructions by the LLM.

Setting	Type	Contents
Easy	Sentences	Positive sentiment: I felt pure joy when I watched the sunset on the beach during our family vacation. Negative sentiment: I was extremely frustrated when I realized that I had lost my wallet on the way home from work. Neutral sentiment: The book on my table has 300 pages and is blue in color
	Instructions	To classify a sentence as positive, negative, or neutral, consider the emotions and evaluations conveyed in the sentence. Positive sentences express happiness, approval, or other positive sentiments. Negative sentences express anger, disapproval, or other negative emotions. Neutral sentences present facts or objective descriptions without expressing any emotion or opinion. Be careful with nuances and context, as some sentences may be subjective or ambiguous in their sentiment
Hard	Sentences	Positive Sentiment: The sun began to peek through the clouds just as we arrived at the beach, casting a beautiful glow on the sparkling water. Negative Sentiment: The sun began to peek through the clouds just as we arrived at the beach, piercing our eyes with its harsh glare. Neutral Sentiment: The sun began to peek through the clouds just as we arrived at the beach, illuminating the shoreline with a soft light
	Instructions	To classify a sentence into positive, negative, or neutral, look for sentiment clues in the words and phrases used to describe a situation or event. Positive sentences will use positive language and express favorable outcomes or emotions. Negative sentences will use negative language and express unfavorable outcomes or emotions. Neutral sentences will be objective and factual, expressing no particular emotion or opinion. Pay attention to adjectives, adverbs, and verb choices, as they often reveal the sentiment in a sentence
Extreme	Sentences	Positive Sentiment: "Even though the road ahead is long and winding, the sun is shining and there's a gentle breeze, making every step feel like a dance with nature". Negative Sentiment: "The silence in the room is deafening, as if the walls are closing in, yet the ticking of the clock is the only sound that breaks the monotony". Neutral Sentiment: "The number of cars passing by on the highway is six per minute, which is an interesting pattern but not particularly noteworthy or emotionally charged". It's worth noting that the sentiment of a sentence can be subjective and depend on the context, so different people might interpret these sentences differently"
	Instructions	To classify a sentence as positive, negative, or neutral, consider the overall sentiment conveyed by the words and phrases used. Positive sentences often contain words that indicate happiness, success, or optimism, while negative sentences might use words associated with sadness, failure, or pessimism. Neutral sentences generally avoid strong emotional language and convey facts or objective information without expressing a positive or negative sentiment. It's important to consider the context and connotations of the words used, as well as any cultural or individual differences in the interpretation of sentiment

Table 2. Accuracy for the close test on three generated sentence sets: easy, hard, extreme, over two prompting settings: simple and enriched. The results for "enriched prompt" are the average over all instruction sets.

Dataset	Prompting setting			
	Simple prompt	Enriched prompt		
		Easy	Hard	Extreme
Easy	100	100	100	100
Hard	90.9	92.0	92.7	92.5
Extreme	82.1	86.1	87.7	87.2

From the base ensemble setting where the same prompt is executed 20 times, we further develop into a more generate ensemble setting with two parameters: N^p (the number of different prompts because of different inserted instructions) $\times\ N^r$ (the number of runs of the same prompts) (Fig. 1).

Fig. 1. Heat-maps of accuracy for various ensemble settings on the self-generated sentences.

The found optimal parameters are: $(N^p, N^r) = (4, 3)$ for "hard" instruction sets, and $(N^p, N^r) = (6, 1)$ for "extreme" instruction sets.

2.3 Performance on Real Data

Here we will evaluate our approach on two datasets: TweetSemEval [8] and Sentiment140 [1]. For keeping the cost of analysis feasible, we randomly sampled 100 instances for each dataset while keeping the same ground-truth label ratio.

We observed that using the close test results on the self generated sentences to select the ensemble setting does give better results than the base setting as shown in Table 3. Additionally, it is also shown that adding the LLM's self generated instructions improves the performance, which is consistent with the observations shown in [5,7].

Table 4 shows that there is a fair correlation in term of the ensemble performance between the LLM-generated data and the real data, which is also evident for the potential of our approach.

Table 3. Accuracy on the real datasets. Base: the base ensemble setting. Opt.: the optimal ensemble setting found using the close test results.

Dataset	Setting				
	Simple prompt	*Instruction Sets*			
		Hard		Extreme	
		Base	Opt.	Base	Opt.
TweetSemEval	70.0	74.5	75.4↑	74.4	75.9↑
Sentiment140	85.0	86.8	87.3↑	86.8	87.3↑

Table 4. Pearson correlation on performance of ensemble settings between the generated data and the real datasets.

	LLM-Generated Data	
	Hard	Extreme
TweetSemEval	0.561	0.672
Sentiment140	0.766	0.724

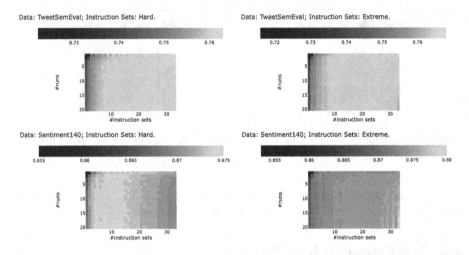

Fig. 2. Heat-maps of accuracy over various ensemble settings on the real datasets: TweetSemEval (top) and Sentiment140 (bottom) with two categories of instruction sets: Hard (left) and Extreme (right).

From Fig. 2, we observed that: increasing the number of the instruction sets in the ensemble makes the accuracy improvement much more effective than increasing the number of runs for the same instruction set, however, the degree of accuracy improvement dismisses quickly as the number of the instruction sets grows large.

3   Conclusion

We have discussed an approach towards improving LLM prompting with ensemble of self-generated instructions while not using ground-truth data for training or instructing LLMs (few-shot learning). Instead, we use the self-generated labeled data to find an optimal instruction ensemble setting. Empirical results show that our approach is promising at improving LLM prompting performance. Future work could address remaining questions, e.g., how to align generated instructions with the characteristics of the target domain data, even when we have no access to the ground-truth labels.

Acknowledgement. This work was supported by "Strategic Research Projects" grant from ROIS (Research Organization of Information and Systems), Japan and JSPS KAKENHI Grant Number JP23K16954. Any opinions, findings, and conclusions or recommendations expressed in this material are those of the author(s) and do not necessarily reflect the views of the author(s)' organization, JSPS or MEXT.

References

1. Go, A., Bhayani, R., Huang, L.: Twitter sentiment classification using distant supervision. CS224N Proj. Rep. Stanford **1**(12), 2009 (2009)
2. Jiang, H.: A latent space theory for emergent abilities in large language models. arXiv preprint arXiv:2304.09960 (2023)
3. Kojima, T., Gu, S.S., Reid, M., Matsuo, Y., Iwasawa, Y.: Large language models are zero-shot reasoners. Adv. Neural. Inf. Process. Syst. **35**, 22199–22213 (2022)
4. Li, G., Hammoud, H.A.A.K., Itani, H., Khizbullin, D., Ghanem, B.: CAMEL: communicative agents for "mind" exploration of large language model society. In: Thirty-seventh Conference on Neural Information Processing Systems (2023)
5. Liu, J., et al.: Generated knowledge prompting for commonsense reasoning. arXiv preprint arXiv:2110.08387 (2021)
6. Lu, S., Bigoulaeva, I., Sachdeva, R., Madabushi, H.T., Gurevych, I.: Are emergent abilities in large language models just in-context learning? arXiv preprint arXiv:2309.01809 (2023)
7. Nori, H., et al.: Can generalist foundation models outcompete special-purpose tuning? Case study in medicine (2023)
8. Rosenthal, S., Farra, N., Nakov, P.: SemEval-2017 task 4: sentiment analysis in Twitter. In: Proceedings of the 11th International Workshop on Semantic Evaluation (SemEval-2017), pp. 502–518 (2017)
9. Schaeffer, R., Miranda, B., Koyejo, S.: Are emergent abilities of large language models a mirage? arXiv preprint arXiv:2304.15004 (2023)
10. Touvron, H., et al.: Llama 2: open foundation and fine-tuned chat models. arXiv preprint arXiv:2307.09288 (2023)
11. Zhou, Y., et al.: Large language models are human-level prompt engineers. arXiv preprint arXiv:2211.01910 (2022)

Author Index

Printed in the United States
by Baker & Taylor Publisher Services